T0302751

DIRTY TRICKS

NIXON, WATERGATE, AND THE CIA

SHANE O'SULLIVAN

HOT BOOKS

Hot Books may be purchased in bulk at special discounts for sales promotion, corporate gifts, fund-raising, or educational purposes. Special editions can also be created to specifications. For details, contact the Special Sales Department, Skyhorse Publishing, 307 West 36th Street, 11th Floor, New York, NY 10018 or info@skyhorsepublishing.com.

Hot Books® and Skyhorse Publishing® are registered trademarks of Skyhorse Publishing, Inc.®, a Delaware corporation.

Visit our website at www.hotbookspress.com.

10 9 8 7 6 5 4 3 2 1

Library of Congress Cataloging-in-Publication Data is available on file.

Print ISBN: 978-1-5107-2958-2
Ebook ISBN: 978-1-5107-2959-9

Cover design by Brian Peterson

Printed in the United States of America

CONTENTS

FOREWORD

By David Talbot

The world is burning, and yet the firelight illuminates the way out. The times are dire, even catastrophic. Nonetheless we can sense a grand awakening, a growing realization all around the globe that "people have the power, to dream, to rule, to wrestle the world from fools" in the prophetic words of Patti Smith.

But in order to rouse ourselves from the nightmares that hold us in their grip, we need to know more about the forces that bedevil us, the structures of power that profit from humanity's exploitation and from that of the earth. That's the impetus behind Hot Books, a series that seeks to expose the dark operations of power and to light the way forward.

Skyhorse publisher Tony Lyons and I started Hot Books in 2015 because we believe that books can make a difference. Since then the Hot Books series has shined a light on the cruel reign of racism and police violence in Baltimore (D. Watkins' *The Beast Side*); the poisoning of U.S. soldiers by their own environmentally reckless commanding officers (Joseph Hickman's *The Burn Pits*); the urgent need to hold U.S. officials accountable for their criminal actions during the war on terror (Rachel Gordon's *American Nuremberg*); the covert manipulation of the media by intelligence agencies (Nicholas Schou's *Spooked*); the rise of a rape culture on campus (Kirby Dick and Amy Ziering's *The Hunting Ground*); the insidious demonizing of Muslims in the media and Washington (Arsalan Iftikhar's *Scapegoats*); the crackdown on whistleblowers who know the government's dirty secrets (Mark Hertsgaard's *Bravehearts*); the disastrous policies of the liberal elite that led to the triumph of Trump (Chris Hedges' *Unspeakable*); the American wastelands that gave rise to this dark reign (Alexander Zaitchik's *The Gilded Rage*); the energy titans and their political servants who are threatening human survival (Dick Russell's *Horsemen of the Apocalypse*); the utilization of authoritarian tactics by Donald Trump that threaten to erode American democracy (Brian Klaas' *The Despot's Apprentice*); the capture, torture, and detention of the first "high-value target" captured by the CIA after 9/11 (Joseph Hickman and John Kiriakou's *The Convenient Terrorist*); the deportation of American veterans (J. Malcolm Garcia's *Without a Country*); the ways in which our elections have failed, and continue to fail, their billing as model democracy (Steven Rosenfeld's *Democracy Betrayed*); the cover-up by the deep state and subsequent fallout after 9/11 (John Duffy and Ray Nowosielski's *The Watchdogs Didn't Bark*); and the commodification and devastation of seeds in our current climate (Mark Schapiro's *Seeds of Resistance*). And the series continues, going where few publishers dare.

Hot Books are packed with provocative information and points of view that mainstream publishers usually shy from. Hot Books are meant not just to stir readers' thinking, but to stir trouble.

Hot Books authors follow the blazing path of such legendary muckrakers and troublemakers as Upton Sinclair, Lincoln Steffens, Rachel Carson, Jane Jacobs, Jessica Mitford, I. F. Stone and Seymour Hersh. The magazines and newspapers that once provided a forum for this deep and dangerous journalism have shrunk in number and available resources. Hot Books aims to fill this crucial gap.

American journalism has become increasingly digitized and commodified. If the news isn't fake, it's usually shallow. But there's a growing hunger for information that is both credible and undiluted by corporate filters.

A publishing series with this intensity cannot keep burning in a vacuum. Hot Books needs a culture of equally passionate readers. Please spread the word about these titles—encourage your bookstores to carry them, post comments about them in online stores and forums, persuade your book clubs, schools, political groups and community organizations to read them and invite the authors to speak.

It's time to go beyond packaged news and propaganda. It's time for Hot Books . . . journalism without borders.

CAST OF CHARACTERS

THE CHENNAULT AFFAIR

Spiro T. Agnew, Vice President of the United States, 1969–73.

Richard V. Allen, senior foreign policy advisor, Nixon–Agnew campaign committee, 1967–8. Senior staff member, National Security Council, 1969.

Jack N. Anderson, investigative journalist and daily newspaper columnist.

William P. Bundy, Assistant secretary of state for East Asian and Pacific Affairs, 1964–9.

George A. Carver, Jr. Special assistant for Vietnamese affairs, Central Intelligence Agency, 1966–73.

Anna Chennault, Vice president, The Flying Tiger Line, Inc. Co-chair, Women's Advisory Committee for Nixon.

Clark M. Clifford, United States Secretary of Defense, 1968–9.

Ray S. Cline, Director of Intelligence, Central Intelligence Agency, 1962–66. Special coordinator and adviser to the United States ambassador to Germany, 1966–69. Assistant secretary of state for Intelligence and Research, 1969–73.

Thomas G. "The Cork" Corcoran, lawyer and lobbyist.

Saville R. Davis, reporter, *The Christian Science Monitor*.

Bui Diem, South Vietnamese ambassador to the United States, 1967–72.

Everett M. Dirksen, United States senator (R—Illinois), 1951–69. Senate minority leader, 1959–69.

Cartha D. "Deke" DeLoach, Deputy associate director of the Federal Bureau of Investigation.

John D. Ehrlichman, White House Counsel, 1969. White House Domestic Affairs Advisor, 1969–73. Served eighteen months in jail.

Thomas W. Evans, Special assistant to John Mitchell, Nixon–Agnew Campaign Committee.

Bryce N. Harlow, Republican political strategist.

H. R. Haldeman, White House Chief of Staff, 1969–73. Served eighteen months in jail for his role in Watergate.

Richard M. Helms, Director of the Central Intelligence Agency, 1966–73.

Ambassador Robert Hill, former United States ambassador to Costa Rica (1953), El Salvador (1954) and Mexico (1957–61) Chairman of the Foreign Policy Task Force of the Republican National Committee, 1965–68.

Hubert H. Humphrey, Vice President of the United States, 1965–69 and nominated Democratic candidate for the 1968 presidential election.

Tom Charles Huston, Nixon aide, 1968–71.

Lyndon B. Johnson, President of the United States, 1963–69.

Thomas H. Karamessines, Deputy Director for Plans, Central Intelligence Agency, 1967–73.

Henry A. Kissinger, National Security Advisor to Presidents Nixon and Ford, 1969–75.

Karl E. Mundt, United States senator (R—South Dakota), 1948–73.

Richard M. Nixon, President of the United States, 1969–74. Resigned from office and was pardoned by President Ford.

John N. Mitchell, Manager of Nixon presidential campaign, 1968. United States Attorney General, 1969–72. Director of the Committee to Re-elect the President (CRP), 1972. Served nineteen months in jail.

Thomas W. Ottenad, political journalist, *St. Louis Post-Dispatch*.

Eugene V. Rostow, Under Secretary for Political Affairs, 1966–69.

Walt W. Rostow, National Security Advisor to President Johnson, 1966–69.

Dean D. Rusk, United States Secretary of State, 1961–69.

Richard B. Russell, Jr., United States senator (D—Georgia), 1933–71. Chairman of the Senate Committee on Armed Services, 1955–69.

Alexander Sachs, economist and banker.

George A. Smathers, United States senator (D—Florida), 1951–69.

Maurice H. Stans, United States Secretary of Commerce, 1969–72. Chairman, Republican National Finance Committee, 1968 and 1972. Fined $150,000.

Nguyen Van Thieu, President of the Republic of Vietnam, 1967–75.

John G. Tower, United States senator (R—Texas), 1961–85. Chairman of the Nixon Key Issues Committee, 1968.

Rose Mary Woods, Personal secretary to Richard Nixon, 1951–74.

WATERGATE[1]

Nick Akerman, Assistant special prosecutor, Watergate Special Prosecution Force (WSPF).

Gerald Alch, attorney for James McCord.

Phillip Mackin Bailley, attorney.

Howard H. Baker, Jr., United States senator (R—Tennessee), 1967–85.

Alfred C. Baldwin, former FBI agent employed by McCord Associates to transcribe bugged telephone conversations and act as "lookout" for the second Watergate break-in.

Bernard L. Barker, Watergate burglar. Served twelve months in jail.

Robert F. Bennett, President, Robert Mullen Company, 1971–3.

Gary Bittenbender, Metropolitan Police Department, Intelligence Division.

William O. Bittman, attorney for E. Howard Hunt.

Douglas Caddy, initial attorney for the Watergate burglars, Howard Hunt and Gordon Liddy.

John V. Cassidento, attorney for Alfred Baldwin.

John J. "Jack" Caulfield, White House investigator, 1969–72.

John W. Coffey, Deputy Director of Support, CIA.

William E. Colby, Executive Director, CIA, 1972–3. Deputy Director of Operations, CIA, 1973. Director of Central Intelligence, CIA, 1973–6.

Charles W. Colson, White House Counsel, 1969–70. Director of the Office of Public Liaison, 1970–3. Served seven months in jail.

General Robert E. Cushman, Jr., Deputy Director, CIA, 1969–71.

John W. Dean III, White House Counsel, 1970–3. Served four months in jail.

Maureen Dean (née Biner), John Dean's wife.

Felipe De Diego, Bay of Pigs veteran who participated in the Fielding break-in.

Leo Dunn, Acting deputy director of Security for Personnel Security, CIA.

Daniel Ellsberg, former military analyst who leaked the Pentagon Papers in 1971.

Jake Esterline, CIA station chief, Miami, 1968–73.

Frederick N. Evans, Personnel Security Division, CIA.

Lewis J. Fielding, Daniel Ellsberg's psychiatrist, 1968–70.

Gerald R. Ford, House Minority leader, 1965–73. Vice President of the United States, 1973–4. President of the United States, 1974–7.

J. Alan Galbraith. Attorney at Williams, Connolly, and Califano, representing the DNC.

Paul Gaynor, Security Research Staff, CIA.

Cleo Gephart, TSD officer who supplied Hunt with CIA equipment.

Millicent "Penny" Gleason, personal secretary to James McCord.

Ramon Esteban Gonzalez III, CIA case officer for Eugenio Rolando Martinez, 1970–2.

Virgilio R. Gonzalez, locksmith and Watergate burglar. Served fifteen months in jail.

L. Patrick Gray III, Acting director of the Federal Bureau of Investigation, 1972–3.

Stephen C. Greenwood, TSD officer who supplied Hunt with CIA equipment.

Tom Gregory, campaign volunteer for the Muskie and McGovern campaigns, secretly working for Howard Hunt.

Alexander M. Haig, Deputy National Security Advisor, 1970–3. White House Chief of Staff, 1973–4.

Sally Harmony, personal secretary to G. Gordon Liddy, CRP.

Seymour Hersh, investigative reporter for the *New York Times*, 1972–5.

Lawrence J. Howe, Personnel Security Division, CIA.

E. Howard Hunt, Jr., White House consultant and former CIA officer. Served thirty-three months in jail.

Richard Kleindienst, United States Attorney General, 1972–3. Received a suspended one-month jail sentence.

Egil (Bud) Krogh, Jr., deputy to Presidential Assistant John D. Ehrlichman and White House Plumber. Served four and a half months in jail.

Richard Krueger, Deputy Chief, Technical Services Division, CIA.

Stephen L. Kuhn, Deputy Director of Security, Personnel Security Division, CIA.

Howard Liebengood, Assistant to Minority Counsel Fred Thompson on the Senate Watergate Committee.

G. Gordon Liddy, White House Plumber, 1971. Counsel, Committee to Re-elect the President, 1972. Served fifty-two months in jail.

Martin Lukoskie, CIA case officer for the Robert Mullen Company.

James W. McCord, Jr., Chief of Physical Security, CIA. Head of Security, Committee to Re-elect the President, 1971–2. Served four months in jail.

George McGovern, United States senator (D—South Dakota), 1963–81. Democratic Presidential nominee, 1972.

Jeb S. Magruder, Deputy Director, Committee to Re-elect the President, 1972. Served seven months in jail.

Bernard Malloy, Chief, Psychological Services Branch, Office of Medical Services, CIA.

Eugenio Rolando Martinez, CIA operative and Watergate burglar. Served fifteen months in jail.

Cord Meyer, Associate Deputy Director of Plans, CIA.

Robert Mirto, attorney for Alfred Baldwin.

Robert Mullen, founder of the Robert Mullen Company, which provided cover for CIA employees.

Lucien N. Nedzi, U.S. House of Representatives (D—Michigan), 1961–81.

Lawrence F. O'Brien, Chairman, Democratic National Committee, 1970–2.

Paul L. O'Brien, attorney for the Committee to Re-elect the President, 1972–4.

R. Spencer Oliver, Executive Director, Association of State Democratic Chairmen.

Howard J. Osborn, Director of Security, CIA.

Henry E. Petersen, Assistant Attorney General, Criminal Division, 1972–74.

Lee R. Pennington, Jr., paid informant for the Security Research Staff, CIA.

Walter Pforzheimer, CIA historian, 1956–74.

Rob Roy Ratliff, CIA liaison to the National Security Council, 1972–77.

Heidi Rikan, friend of Maureen Dean and alleged madam of a call girl ring at the Columbia Plaza apartments.

Robert Ritchie, CIA case officer for Rolando Eugenio Martinez, 1972.

Raymond G. Rocca, Deputy chief of Counterintelligence, CIA, 1972–5.

Felix I. Rodriguez, CIA officer.

Lou Russell, private investigator.

Andrew St. George, journalist.

Edward Sayle, Security Research Staff, CIA.

Theodore Shackley, Chief of Western Hemisphere Division, CIA, 1972.

James R. Schlesinger, Director Central Intelligence, 1973. United States Secretary of Defense, 1973–5.

Earl J. Silbert, Assistant United States attorney and Watergate prosecutor, 1972–3.

John J. Sirica, Chief Judge of the United States District Court for the District of Columbia, 1971–4.

Carl Shoffler, arresting officer, Metropolitan Police Department.

Lawrence Sternfield, chief of Cuban Operations, Western Hemisphere Division, CIA.

Frank A. Sturgis, Watergate burglar.

Dr. John Tietjen, Director of Medical Services, CIA.

Ralph O. True, CIA case officer who ran the Agency proprietaries General Personnel Investigations and Anderson Security.

Anthony T. Ulasewicz, White House investigator.

Jack J. Valenti, President Motion Picture Association of America, 1966–2004.

Louis Vasaly, Security Research Staff, CIA. Case officer for Lee Pennington.

Antonio Veciana, founder and former leader of anti–Castro Cuban exile group, Alpha 66.

Karl Wagner, Executive assistant to General Cushman, CIA.

General Vernon A. Walters, Deputy Director of Central Intelligence, 1972–76. Acting Director of Central Intelligence, 1973.

John Warner, General Counsel, CIA, 1973–6.

Ida "Maxie" Wells, personal secretary to R. Spencer Oliver, 1972.

Frank Wills, security guard, Watergate Office Building, 1972.

Arthur J. Woolston-Smith, private investigator connected to Jack Anderson and the Democratic National Committee.

David R. Young, Special Assistant to the National Security Council, 1971. Special Investigative Unit, 1971. Domestic Council, 1971–3.

INTRODUCTION

The victory of Richard Nixon in the US presidential election of 1968 swung on an "October Surprise"—a treasonous plot engineered by key figures in the Republican Party to keep the South Vietnamese government away from peace talks in Paris, denying Democratic candidate Hubert Humphrey a late surge in support from voters anxious to end the war in Vietnam. Nixon felt President Johnson's decision to call a "bombing halt" on October 31, five days before the election, was itself a blatantly partisan move. Like in the 2016 election, the Republican candidate won by the tightest of margins and claims of election "dirty tricks" on both sides reverberated for years afterwards. The war dragged on and during Nixon's presidency, 21,195 more American lives were lost in Vietnam. After Nixon got away with the "dirty tricks" of 1968, the illicit schemes in his 1972 campaign grew more elaborate. He won the election in a landslide but a bungled covert operation targeting the headquarters of the Democratic National Committee in the Watergate office building on June 17, 1972 and the cover-up that followed led to his resignation in disgrace two years later.[1]

The Chinese-born widow of an air force general, by 1968, Anna Chennault was a protégée of Tommy "the Cork" Corcoran—the most influential lobbyist in Washington and a key figure in the staunchly anti-Communist China Lobby. She hosted glittering parties at her penthouse in the Watergate complex and was one of the founders of the Georgetown Club, fronted by her close friend Tongsun Park and secretly bankrolled by the Korean CIA.[2]

As vice president of the Flying Tiger Line, a cargo airline which transported US troops to Vietnam, Chennault cultivated close ties with Southeast Asian governments. Newly discovered letters from Chennault to Nixon show she offered to use her friendship with the South Vietnamese ambassador in Washington, Bui Diem, to sabotage peace talks on Vietnam until after the 1968 election. Previously unpublished documents show the Nixon campaign's covert meetings with Diem began five months earlier than previously thought. Diem and Chennault met campaign chief John Mitchell, foreign policy advisor Richard Allen, Nixon's secretary, Rose Mary Woods, and Ambassador Robert Hill at Nixon's apartment in New York in February, just weeks after Nixon announced his candidacy. Through Allen, Chennault arranged a "top secret" meeting between Nixon and Diem in July—a meeting Allen insisted never happened until Chennault and Diem confirmed it in eighties memoirs.

Allen has always insisted Chennault was a "loose cannon," never authorized by the Nixon campaign, but newly discovered documents show he was in close contact with her about the "October Surprise" plot just days before the election. The opening two chapters recount this treasonous operation in full and the consternation it caused at the highest levels of government, where President Johnson ordered the FBI to put the "Dragon Lady" under surveillance. Chennault raised a quarter of a million dollars for Nixon's campaign and, for many years, stayed loyal to the president and kept quiet about her secret role in the 1968 election.

Ken Hughes' fascinating book, *Chasing Shadows* (University of Virginia Press, 2014), explores the Chennault Affair through the Nixon tapes and declassified government documents in the LBJ Library, but neglects the personal papers of Chennault, Richard Allen, and Robert Hill, thereby missing the full story.

Presidential historian Luke Nichter and the Richard Nixon Foundation continue to dispute Chennault's role, claiming there is no hard evidence that her actions were authorized by Nixon. In 2017, author John Farrell claimed to have uncovered notes by H. R. Haldeman settling the issue, but the Nixon

Foundation produced a convincing rebuttal and after Anna Chennault's death in March 2018, Professor Nichter called the story a myth but remained open to new evidence. I present that here in these opening chapters.[3]

Following the unauthorized leak of the Pentagon Papers to the *New York Times* by military analyst Daniel Ellsberg in June 1971, the White House hired former CIA officer Howard Hunt and former FBI agent Gordon Liddy to investigate unauthorized leaks of classified information through a special investigations unit later dubbed the "Plumbers." The CIA was commissioned to create a psychological profile of Ellsberg to fuel a planned smear campaign against him in the press. The Agency also provided false identification papers, disguises and equipment to Hunt, which were used in a break-in at the office of Dr. Lewis Fielding—Ellsberg's psychiatrist—in early September. Hunt and Liddy supervised the Fielding operation and two further break-ins at the offices of the Democratic National Committee (DNC) in the Watergate office building in May and June 1972. Hunt remained close to CIA director Richard Helms and four of the five Watergate burglars had CIA connections—Eugenio Rolando Martinez was still on an Agency retainer at the time of his arrest, James McCord had recently retired, and Bernard Barker was a former contract agent. While never recruited by the CIA, Frank Sturgis had been associated with Martinez since the early sixties, and Martinez and Barker were also involved in the Fielding break-in.[4]

On May 11, 1973, the House Armed Services Committee began an inquiry, chaired by Congressman Lucien Nedzi (D—Michigan), into "the alleged involvement of the Central Intelligence Agency in the Watergate and Ellsberg Matters."

A few weeks later, in a statement on Watergate, President Nixon said that within a few days of the second Watergate break-in, he "was advised that there was a possibility of CIA involvement in some way":

It did seem to me possible that, because of the involvement of former CIA personnel and because of some of their apparent associations, the investigation

could lead to the uncovering of covert CIA operations totally unrelated to the
Watergate break-in.

 In addition, by this time, the name of Mr. Hunt had surfaced in con-
nection with Watergate, and I was alerted to the fact that he had previously
been a member of the special investigations unit in the White House.
Therefore, I was also concerned that the Watergate investigation might well
lead to an inquiry into the activities of the special investigations unit itself.

 I also had to be deeply concerned with ensuring that neither the covert
operations of the CIA nor the operations of the special investigations unit
should be compromised. Therefore, I instructed Mr. Haldeman and Mr.
Ehrlichman to ensure that the investigation of the break-in not expose
either an unrelated covert operation of the CIA or the activities of the
White House investigations unit—and to see that this was personally coor-
dinated between General Walters, the Deputy Director of the CIA, and
Mr. Gray at the FBI.[5]

The suspicions of Nedzi and Nixon were shared by Senator Howard Baker
(R—Tennessee), the vice chairman of the Senate Watergate Committee
which investigated the break-in. In 1974, Baker and his minority staff published a report of their investigation into "CIA activity in the Watergate
incident." The Baker Report explores the relationship between the CIA,
Howard Hunt, and the Mullen Company; the CIA "cover" operation Hunt
joined after his retirement; "the extensive contacts" between Hunt and the
Agency while he was a White House consultant; and the support given to
him by the CIA's Technical Services Division (TSD) for an unexplained
"one-time" operation, and "in the preparation of the Ellsberg psychiatric
profile." It also investigates the destruction of evidence at the home of James
McCord by CIA informant Lee Pennington; and the relationship between
the Agency and the only Watergate burglar who was still on its payroll at the
time of his arrest, Eugenio Rolando Martinez.[6]

As the report notes, "the fact that many of those involved in the Watergate break-in were former CIA employees [and] that CIA equipment was used by Hunt" immediately led to newspaper reports of deeper Agency involvement. The Nedzi hearings and the Baker report into possible CIA involvement in the Ellsberg and Watergate affairs form the basis for Jim Hougan's groundbreaking book *Secret Agenda* (1984) and for the remaining chapters of this book.[7]

To my knowledge, I am the first author to examine the personal papers of Senator Baker and assistant minority counsel Howard Liebengood in detail. The Liebengood collection, in particular, has yielded important material never before made public, identifying the previously redacted names of many former CIA personnel referenced in the investigation.

In August 2016, a lawsuit brought by Judicial Watch under the Freedom of Information Act (FOIA) secured the release of the CIA Inspector General's internal report on the "so-called Watergate affair, as it affected CIA." This unfinished draft "history" of the incident was based on a working draft prepared by John Richards in late 1973, to which he added extensive handwritten revisions before his death in December 1974:

It had been planned, prior to John Richards' death, to review certain incidents and developments that are not treated in detail in the working draft. This has not been undertaken. . . .[8]

The FOIA release created great excitement among Watergate researchers but led to a series of articles which made questionable claims about Howard Hunt's role as a "CIA plant" in the White House and Eugenio Martinez' role as a CIA "agent" "planted on the break-in team."[9]

In January 2017, the CIA posted more than twelve million pages of records from its CREST database online, including much material pertinent to Watergate. The release of new or previously redacted JFK assassination records later that year further enhanced our knowledge and this is the first book on Watergate to analyze this new material. The following chapters will use the newly-declassified CIA internal history of Watergate and Agency files not available to Jim Hougan over thirty years ago, to continue the work of the Baker probe. In the process, I reveal the names of many previously unidentified CIA officers and technicians who were in contact with Howard Hunt, Gordon Liddy, and the Watergate burglars in the months preceding the Fielding and Watergate break-ins.

The importance of the Fielding entry has been somewhat neglected in the shadow of the Watergate break-ins, but the handling of the "casing" photographs taken by Hunt and Liddy of Dr. Fielding's car, office and apartment building are central to an understanding of the Watergate story. They were developed by the CIA and Xerox copies showing Dr. Fielding's nameplate above his car and Liddy posing outside Fielding's office building were seen by senior officers, who cut off further support for Hunt on the morning the photos were developed.

Senator Howard Baker once famously asked, "What did the president know and when did he know it?" In the case of the Fielding photographs, I explore in unprecedented detail who saw them, when they saw them, and what information they had to make sense of the images. This chain extends from the photo developers of the CIA's Technical Services Division up to Director Richard Helms on the seventh floor; to assistant Attorney General Henry Petersen and lead Watergate prosecutor Earl Silbert; and to John Dean, General Counsel to the president and the architect of the cover-up, who knew the Fielding photos were a ticking time bomb that would eventually go off.

This book also explores several unresolved mysteries about the Watergate break-ins, moving the focus beyond Nixon's inner circle to the burglars themselves, their CIA connections and their individual perspectives on the purpose of the break-in and why they got caught. According to the conventional narrative, during the first break-in, bugs were planted on the phones of DNC chairman Larry O'Brien and Spencer Oliver, the executive director of the Association of State Democratic Chairmen. But the alleged bug on O'Brien's phone didn't work and was installed in the wrong office; and the targeting of Oliver for political intelligence purposes seemed an odd choice.

In later nomination hearings for US Attorney in the District of Columbia, lead prosecutor Earl Silbert admitted:

> We never were able to determine the precise motivation for the burglary and wiretapping, particularly on the phone of a relative unknown— Spencer Oliver. Baldwin had told us that McCord wanted all telephone calls recorded, including personal calls . . . Many of them [were] extremely personal, intimate and potentially embarrassing. We also learned that Hunt had sometime previously met Spencer Oliver at Robert R. Mullen & Co. and opposed his joining the firm because he was a liberal Democrat. Therefore, one motive we thought possible was an attempt to compromise Oliver and others . . . for political reasons . . . [but] we never had any direct proof of this since neither Hunt or Liddy . . . would talk to us.[10]

In the moments after his arrest, Watergate burglar Rolando Martinez tried to hide a key which the FBI matched to the desk drawer of Oliver's secretary, Ida "Maxie" Wells, ten days later. In the Howard Johnson motel across the street, Alfred Baldwin had been listening to intercepted conversations on Oliver's phone and the key suggests the desk drawer was one of the targets of the second break-in. What was in the drawer?

Baldwin's logs of intercepted conversations were apparently destroyed by the conspirators in the days following the break-in, but his subsequent accounts of what he heard have been generally corroborated by the victims of the wiretapping. According to Earl Silbert, these were principally Spencer Oliver and Maxie Wells. Silbert subpoenaed them to appear at trial to corroborate Baldwin's testimony, but the District Court of Appeals barred the contents of the conversations being discussed for reasons of privacy, a ruling that is still in force today.

Following the arrests, the FBI found no bugs in any of the phones at the crime scene. Three months later, a bug was mysteriously found on Spencer Oliver's phone. Silbert claimed the FBI had missed it in their first search; the FBI concluded it had been placed there after the second break-in. By whom and for what purpose?

CHAPTER 1

THE ANNA
CHENNAULT AFFAIR

IN OCTOBER 1962, at the height of the Cuban Missile Crisis, as President Kennedy prepared for a possible of invasion of Cuba, he telephoned the apartment of Mrs. Anna Chan Chennault—the Chinese-born widow of the late Lieutenant General Claire Chennault. Ray Cline, the CIA's deputy director of Intelligence (DDI), had first alerted the president to the newly-installed Russian offensive missile bases in Cuba nine days earlier and was at a dinner party at Mrs. Chennault's apartment that evening.[1]

Cline had served as station chief in Taiwan from 1958 to 1962, where he and his wife became friends with Mrs. Chennault on her frequent visits home. Chennault had moved from Taipei to Washington after the death of her husband in 1958 and, according to Cline, Tommy "The Cork" Corcoran, General Chennault's legal adviser and a legendary power-broker in Washington, "became her sort of protector and guardian."

Corcoran was a key figure in the China Lobby, a conservative alliance which blamed Truman and the Democrats for losing China to Communism and rallied political support for Taiwan. Corcoran came to see Cline and suggested he meet Mrs. Chennault periodically to benefit from "her fantastic acquaintance with Asians, not only in Taiwan but even more in Vietnam and Korea":

So, what it amounted to was about every six weeks or so we'd find some occasion to have lunch, or [we'd] see each other at a party or something . . . and she'd tell me what she thought about Asian politics . . . Sometimes, I made a little memo of things she told me; mostly it was just exchanging ideas on policy.

Cline cleared it with CIA Director John McCone and while Chennault called it "reporting," Cline saw nothing "very unusual about it . . . As DDI, I had dozens of people with whom I had these open, perfectly overt contacts to exchange ideas and interpretations, not information."[2]

But Cline's association with Chennault and the China Lobby continued long after he was posted to Bonn as chief of station in 1966 and left the Agency in 1969. As author Tim Weiner notes in Cline's obituary, "He believed passionately in the cause of the Chinese Nationalists, and in retirement served as head of the Taiwan Committee for a Free China."[3]

In March 1968, on the day Bobby Kennedy announced his run for the presidency, Anna Chennault dined again with Ray Cline.[4]

In *The Making of the President 1968*, Theodore White compares Chennault to Madame Chiang Kai-shek and "Madame Nhu (the Dragon Lady of South Vietnam)":

A line of Oriental ladies of high purpose and authoritarian manners whose pieties and iron righteousness have frequently outrun their brains and acknowledged beauty . . . In that circle of Oriental diplomacy in Washington once known as the China Lobby, Anna Chennault . . . the Chinese widow of wartime hero General Claire Chennault . . . was hostess-queen.[5]

Chennault had campaigned for Nixon in 1960 after meeting him five years earlier in Taiwan—"first at the presidential banquet given in his honor by

President and Madame Chiang Kai-shek," she recalled in her memoir, "then at another reception held for him by the General and me."[6]

When General Chennault died, she was touched by Nixon's note of condolence and they kept in touch "about Asia and Asian Communism, with which he showed a certain fascination."[7]

In June 1962, she met President Kennedy as president of the newly-created Chinese Refugee Relief (CRR) organization and he gave her his support. She was accompanied by CRR secretary Jack Anderson, who was Drew Pearson's assistant on the influential Washington Merry-Go-Round column at the time: "Jack and I hit it off well from the start. Years later, in 1968 and 1969, Anderson would often check with me before writing any Vietnam-related stories."[8]

Her penthouse apartment on Cathedral Avenue served as "a popular watering hole for ranking Republicans by the time Barry Goldwater decided to run for President." Senator John Tower of Texas was involved in early strategy sessions in her living room.[9]

In March 1967, she moved with her two teenage daughters into a two-story penthouse on the fourteenth floor of the Watergate East apartment building, where she would live for the rest of her life. It boasted a private roof garden and she threw a welcoming reception for four hundred guests a few weeks later.[10]

She was still active as a fund-raiser in the Republican party and around this time, Nixon requested a meeting to sound her out about serving "as an advisor on Southeast Asian affairs" for his presidential campaign. "Vietnam would be a hotly debated issue among the candidates," she later recalled, and Nixon needed her to use her "solid connections to the Vietnamese leaders, to supply him with reliable information." Chennault was "flattered by the request" and told him she would be "happy to help."[11]

She suggested sending two leading Republicans—Senator John Tower (R—Texas) and Ambassador Robert Hill of New Hampshire—on an "advance mission" to Vietnam, preceding a visit by Nixon to President

Thieu. Nixon thought it an excellent idea and later in the year, Chennault met Thieu in Saigon to deliver "a message from Nixon requesting that I be recognized as the conduit for any information that might flow between the two."[12]

At the end the year, Hill wrote a memo anticipating an attempt by Lyndon B. Johnson to settle the Vietnam War during his 1968 bid for re-election. He accused Johnson of deliberately provoking the Gulf of Tonkin Incident in 1964 and acting illegally by declaring war on North Vietnam without Congressional consent. He suggested preparing a study on the incident by "distinguished and objective scholars" which could be used against the president "at the appropriate time."[13]

Newly discovered letters from Anna Chennault to Richard Nixon during his election run in 1968, and previously unpublished documents from her personal papers, show the Nixon campaign's plans to use Chennault's relationship with South Vietnamese ambassador Bui Diem to forestall the Paris Peace Talks began five months earlier than was previously thought.

According to her personal calendar, Anna Chennault introduced Diem to Nixon's people on February 16 in New York, two weeks after Nixon announced his candidacy in New Hampshire. The handwritten entries note a meeting with Ambassador Diem at ten o'clock that morning—"meet at R. Nixon's apartment" (underlined in red) and "met John Mitchell first time."

Mitchell was Nixon's campaign manager and the entries note that foreign policy advisor Richard Allen was also there, along with Nixon's longtime secretary Rose Mary Woods, and Robert Hill, a former ambassador to Mexico who had been chairman of the Republican National Committee Foreign Policy Task Force since 1965. Woods and Mitchell were her neighbors, with apartments on the seventh floor of Watergate East. Maurice Stans, finance chairman for Nixon's campaign, had an apartment on the twelfth.[14]

Hill may have set the ball rolling in mid-January, when Chennault's calendar entry reads "Bob Hill—drop by to talk after dinner on 'Nixon'" and Chennault attended a Foreign Policy dinner at the Mayflower Hotel at the end of the month, where she may have met Allen.[15]

Allen was a senior staff member at the Hoover Institution on War, Revolution and Peace and the editor of its Yearbook on International Communist Affairs. In January 1968, according to the *New York Times*, Allen "approached the C.I.A. for assistance on a research project." He met CIA Director Richard Helms, who agreed to provide Allen with "various unclassified agency reports on the strengths of national Communist parties . . . and Mr. Allen continued to deal with the agency on an informal basis during the spring of 1968."[16]

Allen later insisted his initial approach was merely a request to review the yearbook for "egregious errors" and was "partly precautionary," to avoid CIA interference or offers of funding that would compromise its independence. He claimed he had not asked the Agency for information but then why did he meet Helms in the first place?[17]

Three days after the meeting with Bui Diem and Nixon staff at Nixon's apartment, Chennault had lunch with Senator Tower, and Bui Diem was on her call list the next day.[18]

Mrs. Chennault had recently taken up a job as vice president of The Flying Tiger Line, a cargo airline frequently chartered by the US military to fly troops to Vietnam. She travelled to Saigon in late February and stayed with her sister, Connie, whose husband, James Fong, was the chief of commercial affairs at the Nationalist Chinese embassy in Vietnam. She met informally with President Thieu and General Thiem, whose wife hosted "a huge dinner" for her. "I had known Thiem since his days as ambassador to Taipei," she recalled in her memoir, "and subsequently, from 1962 to 1965, in Washington."[19]

By March 15, she was back in Washington, meeting Bui Diem and the next day, Bobby Kennedy announced his run for the presidency. She had dinner with Diem and the influential lobbyist Bob Gray four days later and her calendar notes a meeting with Rose Mary Woods and lunch with Senator Tower in the days after that.[20]

On March 25, Chennault wrote to congratulate Nixon on his primary win in New Hampshire:

Since we last met in New York, I have been twice to Vietnam and only a week ago I returned from Korea, Taiwan, Japan and Hong Kong. I met with President Thieu, Vice President Ky of Vietnam, President Chiang and Vice President Yen in Taiwan, President Park and Prime Minister Chung Il Kwon of Korea.

I have been in very close touch with our mutual friend, Ambassador Bob Hill . . . and have asked [him] to relay [some] information to you personally.

The Vietnam Ambassador to Washington, Mr. Bui Diem is my very close personal friend. He met with Johnson and Secretary Dean Rusk before he left for Saigon last week. If you wish to talk with me more on Vietnam conditions, I am glad to make myself available.[21]

There's no record of a reply to this or follow-up letters to Nixon sent on April 4 and 12, and copied to Hill.[22]

On March 27, bizarrely, "the C.I.A. decided independently that it wished to make available to [Richard] Allen certain classified publications that bore on his work [and] a background investigation to secure the necessary clearance was ordered." The background check was "farmed out" to Franklin Geraty, an Agency investigator in San Francisco, working under Defense Department cover. As Allen later pointed out, by then, "it was generally widely known" in Republican circles that he would be joining the Nixon campaign and CIA officials later admitted that it looked like "we were watching the other side."[23]

During April, Mrs. Chennault had lunch with columnist Jack Anderson and dinner with Senator Tower and peace negotiator Henry Cabot Lodge respectively.

On May 7, three days before the Paris peace talks began, she sent President Thieu a copy of a recent speech:

> At this most critical time I know you must be deeply worried and concerned of the future of your country as I am deeply concerned about mine, the United States of America. I just want you to know that we are not entirely alone, and as long as there is will, there is hope . . . we just have to keep on fighting until our struggle against Communist aggression is won.[25]

According to Richard Helms' biographer Thomas Powers, during the peace talks, "CIA agents reported regularly on the activities of South Vietnamese observer, Bui Diem." A source in the Agency's Directorate of Operations told him their attempt to "install listening devices in Bui Diem's office and living quarters" failed: "The Agency was simultaneously keeping track of the Saigon government through its bug in President Thieu's office, and in Washington, the NSA monitored radio transmissions from the South Vietnamese Embassy."[26]

In June, over dinner at the Georgetown Club with Corcoran and Senator Tower, Chennault suggested a meeting with Nixon to Diem, who was intrigued by the idea. He agreed but decided against reporting it to Saigon, so "Thieu could later repudiate the move, if necessary."[27]

• • •

On June 1, Richard Allen officially left the Hoover Institution "to handle foreign policy and defense matters" for the Nixon campaign as director of Foreign Policy Research. He also became the point person for Anna Chennault, who wrote several letters to the President later that month.[28]

On June 24, she wrote to advise Nixon on how to handle "the Vietnam issue" and highlighted "one effective man" who has been trying to resolve the power struggle between President Thieu and Vice President Ky of Vietnam:

> He is Vietnamese Ambassador to the United States, Ambassador _Bui Diem_ who is also the South Vietnam representative to the Paris [peace] conference. _A newspaper man by profession and my close friend, he travels constantly between Saigon, Washington and Paris every month and he is one of the most outstanding diplomats and politicians of Vietnam._ Both President Thieu and Vice President Ky rely on him and recognize his ability as a negotiator and a trouble shooter. _I would like very much to suggest you meet him and talk with him if arrangements can be made._ I myself will be leaving for Southeast Asia around July 15th but I could bring him to you either before [then] or after the convention.[29]

Richard Allen underlined the references to Bui Diem (above) and General Khiem, the former Vietnamese ambassador to Washington and Taiwan, who had just been appointed interior minister. Chennault claimed Khiem was "another good friend of mine . . . This general is the highest ranking military man in Vietnam today."

Chennault received weekly reports from her Vietnamese "contact" and would "be glad to give my information to either Ambassador Bob Hill or Mrs. Pat Hitts [sic]" who were copied, along with Senator Karl Mundt (R—South Dakota). Chennault ran a women's advisory committee for Nixon, supervised by Patricia Hitt, co-chair of the Nixon campaign and "a longtime personal friend of the Nixons."[30]

• • •

CIA investigator Franklin Geraty's cover was finally blown the next day, when posing as a representative of Fidelity Reporting Service—and claiming "he had been retained by 'the Republicans' to conduct background checks on some Nixon aides"—he made a clumsy approach to Allen's banker, who immediately alerted the Nixon campaign. Through police contacts, Nixon's security chief Jack Caulfield discovered Fidelity was a "C.I.A. outfit."[31]

Once Allen officially joined the campaign, the Agency dropped its investigation "on the assumption that he would no longer play a role in the yearbook project," but it was a curious episode. If Allen had never asked for classified information, why did the Agency volunteer it as a pretext for investigating him for three months?[32]

Office of Security files prepared for submission to the Rockefeller Commission on CIA Activities within the United States in January 1975 include a folder titled "Alleged Illegal Domestic Activities (Richard V. Allen) (SECRET)." A CIA memorandum from the same period, listing documents in a safe drawer, notes "some material on subject of Richard V. Allen (201–831255), a witting collaborator since January 1968, including a memo from RGR [Raymond G. Rocca, Deputy Chief of Counterintelligence], 16 January 1975." It bears the handwritten notation: "very sensitive, should be restricted. Not for that outside agency [presumably the Commission]."[33]

Allen later told William Safire that he "had been the target of a clumsy CIA probe," a claim briefly mentioned in Safire's book in 1975. While author Ken Hughes calls the claim "unsubstantiated," CIA officials confirmed it at the time and Allen later wore it as a badge of honor, calling it "the first proven illegal investigation of a U.S. citizen by the CIA":

Years later, I told Safire about it and he wrote about it and thought it was much more significant than I did. Now I think it's more significant than he does.[34]

• • •

In the days after Geraty was exposed, Anna Chennault met one of Nixon's secretaries and followed up with Bob Hill before writing Nixon again:

> *President Thieu of South Vietnam's visit to Washington was canceled after Senator Bob Kennedy's assassination but now it has been rescheduled. He will be in Washington for two days. After talking with Ambassador Hill, if you should decide to meet with President Thieu, please let me know and I will work out the detail and make the arrangement.*

"No! No!" is scribbled next to this underlined passage in Allen's copy and linked to a handwritten note "to RN":

> *Allen recommends this not be done for any reason and under no circumstances. Proposal dangerous in the extreme and injurious to our VN position—i.e. to US nat. interests.*

Next to Chennault's conclusion—"There is so much going on in Southeast Asia and so few of us really know the truth"—is scribbled "A.C. included."[35]

On July 2, Senator Mundt discussed Chennault's proposal with Nixon, who dictated a memo for his Chief of Staff H. R. Haldeman following the call:

> *He asked . . . about Anna Chennault's suggestion that either I or a member of my staff talk to General Khiem about Vietnam etc. This might be worth following up and I would suggest that Allen be the man to do the talking. Be sure that Anna Chennault is informed that we did follow up.*

Allen's name is circled and the words "Allen" and "Done" are handwritten in the margin.[36]

The next day, Allen wrote a memo to Nixon, titled "Possible meeting with South Vietnamese Ambassador":

Talked with Mrs. Chennault, who is long-time friend of Saigon's ambassador to US, Bui Diem. He is now in Paris, designated official observer and representative of SVN government to the peace talks. He is due back in here [Washington] next week some time.

Mrs. Chennault has apparently asked him if he would talk to DC [Nixon]. I explained schedule tight, but possible to check on available time.

Meeting would have to be absolute top secret, etc.

Initiative is ours—if DC can see him, I am to contact Mrs. Chennault, she will arrange.

I stressed that it is virtually certain that such a meeting would have to be here in NYC.

This would be a good opportunity to get filled in on events in Paris and other developments.

Referring to the words "Top secret," Nixon scribbled:

Should be but I don't see how—with the S.S. [Secret Service]. If it can be [secret], RN would like to see—if not, could Allen see for RN?[37]

In 1975, Allen told Safire "he thought about it a lot but decided a meeting would be a mistake," but Chennault and Diem's memoirs in the eighties

confirmed the meeting did take place. Allen's misdirection was understand-
able in 1975, in the aftermath of Watergate, but he has consistently distorted
Chennault's ties to him and the Nixon campaign over the years, a subject
we'll return to later.[38]

Anna Chennault's calendar for July 12, 1968 reads: "N.Y. to see Dick Nixon
with Amb. Biu [sic] Diem 2:00 PM."[39]

Her account of who arranged the meeting is questionable. She writes: "I
cannot now remember whether it was Nixon or Mitchell who first suggested
the meeting with Bui Diem." Her letters to Nixon clearly show it was her idea.[40]

"[John] Mitchell received us warmly, reminding me that he had met me
before, with my late husband, whom he admired . . ." reads like she has forgotten or is trying to hide the February meeting. After greeting Bui Diem
with "great warmth," Nixon told him:

> *Anna is my good friend . . . Please rely on her from now on as the only con-*
> *tact between myself and your government. If you have any message for me,*
> *please give it to Anna and she will replay it to me . . . We know Anna is a*
> *good American and a dedicated Republican. We can all rely on her loyalty.*
> *If I should be elected the next President, you can rest assured that I will have*
> *a meeting with your leader and find a solution to winning this war.*[41]

After talking for half an hour, Nixon had an hour-long private discussion
with Diem and Mitchell before emerging to reiterate that Anna would be
"the sole representative between the Vietnamese government and the Nixon
campaign."[42]

Since May, Diem had been commuting weekly to the Paris talks and "con-
ferring almost daily" with William Bundy, assistant secretary of state for

East Asia, and Walt Rostow, Johnson's national security advisor. A summit was planned between Johnson and Thieu the following week. A few days before meeting Nixon, Diem raised the subject with Bundy:

> As a friend and experienced diplomat . . . [he] understood my position and accepted my assurances that I would limit myself to a general discussion with Nixon and would not go into details about the peace talks.[43]

It is very strange that neither Bundy nor Rostow subsequently mentioned this meeting to Johnson and while not discounting it, Bundy had no recollection of doing so in his memoirs.[44]

From then on, Anna Chennault grew closer to Mitchell, the "commander-in-chief of the campaign":

> He had a private number where he could be reached at all times. But so acute was his concern about wiretapping that he would change the number every few days or so . . . At the height of the campaign, I was on the phone with Mitchell at least once a day, much of the conversation consisting of messages I had been asked to relay to him by various people both within and outside the campaign.[45]

She told author Anthony Summers that, "in the weeks that followed . . . Nixon and Mitchell . . . told her to inform Saigon that were Nixon to become president, South Vietnam would get 'a better deal' . . . They worked out this deal to win the campaign," she said. "Power overpowers all reason . . . It was all very, very confidential."[46]

In early August, Chennault told the *Miami Herald* she was concerned at the anti-war protests dividing America: "The Communists take this as a sign of weakness. . . . It is important this nation shows signs of determination, strength and unity. We shouldn't tell our enemies we're going to withdraw. That's childish."[47]

A few days later, Nixon won the Republican nomination at the convention in Miami Beach, appointing Maryland Governor Spiro Agnew as his running mate. Reflecting on the excitement of the convention, Chennault wrote:

What makes men want power? Is it courage? Is it a desire to serve? Or just absolute selfishness? . . . For seven long days and nights, I watched the interaction of heroes and clowns, victors and defeated, challenged and challengers . . . The spectators in the crowd cried, cheered, shouted. So this is American politics!

In a situation like this, we see human behavior uninhibitedly exposed. Friends become enemies—but some enemies always willing to compromise, depending on what the other side has to offer.

I loved the show as much as I despised some of the men and women in it. Some men were born to be leaders; others tried but simply did not have the good sense to stop trying. The powerful, and the powerless, what makes them so different? Confidence, authority seemed to surround the powerful like the air they breathe. Many tried to acquire that air but only a few succeeded.[48]

In mid-August, Maurice Stans, chair of the Finance Committee, wrote Chennault to thank her for a further $3,000 contribution to the campaign. She had already donated $10,000 and later in the month, she persuaded Wayne Hoffman, chairman of the Flying Tiger Line, to make a $100,000 contribution.[49]

• • •

On August 18, Chennault and Tower debriefed Bui Diem after his return from Paris. The next day, she wrote to Nixon again, and in a section underlined by Allen, recommended that "an exclusive team should be sent out to Asia as soon as possible to bring you up-to-date information. I am sure John Tower has already discussed my recommendation with Mr. Mitchell. I volunteer my service if I can be of help." She warned Nixon of possible "dirty tricks" his opponents might pull, "such as the release of prisoners from North Vietnam . . . [or] the release of the crew of the Pueblo [a Navy intelligence ship held captive by North Korean forces at the time]."[50]

On September 3, with no response from Nixon, Chennault sent Richard Allen copies of her "personal and confidential letters to Dick," requesting his comments, particularly on her most recent letter. The letter to Allen has an intriguing handwritten footnote, suggesting Allen may have been sending his own emissaries to the Vietnamese embassy: "P.S. Did you send a Mr McCormick [sic] to the Vietnam Embassy? They called me to check."[51]

Dick McCormack was a foreign policy researcher on Allen's staff who specialized in Vietnam and anticipated Johnson's bombing halt initiative a month ahead of time. After a research trip to Vietnam, he traveled to Washington in early September and met Nguyen Hoan, Diem's deputy at the Vietnamese embassy. They discussed "the general situation in Vietnam" for an hour and planned to meet again on McCormack's next visit to the capital. "After Nixon began taking note of my memoranda and acting on my recommendations," he later said, "one insecure and unscrupulous colleague whispered that I was a secret CIA plant and therefore not to be trusted."[52]

By now, Chennault was co-chair with Mrs. Eisenhower of the party's new National Women's Advisory Committee and the campaign's most successful fund-raiser. She was co-chair for a $1,000-a-plate dinner in mid-September and appointed vice chairman of the Republican National Finance Committee at the end of the month, as its chair gave her a target list of donors for the last five weeks of the campaign. In early October, she donated another $5,000, taking her total raised to $250,000, and she was invited to attend meetings of the Key Issues Committee, a twenty-five-member panel overseeing national security and foreign policy, which included Hill, Mundt, Laird, Baker and Stans, and was chaired by Senator John Tower.[53]

By mid-October, according to Chennault, "Thieu was said to have agreed to a bombing halt, provided his government were included in the negotiation and settlement process." Chennault wrote Nixon—care of his hotel in Kansas City and copying Richard Allen—with her thoughts on the "bombing pause," calling it a "false issue" that masks North Vietnamese reluctance to enter serious negotiations.[54]

Around this time, William Bundy believed Chennault began acting through Thieu's brother, Nguyen Van Kieu, the number two man in the embassy in Taiwan, "who came down to Saigon shortly after October 15 and pulled out all the stops with various leaders about the dangers of going along with the halt and new negotiations"[55]:

According to the cables of the period, his influence was just utterly baleful from the moment he landed. And knowing Madame Chennault's very strong influence in Taipei and the fact that the Taipei government was the one in all of Asia that didn't even clap politely when this bombing stoppage was announced, I think that channels were set afoot to tell him, "Get down there and don't let this happen."[56]

As Johnson's plans for a bombing halt gathered pace, Nixon aide Bryce Harlow had a "double agent working in the White House," reporting on all the meetings and keeping Nixon informed about Johnson's "next move."

"Boss, he's going to dump on you," Harlow told Nixon.

"He has sworn he would not," replied Nixon.

"It's in preparation," replied Harlow, reporting that Johnson was "having a hell of a time" convincing the joint chiefs of staff but "he's forcing them to go with it . . . As soon as he gets them over, and the time is right, he's going to dump. That's the plan." Nixon couldn't believe it.[57]

According to the Nixon Foundation, Harlow sent the following memo to Nixon on October 22, "from an impeccable source in President Johnson's innermost circle":

The President is driving exceedingly hard for a deal with North Vietnam. Expectation is that he is becoming almost pathologically eager for an excuse to order a bombing halt and will accept almost any arrangement . . . . Careful plans are being made to help HHH [Democratic presidential candidate Hubert H. Humphrey] exploit whatever happens. White House staff liaison with HHH is close. Plan is for LBJ to make a nationwide TV announcement as quickly as possible after agreement; the object is to get this done as long before November 5 as they can . . . White Housers still think they can pull the election out for HHH with this ploy; that's what is being attempted.[58]

In H. R. Haldeman's handwritten notes from this period, author John Farrell recently discovered several notations corroborating the official sanction given to Chennault's scheming. On October 22, Nixon asks Haldeman to tell Mitchell: "Keep Anna Chennault working on SVN [South Vietnam]—insist publicly on the 3 Johnson conditions." There is an exclamation mark next to the note, highlighting its importance. After months of deadlock, Hanoi had recently accepted Johnson's three conditions for a bombing halt—entering peace talks, respecting the demilitarized zone (DMZ) on its border and ending the shelling of cities in South Vietnam.[59]

The Nixon Foundation convincingly argues that Nixon's instructions were in direct response to the Harlow memo that day. Nixon was "mad as hell" that Johnson appeared to be dropping his three conditions to support Humphrey and wanted the President to know if he didn't "get 3 conditions N [Nixon] will blast bomb halt."[60]

Haldeman was also to instruct Spiro Agnew to "go see Helms—tell him we want the truth [presumably about Johnson's plans for a bombing halt]— or he hasn't got the job [won't be retained as CIA Director]."[61]

According to author Thomas Powers, "sometime that fall, CIA surveillance began to pick up references to Madame Chennault's activities. Because she was a U.S. citizen . . . the reports were written up in the office of the DDP [Deputy Director of Plans], Thomas Karamessines, and then forwarded to Richard Helms. Helms passed them on to Walt Rostow, the President's National Security Adviser, who in turn sent them to Johnson, who liked to know what was going on."[62]

On June 26, 1973, Rostow sent a sealed envelope, containing many of these CIA cables and his memos to President Johnson, to the director of the LBJ Library with the note:

> Sealed in the attached envelope is a file President Johnson asked me to hold personally because of its sensitive nature . . . The file concerns the activities of Mrs. Chennault and others before and immediately after the election of 1968. At the time, President Johnson decided to handle the matter strictly as a question of national security. . . . It is, therefore, my recommendation to you that this file should remain sealed for fifty years . . .[63]

The "Top Secret" "X envelope" was finally opened for research in 1994 by LBJ Library director Harry Middleton, after security clearance by the intelligence agencies, and sheds considerable light on what happened next. It includes an accompanying memorandum from Rostow on "the activities of

Mrs. Chennault and other Republicans just before the presidential election of 1968." Rostow notes that after a "diplomatic breakthrough" with Hanoi about a bombing halt in the second week of October, the North Vietnamese "backed away" until the agreement was "re-established towards the end of the month":

> *From October 17 to October 29, we received diplomatic intelligence of Saigon's uneasiness with the apparent break in Hanoi's position on a total bombing cessation and with the Johnson Administration's apparent willingness to go forward. . . .*

In mid-October, President Thieu had agreed to peace talks and "as late as October 28," despite continuing unease, he told the US Ambassador to South Vietnam, Ellsworth Bunker, he was still willing to proceed.[64]

According to Powers, in the week ending Sunday, October 27, "the National Security Agency intercepted a radio message from the South Vietnamese Embassy to Saigon explicitly urging Thieu to stand fast against an agreement until after the election."[65]

On October 23, Bui Diem cabled President Thieu: "Many Republican friends have contacted me and encouraged us to stand firm. They were alarmed by press reports to the effect that you had already softened your position." Four days later, according to Diem's memoir, he wrote, "I am regularly in touch with the Nixon entourage," who he identified as "Anna Chennault, John Mitchell, and Senator Tower."[66]

But Diem went further than this, according to State Department official, Benjamin Read, who kept notes of the unredacted cable:

> *I explained discreetly to our partisan friends our firm attitude . . . [and] plan to adhere to that position . . . The longer the situation continues, the*

more we are favored, for the elections take place in a week and President Johnson would probably have difficulties in forcing our hand.[67]

Diem noted that Nixon was still "the favorite despite the uncertainty provoked by the news of an imminent bombing halt." If Nixon won, "he would first send an unofficial person [redacted] and would himself consider later going to Saigon before the inauguration."[68]

The intercepted cables were sent to the White House by NSA early Monday evening, October 28. Earlier that day, Alexander Sachs, a renowned economist at Lehman Corporation, had a working lunch with a group of colleagues in Wall Street, including two bankers who were "very close to Nixon." One of them explained that Nixon was trying to "block" Johnson's attempts to find peace in Vietnam, so he thought "the prospects for a bombing halt or a cease-fire were dim." Nixon was inciting "Saigon to be difficult, and Hanoi to wait": "He was trying to frustrate the President, by inciting Saigon to step up its demands, and by letting Hanoi know that when he took office 'he could accept anything and blame it on his predecessor.'"[69]

That evening, Sachs shared this information with an old friend, Eugene Rostow, who in turn telephoned his brother, Walt, national security advisor to the president. Rostow took the news to a late-night conference with the president, his advisors and General Creighton Abrams, the American commander in Vietnam, who had just been summoned back to Washington.

As Hughes notes, on Monday, President Thieu had agreed to a joint announcement on peace talks, not recognizing "the so-called National Liberation Front as an entity independent of North Vietnam" but allowing them a place at the table. Abrams voiced no objection to the bombing halt but when Johnson sought final approval from Saigon in the early hours of Tuesday morning, "Thieu said three days was not enough time to get a delegation to Paris." As Rostow later observed:

> *During the meeting with Abrams word came from Bunker of Thieu's sudden intransigence. The diplomatic information previously received plus the information from New York took on new and serious significance.*[70]

Putting the intelligence from the cables and Sachs together, Rostow wrote the president early the next morning, "considering the explosive possibilities of the information that we now have on how certain Republicans may have inflamed the South Vietnamese to behave as they have been behaving":

> *There is no hard evidence that Mr. Nixon himself is involved. Exactly what the Republicans have been saying to Bui Diem is not wholly clear . . . [but] the materials are so explosive that they could gravely damage the country whether Mr. Nixon is elected or not. If they get out in their present form, they could be the subject of one of the most acrimonious debates we have ever witnessed.*

For the good of the country, Rostow suggested Johnson speak with Nixon and share the information without suggesting he was personally involved:

> *This kind of talk is inflaming the inexperienced . . . and impressionable . . . South Vietnamese who do not understand our constitution or our political life.*[71]

• • •

The president ordered the FBI to begin physical and electronic surveillance on Madame Chennault and the South Vietnamese embassy. Bromley Smith, assistant to National Security Advisor McGeorge Bundy, called Cartha "Deke" DeLoach, the number three man at the Bureau:

We urgently need to know the identity of every individual who enters the South Vietnamese embassy in Washington for at least the next three days. In addition, we want an accounting of every phone conversation—an English translation, both incoming and outgoing calls. Call the attorney general if you need wiretap approval. Also, place a wiretap on Mrs. Claire Chennault at the Watergate Apartments. Follow her wherever she goes.[72]

Within hours, the wiretap on the embassy was approved and physical surveillance on the embassy and Chennault began, but her telephone was not monitored.[73]

Meanwhile, according to Powers, "Walt Rostow pressed the CIA for what it knew about Madame Chennault's activities":

Helms' Special Assistant for Vietnamese Affairs, George Carver, argued that Saigon did not need a deal with Nixon in order to resist the agreement Johnson was pushing. Thieu thought he was being sold down the river, and if Carver had been in Thieu's position, he'd have felt the same way. But Rostow, reflecting Johnson's anger, wasn't having any; he wanted the CIA to move on this, and the CIA did so.[74]

In a further memorandum that afternoon, Rostow wrote:

Seen as coolly as I can, this is Saigon's view: Hanoi and Moscow [and President Johnson] have tried to time the bombing halt to help Humphrey . . . They are afraid of Humphrey and want Nixon elected. They believe it is fair, under these circumstances, to use their bargaining leverage to prevent a bombing halt before November 5. In this position, they may have been encouraged, to an extent we cannot specify yet, by some in the Nixon entourage.[75]

The following day, October 30, FBI surveillance picked up an early morning call from Anna Chennault to Ambassador Bui Diem at the South Vietnamese embassy seeking an update on the current "situation." Diem told her something "is cooking" and suggested she "drop by and talk with him" that day "as time is running short." She agreed to stop by after a luncheon for Mrs. Agnew, and the FBI followed her to the embassy that afternoon.[76]

Deke DeLoach reported the call to the White House and Walt Rostow had it on the president's desk within two hours. Chennault's diaries suggest the luncheon for Mrs. Agnew was a lavish affair at the Presidential Ballroom of the Statler Hilton, but Rostow read the meeting as a more intimate and conspiratorial encounter that would implicate Vice President Agnew in the Chennault Affair in days to come.[77]

When Johnson heard about the call, he tried to reach his old friend, Senator Richard B. Russell (D—Georgia). When Russell called him back at 10:25 a.m., Johnson told him:

We have found that our friend, the Republican nominee . . . has been playing on the outskirts with our enemies and our friends both, our allies and the others. He's been doing it through rather subterranean sources here . . .

One of his associates, a fellow named Mitchell, who's running his campaign . . . said to a businessman . . . "We're going to frustrate the President by saying to the South Vietnamese, and the Koreans, and the Thailanders, 'Beware of Johnson.' At the same time, we're going to say to Hanoi, 'I can make a better deal than he has because I'm fresh and new, and I don't have to demand as much as he does in the light of past positions.'"

And Mrs. Chennault is contacting their ambassador from time to time. Seems to be kind of the go-between. In addition, their ambassador is saying to him that Johnson is desperate and is just moving heaven and earth to elect Humphrey, so don't you get sucked in on that. He is kind of these folks' agents here, this little South Vietnamese ambassador. Now, this is not guesswork . . . I know it's her . . . Mrs. Chennault, you know, of the Flying Tigers . . . She's young and attractive. I mean, she's a pretty good-looking girl.

"Certainly is," replied Russell.

"And she's around town and she is warning them to not get pulled in on this Johnson move," continued the President. "Then he, in turn, is warning his government . . . to play it for time and get it by the next few days."

"I'm surprised at Nixon," said Russell. "I never did have any confidence in him, but damn if I thought he'd stoop to anything like that."

"Well . . . it may be his agents," said Johnson.[78]

Late Thursday afternoon, October 31, Chennault called Diem but was told he was busy. She asked if "the Ambassador intended to leave town . . . [or] go to Vietnam" and was told he did not. She left a message asking him to notify her if he did. The next morning, Rostow sent details of the call to the president: "Herewith the Lady tries again but gets something of a brush-off . . ."[79]

The same day, Haldeman's notes indicate he received a report from the "Dragon Lady": "D. Lady says Abrams screamed like stuck pig [presumably about the bombing halt]."[80]

On Friday evening, Johnson briefed the three presidential candidates before announcing a bombing halt to support the Paris peace talks in a televised address.[81]

Chennault was dining with Tom Corcoran in socialite Perle Mesta's suite at the Sheraton Park Hotel when she received a call from John Mitchell, asking her to call him back on a more secure number.[82]

"Anna, I'm speaking on behalf of Mr. Nixon," Mitchell told her. "It's very important that our Vietnamese friends understand our Republican position and I hope you have made that clear to them." Chennault told him she had relayed messages, but they had their own national interests and she didn't think it wise to try to dictate their decisions or "force them to act one way or another."

"Do you think they really have decided not to go to Paris?" Mitchell asked.

"I don't think they'll go. Thieu has told me over and over again that going to Paris would be walking into a smoke screen that has nothing to do with reality." Mitchell asked her to keep him posted.[83]

On Saturday morning, in a speech to the National Assembly, President Thieu announced he would not be joining the peace talks in Paris scheduled for the day after the election, "because three key conditions had not yet been met by Hanoi." Chief among these was that the North Vietnamese "agreed to negotiate without the participation of the National Liberation Front [Viet Cong] as a separate delegation," a ploy which Thieu suspected "would be just another trick toward a coalition government with the Communists in South Vietnam."[84]

CHAPTER 2

TELL YOUR BOSS
TO HOLD ON

That same Saturday morning, November 2, the FBI telephone tap on the South Vietnamese embassy picked up an important call:

> *Mrs. Anna Chennault contacted Vietnamese ambassador, Bui Diem, and advised him that she had received a message from her boss (not further identified), which her boss wanted her to give personally to the ambassador. She said that the message was that the ambassador is "to hold on, we are gonna win" and that her boss also said, "hold on, he understands all of it." She repeated that this is the only message. "He said please tell your boss to hold on." She advised that her boss had just called from New Mexico.*

Walt Rostow forwarded the FBI report to the president that evening with the note: "The New Mexico reference may indicate Agnew is acting." Nixon's running mate, Spiro Agnew, was campaigning in Albuquerque that day.[1]

FBI physical surveillance on Mrs. Chennault noted that she was at home all morning and that, at 1:45 p.m., she stepped into her chauffeur-driven Lincoln Continental, which was last observed heading north on the Baltimore–Washington Parkway at 2:15.[2]

• • •

At 5:30 p.m. on Saturday evening, Chennault's calendar records a meeting with the "U.S. Ambassador to Taipei," Walter McConaughy.[3]

In a note to the president just before six, Special Assistant Jim Jones reported that both Walt Rostow and Secretary of State Rusk "believed that the press should be given a background briefing on the China Lobby's interference as the reason for the uncertainty regarding South Vietnamese participation at the Paris conference." Rostow added:

If the story is played significantly tomorrow, Mansfield and Dirksen should be brought in and shown all the evidence we have concerning [the game] that someone in the Nixon entourage (but not accuse Nixon himself) is playing with South Vietnam . . . They should tell Nixon that if he does press forward in this, then he will reveal the evidence which will destroy him and any effectiveness he would have if he's elected. His first duty is to tell Saigon to get their delegation to Paris as fast as possible.[4]

Late that evening, at the suggestion of Secretary of Defense Clark Clifford, Johnson called Senate Minority Leader Everett Dirksen "re stories going around that Nixon people are spreading rumors to wait on peace negotiations":

We're skirting on dangerous ground, and I thought I ought to give you the facts and you ought to pass them on if you choose. If you don't, why then I will a little later.[5]

According to a summary of the conversation, "several times during mid and late October, Thieu had agreed to a bombing halt . . . [until] actions on the Republican side had impacted upon the negotiations." These involved the "old China crowd," and Johnson shared the last FBI report about Chennault's message from her "boss" in New Mexico. "This is treason," said the president:

Now I can identify them because I know who's doing this. I don't want to identify it. I think it would shock America if a principal candidate was playing with a source like this on a matter this important. I don't want to do that. But if they're going to put this kind of stuff out, they ought to know that we know what they're doing. I know who they're talking to and I know what they're saying. And my judgment is that Nixon ought to play it just like he has all along, that I want to see peace come the first day we can, that it's not going to affect the election one way or the other . . . Now, if Nixon keeps the South Vietnamese away from the conference, well, that's going to be his responsibility. Up to this point, that's why they're not there. I had them signed on board until this happened.

Dirksen said he'd tell Nixon about it.

"I think they're making a very serious mistake," continued Johnson. "They're contacting a foreign power in the middle of a war . . . [and] you better tell them they better quit playing with it. And the day after the election, I'll sit down with all of you and try to work it out and be helpful. But they oughtn't to knock out this conference."

"Whoever they are, I'll try to get ahold of them tonight," said Dirksen.

"They ought to stop this business about trying to keep the conference from taking place," said Johnson. "It takes place the day after the election . . . you just tell them their people are messing around in this thing, and if they don't want it on the front pages, they better quit it . . . and they ought to tell their people that are contacting these embassies to go on with the conference."[6]

•   •   •

Nixon aide Bryce Harlow immediately told Chief of Staff, H. R. Haldeman:

> *Harlow—LBJ called Dirksen—says he knows Repubs thru D. Lady are keeping SVN in present position. If this true—and persists—he will go to nation and blast Reps. & RN. Dirksen very concerned.*[7]

Harlow then ran upstairs and over Haldeman's objections, woke Nixon and told him, "You've got to talk to LBJ. Someone has told him that you're dumping all over the South Vietnamese to keep them from doing something about peace and he's just about to believe it. If you don't let him know quickly that it's not so, then he's going to dump . . . Ev is just beside himself. He says that Lyndon is simply enraged and we ought to do something."

Nixon called the President and told him "there was absolutely no truth in it, as far as he knew." Harlow had no firsthand knowledge but was not convinced it wasn't true:

> *It was too tempting a target. I wouldn't be a bit surprised if there were some shenanigans going on . . . As a matter of fact, I wasn't sure what Nixon was going to say to Johnson. But at any rate, Nixon told him no and Johnson put down his pistol, except probably Johnson didn't believe it. But he probably couldn't prove it, I suppose.*[8]

Researching Richard Allen's papers at the Hoover Institution Archives in Stanford, California, I discovered a tantalizing note in the file on Anna Chennault, handwritten on Allen's campaign stationery (see Figure 1). A notation in the top right-hand corner reads: 'Saturday—early a.m. before election.' Meaning Saturday, 2 November, the day Chennault sent Diem the infamous message from her boss. Next to that is written "Box 19 363-8670" and here are the rest of the notes in full:

11-

⟶ 4–5 times daily

Cork ⟶ Tommy the Cork

- Deadlines in Miami – front page

- Thurs in N.H. ⟶ 11:00 AM no longer reach (?)

Mr. M – go thru – RCH 11.45 AM M & H

- 12 N – Shaffner, ~~Stephen~~ Phil

will be contact with you

Since Thurs 12N tried 4–5 times. never been successful.

Look what she had accomplished ⟶ namely 11 senators[9]

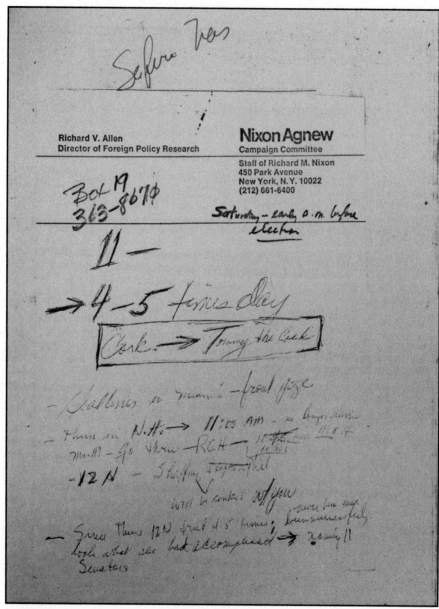

FIGURE 1: Handwritten notes of Richard Allen, November 2, 1968
(Hoover Institution Archives)

While deciphering these notes, it's important to remember that Chennault told her biographer Catherine Forslund that in her Saturday afternoon call to the South Vietnamese embassy, the FBI wiretap technicians had misheard her say "New Mexico." She insisted she said, "New Hampshire, where John Mitchell was at the time, and [that] anything Mitchell knew or told her to do would have been known or come from Nixon."[10]

These notes are consistent with that. She was to contact Mr. M [Mitchell] through RCH [Robert C. Hill]. Hill lived in Littleton, New Hampshire (N.H.) and Phil Shaffner was Mitchell's administrative assistant.[11]

The notes seem to indicate that Chennault (or Tommy "The Cork" Corcoran calling on her behalf) had tried to reach Mitchell through Hill "4–5 times" since Thursday. It was now the Saturday morning before the election and she was trying to get Allen to help. Within hours, her boss would give her the message for Diem.

This document—and Richard Allen—seem to have been the source for a *Sunday Times* exposé, "The Woman Who Scared Nixon" by Godfrey Hodgson, published in March 1969. Hodgson describes handwritten warnings to Nixon from a "foreign policy adviser" about Chennault's June 28 proposal for him to meet President Thieu:

Mrs. Chennault did not give up easily. In the course of the summer she called several of Nixon's staff repeatedly. They were adamant that Nixon should not be mixed up in the peace talks. On Wednesday, October 30, John Mitchell, Nixon's campaign manager (now Attorney General), made a series of calls to certain members of his staff . . . [and] was able to assure the White House that no member of Nixon's campaign staff had been in touch with the South Vietnamese . . .

On Thursday, October 31, Mrs. Chennault made a lot of phone calls. She complained in one of them that she could no longer get through to John

Mitchell. She boasted about her influence within the Nixon team and claimed that she had played a role in the recent endorsement of Nixon by 11 Vietnamese senators. But she got no encouragement.[12]

The newly-discovered notes indicate she did receive encouragement and the reference to "11 Vietnamese senators" clearly chimes with the line "Look what she had accomplished —► namely 11 senators." The notes— and Allen's skewed interpretation of them for Hodgson—tend to confirm Chennault's claim that "her boss" was Mitchell calling from New Hampshire, not Agnew calling from New Mexico. As Forslund notes:

That Agnew would have been in on Nixon's best kept secret—his inside connection to the GVN leaders—is implausible. When queried on the seeming contradiction, Chennault believed the FBI wiretap technician must have misunderstood her. She believes she said, "New Hampshire," where John Mitchell was at the time of the conversation.[13]

In the late nineties, Chennault's biographer Catherine Forslund questioned her about a recently-released memo from Walt Rostow, which briefly seemed to indicate "that a call from Albuquerque did go to Anna Chennault, and that it could have been made by Agnew":

Chennault wavered on these conversations while never faltering in her position that Nixon knew of and/or directed her actions. . . . When confronted directly with phone records indicating a call to her from New Mexico, she was less sure of her memory . . . Her objective was to keep Nixon and GVN leaders informed of each other's intentions with whatever tactics she deemed best.[14]

Chennault told Forslund that "just Nixon, Mitchell, Tower, and Robert Hill . . . all [then] dead, knew of the campaign's connections to the GVN through her" and as we'll see, an FBI investigation would soon discount the Agnew connection.[15]

Above Allen's notes, "Safire has" is written in blue ink, indicating Allen gave a copy of the notes to William Safire, but they aren't mentioned in his book.

On Sunday morning, November 3, George Smathers, a Democratic senator from Florida who was close to Nixon, called the White House to report a call from the Republican candidate:

> *Nixon said he understands the President is ready to blast him for allegedly collaborating with Tower and Chennault to slow the peace talks. Nixon says there is not any truth at all in this allegation. Nixon says there has been no contact at all. Tonight on "Meet the Press" Nixon will again back up the President and say he (Nixon) would rather get peace now than be President.*[16]

Early that afternoon, Smathers told the president that Nixon was worried that "you were getting ready to charge him with the accusation that he connived with John Tower and Anna Chennault to bring about the action of the Saigon government not participating"—a charge Nixon described as untrue, unfair, and unfortunate.

Nixon pledged "his full cooperation" to successfully resolve the impasse in Paris, offering to travel to Vietnam, if it would help. "The problem is not his traveling somewhere," the President told Smathers. "The problem is the people on both sides of this fence getting the impression that they can get a little more for the house if they'll wait a week to sell it." According to a State Department summary of the call, Johnson "insisted that he had proof of Republican involvement with the South Vietnamese

Government . . . and intercepted telegrams revealed that the South Vietnamese were being told 'that Nixon is going to win; therefore, they ought
to wait on Nixon.'"

> *On the surface, [Nixon] was playing that he didn't want to undercut me.*
> *Under the table, his people . . . were saying that you ought to wait on Dick.*
> *Now, that's got it pretty well screwed up. . . .*

Johnson wanted Nixon to get his sources to tell Thieu "you better get on to
that damn conference" or lose US support.

"Your people think that Tower and Chennault have made these contacts,"
said Smathers. "But [Nixon] said he doesn't know whether they have or they
haven't. He doesn't think that they have."

"The South Vietnamese have gotten the word that Nixon feels that it's
better to wait on him, and I know their President has taken that and reversed
himself . . . He's got to keep his Finches and his Lairds and his Chennaults
and the rest of them from running around and messing up this broth."

"Well, I'll pass this word back to him, that, goddamnit, you had it set, and
that someone—his people—are screwing it up," replied Smathers.[17]

Nixon called Johnson shortly afterwards to tell him that "any rumblings
around about somebody trying to sabotage the Saigon government's
attitude . . . certainly have . . . absolutely no credibility, as far as I am
concerned."

"I'm very happy to hear that, Dick, because that is taking place," replied
Johnson. Nixon made brief reference to "that China Lobby thing" before
Johnson cut him off and recapped the agreement with Thieu about the
bombing pause which had been undercut by "traffic [going] out that Nixon
will do better by you. Now, that goes to Thieu . . . I didn't say that it was
with your knowledge. I hope it wasn't."

"Ah, no," said Nixon, laughing before reaffirming his position, "My God, I would never do anything to encourage Hanoi—I mean Saigon—not to come to the table. . . . We've got to get them to Paris, or you can't have a peace."[18]

In his morning meeting on election eve, Clark Clifford observed in his notes:

> *The mess we're in now is wholly of Saigon's making—& is solely due to Republican pressure on Viet Nam thru Bui Diem (SVNamese ambassador to U.S.).*
>
> *(Republican channel is Mrs. Claire Chennault. Chinese-born widow of Gen. [Claire Chennault], whose code name for this action "Little Flower"!!)*
>
> *CMC [Clifford] thinks he's got it stopped.*[19]

In the late morning, an "unknown white male" spent forty-five minutes at the South Vietnamese embassy before taking a cab to the west gate of the White House. He arrived at noon and was identified by White House police as Saville Davis of the *Christian Science Monitor*.[20]

According to FBI wiretaps, he had called the embassy that morning, requesting an appointment with the ambassador, "to check out a story received from a correspondent [Beverly Deepe] in Saigon." He was told the ambassador was busy but insisted on coming to the embassy to "wait for the ambassador to see him" as he had an urgent deadline:

> *Davis said the dispatch from Saigon contains the elements of a major scandal which also involves the Vietnamese ambassador and which . . . [if published], will affect presidential candidate Richard Nixon . . . [and] create a great deal of excitement.*[21]

At 12:10 p.m., Rostow was informed that Davis was "upstairs," awaiting comment on "a sensational dispatch from Saigon," the first paragraph of which read:

> *Purported political encouragement from the Richard Nixon camp was a significant factor in the last-minute decision of President Thieu's refusal to send a delegation to the Paris peace talks—at least until the American Presidential election is over.*[22]

Anna Chennault had visited the South Vietnamese embassy before Davis that morning before proceeding to Nixon campaign headquarters. She was summoned back after Davis left to confer briefly with the ambassador. She then walked to the Chinese embassy, and within minutes, took a cab back to her office.[23]

As Davis waited upstairs, Walt Rostow briefed the president at his Texas ranch. Johnson said, "he had his suspicions" but couldn't confirm Davis' story, and asked Rostow to refer him to the State Department, who refused to comment. Rostow reported the following details:[24]

> *The story was headed by Beverly Deepe: "This must be checked with the Nixon people before publication." Saville Davis volunteered that his newspaper would certainly not print the story in the form in which it was filed; but they might print a story which said Thieu, on his own, decided to hold out until after the election. Incidentally, the story as filed is stated to be based on Vietnamese sources, and not U.S., in Saigon.*[25]

The FBI wiretap report was received by the White House Situation Room at 12:42 p.m. and delivered to Johnson ("Literally Eyes Only for the President") forty-one minutes later, with a note from Rostow: "I assume that Bui Diem brought her in to tell her about Saville Davis' visit."[26]

• • •

Shortly after that, Johnson held a conference call with Clifford, Rusk, and Rostow and told them "this Saville Davis thing . . . concerns me a great deal." He had reports the "old China Lobby" had sabotaged the peace talks but he couldn't "get much more specific than that, (a) because of the sensitivity of the source . . . and (b) because of the limited nature of the information."[27]

He had two pieces of evidence—"the intercept from the Ambassador saying that he had had a call and the boss said 'wait' and . . . this China Lobby operation, the Madame involved. Now, I don't want to have information that ought to be public and not make it so . . . On the other hand . . . I know we'll be charged with trying to interfere with the election."

Rusk was adamant that no President should make use of "interceptions or telephone taps in any way that would involve politics." Clifford thought "some elements of the story [were] so shocking," disclosing them would cast any future Nixon administration "under such doubts that I would think it would be inimical to our country's interests."

The President worried that if the story was published, and they knew about it, they might be "charged with hushing it up." Clifford didn't see a problem, due to "the sensitivity of the sources . . . [and] the absences of absolute proof . . . I don't believe we have the kind of story that we'd be justified in putting out."[28]

Late that evening, following a meeting with Clifford and Rusk, Rostow sent a telegram to Johnson with their recommendations. They agreed that the intercepts were collected "for the purposes of national security" and "must be protected and not introduced into domestic politics." They reasoned that "even if the story breaks, it was judged too late to have a significant impact on the election" and the new president's "viability" and future relationship with Johnson was also at stake. They advised Johnson to sit on the story and "hold tight the data we have."[29]

Meanwhile, another report came in from Gene Rostow's "man in New York," who said the object of Nixon's blocking tactics was to "nullify the political impact" of the bombing halt "by making it dubious":

> *The damage was done via Thieu in Saigon, through low-level Americans . . . Thieu, in their judgement, will continue on his present line until it becomes impossible. Mitchell's strategy is for Nixon now to be a statesman. He can't do any more mischief politically at home, although his troops will continue to use the line here.*[30]

On the morning of Election Day, Secretary of Defense Clark Clifford again complained to senior Defense Department officials about "the Republican Party efforts to sabotage any progress—the FBI telephone taps, the intercepts of messages from Bui Diem to Saigon, the surveillance and taps on Mrs. Claire Chennault, etc."[31]

Chennault met Mitchell in his private office at election headquarters and he was confident of victory:

> *The whole campaign has emphasized Vietnam, and you've done a great deal to help Mr. Nixon. You've done a great job. We'll never forget that. I'm sure Mr. Nixon will want to see you after the election, so let's keep in touch the rest of the day.*[32]

Nixon won the election, with 43.4 percent of the popular vote, to Humphrey's 42.7 percent—just over a half a million votes. As Theodore White later wrote:

> *Having raised . . . some $250,000 for the Nixon campaign . . . [and] having learned of the October negotiations by gossip and rumor and press speculation . . . [Anna Chennault] had undertaken most energetically to*

sabotage them. In contact with the Formosan, the South Korean and the South Vietnamese governments, she had begun early, by cable and telephone, to mobilize their resistance to the agreement—apparently implying, as she went, that she spoke for the Nixon campaign.

Fully informed of the sabotage of the negotiations and the recalcitrance of the Saigon government, Humphrey might have won the Presidency of the United States by making it the prime story of the last four days of the campaign. He was urged by several members of his staff to do so. And I know of no more essentially decent story in American politics than Humphrey's refusal to do so; his instinct was that Richard Nixon, personally, had no knowledge of Mrs. Chennault's activities; had no hand in them; and would have forbidden them had he known. Humphrey would not air the story.[33]

In the last two weeks of the campaign, Nixon's eight-point lead over Humphrey shrank to two by the Saturday before election day—primarily, women who wanted peace in Vietnam, shifting away from Nixon to support the bombing halt. As White noted:

Had peace become quite clear, as fact, in the last three days of the election of 1968, Hubert Humphrey would probably have won the election . . . Through the confusion of those last three days, however, it became apparent that the bombing halt, begun on Friday morning, would not end the killing of Americans in Asia; and the tide of opinion that had begun to flow to Hubert Humphrey began, at the end of the weekend, to flow back to Nixon. The opinion of the Nixon leadership is that, had the election been held on Saturday or Sunday, Nixon might have lost. . . .[34]

The day after the election, George Carver, Richard Helms' special assistant for Vietnamese Affairs, had lunch with Bui Diem. At the request of William Bundy, assistant secretary of state for East Asia, Carver probed Diem for

"South Vietnamese intentions" and tried "to convey bluntly some home truths about American politics," but Diem "refused to discuss or comment on recent events that had led to current differences between Saigon and Washington."[35]

Researching Ambassador Robert Hill's papers at the Hoover Institution Archives, I discovered an intriguing handwritten note, recording nine items discussed by phone with Nixon's secretary, Rose Mary Woods, on the day after the election (see Figure 2). To the left of item one, and underlined, is written "For Boss" and, underneath it, "for Saigon":

Amb of Vietnam needs appt before leaving

a) Try [?] out to Saigon

b) who to Paris

Hill's use of "Boss" echoes Chennault's and shows clearly that he was the intermediary between Nixon, Chennault, and Diem at this point.[36]

Chennault returned to Washington that evening and received a call from the South Vietnamese embassy the next morning, asking what time she would be coming to see the Ambassador:

Mrs. Chennault advised that she had to make a few important telephone calls before she could come . . . [and] that she had talked to "him" very late when she came back. Mrs. Chennault requested that Ambassador Diem be advised that she . . . had been talking to "Florida" and has to make a few other calls before she can move.[37]

Restaurant reservations were made for one thirty. Late that evening, Chennault called Diem to advise that the message received from President

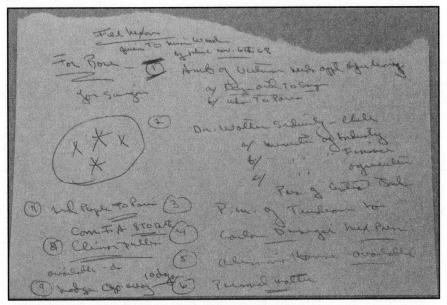

FIGURE 2: Handwritten notes of Robert Hill, November 6, 1968
(Hoover Institution Archives)

Thieu that day—"which our boss"—"was alright." After lunch, she had
returned to her office and "given 'them' everything" and that "they got the
whole message":

> *The person she had mentioned to Diem who might be thinking about "the*
> *trip" went on vacation this afternoon and will be returning Monday morn-*
> *ing, at which time she will be in touch again and will have more news for*
> *Diem . . . "They" are still planning things but are not letting people know*
> *too much because they want to be careful to avoid embarrassing "you,"*
> *themselves, or the present U.S. government. Therefore, whatever we do*
> *must be carefully planned.*[38]

She said she was still planning to "go out" to Vietnam but would do so "just
as a friend and . . . as vice-president of her airlines, so that would not upset
anything." She had talked to Senator Tower today and they hoped to meet
Diem on Monday before he left for Saigon that evening.[39]

At 7:35 a.m. on Friday, November 8, in a covering note to these reports, Rostow wrote the president: "First reactions may well be wrong. But with this information I think it's time to blow the whistle on these folks."[40]

Also on November 7, an "unidentified male" called Major Bui Cong Minh, assistant armed forces attaché at the Vietnamese embassy, and advised "that he had just received a call from General Westmoreland's office" requesting a meeting that evening, so he would have to postpone his visit to see Major Minh until Saturday. He asked "how the peace talks were coming":

Major Minh expressed the opinion that the move by Saigon was to help presidential candidate Nixon, and that had Saigon gone to the conference table, presidential candidate Humphrey would probably have won.[41]

According to Chennault's memoir, *The Education of Anna*, after the election, Thieu pressed her, through Bui Diem, to remind Nixon of his campaign promise to visit Vietnam but she couldn't reach Mitchell in Key Biscayne until he called back on Monday, November 11. Two days later, as Nixon sought to heal political divisions by announcing a joint Vietnam policy with Johnson, she finally met Mitchell in New York and he asked her to "persuade [her friends] to go to Paris."

"You must be joking," she said, flabbergasted. "Two weeks ago, Nixon and you were worried that they might succumb to pressure and go to Paris. What makes you change your mind all of a sudden?"

"Politics," Mitchell replied, and she took up her coat and left.

Later that evening, she received a call from Nixon's press secretary, Herb Klein:

Anna, you must promise to say to the press that our friend [Nixon] does not know about our arrangement with President Thieu . . . We know you're a good soldier; we just want to make sure that our friend is protected.[42]

Shortly afterwards, Tom Evans, Mitchell's assistant, called:

We want you to deliver a message to the Vietnamese ambassador urging President Thieu to send a delegate to the Paris Peace Talks, and also to tell him that Nixon won't have time to visit Vietnam just yet.[43]

She refused, so the next day, Everett Dirksen came to see her, to tell her Nixon was sending him to see Diem instead. Senator Tower and Ambassador Hill continued to be supportive as "the anxiety over news leakage kept festering."[44]

But documents in the "X envelope" cast doubt on Chennault's version of events. In fact, Diem met Dirksen on Saturday morning (November 9), flew to Vietnam Monday evening, and arrived in Saigon Wednesday morning.[45]

This train of events was set in motion by a call between Johnson and Nixon late Friday evening.[46]

"These people [the South Vietnamese government] are proceeding on the assumption that folks close to you tell them to do nothing until January 20th," began Johnson. "Now, we think—"

"I know who they are talking about too. Is it John Tower?" interrupted Nixon.

"Well, he is one of several. Mrs. Chennault is very much in there."

"Well, she is very close to John," replied Nixon.

"And the Embassy [Diem] is telling the President [Thieu] and the President is acting on this advice . . . about the eighteenth [of October] . . . these messages started coming out from here that Johnson was going to have a bombing pause to try to elect Humphrey and that they ought to hold out because Nixon will not sell you out like the Democrats sold out China . . . I think they've been talking to Agnew—I think they think they've been quoting you indirectly—that the thing they ought to do is just not show up at any conference and wait until you come into office."

"Right," said Nixon.

"They're killing Americans every day," continued Johnson. "I have that documented. There's not any question but that's happening . . . I don't believe you know it or you're responsible for it. . . ."

Nixon twice admitted to meeting Ambassador Diem in New York "5 or 6 months ago . . . in April or May" and asked if Diem had "any influence." Johnson said he did:

> *He is giving them these signals and he is telling them that he has just talked to New Mexico, and he has just talked to the Nixon people, and they say, "Hold out—Don't do anything—we are going to win—we'll do better by you." Now, that is the story, Dick. And it is a sordid story . . . Now, I don't want to say that to the country because that's not good.*

Nixon suggested sending his most trusted advisor Senator Everett Dirksen over to see the ambassador with a joint message "that he speaks for Nixon and Johnson" and again pledged, "There's nothing I want more than to get these people to that [conference] table."

The next morning, Rusk briefed Dirksen before his meeting with Diem. In an early morning call, Johnson advised Rusk to express "indignation" to

Dirksen "without being unpleasant" and sensed that Nixon "sees the danger of it now." "If this thing ever got out, the war is over as far as the American people are concerned," replied Rusk. Johnson agreed.[47]

The FBI intercepted Diem's call to Thieu after the meeting:

Dirksen had assured Ambassador Diem that the U.S. could give positive assurances that: one, there would be no coalition, and two, there would be no recognition of the NLF as a separate entity.

[Diem] reported that Dirksen emphasized several times that he was speaking on behalf of both President Johnson and Nixon.

The Ambassador said he had told Dirksen that the Government of Viet Nam's reasons for not attending the Paris conference were based on its own interests and had nothing to do with the internal political situation in the U.S., vis-à-vis a Nixon victory at the polls or anything of that nature. President Thieu confirmed that this is true.

Thieu agreed Diem should return to Saigon for consultation within the next few days.[48]

On Sunday morning, Diem called on Bundy to say he had spoken with Thieu overnight and he was reassured by Dirksen's message that "there was bipartisan agreement that no coalition government would be imposed on Viet-Nam and NLF would be not given status as a separate entity in Paris":

Bui Diem expressed gratification that there now seemed to be [a] way of moving out of [the] present impasse . . . President Thieu had emphasized that this was a matter of principle and there was no intention on the part of Saigon to sabotage Paris talks.[49]

• • •

On Tuesday, after asking the FBI "for the exact arrival and departure times for Agnew's visit to Albuquerque on November 2," Johnson asked DeLoach to check all calls placed from Agnew's plane or pay phones at Albuquerque airport to Washington, D.C., that day. Johnson thought Agnew was the "conduit" for Mrs. Chennault and was suspicious that "the Little Flower" had been "out with Mrs. Agnew" three days before. DeLoach offered to check every one of Agnew's calls but, "for the security of our country," Johnson insisted on details of all long-distance calls from Albuquerque to Washington that day and all calls in and out of the embassy.[50]

The next morning, DeLoach reported that as soon as Agnew's plane landed in Albuquerque, three phones were brought aboard but only one was used. Five calls were made. The first was to Secretary of State Dean Rusk at 1:59 p.m. EST and lasted three minutes.[51]

Haldeman's notes for November 2 include the notation:

1:30–2 M St.—at airport 505-247-1448,9 1440
Agnew—call Rusk—what's story on SVM?[52]

Nixon was telling Haldeman: get Agnew to call Rusk for an update on South Vietnam. The numbers provided are from the airport in Albuquerque, New Mexico, where Agnew's plane was at the time. Haldeman was coordinating the Agnew–Rusk call and received a summary of the conversation later in the day.

Further calls were made by staffer Kent Crane to Cal Purdy in Harlingen, Texas (their next campaign stop); sculptor Bruce Friedle in New York City; and Jim Miller in New York City:

The fifth and last call [at 3:03 p.m. EST] was made to a Mr. Hitt at Nixon–Agnew campaign headquarters by [Kent Crane] . . . [and] lasted for a minute and 51 seconds. And this is the phone chargeable to Maurice Stans, there at the Willard Hotel, which they used for Nixon–Agnew campaign headquarters. Now, there were no toll calls to the South Vietnamese embassy on that date. There were none to the Little Flower or the Dragon Lady, as we call her, from Albuquerque.[53]

As Hughes points out, "Robert J. Hitt was the husband of Patricia Reilly Hitt, the co-chairman of the Nixon–Agnew campaign committee and the first woman to co-chair an American presidential campaign. Mrs. Hitt had appointed Chennault and former First Lady Mamie G. Eisenhower as co-chairs of the Women for Nixon–Agnew Advisory Committee."[54]

The president wasn't giving up. He still thought "somebody from that plane talked to the woman . . . and talked to Rusk . . . [about] the same thing." No toll calls were made to Chennault by name, so the alleged Agnew call was only possible if Mrs. Chennault was using Mr. Hitt's telephone at the Willard. But Johnson stood his ground:

Rusk told Agnew what the facts were . . . Now, I believe that Agnew told her that, because she says, "I have just talked—" . . . And there must be an incoming call to her.

"Well, the toll calls don't show that," insisted DeLoach. Johnson asked if they were bugging her house.

"No, we had a physical surveillance on her, and we had a wiretap on the South Vietnamese embassy."

"But you didn't have one on her [phone]?"

"No, sir. We can still put it on if. . . ."

Johnson didn't want that but he did want the South Vietnamese embassy watched "awfully careful, because this may determine whether we go back to bombing and whether we have another war or not." His priority was to find out "who her boss is." He suspected Agnew because she mentioned a call from New Mexico and he had been in Albuquerque: "we ought to look at that log awfully careful, because if . . . she talked to Albuquerque. That is a cinch."

"Well, I think the key is, then, that she probably was at the campaign headquarters," said DeLoach. "This 1:02 p.m. call was to her . . . It may have been made to Mr. Hitt by name, but she got on the phone . . . I'll check the physical surveillance log."[55]

In February 1970, White House aide Tom Charles Huston produced a report for Nixon titled "Vietnam Bombing Halt—The Chennault Affair," summarizing the contacts between Chennault and Bui Diem during October and November 1968. He called on William Sullivan, the head of the FBI's intelligence operations for help. "[Bill] and Chuck DeLoach, who was the number three guy in the FBI, were bitter rivals. . . ." he later recalled. "DeLoach was literally Johnson's bagman. Whatever Lyndon Johnson wanted, DeLoach would see he got . . . [so], Bill was perfectly happy to let me see the whole thing because DeLoach's fingerprints were all over the damn thing."[56]

Huston acknowledged that "the November 2nd phone call from Mrs. Chennault to Ambassador Diem was the most incriminating evidence which the investigation turned up":

> It certainly suggested that officials high in the campaign (perhaps the candidate himself or his running mate) were attempting to convince the South Vietnamese to hold out against a bombing halt until after the election. The fact that Mrs. Chennault said the call came from her "boss" who was in New Mexico and the fact that Vice Presidential candidate was in Albuquerque, New Mexico, the day of the call prompted LBJ to suspect that he had finally located the culprit, but the FBI was unable to turn up sufficient hard information to make the indictment stick . . . After this intensive investigation into the activities of the Vice President-Elect, LBJ had to

conclude that there was no hard information available to identify Agnew
as Mrs. Chennault's "boss."[57]

Huston concluded that, despite Johnson and DeLoach's best efforts to investigate Chennault's reference to her "boss" in New Mexico, "they had no
evidence whatsoever that Agnew had anything to do with it" and "they really
couldn't make the times [of the calls from Albuquerque] match . . . And she
later says, 'I misspoke. I really meant New Hampshire' or something. Of
course that was where Ambassador Hill was from . . . so my best judgment
is that Chennault . . . and Ambassador Hill, who was linked to this . . . [and
was] one of the leading foreign policy people and who [Nixon] sent to Paris
to be the observer . . . [were the key contacts]."[58]

In Haldeman's handwritten notes for November 2, we see the notation:

M – DL – "only thing J [Johnson] got was right of SVN at
conference table."[59]

This suggests Mitchell and the "Dragon Lady" spoke that day, strengthening
Chennault's claim that her notorious conversation was with Mitchell, not
Agnew. The only evidence we have for a call with Agnew is the "New Mexico" reference but information from Chennault usually came to Haldeman
through Mitchell, and Chennault's personal papers contain very little mention of Agnew. I think Mitchell and Bob Hill were clearly her main conduits
to Nixon, with Richard Allen acting as a "listener."

On November 7, physical surveillance of Mrs. Chennault and the South
Vietnamese embassy was abandoned, but the wiretap on the embassy continued for another two months.[60]

In retrospect, DeLoach felt that, "despite assurances we were acting in
behalf of national security when we were ordered to tap Mrs. Chennault's
phone, we were in fact on a political mission for the Democratic party.
There's no doubt in my mind that any damaging evidence uncovered in our

investigation would have been promptly leaked to the nation's press to embarrass the Republicans."[61]

At a dinner in Saigon on November 11, "self-assured strong man," President Thieu criticized the "unprecedented pressure to which the US government had subjected him during the pre-bombing halt discussions," citing a "half million troops . . . [and] the size of the U.S. commitment in blood and money as justification for insisting that U.S. interests prevail." He saw the US action "as a 'betrayal' comparable to the US abandonment of Chiang Kai-Shek" in the forties, and "complained that the Americans had sent the Australian and Korean ambassadors to badger him into accepting the U.S. point of view." One sentence in the CIA cable is highlighted:

> *Thieu told his guests that during the U.S. election campaign, he had sent two secret emissaries to the U.S. to contact Richard Nixon.*[62]

Four days later, the *Chicago Daily News* reported that "top Saigon officials are boasting privately they helped assure the election of Richard M. Nixon" by "sabotaging President Johnson's attempt to call a bombing halt two weeks before the election." "Fifteen days would have done it, but four days wasn't enough, and we saw to that," said one cabinet minister.[63]

On November 27, Chennault contacted the South Vietnamese embassy to inform Diem's secretary that she had a message for the ambassador when he returned to Washington and "was very anxious to meet with him." She also invited Nguyen Hoan, a counsellor at the embassy, to her Watergate apartment to relay "some messages."[64]

On December 8, 1968, the head of the South Vietnamese delegation finally arrived in Paris.[65]

The next day, Chennault phoned Hoan to advise him that "her very good friend," Melvin Laird, had been appointed secretary of defense in the new administration. She said she was going to New York to see Bob Murphy, the experienced diplomat who served as Nixon's liaison to the White House on foreign policy during the transition. Rostow sent the FBI memo detailing this to Johnson with the note: "The Lady is still operational."[66]

On December 10, Chennault wrote a three-page letter "for President Elect Nixon" and gave it to Thomas Evans in a sealed envelope with a three-page biographical sketch, a photo, and a personal invitation to her from President Marcos to visit the Philippines to discuss "Philippine–American relations."

While friends had volunteered to "ask for something for [her] in the new Administration," she began, "I think it much better . . . that I discuss this directly with you." She stressed she did not want to be "paid off" with a token position or "merely a 'woman's' place in government requiring my abandoning my present significance and the earned part of my income, which is substantial."

She hoped she had "something unique to contribute in the field of foreign affairs" and could use her "friends in high places in this country and in Asia . . . to be one of the effective bridges between the Asian people and the American people," acting as a liaison to the governments of Southeast Asia and continuing her work "with proposed Defense Secretary Laird, Ambassador Robert Hill and Senator Tower."

She sought a position as "an Assistant Secretary of State for Cultural Affairs"—an "apparently neutral" role, "theoretically dealing only with cultural affairs" that would give her an office in the State Department, and "a channel for operations" and "inconspicuous consultation."

On December 13, Tom Evans passed the envelope to Rose Mary Woods "to pass on to RN." Five days later, according to FBI wiretaps, Chennault arranged for Diem to meet Senator Karl Mundt of South Dakota, who she described as "a close friend" of Nixon, who "will make all the arrangements for the Ambassador to see the other people, not further identified."[67]

On January 3, 1969, Tom Ottenad of the *St. Louis Post-Dispatch* called Walt Rostow for a background comment on Chennault's contact with South Vietnamese officials, "urging them to go slow in the hope that . . . they might get a better shake under Nixon than they would otherwise." Rostow refused to comment but, within hours, sent a transcript of the conversation to the president, with the note: "As you will see, the Lady is about to surface."[68]

Diem denied the reports, reaffirming that Vietnamese decisions were not "based on internal politics in the United States." He denied receiving complaints from the Humphrey campaign or having any recent contact with Nixon. He admitted Mrs. Chennault had been an occasional visitor to the Embassy but he couldn't recall exact dates in the weeks before the election.[69]

The story broke three days later in the *Boston Globe*, under the headline "Was Saigon's peace talk delay due to Republican promises?" It contained a teasing quote from Anna Chennault: "You're going to get me in a lot of trouble. I can't say anything . . . we're at a very sensitive time . . . I know so much and can say so little."[70]

Nixon's secretary, Rose Mary Woods, remained unperturbed. In a memo to Nixon's deputy campaign manager Peter Flanigan later that day, she opposed Senator Dirksen's recent letter, "recommending Anna Chennault for the post of Assistant Secretary of State for Public Information. This would be a disaster. The sooner we can keep her as far away as possible from the Administration—the better."[71]

In a note to Robert Hill that day, Richard Allen seems to allude to their liaison with Chennault: "I miss our frequent telephone conversations—is there nothing new to report?"[72]

On January 20, Nixon was sworn in as president. After directing Nixon's election campaign and acting as the liaison to Anna Chennault, John Mitchell was appointed Attorney General—the chief law enforcement officer in the country.

By late February, Haldeman was still worried about Ottenad's investigation into the "Mrs. Chennault episode." According to his handwritten notes, Ottenad had recently identified "Repub ldrs approved activity" and was pursuing the story as "an impt. footnote on Am history," but President Johnson and Tom Corcoran refused to see him and top Johnson aides like Walt Rostow were "told to avoid seeing + if so, say not one word." "They are not playing ball," Haldeman concluded, "but someone may cause a problem."[73]

According to Chennault, months later at a White House function, Nixon took her aside and, "with intense gratitude, began thanking me for my help with the election."

"I've certainly paid dearly for it," she said.

"Yes, I appreciate that," he murmured, suddenly uncomfortable. "I know you are a good soldier."[74]

In an oral history interview with the LBJ Library in June 1969, William Bundy felt sure that "Republican voices" were saying to the South Vietnamese, "Why are you handing this thing to Humphrey on a plate? If you let yourself go along with . . . a bombing stoppage that is not right any way, you are crazy." He thought the channel was through Madame Chennault and that Diem was reporting what she was telling him, but he didn't think Nixon was involved.[75]

In July, when *The Making of the President 1968* was published, Hubert Humphrey agreed that Theodore White's charge of "sabotage" against Chennault and company was "accurate." At a press conference in Taipei, Chennault called the charge "an insult to my intellect and the integrity of the South Vietnamese Government. . . . Someday, when the right time comes, all the facts will be made known . . . To me, America's interest comes first and the Republican party second."[76]

Chennault and Tom Corcoran remained evasive in subsequent press interviews. Corcoran admitted Johnson and Clark Clifford had asked him to find out what Anna "was up to" but he "was very careful not to ask her":

If I had been Anna, I'd have done what they say she did. But I'd have been goddamn careful I didn't do it without orders from the top.[77]

Chennault insisted the speculative press reports were "completely untrue" and that whatever she did during the campaign, "Mr. Nixon knew about [it]."[78]

But her resentment at being overlooked continued to fester. In early August, at "the urgent request of Senators Tower and Mundt," Nixon aide Bryce Harlow invited Mrs. Chennault to the White House, where she complained bitterly of "being cut up by press etc. for her alleged activities during the campaign involving South Vietnam." "Certain aspects of this you and I know," Harlow reported to Haldeman. "She asserts that everything she did was with the full knowledge of John Mitchell and Bob Hill and, in some other respects, Dick Allen. . . ."

Chennault told Harlow she was "under attack" for alleged misdeeds that were "contrary to the desires of the Nixon organization":

She was particularly hurt by John Mitchell's reported comment to the press, "Who's Anna Chennault?" . . . when he was recently braced about his relationships with her during the campaign.

So now she feels forsaken and humiliated by the RN folk, even as she is subjected to severe criticism for activities which she insists were undertaken at the direct request of the Nixon campaign group. To rectify all this, she pleads for some overt indication that the Nixon people still regard her favorably. In particular, she recommends that she be invited right soon to some White House functions so people can see that she is still sympatico vis-a-vis the Nixons and their entourage.

Both Tower and Mundt strongly urge that her appeals be suitably met. They stress her emotional upset over all this (she got right weepy telling me this story), and they are both convinced that the President would not want her to believe that he is now antagonistic toward her, or wants to ignore her, after her campaign activities, financial and otherwise.

I mentioned this problem to Rose Woods. Rose believes Mrs. Chennault is a pretty bad apple and strongly feels she should not be included in any White House function, at least not anytime soon.

Harlow suggested they "respond favorably to the concern expressed by Tower and Mundt" and make "an official friendly gesture toward her" on the premise that they'd need "her cooperation in the future."[79]

Nixon saw Harlow's memo to Haldeman at the end of August, but by early October, nothing had been done and Chennault tried another appeal through Maurice Stans. Peter Flanigan wrote Rose Mary Woods:

I'm informed by Maury Stans that Anna Chenault [sic] was responsible for raising $200,000 for the campaign . . . [but] has not been included at a White House Dinner and feels very unhappy that she has not received any recognition from the Administration. Would it be possible to include Mrs. Chenault [sic] in the near future at one of the dinners.[80]

The same day, Flanigan wrote a similar message to Mitchell:

Since you had the liaison (if it can be called that) with this good lady I'd like your suggestions as to whether we should take some action to recognize

her. If the answer is "yes" should this be in terms of an invitation to dinner
at the White House or something more important . . . [?][81]

On March 13, 1970, two weeks after completing his report for Nixon on "The Chennault Affair," Tom Huston wrote Haldeman, claiming the Defense Department had produced a top-secret report "on all events leading up the bombing halt" that had almost cost Nixon the 1968 election. Huston claimed Leslie Gelb, an aide in Clark Clifford's Defense department, had brought a copy of the report to the Brookings Institution, where he now worked. As author Ken Hughes notes, there's little evidence the report existed but when Haldeman reported it, Nixon "slammed a pencil on the desk and said, 'I want that goddamn Gelb material and I don't care how you get it.'"[82]

In June, Huston convened an "Interagency Committee on Intelligence," where Hoover, Helms, and representatives from NSA and DIA met to coordinate intelligence-gathering in response to a bombing spree by the Weather Underground and escalating "revolutionary youth activities." It proposed "maximum use of all special investigative techniques, including increased agent and informant penetration" and "maximum coverage" of the communications and activities of "revolutionary leaders and groups."

On July 23, after receiving the group's report, Huston recommended that restraints on electronic surveillance, mail coverage, and surreptitious entry on targeted citizens be relaxed. While CIA Director Richard Helms voiced no objections, FBI Director J. Edgar Hoover made his opposition clear. Four days later, he wrote to Attorney General John Mitchell and the so-called "Huston Plan" was quietly shelved.[83]

On April 12, 1971, Nixon and his National Security Advisor Henry Kissinger "welcomed Anna Chennault into the Oval Office for a short talk" after meeting the outgoing Taiwanese ambassador. After her visit, Nixon told his aides to give Chennault a "high-level title . . . [but] it can't be in govern-ment." A month later, he told Kissinger, "We have to finesse her."[84]

On June 17, four days after the *New York Times* began publishing extracts from the Pentagon Papers, leaked by former military analyst Daniel Ellsberg, Haldeman raised the issue of the elusive "bombing halt file" with Nixon and Kissinger, suggesting it could be used to blackmail Johnson. Kissinger told the president, "Bob [Haldeman] and I have been trying to put the damn thing together for three years."

"We have a basic history of it—constructed on our own," said Haldeman, referring to Huston's report, "but Huston swears to God there's a file on it at [the] Brookings [Institution] in the hands of the same people [as Ellsberg]."

"Brookings has no right to have classified documents," said Kissinger.

"Goddamn it, get in and get those files. Blow the safe and get it," said the President, advocating a black bag job.

"But what good will it do you, the bombing halt file?" asked Kissinger.

"To blackmail him. Because he used the bombing halt for political pur-poses," replied the President.

"The bombing halt file would really kill Johnson," said Haldeman, "On the timing and strategy of how he pulled that."[85]

Two weeks later, Nixon again told Haldeman, "You're to break into the place, rifle the files, and bring them in . . ." "I don't have any problem with breaking in . . ." replied Haldeman. "Go in around eight or nine o'clock . . . break into their files and get that stuff out."[86]

As author Ken Hughes notes, in the hundreds of hours of declassified Nixon White House tapes, this is the only break-in you can hear the presi-dent order and "he ordered the Brookings burglary at least three more times over the next two weeks." Later that summer, he created the Special Investi-gations Unit (later known as "the Plumbers") to plug unauthorized leaks, employing G. Gordon Liddy, "a former FBI agent with experience doing 'black bag jobs' (that is, government-conducted break-ins) and a former CIA agent [E. Howard Hunt] experienced in covert operations." Exactly one year later, another break-in planned by Hunt and Liddy led to his downfall.[87]

In July 1971, when Nixon asked his Domestic Affairs Advisor, John Ehrlichman, to recruit someone to investigate the Pentagon Papers leaks and "handle the Ellsberg case," Richard Allen was his suggested choice, as someone who could "lead and prod people in the Departments and Agencies, without direct White House involvement."[88]

Since leaving the Nixon administration, Allen has continued to distort the historical record about the Chennault Affair. In the mid-seventies, he told William Safire that "he thought about [the offer in Chennault's July 3 letter] a lot but decided a meeting would be a mistake." William Bundy concluded that Allen was "deliberately kept in the dark by Nixon, who found some other channel to set up the meeting" (highly unlikely, given his close involvement).[89]

Allen seems to be the unreliable source for Safire's conclusion:

The indications are that the Dragon Lady . . . had not been restrained by the Nixon campaign, but had not been able to reach anybody at the top in the crucial last days—which meant the Candidate and his top staff were keeping hands off, leaving only Allen as a "listener."[90]

In sum, Anna Chennault was in close and frequent touch with the Nixon campaign and in close touch with the South Vietnamese ambassador; she was not able to reach the top of the campaign for authorization to my knowledge, though it is possible she talked to Mitchell or Haldeman; she was not discouraged from her efforts, but she was frustrated in not being able to reach anybody other than Hill, Tower, and Allen at the crucial moments at the end.[91]

In 2008, the year before his death, Safire told Nixon Library Director Timothy Naftali:

Anna Chennault was a go-between, there's no doubt about it. And John Mitchell, the Campaign Manager, was using her . . . Was there an attempt to say, "Do not make peace until after Nixon gets in?" I never saw anything that would suggest that.[92]

In 2002, long after the release of the Chennault and Diem memoirs and the "X envelope," Allen was still "blowing smoke":

Anna Chennault . . . was interfering with Diem in South Vietnam, urging the South Vietnamese not to go to the peace table, saying they'd get a better deal with Nixon. That eventually led to a lot of confusion. She had no authority, no brief . . . She tried to get to me. I wouldn't permit her to talk to me, but President Johnson then tapped our telephones . . . he may have thought he had a legitimate right to if he suspected national security, but it was a political campaign after all, and he did tap our telephones—illegally.[93]

In 2003, Allen was at it again, in a series of email exchanges with Mitchell's biographer James Rosen. Rosen cites "a source close to the affair—who demanded anonymity" and fits the description of Richard Allen—"a senior policy adviser to Nixon and other GOP politicians in later years."[94]

"Simply do not trust what Anna Chennault says about this incident," the source told Rosen. "She manufactured the incident, then magnified her self-importance":

She caused untold problems with her perpetual self-promotion and, actually, self-aggrandizement, because she was ultimately interested only in the money. I do not put it in the realm of fantasy that she was being paid by

the SVs [South Vietnamese]; she had them bamboozled, believing she was
an "important" channel to the campaign. John Mitchell . . . did not have
the bullocks to kiss her off, a tough and persistent woman who could grind
you down . . . Anna thought of herself as a puppet master. She had no
assignment, no tasks, and was an over-the-transom type that can never be
suppressed in a campaign.[95]

"An over-the-transom type" is a phrase often used by Allen to discredit impromptu approaches from supposed "freelancers" like Chennault. It is very strange that he has never been seriously challenged on any of this and he did not respond to an interview request.

Nixon's 1978 memoir doesn't mention Anna Chennault but he did mention her in his interview with David Frost a year earlier:

As I told President Johnson on the phone when he informed me on October
the thirty-first that he was going forward with the bombing halt . . . I
would support the talks . . . I did nothing to undercut them. As far as
Madame Chennault or any number of other people . . . I did not authorize
them and I had no knowledge of any contact with the South Vietnamese at
that point, urging them not to [go] . . . I couldn't have done that in
conscience.[96]

As Rosen notes, "amazingly . . . Mitchell seems never to have been questioned on the record, or under oath, about the Chennault affair." Richard Holbrooke, one of the negotiating team in Paris and a future US ambassador to the United Nations, believes the Nixon team "massively, directly, and covertly, interfered in . . . probably one of the most important negotiations in American diplomatic history."[97]

In a 2008 oral history interview, Tom Huston concluded "there was no doubt that Nixon . . . would have been directly involved, that it's not something that anybody would've undertaken on their own":

> *To what extent was he urging directly or indirectly to Thieu to not participate? Nixon insists in his memoir, and I think with some credence, that he didn't have to do that. Thieu had his own reasons not to participate, but Nixon was not one to leave things to chance.*[98]

In 1981, after the publication of Chennault's memoir, Thomas Corcoran told *The Washington Post:*

> *People have used Anna scandalously, Nixon in particular. I know exactly what Nixon said to her and then he repudiated her. But Anna said nothing; she kept her mouth shut.*

Chennault said her role as "Nixon's secret envoy to Thieu taught her a lesson":

> *If people like this ask me to do something again I'm going to make them put it in writing. I was younger, and maybe I was also naive. I was very anxious to do what they asked me to do because I felt so strongly about working with the Republican Party.*[99]

In May 2016, I met Anna Chennault and her daughter in her Watergate penthouse, still full of paraphernalia from the Nixon years. She was ninety years old and in declining health but insisted she did not initiate the plot—the Nixon people around her did—Mitchell, Tower, etc. She was close to Ray Cline but when it came to the plot, they didn't talk about it. "Only a few people knew," she told me. "Even the ambassador didn't know everything about the messages being passed to Thieu." She remained bitter about Nixon just using her, "like all the other politicians" and abandoning Vietnam. She died in March 2018.[100]

In a recent response to *The Vietnam War* television series, the Nixon Foundation insists, "there is no proof that candidate Nixon had any involvement with, or even knowledge, of any such activities . . . [or] that any Nixon campaign aide told the South Vietnamese government not to participate in the Paris talks . . . [and] there is no evidence that candidate Nixon was involved in any way in any untoward, much less illegal or treacherous dealings with South Vietnam."[101]

On the evidence of these opening chapters, clearly, I disagree. At the same time, John Farrell's misconstrued "discovery" of instructions from Nixon to "keep Anna Chennault working on SVN" has been the subject of much hyperbole. John Dean, Nixon's White House Counsel and the architect of the Watergate cover-up, claimed in an article, ironically titled "Nixon Was Evil: Getting the Historical Evidence Right," that "Farrell's findings establish beyond question that Nixon was not merely a serial liar, but evil" and are proof of "Nixon's direct involvement . . . in this traitorous skulduggery," sabotaging Johnson's efforts to end the war.[102]

The last word on the Chennault Affair goes to Johnson's National Security Advisor Walt Rostow, who in the midst of the Watergate investigations of 1973, wrote his memo about the "X envelope" and reached the following conclusion:

I am inclined to believe the Republican operation in 1968 relates in two ways to the Watergate affair of 1972.

First, the election of 1968 proved to be close and there was some reason for those involved on the Republican side to believe their enterprise with the South Vietnamese and Thieu's recalcitrance may have sufficiently blunted the impact on U.S. politics of the total bombing halt and agreement to negotiate to constitute the margin of victory.

Second, they got away with it. Despite considerable press commentary after the election, the matter was never investigated fully.[103]

At 9:30 a.m. on June 16, 1972, Anna Chennault paid a final visit to the South Vietnamese embassy, to say goodbye to Bui Diem, on his last day as ambassador. She had lunch with Ray Cline and had been a guest at a state dinner at the White House the evening before. The Nixon campaign got away with election dirty tricks in 1968, but four years later, they were about to get caught.[104]

CHAPTER 3

HUNT KNOWS TOO
DAMN MUCH

This fellow Hunt, he knows too damn much. . . . If it gets out that this Cuba thing is all involved, it would be a fiasco. It would make the CIA look bad . . . Hunt look bad and it is likely to blow the whole Bay of Pigs thing which we think would be very unfortunate for CIA and the country at this time.

—President Nixon to chief of staff
H. R. Haldeman, June 23, 1972[1]

E. Howard Hunt was born on October 9, 1918 in Hamburg, New York. After graduating from Brown University in 1940 with a major in English Literature, he spent a couple of years in the US Navy. From October 1942 to October 1943, he scripted naval training films for *The March of Time* newsreel and served as a war correspondent with the Navy in the South Pacific for *Life* magazine. After enlisting in the Air Force in late 1943, he was detailed to the Office of Strategic Services—the forerunner of the CIA—in January 1945. After attending the OSS Clandestine School on Catalina Island, he was assigned to the OSS in China.[2]

After returning from the Far East in January 1946, he spent a couple of years writing novels and magazine stories for *The New Yorker* and *Cosmopolitan* before taking a job in Paris in May 1948 with the Economic Cooperation Administration (ECA), which managed the European post-war recovery program, the Marshall Plan. Ambassador Averell Harriman headed up the program in Paris and Hunt worked as an information officer under *Washington Post* reporter Fred Friendly in the Information Division, "producing propaganda films and radio programs in France and Austria." He began dating one of Harriman's secretaries, Dorothy de Goutiere, and met his future employer Robert Mullen, who ran the Marshall Plan's information service.[3]

In January 1949, Hunt was denied a raise in salary and resigned from the ECA to revive his publishing career in the United States. He received a glowing farewell letter from Averell Harriman, praising his "prompt, efficient handling of assignments" and "quick and imaginative grasp" of the ECA mission. Hunt was described by FBI informants in Paris as "highly intelligent and imaginative but also blindly selfish and egotistical to colleagues and superiors." By now, he had published four novels. "My royalties yield me an average of $3000 a year above my salary," he wrote on his CIA application form in May 1949, "and this year, an estimated 1 million copies of two books in pocket editions will be in circulation."[4]

After a full FBI field investigation, Hunt joined the CIA's Office of Policy Coordination (OPC) on November 8, 1949 as a thirty-one-year-old Intelligence Officer. He had married Dorothy two months earlier. General John Singlaub had known Hunt since his OSS days in China and later claimed he helped Hunt get his job at the Agency.[5]

Hunt was assigned to the Political and Psychological Warfare (PP) staff under Joseph Bryan III, who immediately advised him to submit a memo to clarify that in June 1949, he had completed a novel, *Day of the Serpent*, based on his OSS activities in China. As Hunt's agent at the Famous Artists Agency in Beverly Hills was now shopping it around, Hunt stressed it "was completed some months prior to my association with [the] CIA."[6]

In December 1950, Hunt was assigned to Mexico City under State Department cover—using the pseudonym "Bernard Chumley"—after volunteering to open an OPC station there. He invited William Buckley to be one of his agents outside the embassy and Buckley was later godfather and guardian to his children, taking care of several of them after Hunt's arrest in the aftermath of Watergate.[7]

During his time in Mexico, Hunt's "most daring mission" was a break-in at the Guatemalan embassy, which bore startling resemblance to the later Watergate operations. The CIA office in the embassy "had a direct line of sight to the front windows of the embassy" and with binoculars, Hunt could monitor the ambassador's office. They "cased the target office and mounted round-the-clock surveillance on the principal embassy officers." A cleaning lady inside the embassy bugged the ambassador's office, which was monitored from a listening post in an apartment one floor above, and NSA intercepts of tapped embassy telephones helped fix the date for the surreptitious entry by "a team of CIA safecrackers." They had "a floor plan of the offices, a description of the safe, and a putty imprint of its keyhole," as well as a duplicate key to the "embassy service door," courtesy of the cleaning lady. After covering the windows in black muslin, the team took out their flashlights and broke into the safe, taking a Polaroid of the contents for continuity and photographing a codebook and lists of Mexican spies and targets while an agent played cards and drank tequila with a guard in the basement.[8]

Inspired by such escapades, Hunt continued to write fiction in Mexico. In December 1950, a "whodunit" novel, *The Judas Hour*, was approved for publication by the Agency's Office of Security and a previous novel, *The Violent Ones*, was published in 1951. Four more books were approved by the Office of Security during 1952—*Appointment with Yesterday, Paris VIII, Whisper Her Name,* and *Lovers Are Losers.*[9]

In the Spring of 1953, Colonel Sheffield Edwards objected to the publication of *Darkness on the Land.* While the manuscript revealed no classified information, Edwards was concerned that Hunt planned to publish under his true name and that several passages were "uncomplimentary . . . to the Latin-American type . . . [and] threaded with the inference that the Nordic is superior to the Latin."[10]

Around this time, the Agency's OPC and Office of Special Operations (OSO) stations merged and Hunt was overlooked for the post of Chief of Station. Not happy to be merely Deputy Chief, Hunt requested reassignment and returned to Washington to work on a special project for Tracy Barnes, the new chief of the Political and Psychological Warfare Staff and brother-in-law of his predecessor Joseph Bryan. As Hunt was no longer working in Mexico and no further Latin American posting was envisaged, Edwards withdrew his objection and Barnes approved publication.[11]

In 1954, Hunt worked for Barnes on PBSUCCESS, a project approved by Eisenhower to overthrow the "Communist regime" of Jacob Arbenz in Guatemala, whose land reform programs had incurred the wrath of United Fruit and powerful lobbyist Thomas Corcoran. It was here Hunt met David Atlee Phillips, who was his co-director on the project: "He was the Chief of Propaganda and I was the Chief of Political Action." Psychological warfare was key to the success of the coup by a small rebel force of 480 men, with the Voice of Liberation radio station's anti-government propaganda and "fake news" exaggerating the success of the rebels, creating civilian unrest and demoralizing the army.[12]

In June, after engineering a successful coup in Guatemala, Hunt shipped out to Tokyo as chief of operations for the North Asia command. By now, he had three children—Lisa (three), Kevan (sixteen months), and his first son, Howard St. John, born three months before his departure.[13]

In February 1957, Hunt was reassigned as chief of station in Montevideo, Uruguay, under State Department cover. In late 1958, he saw Phillips again in Havana "at a meeting of chief of stations just before the Castro takeover." Phillips was an undercover agent there. In 1960, Hunt infuriated Robert Woodward, the US ambassador in Montevideo, by lobbying the president of Uruguay to ask Eisenhower to extend his tour. Hunt returned to the United States that summer and was assigned to Mexico City on Project JMARC, the codename for the Bay of Pigs invasion. He met Phillips again in Mexico City before they worked on the Cuba project together—Phillips in Washington and Hunt soon returning to Miami.[14]

In the summer of 1960, Hunt was assigned as the political liaison to a "government in exile" being formed by anti-Castro Cubans in Miami—the Frente Revolucionario Democrático (Revolutionary Democratic Front, or FRD). Hunt met its leaders, including Manuel Artime, at the Hotel Ambassador in New York City and the CIA funded the organization through Hunt. He set them up in Mexico City and sponsored their military activities and liaison with "friendly governments." Eisenhower had "called for the formation and training of a brigade of Cuban exiles who would invade Cuba, establish a provisional government, receive [US] recognition . . . and overthrow the Castro government." This was to be done without overt US participation from training bases in Nicaragua and Vice President Richard Nixon worked closely with the CIA on the project.[15]

In the fall, the Mexican government asked the FRD to leave and they moved to Miami, where Hunt took over as their case officer. Hunt's predecessor assigned Bernard Barker—a former asset of the Havana station and future Watergate burglar—as his liaison with the Cubans.[16]

When John F. Kennedy became president in January 1961, he decided the FRD was "too archaic" and tried to broaden the group to include more progressive politicians from Cuba, some of whom Hunt saw as "radical left-wingers" too close to Castro. The FRD was staunchly anti-Castro and anti-Communist and Hunt found it impossible to broaden the political structure, so he requested reassignment and returned to Washington to work alongside David Phillips on propaganda aspects of the invasion.[17]

Hunt subsequently blamed the failure of the Bay of Pigs invasion on Arthur Schlesinger, Adlai Stevenson, and Robert Kennedy for advising the president to cancel the second air strike and deny air cover to the invasion force. Hunt left Miami shortly before the invasion but stayed in touch with Barker and later asked the Agency's Office of General Counsel "to help him regain his American citizenship." After Barker left the Agency in 1966, Hunt lost track of him and didn't resume contact until he took a trip to Miami on the tenth anniversary of the Bay of Pigs invasion in April 1971.

In the wake of the disastrous Bay of Pigs invasion, Richard Bissell transferred Hunt to the office of CIA director Allen Dulles for about six months until Dulles and Bissell were forced into retirement. Hunt drew on his knowledge of the operation to help Dulles answer questions from Bobby Kennedy and the Cuban Study Group set up to investigate its failure. "Bobby Kennedy was harassing [Dulles] almost daily at these meetings," recalled Hunt. While the Kennedys and the press were calling the operation "a CIA failure, none of us associated with the project, least of all Mr. Dulles, believed that for a minute":

We looked upon it as a failure of nerve by the New Frontier . . . the President had given certain undertakings to Cuban leadership and to our own

paramilitary people, and had failed to carry them out . . . This fact was
successfully disguised for a number of years, but Dulles and Dick Bissell
paid the price.[18]

Hunt had had some contact with Dulles while stationed in Japan and was an "unrepentant admirer." Dulles brought to the CIA "the same feeling of esprit de corps that we had all enjoyed in the Office of Strategic Services" under General Donovan. Both men were "open to all sorts of suggestions . . . and this was a great feeling for creative minds within the Agency . . . if you had a good idea, it would be reviewed, considered and accepted or rejected on its merits." Hunt felt that creative freedom "was largely lost" under Dulles' successors, "until Dick Helms came back in [1966]."[19]

During the Fall of 1962, Helms called Hunt in to brief General Edward Lansdale on "what went wrong" with the Bay of Pigs and lauded Hunt's twenty-minute presentation on the subject. But while working on Dulles' staff, "it was made abundantly clear to [Hunt] in a very pleasant way that, having been stained with the failure of the Bay of Pigs, that [he] was to have nothing further to do with Cuban operations, and that it would be probably a good many years before [he] could expect reassignment to Latin America, if ever."[20]

After Dulles' resignation and retirement, Hunt worked for David Phillips' covert action staff at headquarters before joining Tracy Barnes' new Domestic Operations Division as its first chief of Covert Action in July 1962.[21]

He inherited the case files for several projects "that had been run by the commercial staff of the Agency" and various geographic divisions. Contact with publishers in the United States was now centralized through Hunt and if a division wanted a certain book published, they could submit a request to Barnes. The Agency had a long-standing relationship with the Frederick Praeger Publishing Company—which had been previously managed by Cord Meyer in the International Division—and a publishing proprietary, which operated out of the National Press Building in Washington.[22]

Praeger would pitch Hunt and Barnes books he wanted to publish which aligned with Agency interests abroad but were not "economically feasible" for him on his own. The Agency subsidized the production and marketing of some of them and under Hunt, the project was brought under Defense Department control, managed for the first time by a man who knew something about the publishing industry. Hunt quickly realized the deal was overly favorable to Praeger and spent so much time tidying up the accounts, it distracted from what the program was supposed to be doing.

According to Hunt, Thomas Karamessines signed off budget items up "up to $50,000 and beyond that, it had to be signed off on by Helms." He also liaised with the book division of the US Information Agency (USIA) regarding which agency should publish selected titles. Cord Meyer's International Organizations Division also did a lot of work in this area with the Congress for Cultural Freedom and Radio Free Europe.[23]

When President Kennedy was assassinated in November 1963, Hunt was working on these publishing projects. When later accused of being involved in Kennedy's murder, Hunt denied visiting Dallas until 1971 and said he was not in Mexico or New Orleans in 1963 and had never met Lee Harvey Oswald. Hunt claimed he heard the president had been shot on the car radio after picking up some Chinese groceries with his wife. It was either his day off or he was "recuperating from a hospitalization for ulcers." When they picked up his eleven-year-old daughter Kevan from school, she told them two of Robert Kennedy's children had just been picked up from her school by the Secret Service. His daughter, Lisa, who was twelve at the time, confirmed Hunt was at home on the day Kennedy died, watching television with his shocked family.[24]

• • •

In 1964, Hunt's publisher at the New American Library suggested Hunt write "an American counterpart to the James Bond series, which his firm also published":

> *I submitted the idea to Dick Helms, who agreed that certain public-relations advantages would accrue to CIA if such a series were well received. His sole proviso was that I clear each manuscript in advance with him or his deputy, Tom Karamessines.*

Eight paperbacks were subsequently published in the "Peter Ward" series of "fictional CIA adventures" under the pen name David St. John—an amalgam of the names of Hunt's two sons (his youngest, David, was born in 1962).[25]

In the Fall of 1964, according to Frances "Fig" Coleman, who managed the Iberian desk at headquarters, Helms assigned Hunt as deputy chief of station (DCOS) in Madrid but the move was blocked by Robert Woodward, now ambassador to Spain, who "would not have Hunt in the embassy." Woodward had been "outraged" when Hunt asked the president of Uruguay to lobby Eisenhower to extend his tour in 1960 and "had his revenge in 1964."[26]

In October 1964, Hunt was hospitalized with a duodenal ulcer, which he attributed to "three years of work frustration and professional dissatisfactions" caused by the Agency failing to assign him to "an appropriate post abroad" after the ill-fated Bay of Pigs operation, and "the passive, nonchallenging nature of the domestic work I was given." He compared his position as chief of Covert Action in the Domestic Operations Division to a similar assignment in the Southeast Europe (SE) Division eleven or twelve years earlier, "but with a smaller staff and many fewer responsibilities." He felt he had hit a "professional dead-end, without hope of promotion or foreign assignment, a situation which preoccupied [his] mind and in due course found physical reflection in duodenal hemorrhage."[27]

In February 1965, Hunt was assigned to the Office of the Deputy Director of Plans (DD/P), Richard Helms, and Helms became deputy director of the CIA two months later. After Woodward retired and with the approval of Helms, Karamessines sent Hunt to Spain in the summer of 1965 "for a special undertaking in behalf of the DD/P." He was converted to contract employment and returned in June 1966, "having completed his assignment successfully." Karamessines rated his work during his period as "strong" but only himself and Helms seemed to know what Hunt was doing.[28]

Hunt was sent to Spain under "non-official cover" but Agency documents disagree about whether this was as a writer or a foreign service officer. Hunt had the telephone number of the chief of station and his expenses were paid, but he did "no operational reporting" to the station. Karamessines told Coleman he didn't know much about Hunt's assignment—"Helms said send him out." Hunt was converted to contract agent status on July 4 and sailed for Spain a month later, arriving in mid-August.[29]

Helms' papers include a letter dated August 13, 1965, addressed to Hunt at the Buckley residence in Espalter, Madrid—owned by Bill Buckley's brother Reid—thanking him for a box of what sounds like cigars ("strips of pure gold") and hoping "you had a good trip over and get settled with a minimum of difficulty."[30]

In his autobiography, Hunt divulged the purpose of his highly sensitive Spanish mission—"to develop [confidential] working relationships . . . with people who would be in a successor government to [Spanish dictator, General] Franco." Just as he had worked with a Cuban government in exile in the early sixties, now he would work with the envisaged post-Franco government in Spain. Hunt confirmed the project "had been laid on by Dick Helms" and he reported directly to Deputy Director of Plans Tom Karamessines, who segregated the records of his activities in Spain in a tightly-held "bigot file," with a very limited distribution.[31]

• • •

Another reason for Hunt's Spanish assignment was uncovered by CIA staff probing anomalies in his Agency career during the internal investigations that followed Watergate. In 1974, when questioned about "his knowledge of Mr. Hunt's fictional writings under the pen name, David St. John," CIA historian Walter Pforzheimer recalled trying to identify "the true name of the author . . . when the first St. John book, *On Hazardous Duty*, appeared in 1965." A source in the copyright office informed him "the true name was not given on the copyright application . . . [but] the address . . . was identified with Mr. E. Howard Hunt."

After discovering Hunt's nom de plume, Pforzheimer brought it to the attention of Karamessines and realized from his reaction that he had "uncovered a sensitive matter of senior officer concern." He recommended that "if the Agency is involved in this thing, why not see to it that Hunt leaves his address off the copyright applications in the future." Within five minutes of his conversation with Karamessines, he was called in by Helms, who said: "For Christ sake Walter, this is the first book to come along and say something good about the Agency. Why not leave the goddamn thing alone?"

Pforzheimer "was never officially briefed on the matter" and believed that only Helms or Karamessines had full knowledge of it.[32]

In his autobiography, Hunt confirms that once his cover was blown, "the only solution that seemed feasible . . . was to get me out of the United States for a period of time" and "a delicate but hardly time-consuming mission political-action assignment was found for me in Madrid." Copyright was registered for *On Hazardous Duty* on June 24, 1965 and he was converted to contract status ten days later, so this seems plausible.[33]

When Hunt was assigned to Madrid, "the statement disseminated within the Agency was that Mr. Hunt was retiring . . . [but] this was not generally believed," notes a CIA memo. "Government sources" told author Jim Hougan that Hunt's "false retirement" was part of a counterintelligence

scheme to make the KGB think the St. John spy novels "alluded to actual
CIA operations . . . [and] contained security breaches" but Deputy Chief of
Counterintelligence Ray Rocca later denied working with Hunt.[34]

Hunt also denied any knowledge of Rolando Cubela or the AMLASH
operation to assassinate Fidel Castro, even though "a Senate investigation
determined that [Hunt's] close friend, Manuel Artime, was involved in
Castro assassination plans in Spain during the period 1964 to 1967." Hunt
denied any contact with Artime in Spain or ever discussing the AMLASH
operation with him, but his son, St. John Hunt, vividly remembers Artime
visiting his father in Madrid.[35]

Three St. John books were published in 1966 and three more followed over the
next three years. When Hunt returned to Langley as a staff employee in September 1966, Helms was CIA director and they kept in regular touch. Three
days after Thanksgiving, tragedy struck when Hunt's daughters, Kevan and
Lisa, were seriously injured in a car crash. Lisa was hospitalized for two and a
half years until Hunt couldn't afford to keep her in the hospital any longer:[36]

*Dick Helms approved legal and psychiatric counseling from the agency,
and he distributed some low-interest loans from a special employee fund,
which kept our family afloat until we received a settlement in a civil suit
for the accident two years later. Unfortunately, the judgement was for
much less money than the cost of Lisa's hospitalization, so it still left us
deeply in debt. . . .[37]*

Just before Christmas 1968, Hunt wrote to congratulate Helms on his second
marriage: "Having some experience myself with the institution of divorce, I
also know how rewarding and fulfilling another marriage can be." Several
weeks later, Helms thanked Hunt for "the handsome Christmas present" and
the perfume for his secretary Elizabeth: "I must confess I am awed by your

ability to produce these particular goodies, but then I remember that you have never failed to extricate your heroes from impossible situations."[38]

Over the next four years, Hunt served in various "DDP Staff assignments" under State Department cover. During this period, Richard Helms developed a close friendship with Jack Valenti, a former Special Assistant to President Johnson, who was now head of the Motion Picture Association of America (MPAA). In the Spring of 1966, before leaving the White House, Valenti gave an unspecified briefing to "the most capable intelligence craftsmen in the world," at Helms' request. By 1968, Helms was pitching the David St. John novels to Hollywood studios through Valenti.[39]

On September 19, 1968, Valenti sent Helms feedback from Paramount's Story Department on the "David St. John CIA Project":

While the David St. John paperbacks may be quite acceptable to readers of this sort of international intrigue action melodrama, they are indifferent screen material. Both books have plot and substance enough for a single TV episode; neither has enough for a feature length picture. The emphasis is not on people or action, for all that the books are filled with murder, bloodshed, and casual sex. All these values are handled in pretty cliché terms. What is somewhat interesting is essentially less easy for films than for the printed page—the rather detailed "inside" CIA talk between agents and explanations of procedures. Even this sort of thing, after the several TV series like THE FBI STORY and DRAGNET and others which have explained law enforcement procedures, isn't too fresh or exciting.

And more particularly, series like MAN FROM UNCLE, SECRET AGENT, THE AVENGERS and MISSION IMPOSSIBLE have had far more interesting central characters, not to mention I SPY; Peter Ward does seem pretty dull—and he has no one to talk to—when you think of Crosby and Culp. The idea of doing a straight undercover agent story, without Bondesque spoofing or camping it up, is sound and the public may be ready for it, in both a feature and on TV, but Peter Ward, a loner, without humor, with little or no personal life or personal charm is not a character to win an audience easily. We must therefore pass the project for the present, but I will be on the lookout for a viable story to "marry" to Mr. St. John's area of expertise.

Valenti didn't agree and offered to shop St. John's books to other studios, asking Helms for more copies of the better ones, so he could "keep this exercise going." A month later, Valenti sent Helms more negative feedback from Warner Brothers:

As promised, I read the 4 books by the C.I.A. agent about a fictitious C.I.A. man, and while I agree with you that they make interesting reading, my feeling about them, and especially the character of Peter Ward, is that they would be great for a television series. As you are aware, spy stories at the moment are not great box office attractions. . . .

Valenti planned to contact "two more studios . . . but thus far to my chagrin," he wrote Helms, "we have not scored any points."[40]

After returning from lunch with Valenti on October 24, 1969, Helms wrote, "I spoke to our mutual friend who says that he has a book coming out shortly entitled *The Sorcerers*. When a copy is available, we will see that you get one." In 1970, CIA's Domestic Contact Service (DCS), apparently without Helms' knowledge, also approached Paramount about the David St. John novels but again, they passed.

When the Agency probed the mystery behind the David St. John novels in 1974, there was no indication in Office of Security records "that any of the

David St. John manuscripts were ever submitted for review in accordance with Agency regulations."[41]

General Paul Gaynor—by then retired from the Office of Security's Security Research Staff (SRS)—had noticed that Hunt "was accomplishing a steady flow of spy books, and that security approval was not being requested on the manuscripts before submission to publishers." Gaynor raised the matter on several occasions but was effectively told to "keep your stinking nose out of this business . . . [and] led to believe that Mr. Helms desired to improve the image of the intelligence profession, and the Agency, and that Hunt's books were a part of the program to do so."[42]

Gaynor thought Ray Rocca and Walter Pforzheimer were involved in the "image" materials and might know more. Gaynor also "kept Mrs. Ethel Mendoza fairly current on what he was learning about Hunt's activities because she followed the case for him." Jim Hougan claims Mendoza "analyzed Howard Hunt's 'David St. John' novels to assess the likely reaction of the KGB to those works," but Rocca later denied any counterintelligence involvement in the project.[43]

In July 1968, Hunt took over as chief of Covert Action for the European Division after a period working with the Special Activities Staff. In both jobs, he countered Soviet political action and monitored Communist Party operations, perhaps explaining the Office of Security's suspicions of a counterintelligence operation. Hunt's recently declassified fitness reports for his final years at the Agency remain strong. The division's chief of Operations praised him as "a very competent, tough-minded senior professional," showing imagination, persistence and vigor. But the deputy chief felt that "a series of personal and taxing problems, beyond his control . . . have tended to dull his cutting edge just enough to be noticeable."[44]

On January 26, 1970, as Hunt's retirement paperwork was being processed, there was a flap when it emerged that Bill Buckley had been shopping

Hunt's unpublished Bay of Pigs memoir, *Give Us This Day: CIA and the Bay of Pigs Invasion,* to publishers under the pen name "Edward J. Hamilton," the operational alias he had used during the Bay of Pigs project.[45]

Charles Wiley, a Security Research Staff source, had received a copy of the manuscript from a publishing acquaintance and forwarded a copy to the Agency. Wiley "saw nothing new nor exciting" in the book but did note that General Cabell "appears as the villain" in the Bay of Pigs episode for "allegedly [cancelling] the second or third air strike against the Castro forces."[46]

In July 1968, several publishers rejected the manuscript as "far too controversial," leaving them open to libel suits. A CIA analysis noted immediate similarities in the first few pages between biographical details in the manuscript and Hunt's file, and agreed the text included "minor compromises of security" and personal opinions on prominent former Agency employees which "could be considered controversial if not actually damaging" and "provocative" to those "concerned or described." In a cover note to Mr. Gaynor, one of his staff noted that publishers might be reluctant to get involved in what they might see "as an Agency effort to covertly tell 'the true story.'"[47]

On February 17, 1970, Hunt met with DDP Tom Karamessines, and Paul Gaynor, chief of the Security Research Staff, to discuss the manuscript. At first, he "professed ignorance but . . . [later] admitted he had written it for his own benefit as a historical record."[48]

Two days later, they met again and Hunt "reiterated he had sent the manuscript to [his agent] and Buckley for critique only and cited the use of his agency pseudonym as author as proof that he had no intention of publishing the work." He was warned of the dangers of publishing such a manuscript and asked to find out "how many copies of it might be in circulation."[49]

Hunt brought with him a sealed package returned to him by Buckley, and postmarked October 29, 1968. Hunt's agent denied showing the manuscript to anyone in the publishing world but as Gaynor pointed out, one publisher "had returned the manuscript to Buckley with a refusal in July 1968" and three other publishers had subsequently received copies.[50]

Three days before the meeting, Walter Pforzheimer sent a detailed commentary on the manuscript to Director of Security, Howard Osborn, noting that "this manuscript has evidently been kicking around in publishing circles since at least mid-1968, presumably without CIA clearance." He concluded:[51]

> *It is apparent that Hamilton feels very deeply about the Bay of Pigs and its aftermath, to the extent that he is willing to put his career on the line by circulating this manuscript to several publishers without apparent clearance or authorization.*

By using his CIA pseudonym for the Cuban project as his nom de plume, Hunt made identifying the author far too easy. Pforzheimer called the manuscript "the most comprehensive story of a CIA operation that has ever been written for publication . . . with all the authority of an 'insider' who was there . . . The author's claim that this book would provide no information not known to Castro's intelligence service, or that details this late are of no value to the opposition, is, in my view, seriously open to question":

> *The book is, in general, favorable to CIA actions in the Bay of Pigs. The villains of the piece are certain liberal figures in the Kennedy administration (Schlesinger, Goodwin, Stevenson) and, to some extent, the President himself. In his concluding chapter, the author's bitterness is undisguised against those in the Administration and the press who took the opportunity of the Bay of Pigs incident to attack and denigrate CIA.*[52]

The book was eventually published in 1973 by Arlington House, one of the publishers who had initially rejected it. In Hunt's Foreword, he notes that his memoir of nineteen months on the CIA's doomed "Cuba Project" was written "reluctantly and in a mood of nostalgic bitterness" in 1967, "as a private legacy to [his] children; perhaps eventually to be lodged in a university library."[53]

Hunt retired voluntarily on April 30, 1970, as a GS-15 Operations officer in the European division, on a salary of $26,629: "He was rated superior in all of his fitness reports and is eligible for rehire as far as his performance is concerned."[54]

In his autobiography, *Undercover,* Hunt writes that his desire to retire was linked to his need to "become financially solvent again" after his daughters' crash. In his retirement interview, dated April 24, Hunt revealed that he planned to join the Mullen Company and knew the company provided cover for at least one Agency employee. He also said Karamessines had asked him to "stay in touch."[55]

The day before his retirement, he received a letter of appreciation from Helms, thanking him for his service:

You have every reason to feel great pride and satisfaction in your accomplishments. Your record of service is both example and goal for the young people who are now just beginning their careers in intelligence. May I extend to you, personally and officially, my sincere appreciation for the important work you have done and my warmest hopes that you will find full enjoyment in the years ahead.[56]

But not everyone was convinced Hunt was really retiring. After discussions with Walter Pforzheimer, General Gaynor believed "Hunt was merely moving his desk outside the building, but being paid by the same source as before."[57]

Hunt stayed on good terms with Helms and returned to CIA headquarters the following March, when Helms threw a birthday party for his secretary, Elizabeth Dunlevy, in his private office.[58]

Robert Mullen had known Hunt since 1948, when they worked together on the Marshall Plan and they kept in touch socially during the sixties. According to CIA records, Mullen "was instrumental in the formation of the Cuban Freedom Committee [in late 1960]" and his company "had been utilized by the Central Cover Staff since 1963" to provide cover for Agency employees.[59]

Frank O'Malley worked in the External Employment Assistant Branch of the Retirement Activities Division within the Agency's Office of Personnel, helping "personnel retiring from the Agency in finding post-retirement employment" and was "instrumental" in placing Hunt with Mullen's public relations firm. O'Malley had known Hunt since the early sixties when he served with the Central Cover Staff funding "covert action projects" and Hunt was involved in propaganda activities for the Covert Activities staff. The Mullen Company handled public relations for the Cuban Freedom Committee, which sponsored anti-Castro radio broadcasts, and O'Malley became close to Robert Mullen, who confided that the Howard Hughes organization was a client.[60]

Given Hunt's experience in public relations, O'Malley asked Mullen's advice. Hunt listed Richard Helms as a character reference on his résumé and Helms "signed a letter of recommendation to the Kennecott Copper Company on . . . Hunt's behalf." But Hunt didn't sell himself very well in interviews with Kennecott, *Reader's Digest*, and General Foods (a Mullen client) and still couldn't find a job.[61]

During Hunt's last month at the Agency, according to O'Malley, Mullen called to say his company had plans to expand and could offer Hunt a position immediately. But Mullen later told Robert Bennett—who would soon buy the company from him—that O'Malley "twisted [his] arm pretty hard" to hire Hunt:

> Mullen believed that Helms wished him to employ Hunt, especially after receipt of a splendid letter of recommendation of Hunt from Mr. Helms who later personally expressed his appreciation to Mr. Mullen for hiring Hunt. Mr. Mullen said he honestly believed, as a result of the pressure exerted by [O'Malley] that the Agency wished him to resolve problems attendant to Hunt's retirement by hiring Hunt.[62]

Hunt joined the company on May 1, 1970 and began writing short films promoting "special education" for gifted disabled children for the HEW account. The Agency did not brief Hunt "on certain sensitive cover arrangements," assuming he was already aware of them "based on his senior position and his long-time personal association with Mr. Mullen."[63]

On May 28, Martin Lukoskie, the case officer for the Mullen Company within the Central Cover Staff (CCS), requested a Covert Security Approval (CSA) for Hunt for utilization "under Project QKENCHANT." But the Office of Security were still investigating Hunt's novels and Lou Vasaly in SRS advised that clearance could not be granted without Karamessines' personal approval. Hunt's proposed corporate cover status was put on hold, pending discussions between SRS and Karamessines regarding his manuscript.[64]

On July 7, Hunt contacted CCS, suggesting the Mullen Company "could provide cover as a result of its connections with *The Brussels Times*." The Belgian newspaper was owned by long-term Agency asset Sam Meek and edited by James Everett, a deep-cover CIA officer who ran the Mullen Company office in Amsterdam. In subsequent discussions with Mullen and Hunt, it emerged that Mullen "had informed Mr. Hunt of the existing cover arrangement without authorization from CCS."[65]

In mid-October, Willard Burke, chief of CCS, wrote to Karamessines, requesting clearance for Hunt, who was expected to "succeed Mr. Mullen as principal officer of the company." Hunt was "already witting of the current cover arrangement" and would be needed to help with ongoing and potential cover abroad. Karamessines approved and Hunt was granted clearance three weeks later.[66]

Mullen had planned to retire and hand over the running of his business to three younger successors—Howard Hunt; attorney Douglas Caddy, the Washington representative for General Foods, who worked out of the Mullen office but soon quit to practice law; and Robert Bennett, the son of Wallace Bennett, a Republican senator from Utah. In early November, Mullen casually told Hunt that his lawyer had advised him "to sell out to one person rather than [three], and so he was making arrangements to sell his 90% of the company stock to Bob Bennett who was to have been one of the original triumvirate." "I confronted Mullen with his breach of faith," Hunt recalled, "and from that time on, our relations were cool."[67]

In December, Howard Hughes fired Robert Maheu, the manager of his Las Vegas operations, and Maheu sued his former boss for fifty million dollars, claiming they had "a verbal contract for life." William Gay, a senior vice president at Hughes Tool Company, called Bennett and suggested he replace Larry O'Brien as Hughes' man in Washington. Bennett accepted and around the same time, Charles Colson told him Robert Mullen was looking to sell his company. Bennett had previously served as Colson's liaison at the Department of Transportation."[68]

In January 1971, Bennett joined the Mullen Company and became its president, prior to finalizing his acquisition of the company. When Bennett examined the books, he found a number of mysterious entries and was told by Mullen that the company "had a contract with the CIA under which the CIA would place their employees on our payroll at selected cities abroad . . . [and]

use our name as a cover for their CIA activities." Mullen told him it was a non-profit service "performed for the Government as a patriotic gesture." Within the company, only Mullen, Hunt (a former CIA officer) and bookkeeper Edward Naeher (a retired CIA Finance Officer) knew about it.[69]

Bennett brought the Hughes Tool account with him, assuming Maheu's previous responsibilities for "dealing with Government affairs." Maheu had told Hughes he was "a CIA operator," so Hughes asked Bennett to investigate if he was or not:

> Having just joined the Mullen Co. and having discovered that they had a CIA connection and that Howard Hunt was a former CIA officer that had worked on the Bay of Pigs operation, I thought that I would ask Howard if he ever heard of him.

Hunt claimed he had never heard of Maheu and that there was no trace of Maheu having ever done anything for the CIA.[70]

Nixon had reason to fear Maheu and O'Brien, as Hughes had contributed one hundred thousand dollars to the Nixon campaign through Charles "Bebe" Rebozo during his first term. If O'Brien knew about this, as chairman of the Democratic National Committee (DNC), he might now use it against Nixon, leading some to argue this was why O'Brien's phone and the DNC offices were targeted by the Watergate burglars.[71]

At the end of April, Mullen introduced Bennett to the company's case officer, Martin Lukoskie. Lukoskie's report of the meeting notes that he and Maheu had known each other as FBI agents in New York many years earlier and that Maheu was then working for the Agency on a cover operation in Chile named "Peltier," which he didn't mention to Bennett or Mullen.[72]

By the next meeting in early June, Bennett had received his security clear-ance. He reported that Maheu openly "bragged about his relationship with Sam Giancana and with the CIA and the Bay of Pigs" and that "Maheu was owned by the Mafia and that the Hughes people feared they might end up in the river due to their law suit."[73]

CIA records indicate that Agency consideration was given to utilizing Mullen's relationship with Hughes for a matter relating to a cover arrange-ment in South America, and to garner information on Robert Maheu.[74]

On April 5, 1971, Hunt began a lengthy exchange with CIA General Coun-sel Lawrence Houston about an "annuity problem":

> *At the time of retirement Mr. Hunt did not elect survivorship benefits.*
> *This meant that upon his death, his wife would not draw a survivorship*
> *annuity.*[75]

Houston had first met Hunt during a short assignment to Tokyo in 1954 and was invited over to Hunt's house with his wife for cocktails in the mid-sixties. They would see each other "from time to time in or around the office" until Hunt's retirement and now, Hunt asked Houston to intervene to change his choice of survivorship benefits. After careful consideration with colleagues, Houston wrote back a month later to say that, regretfully, he was bound by the regulations and it couldn't be done. "I thoroughly appreciate the thought and study you gave my problem," replied Hunt, "and while your findings are disappointing to me, I must regard them as defini-tive." He floated the possibly of a class action suit with fellow annuitants before thanking Houston for his efforts "to help me once again." While Hunt didn't sue the CIA, it wasn't the end of the matter and four months later, Hunt called again on the Agency for support that led it into the great-est crisis in its history.[76]

CHAPTER 4

THE ELLSBERG AFFAIR

On Sunday, June 13, 1971, the *New York Times* began publishing extracts from the Pentagon Papers, leaked by former military analyst Daniel Ellsberg. They had already been turned over to the Soviet embassy, according to a Soviet double agent working for the CIA. Within days, with Nixon's approval, a special investigative unit was set up within the White House "to stop security leaks and to investigate other sensitive security matters." They later became known as "the Plumbers." John Ehrlichman's deputy, Egil "Bud" Krogh, ran the unit with former Kissinger aide David Young, under the direction of Ehrlichman and Charles Colson, special counsel to the president. They soon recruited G. Gordon Liddy, a former FBI agent later described by Hunt as a "taut, wisecracking extrovert." Nixon asked Young to make investigating Ellsberg's motives and possible further disclosures his top priority but later insisted he "did not authorize and had no knowledge of any illegal means to be used to achieve this goal."[1]

Ellsberg had enlisted his children, aged ten and thirteen, to help him copy the documents, infuriating his ex-wife Carol Cummings. She agreed to cooperate with the FBI four days after the papers were published, on the basis that if Ellsberg had disclosed classified information, he should go to jail. Cummings provided incriminating evidence on the copying of the documents and the names of Ellsberg's former girlfriends and most recent psychiatrist, Dr. Lewis Fielding.[2]

On June 28, Ellsberg turned himself in and the next day, Nixon told Attorney General John Mitchell: "We've gotta get this son of a bitch." The Left would make Ellsberg a "martyr" but Nixon couldn't allow him "to get away with this kind of wholesale thievery, or otherwise it's going to happen all over the government."[3]

"Let's get the son of a bitch into jail," he told Mitchell and Kissinger the next day. "Don't worry about his trial. Just get everything out. Try him in the press . . . Everything, John, that there is on the investigation . . . leak it out. We want to destroy him in the press . . . That's where we won the [Alger] Hiss case. I didn't try it in the goddamn courtroom. But I won it before it ever got to court."[4]

Charles Colson had been friends with Howard Hunt for several years, they were president and vice-president of the Brown University Club in Washington. When Colson became involved in Nixon's 1968 campaign, Hunt recalled Nixon's interest in his Bay of Pigs activities and when Colson joined Nixon's White House staff, they "lunched occasionally to mull over possible employment opportunities" for Hunt in the new administration.[5]

On July 1, Hunt received a call from Colson that would change his life. Colson sounded him out about the Ellsberg prosecution and asked if, "with the right resources . . . this could be turned into a major public case against Ellsberg and his co-conspirators." Colson was intent on "nailing any son-of-a-bitch who would steal a secret document of the Government and publish it" but realized the case "won't be tried in court, it will be tried in the newspapers" and that's where Hunt came in. When Colson raised the question of possible conspirators, Hunt mentioned DNC chairman Larry O'Brien but Colson suspected a Soviet hand behind Ellsberg. Either way, Hunt wanted "to see the guy hung if it can be done to the advantage of the Administration."[6]

The next day, Colson sent Haldeman a transcript of the conversation, recommending he meet "the CIA mastermind on the Bay of Pigs." He also called Bob Bennett and asked him to make Hunt available for a White House assignment on a part time basis. Bennett was happy to oblige and changed Hunt's contract from a monthly salary to a $125-a-day consultancy. On July 6, Hunt met Colson at the White House and was appointed as a security consultant at a day rate of $100.[7]

The following day, Hunt was introduced to Ehrlichman and asked Colson to provide "flash alias documentation and physical disguise material" for an interview with Kennedy insider Clifton DeMotte, so Hunt couldn't be traced to the White House. Later that day, Ehrlichman called General Cushman, deputy director of Central Intelligence, to inform him of Hunt's appointment as a security consultant and to tell him to expect a call from Hunt soon: "He may want some help on computer runs and other things. You should consider he has pretty much carte blanche." Cushman promised "full cooperation from CIA."[8]

Cushman called Director of Security, Howard Osborn, with the news and his reaction "was one of wonderment . . . since, to [his] knowledge, [Hunt] knew nothing of security." Hunt and Osborn had been high-school classmates at Hamburg High School in New York and Osborn would soon be the Agency liaison to the Plumbers. Cushman reported the news of Hunt's appointment at Helms' morning meeting with senior staff the next day and while the FBI reviewed Hunt's Agency security file a month later, Helms was never consulted by the White House on Hunt's suitability for the new role.[9]

Colson's appointment book for July 8 reads: "Bottle of Scotch—Lucien Conein—Howard Hunt Project—E's [Ehrlichman's] Office." The aim of the boozy session was "to elicit . . . derogatory information about Ellsberg's activities in Vietnam" from retired CIA agent Lucien Conein but Hunt's attempt to tape-record the conversation failed (Conein sat on the tape recorder) and he remembered little of it the next morning, so he called

Conein to refresh his memory. Osborn received a call from Hunt, asking for Conein's number around this time and never heard from Hunt again.[10]

A week later, Hunt met CIA General Counsel Larry Houston and discussed, "among other things," another possible resolution to his annuity problem. He had been asked to write up an award recommendation for the Agency six months after his retirement. If he was invited "to assist in writing up [another one]," he asked, "could I be re-employed for a few days for the purpose of doing the writing?" While this was within the rules, Executive Director Colonel White and Director of Personnel Harry Fisher felt it would establish "an unfortunate precedent" and strongly opposed it.[11]

One day, when Hunt asked Colson for a classified document, he was told to visit Gordon Liddy in Room 16—the hub of the "Plumbers" operation in the Executive Office Building, where FBI reports on Ellsberg were received. Hunt was twelve years older than Liddy but they "clicked immediately" and started having lunch in the White House cafeteria.[12]

Hunt didn't let his new White House position divert him from lucrative business opportunities. One weekend in July, he was flown to Nicaragua with his wife and daughter as a guest of Dr. Manuel Artime, who had large investments in the country and "was an intimate friend of President Somoza."[13]

On Thursday, July 22, Hunt visited General Cushman at CIA headquarters. He asked for privacy, so Cushman's executive assistant Karl Wagner left the room but Cushman recorded the conversation, without Hunt's knowledge.[14]

"I've been charged with quite a highly sensitive mission by the White House to visit and elicit information from an individual whose ideology we aren't entirely sure of," began Hunt. "They asked me to come over here and see if you could get me two things: flash alias documentation . . . and some degree of physical disguise for a one-time op—in and out."

"Flash alias documentation" meant a driver's license and some "pocket litter" (other ID documents) in the name of "Edward."

"I don't see why we can't," replied Cushman.

Hunt wanted to keep the mission "as closely held as possible" and asked for a disguise for a trip that weekend, so "I just don't exist, and it's not possible to describe me." He suggested meeting the "cover people" at a safehouse to pick up the flash documents and disguise but "they wouldn't need to know my name. . . ."

Cushman agreed to Hunt's request and was later heavily criticized for not pressing Hunt for "the details of his mission." Hunt said he could be contacted through Charles Colson's secretary Joan Hall, and complimented Cushman on losing a little weight, which the general put down to going to the gym with Helms after work, which "discouraged mid-afternoon snacking."[15]

After a briefing from Cushman, Karl Wagner cleared Hunt's request with Samuel Halpern (Karamessines' assistant) and instructed Richard Krueger, the acting chief of the Technical Services Division (TSD) to furnish "a physical disguise and alias documentation to an individual who didn't want his identity known to TSD officers." Wagner told Krueger "the matter was extremely sensitive and was being done for the White House."[16]

The next day, TSD officer Stephen Greenwood met "Edward" in a safehouse and gave him alias documents, "including a social security card, driver's license, and several association membership cards, in the name of 'Edward Joseph Warren' . . . and disguise materials, a wig, glasses, and a speech alteration device."[17]

On July 28, Hunt assumed the disguise and "ill-fitting wig" to interview Clifton DeMotte, who had promised information on the Kennedy family that didn't prove particularly helpful.[18]

The same day, Hunt sent Colson a "skeletal operations plan," titled "Neutralization of Ellsberg," setting out a wish list of materials that would help "to destroy his public image and credibility." They included an interview with his ex-wife Carol Cummings and his mistress in Saigon, and obtaining a psychological assessment from the CIA and "Ellsberg's files from his psychiatric analyst."[19]

The CIA's Office of Medical Services (OMS) had been producing "personality assessments" of foreign leaders for many years and in December 1970, Tom Huston had contacted Dr. John Tietjen, the Agency's director of Medical Services, to discuss how such "personality studies . . . could be applied to domestic problems, particularly as related to dissidents."[20]

David Young was also familiar with CIA profiles of foreign leaders from his time as an assistant to Henry Kissinger on the National Security Council (NSC) staff. Hunt soon suggested Young make use of the Agency's psychiatric unit, giving him the name of Dr. Bernard Malloy, the chief of the unit.[21]

In mid-July, Young called CIA Director of Security Howard Osborn and told him, "Dr. Kissinger and Mr. Ehrlichman had been very impressed with a psychological profile prepared by the Agency's Office of Medical Services on Fidel Castro." Young requested "a similar profile on Daniel Ellsberg." As Ellsberg was a US citizen under indictment by the US government, Osborn said only Helms could approve the request.[22]

Helms subsequently called Young to query his request: "We didn't know Mr. Ellsberg. We didn't have any information about him . . . why were we being asked to make a study of this kind?" According to the Agency's internal history of Watergate, Young "pleaded" with Helms, stressing that the study had been given the "highest priority" by Ehrlichman and Kissinger "and that CIA was the only Agency with such a capability."[23]

On July 29, Osborn visited Dr. Tietjen to inform him that, "with considerable reluctance," Helms had agreed to a White House request for a personality study on Ellsberg. Tietjen noted that the information available was "very sparse" and passed the request to Dr. Malloy, chief of the Psychiatric Staff. Helms told Osborn to send nothing to the White House on the matter without his approval.[24]

Dr. Malloy and his colleagues expressed serious "reservation and concern" that such a "potentially controversial and highly speculative" project targeting an American citizen "might be outside of the Agency's purview." Malloy directed Dr. Jerrold Post to prepare an initial draft, based on press articles about Ellsberg and FBI interview reports with informants about him supplied by the White House.[25]

As the Senate Watergate Committee later noted, the provision of "CIA equipment and assistance in developing a psychological profile of Ellsberg overstepped the Agency's legal bounds by being involved with domestic intelligence-gathering and internal security."[26]

As Young was discussing the Ellsberg profile with the Agency, the FBI was investigating Dr. Fielding, the psychiatrist who had been seeing Ellsberg from the fall of 1968 until July 1970. On July 20, 1971, two FBI agents visited Dr. Fielding's office to discuss Ellsberg. After consulting his attorney, Fielding refused to discuss his former patient, invoking client confidentiality. After trying again, the FBI informed the White House of Fielding's decision a week later.[27]

On August 5, the first "indirect assessment" on Ellsberg was completed and after revisions by Tietjen and Malloy, the final draft was cleared by Deputy Director for Support John Coffey four days later.[28]

The same day, Helms and Howard Osborn met David Young in Ehrlichman's office to discuss "unauthorized disclosures of unclassified information" in the news media and Young ordered an analysis of the frequency and gravity of recent leaks within a week. Osborn later described Young as a frequent visitor to Langley and "any reluctance to comply with his requests were invariably met with the rejoinder 'I will have Mr. Ehrlichman call Mr. Helms.'" Osborn "provided him with extensive material from [CIA] files and performed several specific damage assessments at his request."[29]

The next morning, Dr. Tietjen hand carried the first Ellsberg profile to Howard Osborn, with a note bearing the proviso:

> *This indirect assessment should be considered impressionistic and speculative, the data on which it is based are quite sparse. If more reliable family history and personal data become available, we should be able to provide a more solid assessment.*[30]

After forwarding a copy to Helms, Osborn sent Young the assessment the next day, with a reminder that "however this is used, the Agency should not become involved."[31]

The assessment depicted Ellsberg as "an extremely intelligent and talented individual" with an "insatiable need for success and recognition" who saw the release of the Pentagon Papers as the act of a patriot, not a traitor. It described him as a man "whose career had taken off like a rocket, but who found himself at mid-life not nearly having achieved the prominence and success he expected and desired. Thus, it may well have been an intensified need to achieve significance that impelled him to release the Pentagon Papers."[32]

A memorandum from Krogh and Young to Ehrlichman the same day acknowledges receipt of the "CIA preliminary psychological study," which they found disappointing and "very superficial." They resolved to impress on Dr. Malloy "the detail and depth" expected and give him additional FBI reports on Ellsberg:

> *We would recommend that a covert operation be undertaken to examine all the medical files still held by Ellsberg's psychoanalyst covering the two-year period in which he was undergoing analysis.*[33]

Underneath this, Ehrlichman was invited to approve or disapprove. He initialed "Approve" with the handwritten caveat, "if done under your assurance that it is not traceable."[34]

Young called Osborn to express his disappointment with the assessment and suggested they "try again." On August 12, Malloy met Young and a "Mr. Linney" (later identified as Gordon Liddy) for an hour in Room 16 of the Executive Office Building to discuss "a psychiatric write-up on the case of Daniel Ellsberg." Young told Malloy that "the Ellsberg study had the highest priority and had been requested by Mr. Ehrlichman and Dr. Kissinger" and approved by the president. Young understood Malloy's unease but assured him that "great care would be given to make it non-attributable to the Agency."

Howard Hunt joined the meeting late and greeted Dr. Malloy warmly as a former colleague. Young and Liddy were very concerned that Ellsberg was sitting on a lot of sensitive information for further leaks, so Hunt wanted to "try Dr. Ellsberg in public" to neutralize his effectiveness and "make him the object of pity as a broken man."

Young asked Malloy what kind of information he needed to construct a study like the one on Castro. Malloy requested data from Ellsberg's early years—"from nurses or close relatives . . . school progress, including testing . . . year books, his years in college and in the military [and] comments from friends." Hunt suggested interviewing Ellsberg's first wife "under an operational alias," as she was thought to be "cooperative." He also wanted to see the kind of data that "psychiatrists found out about Barry Goldwater in 1964," with a focus on "Dr. Ellsberg's oedipal conflicts or castration fears."

According to FBI reports, after leaking the Pentagon Papers, Ellsberg had called his analyst and said, "Now I am free." Liddy was keen to probe the background to this statement and Hunt promised to send "further biographic information" on Ellsberg to Malloy and to schedule further meetings but

Hunt wanted to avoid visiting CIA headquarters. At the end of the meeting, Hunt asked Malloy not to divulge "his presence and participation in the meeting" to his Agency colleagues. An internal memo by Malloy gives the reason for this not shared in his affidavit:

> *[Hunt] stated that his house was in the process of being repainted by the son of the Director of Security and "[Osborn] has been trying all summer to find out what I was doing."*[35]

After arriving back at the Agency, Malloy called Hunt and told him it was necessary to tell Dr. Tietjen about Hunt's presence at the meeting. Hunt didn't agree and "expressed great regret," insisting "he had adequate contact with General Cushman and was on good terms with the Director."

"Couldn't this be treated as confidential medical information?" asked Hunt, clutching at straws.

"In what way?" replied a bemused Malloy, who subsequently discussed "the dangers and the reservations and the gravity of the situation" with Dr. Tietjen, his deputy and the deputy chief of the Psychiatric Staff.[36]

According to the Agency's draft Watergate history, Malloy "did not mention Hunt's presence at the conference to Howard Osborn. He may have mentioned it to Mr. Coffey but if so, Coffey did not so advise Helms." Helms claimed he didn't know about Hunt's involvement in the profiles until May 1973. "It is thus apparent," the report's author, John Richards concludes, that "Hunt's dual involvement with the Agency, i.e. with Cushman and TSD and with OMS was not known by any one officer in the Agency."[37]

The day after the White House meeting, Malloy received "poorly Xeroxed classified FBI reports and Department of State documents" from Hunt and shared "his general uneasiness" about Young, Hunt, and Liddy with Dr.

Tietjen, feeling they put "undue store on what psychiatry might do and what we might produce."[38]

A week later, on August 20, Malloy and Tietjen met with Deputy Director for Support John Coffey to discuss "the continuing pressure and desire for a psychiatric study" from the White House, "the problems associated with developing the study" and their "continuing reservations," which Coffey shared.[39]

The documents provided by Hunt suggested Ellsberg "was under emotional pressure" but were not enough for a "comprehensive understanding of [his] personality." Ellsberg had allegedly revealed "quasi-Secret Information while still in the service when . . . applying for a Ph.D. fellowship"; had volunteered for State Department service in Vietnam in 1965 "while under the stress of obtaining a divorce from his first wife"; and had seen a psychoanalyst in California from the fall of 1968 to 1970. Around this time, Dr. Malloy did a background check on Dr. Fielding and described him as "a solid, capable, talented and responsible psychoanalyst."[40]

It was agreed that Malloy would discuss "the implications" of this data with Hunt, Liddy, and Young but the Agency staff were extremely reluctant to interview Ellsberg's ex-wife. Coffey considered notifying Helms at this stage but decided to wait until after Malloy's next meeting with Young to bring the director up-to-date. Malloy planned to tell Young that the additional material wasn't very helpful and "it was hoped that this would put an end to the situation."[41]

Three days later, Malloy called Young to arrange a meeting but Hunt wasn't available. As Richards notes, while Young seems to have delegated the profiles to Hunt at that point, he may have been playing for time, since "the decision probably had already been taken to burgle Fielding's office in the hope of making more material available." Malloy didn't hear from Young again until September 30. Hunt was "away," so Young called Osborn to get Malloy's number and left a message from Hunt, suggesting a meeting with Malloy at the end of October.[42]

Dr. Malloy subsequently mentioned to Osborn that he had briefed Coffey on the matter. When Coffey called Osborn "shortly thereafter," Osborn reminded him that Helms "wanted to approve personally all material forwarded to the White House on this matter." Coffey "was unable to recall when asked in June 1972, after Watergate, that Howard Hunt was involved with the psychiatric profile of Ellsberg."[43]

A former staff member of the Senate Watergate Committee later showed copies of the background material given to Malloy for the psychological study to author Jim Hougan. He was struck by "marginal notations, circled phrases and exclamation points that crowded the pages whenever Ellsberg's relationship to a writer named Frances FitzGerald was mentioned." FitzGerald befriended Ellsberg as a reporter in Vietnam in the mid-sixties and may have dated him. She was the daughter of Desmond FitzGerald, Karamessines' predecessor as deputy director of Plans, who arranged for Rolando Cubela to be given a poison pen in Paris to assassinate Castro on the day JFK was killed in Dallas. Frances FitzGerald wrote "favorable reports" on Ellsberg to her father before his death in 1967 and the Agency worried about what she might have "leaked" to Ellsberg about her father.[44]

Howard Hunt's demands on Agency resources didn't stop there. On July 16, he had written to the twenty-four-year-old secretary for the CIA station chief in Paris, whom he had become friendly with while chief of covert action for the Europe Division. Hunt told her "she might receive TDY [temporary assignment] orders to return to Washington . . . at his request" soon. He advised her to "let it come as a complete surprise and not to mention his name or the fact that he was working at the White House." Two weeks later, he wrote her again, saying he was still awaiting a decision.[45]

Oddly, Hunt didn't formally request her reassignment to work with him at the White House until he called General Cushman's assistant Karl Wagner on August 18. Hunt said it was for a "highly sensitive assignment" and that

"White House involvement should not be mentioned to anyone but General Cushman or the Director." When Cushman denied the request the same day, Hunt protested and Cushman forwarded a memo on the incident to Helms with the note, "FYI and guidance on how to handle." Helms immediately replied, "If Hunt renews the request . . . please let me know and I'll speak to Ehrlichman at once."[46]

According to Helms, Hunt wanted the transfer "to be done secretly and he didn't want anybody to know about it . . . so I got hold of General Cushman and told him that I thought this was totally unacceptable and I wouldn't stand for it."[47]

The same day, TSD officers Stephen Greenwood and Cleo Gephart met Hunt to deliver business cards he had requested and to adjust his disguise spectacles. Hunt asked for a tape recorder and two microphones, which Gephart delivered, concealed in a typewriter case, two days later.[48]

Gephart knew Hunt as "Edward" and thought he was a "case officer detached to the . . . White House for [a] special mission," possibly interviewing or debriefing defectors. He regarded Hunt's request for a commercially available tape recorder as "an unmitigated pain in the neck" and "judged 'Edward' as an over-graded semi competent case officer, making an entirely unnecessary clandestine operation [out] of a simple support request."[49]

Early the following week, Greenwood met Hunt to deliver a new speech alteration device and Hunt asked for a disguise and "pocket litter" for an associate, and a backstopped address and telephone number in New York. Krueger asked Greenwood to prepare the disguise and documentation for Hunt's associate, pending authorization, but Greenwood misunderstood and thought he had approval.[50]

On Wednesday, August 25, "Mr. Edward" met Greenwood at a safe-house and introduced him to a "Mr. Leonard" (Liddy), who provided details for his alias documentation. Hunt also requested a concealed camera suitable for indoor photography and later that day, TSD technician Ronald James arrived with the alias documents and a Tessina camera disguised in a tobacco pouch. James showed Hunt how to use the camera, which Hunt said he needed for a "new assignment" related to drug control. Hunt and Liddy were about to catch a plane to Los Angeles but, first, they had to stop by the Pentagon.[51]

When later questioned about his knowledge of the support for Hunt, Helms said Cushman informed him "he had authorized giving to Howard Hunt a tape recorder and a camera. I asked for what purpose and he said he wanted to conduct a one-time interview, and that he had been properly authenticated by the White House and that he was working at their behest." He was told the camera was "carried in a tobacco pouch" and knew Hunt was a consultant at the White House, working for Ehrlichman.[52]

That evening, Hunt and Liddy checked into the Beverly Hilton Hotel and walked a few blocks to Dr. Fielding's office building at 450 North Bedford Avenue, Beverly Hills. The next morning, they had breakfast with Morton "Tony" Jackson, a former Agency lawyer and Hunt implied he was in town "on a narcotics mission."[53]

After breakfast, Hunt and Liddy donned their disguises and photographed "the target office building" with Hunt's 35mm camera—"the access and escape routes" and a rear parking lot, where they found a Volvo in a parking space with Dr. Fielding's name on it. "To blunt curiosity among passersby," Hunt asked Liddy to pose in front of the office building, as if for a tourist snap. They also rented a car and "scouted Dr. Fielding's residence," photographing his apartment building in Brentwood from three sides.[54]

• • •

Back at CIA headquarters, Greenwood reported the material issued and Hunt's comments to his supervisor, Richard Krueger, deputy chief of Technical Services Division (TSD). Krueger called Karl Wagner, General Cushman's executive assistant, to advise the material had been issued "without prior notification or approval from [Karamessines'] office" and Wagner wrote up the incident in a memorandum for General Cushman, who was due back in the office the next day:[55]

Mr. [Krueger], Deputy Chief, TSD, called to express concern about the extent of support being requested by Mr. Howard Hunt, former Agency officer who is a White House consultant.

Hunt's original request for Agency technical support—false documentation, a disguise and a tape recorder—had been approved by Ehrlichman, Cushman, and Helms "in connection with an extremely sensitive White House project" and "his contacts with TSD officers were conducted in pseudonym." But Hunt was now requesting additional support, including "a disguise and documentation [for] a colleague whom he identified only by pseudonym":

On 25 August, he asked for and received training in clandestine photography and was given a concealed camera in order to photograph an individual in a poorly lighted corridor . . . [for] a "new assignment".

Krueger noted that Hunt "now possessed a considerable amount of special materials" and "the clandestine camera is particularly sensitive since it could plausibly be associated with the Agency," especially if used in "domestic clandestine activity."[56]

After the call, Krueger "jotted down instructions" for Greenwood to pass to Hunt at their next meeting. Assistance with Hunt's alias documentation, disguise, and tape recorder could continue, but Liddy's documents were to be returned and all other requests were subject to authorization by Green-wood's supervisors.⁵⁷

Later that day, General Cushman called Krueger back, "apparently disturbed that somebody hasn't turned [Hunt] off." He said Helms had received a letter from Ehrlichman "requesting that a [chief of station's] secretary in Europe be detailed to [Hunt] for a year" but reiterated that Hunt had "no authorization on support for an associate" and no further support was to be given to Hunt "without specific authorization."⁵⁸

That night, Hunt and Liddy took more photographs of the exterior of Fielding's office building before going upstairs to his second-floor office, where Hunt used his Spanish to convince the Hispanic cleaning woman that they were doctors and had "an urgent message for Fielding." As Hunt chatted to her, Liddy went inside with his pipe and tobacco pouch camera and took several photographs. They watched her leave at midnight and were surprised to find she left the front and rear doors of the building open.⁵⁹

Young had already told Ehrlichman, "Hunt and Liddy have left for California." As Hunt and Liddy were casing Fielding's office building, they began planning the subsequent smear campaign on Ellsberg. "If the present Hunt/Liddy Project #1 is successful," wrote Young, "it will be absolutely essential to have an overall game plan developed." Ehrlichman sent Colson a memo the next day:

*On the assumption that the proposed undertaking by Hunt and Liddy would be carried out and would be successful, I would appreciate receiving from you by next Wednesday a game plan as to how and when you believe the materials should be used.*⁶⁰

Colson told his secretary it was "stupid to put it in writing" and Ehrlichman subsequently told him to "forget the memo" and not to talk to anybody about Hunt and Liddy's operations.⁶¹

• • •

Despite mounting Agency concern about Hunt's requests, Greenwood was cleared to meet Hunt at Dulles airport at six o'clock on Friday morning (August 27). Hunt gave Greenwood the concealed camera in the tobacco pouch, which he had used to photograph Fielding's office, and a roll of exposed film from his 35mm camera, which had been used for "the external casing":

> *Hunt requested immediate development of the film and asked that the negatives and one print of each picture be delivered to him that day. [Greenwood] agreed to meet Hunt at a safehouse later that morning. The roll of film was developed and a single print was made in accordance with Hunt's instructions. However, a Xerox copy of the prints was made for the TSD files.*[62]

Krueger approved the development of the film and Greenwood made Xerox copies of the pictures and delivered them to Krueger before going to meet "Edward" at the safehouse.[63]

Before the prints were returned to Hunt, Krueger reviewed them and, in later testimony, said he found them "intriguing" and recognized their location as "southern California." He asked TSD technician Ronald James, who had developed the photographs, to enlarge one of them to "identify the name on the parking space in one of the pictures." As seen in Figure 3, the names of Dr. Fielding and Dr. Rothenberg were inked in on the Xerox copy and the Beverly Hills license plate of Dr. Fielding's Volvo is clearly visible.[64]

• • •

Figure 5: Photograph of Dr. Fielding's car, with CIA annotation (National Archives)

In late 1972, Leo Dunn—the CIA officer who had handled the initial FBI requests regarding Watergate—was detached from the Office of Security to work for Executive Director William Colby, as he prepared answers and collected information in response to Justice Department queries about Watergate. On December 5, Dunn interviewed Greenwood and Gephart and collected their notes and materials. A memo written the same day and titled "TSD Photographs," notes:

> At least one photograph shows a Volvo automobile with California license plates # 377 CUJ, in a reserved space for "Dr. Fielding". There is reference to "Beverly Hills" under the auto tags. An appropriate check by the Office of Security has determined that a 1971 Volvo Sedan, California license number 377 CUJ, is registered to Lewis J. Fielding or Elizabeth B. Fielding, 450 N. Bedford Drive, Beverly Hills, California.[65]

According to Hunt, the developed photographs included close-ups of Fielding's office door and the building directory, as well as coverage of the entrance and exit to and from the parking lot "as well as shots of the inside of Fielding's office, including the top of Fielding's desk."[66]

Ten photographs later published by the Senate Watergate Committee include the image of Dr. Fielding's parking space described above; shots of Liddy posing as a tourist with a pipe in front of a Xerox shop and in the rear parking lot of Fielding's office building; interior shots of Dr. Fielding's door and office; exterior shots of Dr. Fielding's apartment building on Darlington Avenue in Brentwood; and photographs of Vassel's Barber Shop and a fashion boutique called Mediterranee, traced to 9637 and 9645 Santa Monica Boulevard in Beverly Hills, just around the corner from Fielding's office. Three are shown in Figure 4.[67]

While the CIA draft Watergate history argues the pictures "seemed routine—surveillance scenes, parking lot, office buildings, etc.," the involvement of Hunt, the name of Dr. Fielding, the Ellsberg profile, and the use of CIA equipment surely made them anything but routine.

•   •   •

Figure 4: Gordon Liddy in front of a Xerox shop, Beverly Hills (top); Gordon Liddy in the rear car park of Fielding's office building (middle); Hunt photo of Dr. Fielding's apartment building (bottom)
(National Archives)

After reviewing the developed film, Krueger called Wagner and Cushman and described "photographs of a doctor's office and medical buildings in Southern California," which looked to him like "a training exercise." Krueger had asked Ronald James to blow up one of the images to reveal the name of "Dr. Fielding" above a parking space but later insisted "he did not convey to either Wagner or Cushman the fact that the name Fielding had appeared in one of the photographs. Greenwood and Krueger both kept a set of Xerox copies of these photographs for file purposes." Krueger kept them and other Hunt materials in a "Mr. Edward" file in his safe.[68]

Senator Howard Baker, vice chairman of the Senate Watergate Committee, later noted with "a degree of incredulity" that Krueger "denies telling his superiors that he blew up one of the photographs and that it revealed the name of Dr. Fielding. Moreover, both Cushman and his assistant [Wagner] denied ever having been told about the content of the photographs by [Krueger] or anyone else."[69]

According to the CIA Watergate History, probably in the same phone call, Krueger told Wagner he had turned down additional requests from Hunt for backstopped documentation and a backstopped telephone answering service. Wagner approved and instructed Krueger "that CIA was to furnish no additional help to Hunt, that TSD should not accept any more requests from Hunt, and that Hunt should be asked to return the sensitive materials from TSD."[70]

That same Friday morning, Wagner attached a buck slip memorandum to his report of Krueger's call for General Cushman, noting two problems with Hunt's requests for TSD support:

1. *Hunt has brought a stranger into the picture who is now privy to TSD's role in this affair. The White House should have cleared this with us and we must be told who the fellow is. He could embarrass us later.*

*2. Hunt's use of unique clandestine equipment in domestic activity of an
uncertain nature also has potential for trouble. The Agency could suffer
if its clandestine gear were discovered to be used in domestic secret operations. I will instruct TSD to clear all of Hunt's requests with this
office. Also, I think it would be desirable to obtain Ehrlichman's assurance that Hunt's latest caper is OK. Even then, this does not relieve the
Agency from its vulnerability if associated with domestic clandestine
operations against Americans.*[71]

Cushman called Ehrlichman at eleven o'clock that morning and noted that
"J. E. indicated he would call a halt to this."[72]

After reading Wagner's memorandum, Cushman called Krueger and
revealed "that 'Edward' was a former employee, E. Howard Hunt, and that
he had immediately stopped all relationships with Mr. Hunt. Cushman and
Wagner had no further contact with Hunt.[73]

In a later memo, General Cushman recalled that Hunt's escalating
requests were drawing the Agency "into the sensitive and forbidden area of
operations against Americans." He told Ehrlichman that Hunt "was becoming most demanding and troublesome and . . . indiscreet" and they agreed
to cease further support.[74]

While this paper trail and testimony suggests a clean break with Hunt that
Friday afternoon, the CIA Watergate History admits "the record does not
fully support the view that the Agency finally did cut Hunt off cleanly":

*TSD did not tell Hunt he would receive no further support, but that
he would not be given the backstopping he requested without further
authorization. Nor was Hunt turned down flatly in his request for a
secretary; he would not accept a substitute for the one he specifically
requested. . . .*

Greenwood met Hunt at the safehouse on Friday afternoon to deliver the prints and "to list the conditions for further support":

> *Edward, who appeared to be in a hurry, interrupted Greenwood about half way through to state he thought he had the Agency's full support and that he would straighten out the matter.*

Richards concluded that Hunt stopped Greenwood before he listed the new conditions, so Hunt wasn't aware aid was being stopped and would call again for help four days later.[75]

Hunt went back to the White House and added the prints to the operational plan he had been working on with Liddy, using transparent overlays. Hunt later told William Merrill—who oversaw the Fielding break-in investigation for the Watergate Special Prosecution Force—the very detailed memo included "a layout of Dr. Fielding's office and an escape plan in case of detection—a [thirty]-foot piece of nylon rope for sliding to the ground":[76]

> *Hunt told us that the original of that memo and the originals of the pictures he and Liddy had taken of Dr. Fielding's office were placed in the safe in his office at the White House. When Hunt's name surfaced in connection with the Watergate break-in in June 1972, the FBI opened Hunt's safe. The memo and pictures were not there. We were never able to prove who removed and destroyed this evidence.*[77]

The following Monday, Wagner wrote a memo to Cushman, reporting Krueger's mounting concern about Hunt's requests, the development of the film and "the pseudonym of Mr. Hunt's colleague":

> *I told [Mr. Krueger] that Mr. Hunt's latest requests drew us even further into the sensitive area of domestic operations against Americans and that*

all such requests should be referred to General Cushman's office. Mean-
while, these requests should not be met.[78]

Cushman forwarded Wagner's memo to Helms, with the note:

I called John Ehrlichman Friday and explained why we could not meet
these requests. I indicated Hunt was becoming a pain in the neck. John said
he would restrain Hunt.

Helms' response can be seen on the buck slip: "Good."[79]

As the CIA Watergate History notes, "despite the reservations about Hunt
expressed to John Ehrlichman by General Cushman . . . the White House
staff apparently took no action to modify their on-going program or to
restrain Hunt and the other Plumbers in their pressure on the Agency to
produce the Ellsberg profiles."[80]

On Monday, after debriefing Liddy about his reconnaissance trip to California and the operational plan for the break-in, Krogh and Young got
Ehrlichman's approval for the mission, on the understanding that it couldn't
be traced to the White House. This meant Hunt and Liddy, who initially
planned to make the entry, could not go "anywhere near the target premises." Hunt called Bernard Barker and asked him to "put together a three-
man entry team, telling him only that the target was a traitor to the United
States."[81]

Barker recruited two Cubans who worked with him in the real estate
business in Miami: Eugenio Rolando Martinez and Felipe De Diego.
They were Bay of Pigs veterans who had worked for the Agency and could
be trusted. We will explore Martinez' Agency career in the next chapter.
De Diego had been a member of Operation 40, a "CIA-sponsored

counterintelligence group . . . of Cuban exiles" and had been trained as an intelligence officer by the US Army.[82]

Hunt cleared the three Cubans for the operation through Young, who did "a five-way index check" on them. According to Liddy, they also viewed the men's CIA training files and their "final exam" was "breaking into a building in New York City—getting in and getting out." They worked for expenses and compensation for lost earnings in their real estate jobs, out of a sense of patriotic duty for the national security of their adopted country and the Cuban cause. Hunt billed the White House for the trip as a "consultant."[83]

On Tuesday, Hunt called Greenwood at home, again asking for the back-stopped credit cards. Greenwood said he couldn't help and didn't hear from Hunt again. According to Helms' successor as CIA Director, James Schlesinger, the Technical Services Division "had no further association with Mr. Hunt."[84]

After cutting off aid to Hunt, Helms subsequently told Ehrlichman that Hunt was "bad news" and they "had perhaps kept Mr. Hunt on a little longer than [they] should have." Several years before, Hunt had been separated "from more operational tasks because he was overly romantic . . . [but] we had continued him because he had some serious financial problems relating to a sick child and we did not want to have a disgruntled ex-employee."[85]

While the CIA insists that "the decision to cut off support to Hunt was made in the face of escalating demands and was not based upon the development of the photographs," the timing is uncanny—the two happened almost simultaneously the same morning.[86]

CIA awareness of the Fielding photos came just a week after Dr. Malloy expressed his concern to his superiors about Hunt's remarks and was told his concerns were shared with Director Helms (who denied ever knowing Hunt was involved in the Ellsberg profile).[87]

As the Baker report notes, "it was only after these photographs were developed and examined that the CIA technician dealing with Hunt [Greenwood] was ordered to cut off all support for Hunt. This decision was made by the Deputy Director of the CIA (Cushman) and/or the Director of the CIA (Helms)."[88]

Bud Krogh requested and received five thousand dollars in cash to finance the Fielding operation and gave it to Hunt and Liddy on Wednesday, September 1 before they left for the airport. Krogh was nervous. "For God's sake, don't get caught!" he told Liddy, asking him to call "as soon as you're out of there and it's safe." Hunt gave the greenlight to Barker and his team flew from Miami to Los Angeles two days later. The break-in was set for Labor Day weekend.[89]

CHAPTER 5

EUGENIO ROLANDO MARTINEZ

The trip to Los Angeles was the first time Rolando Martinez had left the Miami area since moving to the United States twelve years earlier. He was born in Artemisa, Cuba on July 8, 1922, an only child to parents who started out as poor farmers but later became quite wealthy working in real estate. In his youth, he was very athletic and earned the nickname "Musculito"— "muscle man." He studied medicine for four years until his father became ill and he took over the family business. He married his first wife Mercedes in 1940 and they had a daughter—whom he remains very close to today—but they divorced two years later.

His godfather and "uncle by marriage," Perez Galan, was very active in politics, as a state senator for over thirty years and the owner of over 95 percent of Cuba's pineapple business. After a coup returned Fulgencio Batista to power in 1952, Galan got Rolando interested in politics and he joined the underground anti-Batista movement.

Martinez arrived in the United States on a tourist visa in August 1958 and claims to have bought weapons for the anti-Batista movement through the Mafia. He was arrested for overstaying his visa and deported to Cuba "by private aircraft" on January 2, 1959. Castro had seized power in Havana the previous day after Batista left the country. Martinez told Timothy Naftali he was in Mexico City at this time, with a group led by Carlos Prio Socarrás, the former Cuban president ousted by Batista and one of Castro's main rivals for power. They were "planning to invade Cuba through Pinar del Río Province" but Castro got there before them.[1]

In November 1959, Martinez married Jean Walton, an American citizen, and returned to the United States on a residential visa on Christmas Day, 1959, forsaking the Hollywood Yacht Club he owned on the beach in Havana. His new wife had a son by a previous marriage, who became extremely close to his stepfather, changed his name to Martinez, and became a US Marine.[2]

Like many in the anti-Batista movement, Martinez soon felt betrayed by Castro's turn towards Communism. Shortly after arriving in Miami, he joined the newly-formed Movement to Recover the Revolution (MRR), led by Manuel Artime and closely aligned with Carlos Prio, and started working for a small shipping salvage company run by the CIA.[3]

In January 1961, he was formally recruited as a contract agent by the Agency. As a boat captain, he engaged in paramilitary maritime activities against Castro, providing "emergency exfiltration from Cuba of persons of interest to the Agency." According to a post-Watergate CIA summary of his career:

> *Mr. Martinez was a loyal and reliable employee [who] conducted many hazardous infiltration and exfiltration missions often under adverse conditions, willingly endangering his life for the cause of the missions in which he strongly believed.*[4]

Three months after he joined the Agency, he participated in the failed Bay of Pigs invasion, led by Artime, and he reportedly conducted over 350 missions to Cuba in the CIA's "clandestine navy" during the secret war against Castro, until Agency support for the project was terminated in 1969. During this time, he worked for three CIA front companies in Miami: Ace Marine Survey, Gulfland Corporation, and Caribbean Enterprises.[5]

After the Bay of Pigs, these weekly missions smuggled weapons or infiltrated agents into Cuba—often sixty agents at a time. A CIA mother ship would tow him toward the Cuban coast and he would drop commando teams close to shore. The weapons drops often included rifles equipped with silencers and telescopic sights—"rifles only used by snipers," said Martinez. "Everyone in the underground was plotting to kill Castro, and the CIA was helping the underground . . . so you could say I was involved in the plots, too."[6]

He was also involved in sabotage raids and "exfiltration" missions, picking up agents in Cuba and giving the Coast Guard a code word if stopped on the way back to the United States. "These were the most nerve-wracking assignments," he later recalled, with the risk that "the agents had been captured and forced to reveal the time and place of their rendezvous . . . [setting] a trap . . . for the boat crew." His parents were not allowed to leave Cuba and even though exfiltration was his specialty, he never saw them again: "My bosses in the Company—the CIA—said I might get caught and tortured, and if I talked I might jeopardize other operations. So, my mother and father died in Cuba. That is how orders go. I follow the orders."[7]

The Cuban agents only knew their case officers by their first names (or "war names") and information was compartmentalized and shared on a "need to know" basis, demanding extraordinary trust in the "power and good intentions of the CIA":

Your CO [commanding officer] was for you like the priest. You had to rely on him, because he was the one who could solve your problems. You learned to tell him everything, your complete life. The important thing was that you knew they would take care of you, and you knew they would take care of your family if you were captured or killed on a mission. They supported all the families of the Brigade members, and they did the same for the families of the men who were lost on our operations. They are still supporting them.

Once a Castro gunboat came after my boat on a mission off the north coast of Cuba, and I radioed for help. Before we could even decode the return message from the base, I looked up, and there were two Phantom jets and a Neptune flying over us. . . . I still believe today that the Company might be able to do something for me about the Watergate someday.[8]

In August 1969, Jake Esterline, the CIA veteran who oversaw the ill-fated Bay of Pigs invasion, was assigned to Miami as chief of station "to quietly complete the phase-out of the unsuccessful post-Bay of Pigs secret war against Fidel Castro . . . without creating a scandal that might embarrass Washington." According to his obituary, he spent the next four years working on this very delicate operation, "disposing of ships and boats, terminating leases on safe houses, marinas, boat yards . . . [and] laying off the several hundred Cubans still directly on the payroll."[9]

Esterline volunteered for the assignment because he "felt a sense of obligation to the Cubans after the failure of the Bay of Pigs":[10]

I went down there to gently terminate and direct these people into new avenues of life . . . I actually got a couple of these very bright fellows into law school . . . In the case of Rolando Martinez, he'd been a Cuban businessman and was a mature man at this point. We put him on a retirement pension which wasn't very much money obviously . . . [and] I got him into [real estate] brokers school to direct him into the lifestyle he had in Cuba before he got mixed up in all these crazy kinds of things against Castro.[11]

• • •

By the time the maritime project was terminated in 1969, Martinez was earning $8,100 a year as a contract agent and had built up, according to the Rockefeller Commission report, "what the CIA considered a distinguished record . . . in recognition of his services . . . [the Agency] continued his contract payments until early 1970" while he worked as a boat captain for Bayfront Engineering and Development Corporation.[12]

In June 1970, Martinez' case officer met all the men in his unit and handed them "envelopes with retirement announcements inside":

> *But mine was a blank paper. Afterward he explained to me that I would stop making my boat missions to Cuba but I would continue my work with the Company. He said I should become an American citizen and soon I would be given a new assignment.*[13]

According to the Rockefeller report, "the Agency had planned to terminate him but agreed to pay him $100 per month for a year to help him make the transition to civilian life":

> *In return, he was required to report monthly to a CIA case officer in Miami on developments in the Cuban community. In July 1971, it was agreed that his retainer would be continued for one more year because of Martinez' ability to report illegal attempts by Cuban exiles to infiltrate Cuba, but it was intended that it should end in July 1972.*

Another CIA document says Martinez was asked to report on Cubans arriving in Miami who could provide useful information.[14]

After his conversion from contract to retainer status, Martinez became a naturalized citizen in July 1970 and was assigned a new case officer, who handled him until April 1972. Rolando was approaching fifty but his new CO was a young man in his early thirties. Martinez only knew him by a pseudonym but they became very close. The case officer's name has never been disclosed publicly until now.[15]

Ramon Esteban Gonzalez III graduated from the University of Toledo in 1961. His father was a general sales manager for the Owens Illinois Glass Company, covering Latin America, and according to Martinez, Gonzalez' father also worked for the Agency, so Owens Illinois may have provided cover to CIA agents in Latin America during this period. William Niehous, head of the glass company's Venezuelan operations, was famously kidnapped and held in the jungle by leftist guerrillas for three years in the late seventies.[16]

While studying for his real estate license, Martinez began an apprenticeship at Keyes Co. in November. On February 18, 1971, the CIA station in Miami sent a cable to Headquarters, in which Martinez reported on an "exile leader's activities in Miami" (probably Manuel Artime) and on April 6, Martinez advised his case officer of "rumors that people were coming down from Washington recruiting Cubans again."[17]

On April 17, the tenth anniversary of the Bay of Pigs invasion, the rumors materialized when the legendary "Eduardo" appeared at an event to commemorate the fallen Brigade members in Miami. As Martinez later recalled:

> *Eduardo was a name that all of us who had participated in the Bay of Pigs knew well. He had been the maximum representative of the Kennedy administration to our people in Miami. He occupied a special place in our hearts because of a letter he had written to his chief Cuban aide and my lifelong friend, Bernard Barker. He had identified himself in his letter with the pain of the Cubans, and he blamed the Kennedy administration for not supporting us on the beaches of the Bay of Pigs. So, when Barker told me that Eduardo was coming to town and that he wanted to meet me, that was like a hope for me.*[18]

When Hunt couldn't reach Barker by phone that morning, he pinned a note to his door: "If you are the Bernie Barker who worked for me in 1960–61, call me at the Singapore [Hotel]."[19]

Martinez had known Bernard Barker since university in Havana. The day after Pearl Harbor in 1941, as the United States joined the war, Barker was the first person in Cuba to enlist, serving as a bombardier in the Air Force. He was shot down over Germany and was a prisoner of war for sixteen months before returning to Cuba and working for the FBI within the Cuban police force. He migrated to the United States in 1958 and was soon recruited by the CIA as a member of the Cuban underground. Barker worked with Hunt on political action through the Cuban government in exile while Martinez was involved in paramilitary operations.[20]

Ten years after the calamitous invasion, "Eduardo" was relaxing in front of the Bay of Pigs monument, smoking his pipe, when Barker introduced him to Martinez as Howard Hunt and they proceeded to a Cuban restaurant for lunch with Hunt's wife, Dorothy. Hunt struck Martinez as "more like a politician than a man who was fighting for freedom":

Eduardo told us that he had retired from the CIA . . . and was working for Mullen and Company. I knew just what he was saying. I was also officially retired from the Company . . . Not even Barker knew that I was still working with the Company. But I was quite certain that day that Eduardo knew.

Hunt told them how bad he felt about the Bay of Pigs and as they talked about the liberation of Cuba, Hunt assured them "the whole thing is not over." He wanted to meet the Bay of Pigs leaders—Artime and Pepe San Roman—and Martinez felt his visit was "a good sign. We did not think he had come to Miami for nothing."[21]

Martinez usually met up with his CO, Ramon Gonzalez, "at least twice a week" as well as speaking a couple of times on the phone. "Any time anyone from the CIA was in town, my CO always asked me what he was doing," so Martinez informed Gonzalez "right away that Eduardo was back in town . . . but he didn't ask me anything about Eduardo, which was strange." Around this time, CIA officers Adrian Swain and Tom Tripodi were seconded to the BNDD to set up a Special Operations unit, reporting on drug traffickers. They recruited "some of the guys who would later be bagged in the Watergate affair" (probably including Martinez) and Hunt later inherited these operations at the White House as part of Nixon's "war on drugs."[22]

After obtaining his real estate license, Bernard Barker had set up Barker Associates in early 1971, working from a one-room office next door to Carlos Prio's Authentic Party. Soon, Martinez was working for him and in mid-July, "Eduardo" wrote Barker about his new appointment and sent him several memos on White House stationery. Barker explained to Martinez that Hunt was forming an interagency group "to deal with certain national security problems over which the CIA had no jurisdiction and in which the FBI could not become involved due to certain court cases." Martinez was impressed and told his CO, "Hey, Eduardo is still in contact with us, and now he is a counselor of the President":

A few days later, my CO told me that the Company had no information on Eduardo except that he was not working in the White House. Well, imagine! I knew Eduardo was in the White House. What it meant to me was that Eduardo was above them and either they weren't supposed to know what he was doing or they didn't want me to talk about him anymore. Knowing how these people act, I knew I had to be careful. So, I said, well, let me keep my mouth shut. Not long after this, Eduardo told Barker there was . . . a national security job dealing with a traitor of this country who had given papers to the Russian Embassy.[23]

Martinez immediately agreed to the mission, seeing it as "a great honor" and a reward for his "sacrifice for the previous ten years . . . [carrying] out hundreds of [dangerous] missions for the U.S. government." He "was led to believe that this was the beginning of a new underground organization which would eventually perform a Cuban invasion, and he was totally assured that the missions had the sanction of the U.S. Government." Similarly, Barker was told "that if Nixon were re-elected, there would be another assault upon Cuba with better support than the Bay of Pigs Invasion, and this assault would probably succeed in liberating Cuba."

When Cubans working for the CIA were caught by Castro and sent to jail, their families received support, so Martinez assumed the same rules applied to Hunt's operations. When he later got caught at the Watergate building, he "was expecting someone [a lawyer] to show because that is the procedure."[24]

The trip to Los Angeles for the Fielding operation was Martinez' first outside the Miami area and his CO gave him a few days off and the impression that "he did not want to know what I was doing." The Cubans were briefed in "Eduardo"'s room at the Beverly Hills Hotel, where Hunt showed them the voice modification devices, wigs, glasses, and false identification documents the Agency had supplied. In later affidavits, Barker and Martinez swore Hunt told them that the equipment, disguises, and false documents used in the Fielding and Watergate burglaries were supplied by the CIA and Martinez assumed "the Company [knew] of my presence there, because this was not a project in which you wrote an after-action report."[25]

Martinez thought "Eduardo"'s briefing was amateurish. Normally, he would train for an operation, practicing it many times in a similar place, in disguise, using the codes you were going to use. This time, there was no training, "no written plan . . . [and no] mention of what to do if something went wrong."

Liddy was introduced as an "ex-FBI man" Hunt was working with at the White House. It was illegal for the CIA to conduct domestic operations and FBI Director J. Edgar Hoover no longer allowed "black bag" jobs, so Hunt told them he was part of a new group dealing with "national security" problems those agencies couldn't handle. When Martinez complained to Barker that the walkie-talkies were "no good," Liddy replied: "You are here not to think, just to do."[26]

Barker was only told Ellsberg's name half an hour before the break-in. They were to look for any files with Ellsberg's name on them—the "psychiatric records of a traitor." Barker would "spot" the files and Martinez would photograph them. Barker and Felipe De Diego bought delivery man uniforms in Sears and that evening—September 3, 1971—they delivered a footlocker containing camera equipment to Fielding's office, disguised in wigs and glasses.[27]

Barker and De Diego unlatched the back door and then waited in the car with Martinez for the cleaning lady to leave. Barker whispered the name of "Ellsberg" to Martinez, in case he forgot it, and once inside, Martinez had to remind him of the name. When they tried the back door, it was locked, so Liddy (who they knew as "George Leonard") told them to force a window open. The glasscutter supplied by Hunt didn't work, so Martinez smashed it with a small crowbar to gain entry: "Really, it was a joke. They had given us a rope to bail out from the second floor if anyone surprised us; it was so small, it couldn't have supported any of us."

Once inside Dr. Fielding's office, Martinez covered the windows with black cloth and took out the two cameras—a Minolta and a Polaroid. He took continuity Polaroids of the room and the main file drawer—so he could put everything back the way he found it. They forced open a filing cabinet but the only mention of Ellsberg was in Dr. Fielding's telephone book. The other files contained bills, not medical records:

> *The office did not look like a doctor's or a psychiatrist's office. It looks like an import-export company . . . loaded with stacks of bills or letters, but nothing like a clinical history of anyone.*[28]

To explain the damaged filing cabinets, Martinez scattered pills from Dr. Fielding's briefcase all over the floor to make it look like a break-in by drug addicts.

According to Hunt, "Liddy was nearby in a car, providing mobile surveillance against police . . . [or] untoward incidents. We were in touch with the team inside by walkie-talkie . . . I did not know at that time that Mr. Martinez was then an employee or informant of the Central Intelligence Agency on a salaried basis."[29]

When Martinez returned to the car, "Eduardo" was waiting. He had been watching Dr. Fielding's house, but Fielding had gone out and he'd lost him:

> *A police car appeared as we drove away and it trailed behind us for three or four blocks. I thought to myself that the police car was protecting us. That is the feeling you have when you are doing operations for the government. You think that every step has been taken to protect you.*[30]

Back at the hotel, the Cubans felt "very bad" that they had "failed" their first mission but Martinez was shocked to find Hunt and Liddy opened a bottle of champagne and congratulated them. They hadn't found anything "but *they* don't know that," said Hunt. Martinez gave the Polaroids he had taken to Hunt and he thanked the Cubans and they left for the airport:

> *The whole thing was strange . . . I told Diego and Barker that this had to have been a training mission for a very important mission to come or else it was a cover operation. I thought to myself that maybe these people already had the papers of Ellsberg. Maybe Dr. Fielding had given them out and for ethical reasons he needed to be covered. It seemed that these people already had what we were looking for because no one invites you to have champagne and is happy when you fail.*[31]

Martinez felt "very disappointed" after the Ellsberg operation because it was "the first operation we were supposed to start to build this thing for Cuba."[32]

When Liddy called Krogh at 4:00 a.m., he didn't sound disappointed, just relieved they weren't caught. The next day, Hunt and Liddy cased Fielding's apartment building, checking the front door lock and taking photographs, thinking Ellsberg's files were in his basement but according to Liddy, Ehrlichman, Krogh, and Young were "too scared to do it."[33]

At nine o'clock on Saturday evening, the Beverly Hills Police Department called Dr. Fielding to inform him of a break-in at his office. He arrived with his wife to find his papers and records "strewn about" and a police officer searching for fingerprints:

> *I observed that the locks on my office doors had been pried open and that the wood part of the door near the lock had been hacked away. I also observed that the locks on my wood cabinet and on my steel filing cabinet behind it had also been pried open and bent completely out of shape. These cabinets contained information and records concerning my patients including Dr. Ellsberg. The files in my cabinet were in considerable disarray. My personal*

papers, including those pertaining to Dr. Ellsberg, appeared to have been
thoroughly rummaged through . . . I couldn't tell what was missing. . . .

Dr. Fielding later testified he found the Ellsberg papers outside their envelope and knew they had been "fingered." He kept them in the fourth drawer
of the filing cabinet but the Cubans insisted they found nothing.[34]

When he returned to Miami, Martinez "again told [his] CO about Eduardo:
I was certain then that the Company knew about his activities. But once
again my CO did not pursue the subject."[35]

Martinez checked the Los Angeles paper for any mention of the break-in
but found nothing. Fielding thought the burglary was drug-related and
didn't notify Ellsberg. In late October, Beverly Hills police arrested Elmer
Davis, a "convicted burglar and drug addict" and offered him a deal if he
confessed to the Fielding break-in as well as two other burglaries he had
committed. According to the Rockefeller Commission report, "In return for
the dismissal of other charges, he pleaded guilty to the Fielding burglary,
although there is no evidence he had had any part in it." In fact, on November 12, 1971, Davis had written to the L.A. County district attorney, proclaiming his innocence and rejecting the deal offered for his false confession.
He was never prosecuted. Eighteen months later, at the end of the Ellsberg
trial, police records revealed that Davis had spent nine days in jail from
August 28 to September 5, 1971 after an arrest for petty theft and couldn't
have been involved. The police never told Dr. Fielding about Davis' arrest
and false confession and the police file on the case was closed.[36]

Martinez knew Fielding had previously refused to give the FBI Ellsberg's
file on ethical grounds, so when he read later about the psychological profile,
he concluded the mission was either a "training operation" or "Dr. Fielding
had already given [the FBI the file] . . . and it was a cover-up operation
because he never made a big deal about the breaking into his office."

Being told to make it look like there had been a break-in also indicated to Martinez that it was a "cover operation." As with Watergate, the whole operation made Martinez "uneasy" and he told Hunt he wasn't happy with the lack of an operational plan, which was usually so meticulous. Later, he was confused when he read Dr. Fielding's testimony about finding Ellsberg's papers outside their envelope: "No one knows that but Dr. Fielding and us. The documents were not there."[37]

Despite reports to the contrary, the third burglar, Felipe De Diego, testified Ellsberg's records were not found. Publicly, Fielding refused to speak to the FBI, citing patient privacy, but privately, had he already given the file to the Bureau or had they broken into his office with their own "black bag" job?[38]

George Crile and Taylor Branch interviewed Barker and Martinez at length for an article and proposed book in the mid-seventies. According to Ellsberg, the Cubans told Branch they hoped to neutralize Ellsberg by blackmailing him with information he didn't want made public. The hope was that Ellsberg would either "commit suicide . . . not go on the stand . . . [or] leave the country [and] go to Cuba . . . putting [him] out of action."[39]

When the CIA reluctantly provided Senator Howard Baker's staff with the contact reports between Martinez and his case officer, Ramon Gonzalez, during this period, the earliest report written by Gonzalez and seen by Baker's staff was dated November 19, 1971. In the report, Gonzalez admits that "Martinez mentioned Howard Hunt's name several months ago" but that when he ran a trace on Hunt and possible pseudonyms at the station, there were no "hits." He apologizes for "now recognizing Hunt's White House affiliation and the fact that Hunt is a writer."[40]

The report suggests Martinez told Gonzalez about Hunt around the time of the Ellsberg break-in in September and Martinez confirmed this in a later affidavit. As the Rockefeller report notes, Martinez took Gonzalez' earlier denial "to mean that Hunt was on a secret CIA mission of which the Miami station was not to know. On the strength of his past experience maintaining the secrecy of CIA operations, he therefore disclosed none of the Hunt-related activities to his case officer."[41]

In the contact report, Gonzalez justified this lack of information by stating that Martinez "didn't pry into Hunt's affairs" because "he always tried to live with his cover of no longer working for the outfit."[42]

The inexplicable lack of station traces failed to raise a red flag and his case officer's ignorance of Hunt gave Martinez a signal that his CO had "no need to know" about the White House-sanctioned activities. In a later affidavit, Jake Esterline stated he met Martinez on November 19 and Martinez told him, "Howard Hunt had been in the Miami area and attended the Tenth Anniversary of the Bay of Pigs celebration," prompting Esterline to berate Gonzalez for not reporting the contact with Hunt sooner. The Rockefeller Commission's explanation of this episode is unconvincing:

The Miami Chief of Station [Jake Esterline] had been disturbed when he later learned that the case officer had not promptly reported the reference to Hunt's name, a name that meant nothing to the case officer. The Chief felt that he should be advised of the presence of any former CIA officers in his territory. His lingering and undefined concern over Hunt was evidently in his mind in March 1972, when he met Martinez in connection with another intelligence requirement.[43]

Why did Esterline's concern linger undefined for four months and why did he wait until March 1972 to address it?

On the Tuesday following the Labor Day weekend break-in, Hunt walked into Colson's office with an envelope in his hand. "I have half an hour before I have to give a briefing on what we were up to this weekend," he said, "and I would like to show you something." As Hunt started to take photographs out of the envelope, Colson claimed he replied, "I don't have time right now, Howard, and it isn't any of my business." According to Hunt, his words were, "I don't want to hear anything about it." Colson claimed he first heard about the "attempt to get Dr. Ellsberg's psychiatric records" from Ehrlichman, "later that week or the following week."[44]

Snubbed by Colson, Hunt showed the photos to Colson's secretary Joan Hall and told her they had been taken in Ellsberg's psychiatrist's office the previous weekend. According to author Tom Wells, "Hunt also showed David Young's secretary a pair of rubber gloves and pictures of Liddy standing in front of Fielding's building." When Hunt and Liddy met Krogh and showed him their suitcase of burglary tools and pictures of "a very damaged office," he was very distressed and knew he'd made a mistake. Liddy offered to get rid of the equipment but Krogh said, "No, hang on to that. You may need it." Krogh went over to tell Ehrlichman, who was equally disturbed by the reports of the damaged office and evidence left at the crime scene.[45]

The next day, Ehrlichman met Nixon in the Oval Office. He said Krogh was still working on "the narcotics thing but he's also spending most of his time on Ellsberg, declassifications, and the dirty tricks business on getting stuff out . . . We had one little operation that aborted out in Los Angeles . . . which, I think, it's better that you don't know about. But we've got some dirty tricks underway that may pay off."[46]

On October 14, 1971, in preparation for a lunch with Hunt the following day, DDP Tom Karamessines asked Sidney Gottlieb, Chief of TSD, to bring him up to date on Hunt's contacts with TSD personnel, "in case Hunt requested anything."

According to Rockefeller Commission testimony, he "was briefly shown the Xerox copies of the Hunt photographs in the files. He and [Gottlieb] glanced at the pictures which . . . meant nothing to them." To Hunt, the

Fielding photos were clear evidence of a "casing operation to anyone experienced in intelligence operations" and Gottlieb got the same impression.[47]

At lunch with Karamessines, Hunt wanted to discuss "a cover problem with the Mullen Company" and his contacts with TSD were not mentioned. Hougan believes Karamessines was effectively Hunt's case officer at this point.[48]

On the same day, Dr. Tietjen and Dr. Malloy briefed Deputy Director for Support John Coffey on FBI reports Malloy had received from Hunt at the White House three days earlier. The reports were judged not particularly helpful to an in-depth study of Ellsberg but the White House insisted on a second psychological profile: "It was agreed . . . that [Malloy] should try to see Young and explain the continuing problems and deficiencies in trying to satisfy the requirement."[49]

On October 27, Malloy met with Hunt, Liddy, and Young at the Executive Office Building and shared his observations on the documents provided by Hunt and discussed with Coffey two months earlier. Malloy was asked to write these up in a final report "within a week" and interest was expressed "in Ellsberg's sexual proclivities and in obtaining information which could be used to defame or manipulate him." Malloy briefed Coffey the next day, who in turn, briefed Helms over lunch on the "continuing pressure" from Young.[50]

On October 29 and November 3, Liddy sent Dr. Malloy further information on Ellsberg as Malloy drafted the second profile. When Malloy discussed the profile with Coffey and Dr. Tietjen on November 8, Tietjen felt Helms should review it, noting the concern of his staff that it entered "into matters beyond the agency's purview" and might be illegal. Dr. Tietjen later insisted he and his colleagues never received "any psychiatric material" on Ellsberg from Dr. Fielding's office.[51]

On November 9, Coffey sent the old and new Ellsberg profiles to Helms, relating the doctors' concerns. Helms approved the second profile and wrote to Young, reminding him that "our involvement in this matter should not be revealed in any context, formal or informal. I am sure that you appreciate our concern."⁵²

Three days later, Dr. Malloy delivered his final report to the Executive Office. "These men were interested in obtaining information which could be used to defame or manipulate Ellsberg," he later said. Both he and Dr. Tietjen got the impression the reports were not of much use or interest to Hunt, Liddy, or Young and they received no further requests.⁵³

In subsequent testimony, Dr. Malloy said he kept a close record of events because, like his colleagues, he was "uneasy and apprehensive" about what was going on. Karamessines denied all knowledge of the Ellsberg profiles and Colby and Schlesinger claimed they didn't hear about them until early May 1973.⁵⁴

The question remains—were Helms and Osborn aware of Hunt's involvement in the construction of the Ellsberg profiles? Malloy told Tietjen after the meeting on August 12. Coffey knew on August 20 and worked closely with Osborn, who saw the first profile. While Osborn's son was painting Hunt's house, and Hunt was feeding Dr. Malloy information for the Ellsberg profile that David Young had requested and Osborn had approved, Osborn was also the CIA liaison to the Plumbers. Given the unease expressed by the medical team, Osborn had to have known about Hunt's involvement. He spoke to Coffey about the profile in mid-October and Coffey discussed Malloy's meeting with Young, Hunt, and Liddy a few days after it happened. How is it possible that Osborn and Helms did not know Hunt was present at that meeting and feeding Malloy the information for the profiles?

In the foreword to the section of the CIA Watergate History concerning the Ellsberg profiles, Richards writes:

Central to an understanding of the Agency's continuing support to Hunt and the White House on the Ellsberg profiles after the stand-down ordered by General Cushman is the fact that in this case the Agency's right hand did not know what its left hand was doing and vice versa. The doctors in the Office of Medical Services who were involved in preparing the profiles and meeting with Howard Hunt were never aware of Hunt's contacts with Cushman and TSD; nor were Cushman and TSD aware of the Doctors' contacts. Indeed, with the possible exception of the then Deputy Director for Support, John Coffey, and the Doctors, no one, not even Director Helms, was aware of Hunt's participation in the profiles matter.[55]

Howard Osborn is the key person missing from this analysis. He had contact with Young, Hunt, Malloy, Coffey, and Helms. Coffey oversaw both TSD and the Office of Medical Services and knew enough to have reported Hunt's involvement but his executive session testimony remains classified.

In an epilogue to the same section, Richards notes the "adverse publicity" generated when the Agency's involvement in the Fielding break-in surfaced in April 1973, showing "the anxiety and concern . . . [expressed] by the Doctors and other Agency officials was well-founded." The final decision lay with Helms and Richards wonders "whether his decision would have been different had he known that E. Howard Hunt was involved." I would argue Helms did know Hunt was involved and continued regardless.

Richards concludes the section by quoting Helms' August 1973 testimony to the Senate Watergate Committee about the profiles, in which he expressed "genuine regrets about being pressured into that. On Monday morning, there are a lot of football games that if played again might have been played differently, and, you know, I'm not proud of that one."[56]

In early March 1972, Hunt paid another visit to Miami and Martinez again mentioned it to Gonzalez, insisting "that Hunt was involved in some

operations and that he was in the White House, even if they said he wasn't."
On March 10, during a meeting with Miami station chief Jake Esterline,
Martinez raised "a sensitive matter re Hunt/Barker that needs to be put in
writing." During the conversation, according to the Rockefeller Commission
report, "Martinez again mentioned that Hunt had been in and out of Miami
on a foreign business deal":

> *Separately, he asked the Chief of Station whether he was certain that he
> was aware of all CIA activity in the Miami area. These repeated references
> to Hunt, in whom the station chief from past experience had limited con-
> fidence, and Martinez' unusual question led the station chief to contact his
> superior at CIA Headquarters.*[57]

According to Howard Liebengood, assistant minority counsel to the Senate
Watergate Committee, the meeting concerned "a Costa Rican requirement"
and Frank Sturgis was Martinez' source "re: Costa Rican activities." This
seems to relate to a group of twenty-seven Cubans arriving in Costa Rica in
March to help defend the country against a rumored Guatemalan invasion.
President Figueres had allegedly made a trip to Miami in February to obtain
arms "to repel the invaders." The Cuban group claimed they were shrimp
fishermen whose boat had broken down. They allegedly planned to make
Costa Rica a base for raids on Cuba but quickly dispersed. Martinez was due
to travel to Santo Domingo with Gonzalez that spring but according to
Liebengood, the "Santo Domingo trip displeased Hunt and was cancelled by
Speedy [Gonzalez]." Perhaps Hunt's interference with the trip explains how
it came up in conversation.[58]

Martinez told Esterline that Hunt was "discussing business dealings in
Nicaragua with Barker" but did not mention the Fielding break-in, say he
was working for Hunt or "that either he or Hunt were engaged in any domestic clandestine operations."[59]

• • •

After working with Howard Hunt on the Bay of Pigs operation, Esterline later explained why he had "limited confidence" in him:

> When [Hunt] was working for me, I was never quite sure what he was up to . . . What really riled me at that time was here was a guy no longer with us that must have known that the people he was messing with—namely Rolando Martinez, who was a nice, dedicated to his cause Cuban, who was obviously confused by someone saying, "I work for the White House," coming in there. It was totally unethical for Mr. Hunt to come in and touch somebody working for another agency, regardless of where he worked. He had no business touching any of our people. I didn't deal directly with Rolando Martinez. I had a case officer dealing with him. But Hunt obviously convinced them that this was so important that they shouldn't tell the case officer or me that they were doing these White House break-ins. Really cheap shot.[60]

On March 17, after a further meeting with Martinez, Esterline cabled his superior, Lawrence Sternfield, chief of Cuban Operations in the Western Hemisphere Division. He reported that "Hunt had been in the Miami area twice recently contacting old friends," usually through Artime or Barker:

> Hunt seemed to be trying to promote business deals . . . and had indicated to Martinez and Barker that he was a White House counsellor. Hunt tried to create the impression that this could be of importance to his Cuban friends.

Esterline asked Sternfield "if it could be quietly ascertained whether Hunt did, in fact, have such capacity with the White House."[61]

Sternfield discussed the cable with Associate Deputy Director for Plans Cord Meyer, who had previously been told by Tom Karamessines that "Hunt was a White House consultant supposedly engaged in domestic activities having nothing to do with foreign intelligence and that it was neither necessary nor proper for CIA to check into Hunt's activities since domestic activities were involved." Ten days later, Sternfield sent "a strongly worded letter" to Esterline, "on advice of Cord Meyer," informing him that Hunt "undoubtedly is on domestic White House business, no interest to us, in essence, cool it." Esterline later testified that Cord Meyer dictated the letter.[62]

Meyer and Sternfield later justified the letter as "premised not only on concern that the Agency should not become involved in domestic political activity but also on [Meyer's] estimate of Hunt's erratic judgment" and as the Rockefeller report notes, they did not want to "cross paths with the White House." A later CIA summary of the incident describes Esterline's reaction:

> *Stunned by the tone of the reply, and concerned about not being privy to activities going on in his area, Mr. Esterline had Martinez write an account of his knowledge of Hunt's recent activities in the Miami area, in Spanish, in long hand, which Mr. Esterline filed away in his safe at Station WH/ Miami.*[63]

"It set off a very bad relationship between Cord Meyer and me," Esterline later recalled. "In retrospect, when I wrote that letter to Meyer, it hit him like a bombshell. I'm sure they had no idea what Hunt was mixed-up in."[64]

Esterline later testified that "he confronted Meyer with this matter after the Watergate break-in" during "an unfriendly discussion in which Meyer first could not recall dictating the return message but later remembered it . . . While Meyer did not mention the Fielding break-in or the fact that Hunt was contacting former agents around the country, he did tell Esterline that the Agency became uneasy about what Hunt seemed to be doing in March or May of 1972."[65]

The Rockefeller Commission claimed none of "the parties to these communications apparently knew of the prior support to Hunt or of the Ellsberg profile" but given what we have learned in these chapters, how is that possible?

After Sternfield's rebuke, Esterline invited Martinez to breakfast and asked him to write a report in Spanish on Hunt's activities and to "give it to [his] CO in a sealed envelope." Esterline "had no reason to suspect Hunt of unlawful activities" or suspect Martinez "was engaged in domestic espionage activities" but he wanted to know "what a former Agency employee was doing in his territory."[66]

Martinez was "very close" to his CO, whose father had been with the Agency. Gonzalez told Martinez his father once told him, "he should never put anything in writing that might do him any harm in the future." Gonzalez subsequently confirmed that Martinez had been reluctant to write the report and that he had given him this advice. "So," Martinez later admitted, "I just wrote a cover story for the whole thing . . . What I really thought was that Hunt was checking to see if I could be trusted."[67]

Martinez gave his handwritten report, dated April 5, 1972, to Gonzalez, who passed it to Esterline. A CIA index card on the English translation of the report lists the title as "Activities of Howard Hunt and Dr. Manuel Artime in Miami and Nicaragua" and the names referenced as: Martinez, Barker, Mr. and Mrs. Hunt, Tony Varona, Macco [possibly Antonio Maceo], Artime, Carlos Prio and Tino Fuentes [Prio's brother-in-law].[68]

In 2008, Martinez told Nixon Library director Timothy Naftali that the report was a "cover story" about Hunt's daughter flirting with Somoza's son and their parents discussing building a canal through Nicaragua to rival the one in Panama. St. John Hunt confirmed to me that Lisa Hunt and Somoza's son were engaged at the time. The "cover story" did not mention Ellsberg and reported that Hunt was still working for the Mullen Company, even though Martinez knew he was working for the White House.[69]

According to a CIA memo, "Martinez made no mention of what has become known as the Watergate and Ellsberg break ins, nor was the Agency aware of his participation in any secret arrangement or relationship that might have involved any domestic clandestine operations." While the report is still classified, Baker's staff saw the English translation and confirmed it "does not contain any reference to [the] Plumbers or Watergate" but they became increasingly suspicious of Agency involvement in these operations. It should have been clear to the CIA that Hunt was down in Miami again recruiting Cubans while using documents and equipment they had given him to mount domestic clandestine operations on behalf of the White House. Martinez told Hunt "that his case officer had been made aware that I was in the Miami area and had asked him for a report on my activities. I was quite sure that Martinez would not tell the agency what our plans were." The Agency failed to question Martinez more thoroughly about his "cover your ass" report, and his "national security" work for Hunt was allowed to continue.[70]

CHAPTER 6

JAMES WALTER MCCORD

On August 31, 1970, James McCord retired from the CIA after nineteen years of service in the Office of Security. Born in 1924, his career began as an FBI Radio Operator in 1942, monitoring German and Soviet intelligence agencies. After wartime service in the Army Air Corps and a college degree in business administration, he graduated as an FBI special agent in 1948 and three years later, joined the CIA.[1]

From 1955 to 1962, he served with Paul Gaynor's Security Research Staff [SRS]—the counterintelligence arm of the Office of Security—becoming Gaynor's deputy in May 1957. He reconstructed Soviet intelligence operations in Europe in the thirties and forties, developed and debriefed Soviet defectors, and was the case officer in several "double agent cases," in which the Russians tried to recruit CIA personnel. From 1960 to 1962, he was also a case officer for three Cuban agents tasked with entering Cuban prisons where "three CIA staffers were being held" and obtaining "data and photographs concerning their layout and operation." In January 1961, at the request of David Atlee Phillips, an employee in the Agency's Cuban directorate (WH/4) began spying on his former high school classmate, Court Foster Wood. Wood had just returned from a three-week trip to Cuba with the Fair Play for Cuba Committee and "lauded Castro very highly." On February 1, Phillips coordinated a counterintelligence operation against Wood with

McCord at SRS, as Wood started a chapter of the FPCC (as Lee Harvey Oswald would do later in New Orleans).[2]

From 1962 to 1964, McCord served in Frankfurt as chief of the Regional Security Support Staff, responsible for personnel and physical security, and audio countermeasures programs to protect European stations and bases from electronic surveillance. After a year studying Political Science at the Air War College, McCord re-joined the Office of Security as chief of the Technical Division in July 1965, developing "esoteric equipment" to strengthen the Agency's Audio Counter-Measures Program. Supervising a staff of forty, he developed a new device which used X-ray equipment to rapidly scan "large interior wall surfaces, room furnishings, and objects . . . for hostile technical penetrations," which was considered "a major breakthrough in the detection of clandestine microphones and other devices targeted against the Agency."[3]

In October 1968, McCord became chief of the Physical Security Division, supervising seventy staff members and protecting Agency installations (domestic and overseas) "against unauthorized physical penetration and Agency information and material against loss, compromise or disclosure." He also expanded the Agency's Security Command Center, which protected "Agency assets in time of demonstrations, riots and civil disturbance" and it was here he crossed paths with Ralph True and Anderson Security.[4]

The Office of Security was responsible for safeguarding CIA personnel, facilities, and information. When the Agency moved into its Langley headquarters in 1962, a counterintelligence project MHBOUND was established "to prevent hostile penetration and sabotage." It operated through a CIA-owned proprietary, Anderson Enterprises, Inc., based in Arlington, which also offered its services to government and commercial clients for cover purposes. Anderson provided Counterintelligence (CI) and Counterespionage

(CE) support for various components of the Agency and handled a wide range of "sensitive covert operations" and investigations for the Office of Security, as well as offering guard services and document destruction. The commercial arm, Anderson Security Services, Inc. was later merged into General Personnel Investigations.[5]

In February 1967, amid rising protests against the war in Vietnam, the CIA grew "concerned about the safety of its personnel"—from "recruiters on college campuses" to staff in field offices around the country. The Office of Security activated Project MERRIMAC "to provide timely advance notice of impending demonstrations in order to protect CIA assets and installations on a long-range basis . . . multi-racial covert assets were directed to monitor various protest groups in the Washington area considered to be potential sources of demonstrations against the Agency." Agents infiltrated Washington-based pacifist organizations and black activist groups, and participated in demonstrations and marches. The program expanded in 1968, coordinating its effort with the FBI and gathering intelligence about the "leadership, funding . . . activities and policies of the targeted groups."[6]

While Howard Osborn told the Rockefeller Commission MERRIMAC was terminated in December 1968, declassified documents show that "from February 1967 to November 1971, [Anderson Security], an Office of Security proprietary, recruited and handled several Agents for the purpose of covertly monitoring dissident groups in the Washington area considered to be potential threats to Agency personnel and installations. One of these Agents so successfully penetrated one dissident group that she was turned over to the FBI for handling."[7]

The Office of Security provided Anderson Security with a list of organizations "thought to represent potential threats to CIA personnel or installations," so its agents could infiltrate the meetings and events of anti-war and dissident groups and report on their activities. In 1975, Osborn told the Rockefeller Commission:

Anderson Security was, in reality, run by Mr. Ralph True, a CIA Headquarters case officer who also ran a similar wholly-owned proprietary company on the West Coast, General Personnel Investigations Inc. The Anderson company has since folded.[8]

True's background is extremely interesting. A veteran of the OSS, he had worked in Greece under Tom Karamessines in the post-war period, and by October 1960 was acting chief of the Agency's Interrogation Research Division, when he interviewed Agency informant June Cobb over two days.[9]

MERRIMAC employed twelve part-time agents—none of whom were "professionally trained intelligence gatherer[s]." Much of the information gathered was shared with Operation CHAOS, the Agency's most extensive domestic spying program, begun in 1967 by Richard Ober and James Angleton within CIA counterintelligence, and investigating possible foreign sponsorship of anti-racism and anti-war protest groups.[10]

As chief of the Physical Security Division, McCord would have worked closely with Ralph True on the MERRIMAC project—which was coordinated by the Office of Security's Special Activities Division, "the CI/CE support element to the Security Research Staff"—and continued to monitor dissident groups until just after McCord's retirement. McCord would later use the same modus operandi as security chief of the Committee to Re-elect the President (CRP) to target anti-Nixon protestors. Other Anderson activities, from monitoring the construction and security of Agency facilities to the surveillance of suspect staff, dovetailed neatly with McCord's responsibilities in his final years at Langley.[11]

There's also evidence Howard Hunt was in touch with Ralph True. While working at the White House, Hunt contacted Frank O'Malley in the Agency's External Employment Assistance Branch and asked him to recommend "a security service organization to carry out an electronic countermeasures 'sweep.'" O'Malley suggested Anderson Security Consultants and Hunt later told him, "They did a fine job." O'Malley "suspected the electronic counter-measures 'sweep' was to be carried out in the offices of the Committee to Re-Elect the President." This would have reunited Ralph True with McCord in the months before the Watergate break-in.[12]

Anderson Security's CIA connections first surfaced in a *Washington Post* story in July 1974, when Charles Colson outed the company as a CIA propri-etary and two former Anderson Security associates "confirmed Colson's charges" and told reporters "that mysterious checks, written for large amounts, would frequently arrive at the office of the firm's secretary-treasurer":

> *Our sources say that the Anderson firm's industrial security business was also a front to hide another CIA activity . . . Ostensibly, the firm dis-tributed document shredders, conducted security sweeps and planned sur-veillance programs for industrial concerns. But behind this facade, Anderson Security also funneled money to support the CIA's clandestine opera-tions . . . Some of the mystery money was dispatched to Miami banks and was used allegedly to support the CIA's anti-Castro activities . . . One of the firm's primary functions, the sources say, was to shred sensitive documents discarded by defense contractors "so the Russians wouldn't get them."[13]*

According to the sources, "the secret instructions" regarding where to route the money often came from Paul Hellmuth, the managing partner of a Boston law firm, who had been associated with Anderson Security for "the past decade" and was listed as president of the firm when it was dissolved in 1973. Hellmuth's CIA connections were first exposed in 1967, when the Agency's covert funding of the National Student Association through two foundations controlled by Hellmuth was revealed.[14]

On August 31, 1970, the Office of Security downsized and McCord was retired involuntarily after twenty-five years of federal service. His final

fitness report rated him highly, praising his tenacity, "imagination, inge-
nuity and drive" and people management skills but noting his "innate
stubbornness" as "a very principled individual who once convinced he
has hit upon the proper course of action will usually yield only by
direction."

He left on good terms, with a full pension and a Certificate of Distinc-
tion "in recognition of his exemplary performance," praising his "curious and inventive mind" and noting "his achievements in the fields of
audio-countermeasure techniques and physical and technical security."
McCord was also commended by the Secret Service for his Division's work
supporting their mission at the 1968 Republican National Convention at
Miami Beach, Florida; and by Howard Osborn for his role in planning the
visit of Nixon to CIA headquarters in March 1969.[15]

In June 2007, the CIA released the "Family Jewels," a 693-page com-
pendium of the Agency's darkest secrets—and possible violations of its
charter—from 1959 to 1973, compiled in the wake of Watergate. It includes
documents which reveal that "two Office of Security counter-audio technicians [were] loaned to the Secret Service" to protect Presidential candidates amid the violence between police and anti-war demonstrators at the
Democratic National Convention in 1968. While the CIA claimed the
activities of the "two audio surveillance officers . . . were completely under
Secret Service direction," it's hard to imagine McCord not using his presence in Chicago to gather intelligence for his own purposes. One of the
men detailed to both conventions (possibly McCord) spoke about this
at the Agency's Advanced Intelligence seminar in September 1971 and
was interviewed about it by the Inspector General's office on May 31,
1973.[16]

"Because of the possibilities for misunderstanding of such situations,"
wrote Executive Director Colby in January 1972, Director Helms instructed
staff to advise him personally "of any cases in which CIA personnel are
loaned to other agencies for activities within the United States."[17]

On April 10, Helms approved James Angleton's request for CIA support to the Secret Service for the Democratic National Convention in Miami in July. The Agency agreed to provide a safehouse in Miami; conduct name traces on Cubans and other foreign-born persons of interest; and provide counterintelligence briefings on Cuban intelligence operations affecting the security of the convention; but referred "coverage of Latin American exile groups" to the FBI.[18]

After his retirement, McCord called on his contacts in the intelligence world and set up his own security business, McCord Associates. It shared an office in Rockville, Maryland with a non-profit affiliate, the Institute for Protection and Safety Studies, which listed three recently retired CIA officers as consultants—intelligence officer William Francis Shea, who had resigned under a cloud and later worked part-time for CRP; Dr. Jacob Golder, former chief of the Psychological Services Staff; and Dr. Edward "Manny" Gunn, the former chief of Operations in the Office of Medical Services, who had previously supplied poison pills, cigars, and a poison syringe encased in a ballpoint pen for CIA-sponsored assassination attempts on Castro. Shea's wife Therese was also a former Agency employee and worked as McCord's secretary, while George Stanton joined after retiring as an Operations officer with DDP Counterintelligence staff in January 1972.[19]

McCord was also a lieutenant colonel in the Air Force reserve and a member of a "special analysis unit" created by the Office of Emergency Preparedness "to develop a list of radicals . . . [and] contingency plans for censorship of the news media and [mail] in event of war."[20]

There was also an interesting Chilean dimension to McCord's operations. In 1967, Donald Heath, an experienced diplomat in his early seventies who had served as an ambassador in Southeast Asia and the Middle East, was working in Chile as a CIA operations officer under embassy cover. He had been with the Agency since 1952 and according to a post-Watergate status report, "had been acquainted with [Howard Hunt] through the years."[21]

Heath met a young Chilean, Juan Rigoberto Ruiz Villegas, who was just out of school, working as an administrative officer in the Santiago Police Department. Heath hired Ruiz as a "covert asset" and brought Ruiz with him to another posting, from June 1969 to June 1971, apparently as a translator.

In August 1971, Heath sponsored Ruiz to come to the United States, where, according to CIA documents, he "became something of a [Heath] protégé." That fall, the twenty-one-year-old Chilean enrolled in a class in Industrial and Retail Security at Montgomery Junior College in Rockville, Maryland taught by James McCord and through the class, Heath met McCord:[22]

> [Heath's] association with Mr. McCord developed through his interest in a young Chilean protégé . . . [Heath] arranged for Juan Ruiz Villegas to acquire an office position at McCord Associates while the young Chilean continued to live in [Heath's] home, drive Mr. [Heath's] vehicle, and attend school.[23]

McCord later gave Ruiz "temporary (and illegal) employment at McCord Associates as a sort of caretaker." McCord paid Heath by check for "odd jobs" Ruiz performed for him and Ruiz lived with Heath for eight months before moving to a rooming house in Montgomery County that helped him access cheaper tuition. McCord later employed several of his students as security guards at CRP.[24]

McCord recommended Ruiz to CRP General Counsel Glenn Sedam as "the most trustworthy, outstanding student in his class" and during weekends in March and April 1972, Ruiz did some yard work at Sedam's home. He was paid by check to Heath and quit when McCord took him on full-time. When the clearly suspicious FBI re-interviewed Sedam ten days after the second Watergate break-in, they discussed "the possibility of Ruiz electronically 'bugging' or tapping [Sedam's] phone."[25]

McCord joined the Committee to Re-Elect the President (CRP) as its part-time chief of Security on October 1, 1971. He was recruited by Jack Caulfield—a former New York City cop who had handled security for Nixon's 1968 campaign and had coordinated law enforcement at the White House since his election—and approved by White House Counsel John Dean. Over lunch one day, Caulfield told McCord how John Ehrlichman had earned Nixon's respect in 1968 by walking into Rockefeller headquarters at the Republican convention in Miami and "lifting" Rockefeller's entire campaign battle plan from a secretary's desk. Nixon was reportedly "beside himself with elation."[26]

Around the time of the Ellsberg break-in, CRP was looking for its own covert political intelligence–gathering operation. Caulfield pitched Operation Sandwedge but it was rejected by John Mitchell, so John Dean was asked "to find a lawyer to serve as CRP general counsel who could also direct an intelligence-gathering program." Dean recruited Gordon Liddy, who was approved by Mitchell in late November, and moved from the special investigations unit to CRP.[27]

McCord and Liddy were the only former FBI agents at the Committee and swapped "war stories" about their days as G men. McCord went full-time in January as the campaign staff grew from twenty-five people to over a hundred and fifty in offices spread over four floors at 1701 Pennsylvania Avenue, just across from the White House.[28]

John Mitchell would soon resign as Attorney General to direct Nixon's 1972 election campaign. Mitchell and Liddy's key security concern, at a time of fervent anti-war protest, was that the 1972 Republican Convention would avoid a repetition of the bloodshed at the 1968 Democratic convention in

Chicago. The 1972 convention was due to be held in San Diego and Liddy expected up to half a million demonstrators. Bomb attacks on CRP offices in New Hampshire and California had put staff on edge, and, according to McCord, "there were plans for a massive demonstration in Washington in May."[29]

According to Linda Jones, a secretary at the Mullen Company, closed meetings were held at Mullen offices by Bennett, Hunt, and Liddy between December 1971 and April 1972. Hunt was still in contact with the Agency about Mullen cover arrangements and contacted Frank O'Malley "on several occasions requesting referral of retiring Agency employees with specific qualifications." One request was "for an individual having skills in the areas of locks and surreptitious entry." The client involved was the Howard Hughes Organization in Las Vegas and O'Malley got the impression "the duties involved would include the monitoring of a listening device in an undisclosed location." O'Malley sent Hunt a résumé for Thomas Amato and in December 1971, Hunt contacted Amato through Jack Bouman, a former Agency colleague who had also worked with McCord in the Office of Security. Hunt told Bouman he was "assembling a 'capability' in the security field for the Republican Party" and offered both men a job but they declined.[30]

In late January 1972, Liddy sounded out McCord about "listening devices" before presenting his infamous Gemstone plan to John Mitchell, CRP deputy director Jeb Magruder, and John Dean. Liddy used "six professionally drawn color charts" prepared by Hunt's contacts at the CIA to outline "a vast intelligence-gathering and dirty-tricks scheme" budgeted at a million dollars. DIAMOND and GARNET were counterdemonstration plans to deal with anti-Nixon demonstrators at the Republican convention and stage "repulsive" hippy protests to undermine the Democratic campaign.

EMERALD and QUARTZ used "a chase plane" and microwave technology to eavesdrop on "telephone traffic" from Democratic planes, buses, and offices. RUBY infiltrated spies into the campaigns of Democratic contenders. TURQUOISE envisaged a commando team of Cuban exiles sabotaging the air-conditioning unit at the Democratic National Convention. CRYSTAL and SAPPHIRE would operate from a large "opulent" houseboat near the Fontainebleau Hotel in Miami, which would double as both a listening post for electronic surveillance, and a "honey trap" wired for sound, where prostitutes could lure campaign officials into sharing campaign secrets. OPAL and TOPAZ planned four "clandestine entries" to plant "microphone surveillances" and photograph documents. Liddy proposed illicit entries into the campaign headquarters of Democratic presidential candidates, Senator Edmund Muskie (D—Maine) and Senator George McGovern (D—South Dakota); and one of the hotels used for the Democratic National Convention in Miami, using "Cuban help" employed at the hotel.[31]

The crazed ambition of Liddy's plan dumbfounded his audience and Mitchell ruled the budget out of the question. But a few days later, Dean told Liddy the plan was still feasible if it could be scaled down to a more realistic budget; funding could be arranged outside regular channels, and some means of "deniability" could be provided for Attorney General Mitchell, so the operations couldn't be traced back to him.[32]

In early February, Liddy presented a revised $500,000 plan to Mitchell, Magruder and Dean, with the targets scaled back to the office of Larry O'Brien, the chairman of the DNC in Washington; O'Brien's hotel suite in Miami Beach during the Democratic Convention that summer; and the campaign headquarters of the most likely Democratic Presidential nominee. The budget was still too high, so Liddy's proposal was deferred.[33]

In February 1972, through Bob Bennett's nephew, Howard Hunt recruited Tom Gregory, a Mormon studying political science at Brigham Young

University, to infiltrate the Muskie campaign. Gregory received college credit for his volunteer work on the campaign and was paid $175 a week by Hunt to report on campaign schedules, financial contributors, and overheard conversations in the foreign affairs section where he worked. His codename was Ruby II.[34]

At the end of March, under pressure from Colson and Haldeman, the Gemstone plan was finally approved, with a reduced budget of $250,000. According to Magruder, approval was given "for initial entry into the [DNC] headquarters in Washington . . . [and] if the funds were available, we would consider entry into the Presidential contenders' headquarters and . . . the Fontainebleau Hotel in Miami." According to McCord, the three priority targets were Larry O'Brien's office at the Watergate, McGovern headquarters, and the DNC headquarters in Miami. McCord told Liddy he was willing to participate in the Watergate operation and they began to hold planning meetings in Hunt's office across the street in the Mullen Company.[35]

In early April, George McGovern beat Muskie in the Wisconsin Democratic primary and Haldeman asked Liddy "to transfer whatever intelligence capability he had from Muskie to McGovern," so Hunt moved Gregory to the McGovern campaign.[36]

On April 6, the FBI raided the apartment and office of attorney Phillip Mackin Bailley, following a tip-off by a college student who claimed Bailley had blackmailed her into prostitution. They seized address books, phone logs, sex toys, nude photographs of women and pornographic "home movies." Bailley was a charismatic womanizer in his late twenties, who according to Jim Hougan, "specialized in the defense of women charged with prostitution." According to author Phil Stanford, one of his clients was Heidi Rikan, a "lush blonde" and former stripper who allegedly went by the name "Cathy Dieter" and was involved in a call-girl operation at the Columbia Plaza apartment complex, a block away from the Watergate. She paid

Bailley two hundred dollars a week to report any "vice squad" activity affecting her, slept with him without charge and counted "a host of prominent Democrats" among her clients. Her best friend was Maureen "Mo" Biner, the fiancée of John Dean; Biner lived with Dean but often stayed at Rikan's apartment. Biner met Dean in California in November 1970, fell in love, and moved to Washington in January 1971. Through Dean's friend, Mike Sonnenreich, she worked as a clerk for three weeks at the Bureau of Narcotics and Dangerous Drugs (BNDD) before becoming his executive assistant as director of a new National Commission on Marihuana and Drug Abuse. Rikan called Biner "Clout" because she was dating Dean and her name and nickname allegedly appeared in Bailley's address books, alongside, as Hougan notes, the names of "the secretaries and wives of some of Washington's most prominent men—as well as the names of the johns they serviced."[37]

According to Stanford, in late September 1971, Bailley visited Rikan's operation on the sixth floor of the Columbia Plaza. The door was opened by sixty-year-old private investigator Lou Russell and as he waited for Rikan, Bailley looked around. Wandering around the bordello, he opened a closet door to find a man in his fifties sitting there, surrounded by recording equipment, pointing a movie camera toward the bedroom and apparently "filming the johns" through a two-way mirror. Shortly after the Watergate arrests, Russell bragged to private investigators that, with the girls' cooperation, "he was tape-recording conversations between Columbia Plaza prostitutes and their clients," who included campaign staff at the DNC.[38]

According to Hougan, Russell "was a friend to some of the girls, a sometime customer, a free-lance bouncer and a source of referrals." He was a former FBI agent who had spent twenty years working for the House Committee on Un-American Activities and had battled alcoholism most of his life. He had worked for General Security Services (GSS), the guard service with the Watergate contract, from December 1971 until March 1972, when he joined McCord Associates to do background checks on CRP personnel and bought "electronic eavesdropping equipment" from his former colleague, John Leon, presumably on behalf of McCord.[39]

Having worked on Bobby Kennedy's 1968 campaign, Bailley thought they could drum up business from visitors to the DNC during the 1972 campaign season. He was very well-connected politically and claimed he was a friend of Spencer Oliver, the executive director of the Association of State Democratic Chairmen at DNC headquarters. After chatting up DNC secretaries in the Watergate bar, Bailley claims he found one—codenamed "Champagne" in his address book—who agreed to connect DNC visitors to an "escort service" for a commission. She would give visitors a plastic folder of photos kept in her desk and they would select their "date." She would then show them into Spencer Oliver's office, which was usually empty, where they would receive a call from their chosen girl at the Columbia Plaza and make the necessary arrangements. When "Champagne" left the DNC, Bailley told author Phil Stanford, she was replaced by another secretary he knew and "sometimes dated," Ida "Maxie" Wells (who he codenamed "Iron Works").[40]

In September 1971, with the help of former DNC chairman John Bailey, Spencer Oliver had set up the Association of State Democratic Chairmen in the DNC offices in the Watergate office building. Oliver's office had a "wet" bar and refrigerator and adjoined an outside terrace for entertaining visiting chairmen. Maxie Wells was working for his close friend Hodding Carter at the Institute of Politics in Mississippi and Carter recommended he hire Wells as his secretary. She arrived in Washington in February 1972, "very capable, very nice, naïve, wide-eyed and ready to see the big city."[41]

Oliver worked part-time as he had another job with the American Council of Young Political Leaders, an international exchange program he had founded in 1966. According to Wells, Oliver "was only there half days when he was in town" and his other job required a lot of travelling, so "he was frequently absent for two or three weeks at a time . . . So his office was free a great deal of the time and it was frequently used by other staff members or if we had visitors . . . to have a little more peace and quiet to make phone calls." He had three lines and all calls went through the switchboard.[42]

As Oliver was often out of town, Bailley claimed Oliver's telephone was used to arrange liaisons between Rikan's call-girl network and the Democrats. Maxie Wells has always denied all knowledge of a call-girl ring or incriminating pictures in her desk, or that she knew or dated Bailley. Oliver also denies knowing Bailley and didn't have a secretary at the DNC before February 1972, throwing serious doubt on Bailley's "Champagne" story.[43]

During the FBI raid on Bailley's office, investigators missed the tapes recorded at the Columbia Plaza and the Columbia Plaza file in Bailley's briefcase, so the operation was never mentioned in the subsequent indictment. White House Counsel John Dean allegedly panicked because he knew his girlfriend's name was listed in Bailley's address book. As author Ray Locker notes, Dean's telephone logs show he called Nixon campaign staff whose names were later found in Rikan's address books—Mitchell's deputy, Jeb Magruder, Commerce Secretary Maurice Stans and Mitchell aide Fred LaRue, who also lived in the Watergate—and Rikan immediately cut her ties to Bailley.[44]

On April 7, Jeb Magruder approved an initial payment of $83,000 to Liddy and five days later, Liddy gave $65,000 to McCord to spend on electronic equipment for the forthcoming operations. Towards the end of April, Magruder met Liddy and asked him to plant a bug in Larry O'Brien's office at the DNC, "we want to know whatever's said in his office . . . [Bug] the phones, too . . . and while you're in there, photograph everything you can find." O'Brien had an apartment in the Watergate building but his DNC office was considered "a more productive target." After a meeting with Hunt in his Mullen Company office across the street, McCord and Hunt cased the DNC office building over two evenings in April and May, "checking the exits and entry points and . . . building layout." When nobody was around, Hunt also made a "clay impression" of the lock on the front door of DNC headquarters on the sixth floor. They agreed "the building was well-guarded and it presented a difficult target" but, as author J. Anthony Lukas notes, critics called the Watergate complex a "Republican Bastille." Its residents included campaign chief John Mitchell, treasurer Maurice Stans, Nixon's secretary Rose Mary Woods, Anna Chennault, and Robert Mullen. As CRP head of security, McCord regularly checked Mitchell's phone and X-rayed his furniture for bugs, had a key to his apartment and dropped his daughter to school. He had the status to move around the complex with impunity and cultivate a relationship with the guards.[45]

It's worth noting here that CIA historian Walter Pforzheimer lived in a studio apartment on the fourth floor of the Watergate East apartment building and kept a library of three thousand spy books in a one-bedroom duplex on the seventh. Pforzheimer was on the board of directors of Watergate East and the chairman of its security committee. Robert Mullen was president of the board.[46]

On May 1, Alfred Baldwin received a call from James McCord, who identified himself as the security coordinator for CRP. McCord had obtained Baldwin's résumé from the Society of ex-FBI Agents in New York and invited him to Washington to interview for security work with CRP. Baldwin had a law degree and had been teaching a course to policemen in New Haven, Connecticut. They met at CRP headquarters the next morning and Baldwin got the job and was given a .38 caliber revolver and sent off to Detroit and the Midwest for six days as Mrs. Mitchell's bodyguard.[47]

Meanwhile, Colson sent Magruder details of an anti-Vietnam rally scheduled for that week and asked him to "orchestrate" a counterdemonstration—"we can get a couple of Viet Cong flags, several posters and perhaps one or two scalps. Would you put your troops into this and let me know how it is set up in advance so that we can perhaps turn the publicity our way for a change?"[48]

While Liddy gathered intelligence on the demonstrators, McCord described his job as "protecting lives and property against violence." In May, they received reports that a key target group, Vietnam Veterans Against the War (VVAW) was collaborating with the McGovern campaign, and McCord investigated possible collusion "between McGovern headquarters, Democratic National Committee headquarters and such anti-war groups."[49]

On May 2, FBI director J. Edgar Hoover died and Liddy received word that Daniel Ellsberg and other radicals were planning to demonstrate on the west steps of the Capitol building while mourners visited Hoover's coffin, as he lay in state, a short distance away in the Rotunda.[50]

As Watergate Special Prosecution Force (WSPF) researcher Nick Akerman notes, the demonstration "brought together two very explosive elements"— anti-Nixon, anti-war protestors and pro-Administration mourners "paying their respects to . . . a symbol of the political right." The PR-savvy Colson was eager to capitalize on "these two explosive factors to create media exposure which would portray Ellsberg and the anti-war demonstrators in a highly unfavorable light."[51]

Colson's aide, Bill Rhatican, had problems recruiting "demonstrators," so Colson said he would ask Hunt "to bring up his 'boys' from Florida." Because of Hunt's involvement in CIA activities and the Bay of Pigs, Colson explained, he "commanded the unquestioning allegiance of a number of men in Florida who would 'do anything Hunt desired.'"[52]

The next day, Bernard Barker made reservations for himself and nine Cubans to go to Washington "to prevent a demonstration at Hoover's funeral." Their mission was "to guard the casket . . . infiltrate and weaken the demonstrations and prevent desecration." Martinez "was reassured of the legitimacy of the operation because Barker had made all arrangements through Hunt, whose offices were in the Executive Office building and who was known to be on the White House staff."[53]

According to Reinaldo Pico, Barker told the men "their mission was to break up the demonstration and beat up some of the demonstrators" and showed them pictures of Ellsberg and radical lawyer William Kunstler as their key targets. Several Cubans admitted punching demonstrators and Frank Sturgis got into a scuffle which was quickly broken up by the police, with no arrests.[54]

According to prosecutor William Merrill, the Cubans had orders "to incapacitate Ellsberg totally" and he later told Ellsberg "the intent was to have you killed." But Ellsberg recently told NBC News he's "dubious" about that: "I think it was meant to silence me for at least a couple weeks," causing serious injury, not death. Barker told journalist Lloyd Shearer, "My orders were to break both his legs . . ."[55]

Hunt was happy with the mission and the Cubans returned to Miami the next morning. "Keep in shape for another operation soon," Barker told Martinez.[56]

In late April or early May, Hunt introduced Tom Gregory to McCord and asked him for a floorplan of McGovern headquarters, so they could install electronic surveillance. Gregory had been supplying Hunt with McGovern's itinerary and names of contributors but now he was quizzed about the locks on the doors, and "the location of pictures, air ducts and other physical characteristics of the office" with a view to Xeroxing documents and bugging offices.[57]

On May 10, Hunt flew to Miami and briefed Barker on a "double mission" set for the Memorial Day weekend—to break into and plant bugs in the offices of the DNC at the Watergate and at McGovern campaign headquarters. Hunt proposed it as "a matter of national security" and Barker knew he had the training and personnel "available for this type of operation," so he couldn't turn him down. Barker assembled his burglary team: Martinez would again photograph documents, Virgilio Gonzalez would pick locks and Felipe De Diego, Reinaldo Pico, and Frank Sturgis would act as lookouts. The operation would be financed by $114,000 in checks deposited in Barker's bank account in Miami—four checks, totaling $89,000 written out to Manuel Ogarrio and drawn on a bank account in Mexico City; and a $25,000 check made out to CRP's Midwest finance chairman, Kenneth Dahlberg. Six days later, Rolando Martinez met his new case officer, Robert Ritchie, but said nothing about Hunt's activities.[58]

As Hunt planned his "double mission," he was again being discussed at the highest levels of the CIA for two different reasons just weeks before the first Watergate break-in. Back in March, Hunt had sent Charles Colson a memo explaining that, before retiring from the Agency, "he had failed to designate survivor benefits for his wife" and with a history of "severe ulcer attacks, he wondered if this could be changed in view of his present government service." Colson directed Hunt to his administrative assistant, Dick Howard, who discovered, to his surprise, that Hunt was still on the White House payroll, even though he had been assigned to Young and Krogh shortly after Colson brought him aboard. Colson had always assumed Hunt was "charged to someone else's budget . . . [and not] under [his] supervision or responsibility."[59]

In April, Hunt invited his former Mullen Company colleague Douglas Caddy to meet CIA General Counsel Lawrence Houston at a restaurant in Maryland. Two months earlier, Caddy had started doing some volunteer work for the Lawyers Committee for the Re-Election of the President and met Dean and Liddy. Now, Hunt and Houston sounded him out about an assignment with the CIA in Nicaragua—to move there and "build and manage a luxurious seaside hotel that would lure the Sandinista leaders. . . . [and] allow the CIA to learn more about them." Caddy declined.[60]

On May 5, on White House stationery, Hunt wrote to Houston again, telling him "the White House staff" had examined the CIA Retirement Act regarding his "annuity survivorship benefits" and concluded that Director Helms had the authority to briefly recall Hunt to duty "for say a day or a week, after which I could opt for survivorship benefits . . . May I ask that you re-examine my situation in light of the foregoing and if it squares with your own interpretation of the pertinent Sections of the Act, lay the matter before Mr. Helms for his decision?"[61]

Before responding, Houston sent his draft to Executive Director William Colby:

Bill: The Director was well aware of the serious personal troubles Howard had before he left the Agency and our efforts to help him, so if you agree with my approach you might want to mention it to the Director.

Four days later, on May 15, Colby initialed the routing slip with the message "DCI OK'd." The next day, Houston wrote to Hunt, reaffirming that while a recall to duty was possible "if suitable requirements arise . . . to call you back solely for this purpose would be at least a violation of the spirit of the law."[62]

Soon after these exchanges, Houston ran into Hunt at National Airport, "expressing regret that [he] had to turn him down. [Hunt] said he quite understood . . . and went on to say he was doing very well and recovering from his financial reverses resulting from his daughter's injuries and hospital care."[63]

Meanwhile, on May 9, Paramount invited Helms, Ehrlichman, and a White House delegation to a preview screening of *The Godfather*. A year earlier, Paramount had proposed a TV series to Helms about the CIA. The Agency felt it "unwise" but offered Paramount first refusal if they changed their mind.

Wires then crossed after the screening when Jack Valenti gave studio boss Charles Bluhdorn several David St. John paperbacks he'd received from

Helms. Bluhdorn thought this was a sign Helms now wanted to do the TV series. Meanwhile, the CIA's Central Cover Staff (CCS) were developing a "cover placement" with Paramount's parent company, Gulf and Western (LPCHRIS), and began to investigate Helms' secret initiative regarding the David St. John novels. Valenti claimed he had talked to Helms "about six months ago and again two or three weeks ago concerning the possibility of a movie or TV series on CIA based on the David St. John books and/or other material provided by the Agency." Valenti also said "he had interviewed David St. John [Hunt] recently at the request of Mr. Helms."

On May 19, Helms met with the Chief of CCS and the case officer for Gulf and Western, Martin Lukoskie, to clear up the matter. He explained that "approximately three years ago," he had discussed the matter with Valenti, thinking the St. John books "gave a favorable impression of the Agency and might be exploitable for the movies." He heard nothing further "until several weeks ago when Mr. Valenti expressed an interest in the books" and then re-pitched them to an executive at Paramount ahead of the Bluhdorn meeting. A month later, Hunt's name would be in the headlines for very different reasons.[64]

On May 12, McCord moved Baldwin into Room 419 of the Howard Johnson Motel on Virginia Avenue, across the street from the Watergate complex. McCord had already been renting the room for a week in the name of McCord Associates. For the next two weeks, Baldwin "was engaged in surveillance activities" on political figures, including Senator Edward Kennedy. He also infiltrated anti-war demonstrators by posing as a "legal aide" who would help anyone who got arrested, and reported their daily activities to McCord. If questioned by law enforcement, Baldwin was to say he worked in security for CRP under John Mitchell.[65]

A series of demonstrations were planned for Washington in late May, involving seventy-five thousand people, so McCord was concerned about their effect on CRP offices in Washington and the Republican convention in August, which had just been moved from San Diego to Miami.[66]

During the Watergate trial, Baldwin recognized Carl Shoffler, one of the arresting officers, and remembered seeing him also conducting surveillance on the demonstrators. They both wore army fatigues and "crossed paths" several times.[67]

In the second week of May, McCord and Hunt checked out the Watergate Office Building one evening and on May 15, Gregory walked McCord through McGovern headquarters "to acquaint [him] with the office layout" and they "checked the back door lock and alarm arrangement." Gregory was disturbed and "realized he was in over his head."[68]

Earlier that day, Alabama Governor and Democratic Presidential contender George Wallace had been shot five times by Arthur Bremer during a campaign speech and left paralyzed. The next morning, Colson feared an assassination attempt by a "right-wing nut" would hurt Nixon's campaign. He called Hunt into his office and asked him to break into Bremer's apartment to discover his "political orientation." Hunt protested and Colson eventually dropped the idea.[69]

On Tuesday, May 16, the Chilean Foreign Ministry announced there had been a break-in at its embassy in Washington, D.C. between 5:00 and 8:00 a.m. the previous morning and several transistor radios, books, and documents were taken. As the State Department history of US relations with Chile notes:

Although the D.C. Metropolitan Police Department and the Federal Bureau of Investigation subsequently abandoned the case as unresolved and unimportant, other investigators—including newspaper reporters, congressional staff, and federal prosecutors—began by January 1973 to explore a possible connection between the break-in at the Chilean Embassy and the break-in one month later at Democratic National Committee headquarters in the Watergate Office Building, in particular, allegations that the burglars in both cases had been associated with the so-called "Plumbers," the White House Special Investigations Unit.[70]

In late 1972, a senate subcommittee, chaired by Frank Church, investigated the break-in. Telecommunications giant International Telephone & Telegraph Inc. (ITT) had been a conduit for CIA money to the Chilean opposition, so Church probed whether ITT had been involved in the break-in. While the police and FBI "both dismissed [it] as a routine break-in by a juvenile offender," chief counsel Jerry Levinson concluded "it was not routine":

Valuable office equipment and cash were left untouched. The Ambassador's office and the office of the First Secretary were both searched and files were inspected. The thieves walked past several more attractive offices to get to the First Secretary's office, suggesting they knew where they were going. At the same time, a source with excellent contacts in the Cuban community told the Subcommittee staff that Frank Sturgis had told other people that he and [Eugenio] Martinez and [Virgilio] Gonzalez, two other Watergate defendants, had broken into the Embassy to photograph documents.

While there was no "hard evidence" of ITT involvement, a "circumstantial" case could be made. McCord later revealed that in the Spring of 1972, his Chilean employee Juan Ruiz called the Chilean military attaché's residence in D.C. McCord also believed US authorities were tapping the phones in the Chilean embassy and after the arrest of the Watergate burglars, more evidence would emerge to implicate them in the Chilean embassy break-in.[71]

On Friday, May 19, the Weather Underground bombed the Pentagon. Three days later, Barker's team arrived in Washington and checked into the

Manger-Hamilton Hotel under alias. The following evening, they met McCord, Hunt, Liddy, and Gregory for a final briefing on the mission. Barker was identified as the "team captain" for the operation and McCord was introduced as "Jimmy," an "electronics expert" who had worked for the FBI and CIA. "Eduardo told us he had information that Castro and other foreign governments were giving money to McGovern," Martinez later recalled, "and we were going to find the evidence." Barker didn't give his team the details of the assignment or their role until shortly before they entered DNC headquarters.[72]

On Friday, May 26, Barker's team moved to the Watergate Hotel, where Hunt and Liddy were also registered under aliases. According to his trial testimony, Baldwin returned to Room 419 that afternoon after a few days in Connecticut, to find an array of electronic equipment. McCord was tuning a receiver unit and told Baldwin he would be monitoring conversations on it from then on. After explaining how the receiver worked, McCord handed Baldwin a set of earphones. When he put them on, he heard a man and a woman discussing their marital problems. When the call ended, he wrote a rough memo of the conversation and gave it to McCord. He later identified the couple as Mr. and Mrs. Spencer Oliver and the frequency he was monitoring as 118 megacycles. Shortly afterwards, two men in dark suits arrived and McCord introduced Baldwin as "Bill Johnson" and the men as "Ed" and "George." Baldwin later identified them as Hunt and Liddy. McCord showed them the equipment, gave Liddy the memo and the three men left to have dinner across the street. All of which raises the question: how could Baldwin have been listening to a bug on Spencer Oliver's phone on Friday evening if the first break-in hadn't even happened yet?[73]

McCord returned at 11:30 that evening and they left the Howard Johnson in McCord's car and stopped off to buy batteries at an all-night drugstore. That night, McCord and Baldwin drove around the Capitol Hill area and McCord pointed to McGovern Headquarters: "That is what we are interested in . . . We may move you up to this location and have you do the same thing here." McCord said they were trying to rent a house across the street. McCord was communicating by walkie-talkie with another car and then turned around and pulled up alongside it. Liddy got out of the other car and jumped in with Baldwin and McCord. Baldwin saw Hunt in the other driving seat, with others in the back. As they drove around again, McCord explained to Liddy that they couldn't find Gregory.[74]

Baldwin recalled that McCord was deferring to Liddy "as his superior, answering in a 'yes, sir. No, sir' fashion." The lights were still on in the offices, a man was standing in front of the building and they couldn't find Gregory. They drove around looking for him until 3:00 a.m. when Liddy finally told McCord to abort the mission and McCord drove Baldwin back to the Howard Johnson.[75]

The rest of the team made the first of two "frustrated attempts" to gain access to the DNC that evening. Martinez was not impressed by the final "improvised briefing" in "Eduardo's" room:

> *Eduardo told us he had information that Castro money was coming into the Democratic headquarters, not McGovern's, and that we were going to try to find the evidence there. Throughout the briefing, McCord, Liddy, and Eduardo would keep interrupting each other, saying, "Well, this way is better," or "That should be the other way around."*[76]

The plan was sketchy, but the Cubans trusted Hunt and thought he knew what he was doing. They reserved a private dining room in the basement of the Watergate which had access to elevators that could bring them up to the DNC on the sixth floor. After their meal, they would project a film until all the food was cleared away, staff left and they could safely proceed to the sixth floor. But the staff in the DNC stayed late and the night guards asked them to leave at 2:00 a.m. "Eduardo said he would hide in the closet of the banquet room with Gonzales, the key man, while the guard let the rest of us out," Martinez recalled. "As soon as the coast was clear, they would let us back in." But the door leading to the corridor was locked and alarmed, so Hunt and Gonzales were trapped in the closet all night and sneaked back to their hotel rooms past the guards when the doors were unlocked at seven the next morning.[77]

The next night, according to Martinez, they waited until all the lights were out in the DNC offices on the sixth floor:

> *All seven of us in McCord's army walked up to the Watergate complex at midnight. McCord rang the bell, and a policeman came and let us in. We all signed the book, and McCord told the man we were going to the Federal Reserve office on the eighth floor. It all seemed funny to me. Eight men going to work at midnight . . . Then we went up to the eighth floor, walked down to the sixth—and do you believe it, we couldn't open that door, and we had to cancel the operation. . . .*

While Gonzalez was working on the door, McCord kept going up to the eighth floor. "It is still a mystery to me what he was doing there," recalled Martinez. At two o'clock, he went up there with the bad news and saw McCord talking to two guards. "What happened? Have we been caught?" he thought, but McCord seemed to know the guards. Martinez assumed he worked there and was their "man on the inside."

"Pretty soon," he wrote, "we picked up our briefcases and walked out the front door":

> *Eduardo was furious that Gonzalez hadn't been able to open the door. Gonzalez explained he didn't have the proper equipment, so Eduardo told him to fly back to Miami to get his other tools.*

Martinez complained to Barker that the operation was poorly planned—they had no floor plan of the building and didn't know where the elevators were, how many guards there were, when they checked the building or what type of door Gonzalez had to open; and there were no contingency plans. When Barker told Hunt, his reply to Martinez was: "Your mission is to do what you are told and not to ask questions."[78]

Late Sunday afternoon, Gonzalez arrived back from Miami, with almost "his whole shop" in tow. By eleven o'clock, all lights were out at the DNC and the team went in again. Gonzalez picked the lock of the rear basement door to the DNC building and taped the door, so the rest of the team could enter. Fifteen minutes later, Gonzalez picked the lock to the sixth-floor offices of DNC headquarters upstairs and they were finally in.

As Hunt and Liddy monitored the operation by walkie-talkie from a hotel room at the Watergate, Barker led the burglary team. Once inside the DNC, McCord set about planting the bugs and Martinez photographed documents selected by Barker.

"I took a lot of photographs," recalled Martinez, "maybe thirty or forty—showing lists of contributors that Barker had handed me. McCord worked on the phones. He said his first two taps might be discovered, but not the third."[79]

According to McCord's testimony, Mitchell set Liddy two priorities for the bugs: Larry O'Brien's office and the office of another senior official. The Senate Watergate Committee's final report notes that "McCord placed electronic bugging devices (miniature transmitters) in the telephones of DNC chairman Larry O'Brien and another official Spencer Oliver."[80]

But in his book, McCord writes that he "had been asked to install only one device but had brought a second "for insurance" in case needed:

I found an office with a direct view across the street at the Howard Johnson Motel, pulled the curtain and made the installation in the telephone . . . I did the same on an extension off a telephone call director carrying Larry O'Brien's lines in an adjoining room. Surprisingly, both devices were to remain in place and both to operate for months after the arrests.

As we will see, Baldwin revealed the location of the Oliver bug to the FBI in July but no device was found in Oliver's phone until a telephone repairman was called in September. According to McCord, the O'Brien bug remained operational until April 1973, when McCord told prosecutors its exact location.[81]

McCord's description of how he selected Oliver's phone and its "direct view across the street at the Howard Johnson Motel" is intriguing. McCord claimed the receiver needed a "line of sight" to pick up the signal clearly but at the time he bugged Oliver's phone, neither he or Baldwin knew who Spencer Oliver was. Years later, Martinez confirmed "that the tap was not placed on Larry O'Brien's telephone, but on one in the Oliver/Wells/Governors' area" and that the photographs were also not taken in O'Brien's office. McCord's reference to "an extension off a telephone call director carrying Larry O'Brien's lines in an adjoining room" suggests he didn't know where O'Brien's office was, or thought he could access O'Brien's phone lines in a room adjoining Oliver's office. Twenty years after Watergate, arresting Officer Barrett returned to Larry O'Brien's office and said, "Many people believe this to be the original target of the break-in . . . However, no burglars were found in here, no listening devices; nothing. This room was clean."[82]

The choice of R. Spencer Oliver, the executive director of the Association of State Democratic Chairmen, as a target puzzled Larry O'Brien. "Spencer Oliver would be low on the list of priorities if you were seriously trying to garner information," he said. The treasurer made more sense, as he solicited campaign contributions. O'Brien felt "there had to be some reason for Oliver being selected."[83]

Oliver's father, Robert Oliver, was a Washington lobbyist with a background in the labor movement, where he had been legislative director of the AFL–CIO and had worked on the Marshall Plan with Robert Mullen in the early fifties. They remained close friends and when Mullen's PR clients needed a lobbyist, he recommended Robert Oliver and Associates. Oliver handled the General Foods and Hughes Tool accounts as a consultant to the Mullen Company. In his autobiography, Hunt recalls a dinner with Mullen, Bennett, and Spencer Oliver:[84]

> *A Democrat, Oliver had been engaged for some time in an international student exchange which I suspected to be financed by CIA . . . Oliver mentioned several active CIA officers who I knew. When Mullen and Bennett asked me what I thought of Oliver as a possible partner, I was less than enthusiastic. . . .*[85]

It's the only mention of Oliver in the book and a very odd reference by a man who was involved in bugging Oliver's phone for still obscure reasons. Hunt refers to Oliver's involvement with the American Council of Young Political Leaders, a bipartisan exchange program designed to bring young leaders from all over the world and across the political spectrum together "to foster mutual understanding, respect and friendship among the next generation of leaders." Oliver served as its first president and executive director and it was supported by the Ford Foundation and the State Department, and would have been of great interest to Cord Meyer, who was sponsoring similar programs at the time. Hunt later testified that he knew "some of Spencer Oliver's activities were covertly, at least, financed by CIA, whether Mr. Spencer Oliver knew it or not . . . [and he] was performing a CIA function, wittingly or unwittingly." But he saw no relationship between that and the bugging of

Oliver's phone. Until Liddy told him whose phone they were bugging, he didn't even know Oliver worked at the DNC: "It came as a total surprise to me . . . I couldn't conceive why his phone had been bugged. I thought it must have been by error and Mr. Liddy indicated to me that he thought, too, that McCord probably made a mistake."[86]

According to Oliver, his father told him Bob Mullen wanted himself and Bob Bennett to join the Mullen Company as vice presidents and to eventually buy him out, so he could retire. Oliver Jr. was trying to pass the bar at night and wasn't interested but he agreed to meet Mullen at the Metropolitan Club. After lunch, Mullen invited Oliver back to his office, where he introduced him to Hunt. Thirty minutes after he left, Hunt went into Mullen's office and said, "Don't hire that liberal democrat, hire me!"[87]

Soon, federal prosecutors were convinced Hunt was trying to blackmail Oliver with the content of the intercepted conversations.

According to McCord, the burglary team all left together in the early hours of Monday morning, "down the back stairway to the basement, removing tape as we went until the last one had been removed on the rear basement door. Liddy was elated. . . ." The group then went to McGovern headquarters, hoping to bug the offices of campaign manager Gary Hart and national political director Frank Mankiewicz, but McGovern staff were working late. On Hunt's orders, Gregory was waiting outside to "report when they left [but] was asked by a policeman to leave the area," so the mission was aborted.[88]

The team returned to the hotel around 5:00 a.m. with their primary mission accomplished. "Eduardo" was happy and Martinez gave him the film and left for the airport, hoping the photographs of campaign contributions might substantiate "rumors in Miami that McGovern was receiving money from Castro."[89]

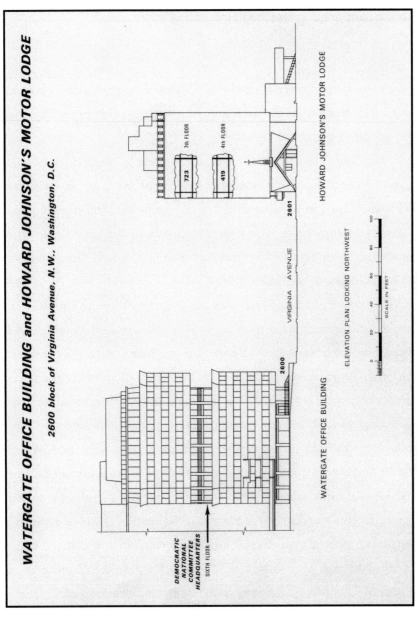

FIGURE 5: Chart showing Alfred Baldwin's lookout position in relation to the DNC
(National Archives)

At 8:15 a.m. that morning, a security guard discovered the lock on the door to the DNC offices had been tampered with and the police dusted for fingerprints, but nothing was missing from the office area.[90]

Once the bugs were in place at the DNC, McCord taught Baldwin how to use the receiver to monitor the wiretaps at the listening post in the Howard Johnson Motor Lodge across the street.[91]

When McCord tuned to 118.9 megacycles, Baldwin could monitor telephone conversations from three extensions on the phone in Spencer Oliver's office. He also tuned to 135 megacycles, trying to pick up the other bug but only heard a radio station. "We'll have to move to a higher level," said McCord and on Monday, Baldwin moved to Room 723 on the seventh floor to get better reception (see Figure 5).[92]

McCord discovered his tape recorder was incompatible with the receiver, so strangely, the intercepted conversations were not taped. McCord ignored Liddy's request to either source a compatible recorder or tape the conversations through a microphone and asked Baldwin to transcribe a log of intercepted telephone conversations but as Hougan notes, if blackmail was the intent, "Baldwin's scribbled notes were useless as evidence of anything."[93]

On the first day, Baldwin used a yellow legal pad but the next day, McCord brought in an electronic typewriter. From then on, Baldwin typed out the conversations "almost verbatim" and gave the logs to McCord, who passed them on to Liddy's secretary, Sally Harmony. Baldwin was a poor typist, so Liddy had Harmony retype several logs to correct typos and make them more presentable for Magruder and Mitchell. He also shared them with Hunt. According to the final Senate Watergate Committee report:

> *The Gemstone project had its own stationery with the word "Gemstone" printed in large letters at the top. Sally Harmony testified she used Gemstone stationery when she retyped the telephone logs. Harmony also said she*

saw a stack of 8 by 10 photographs of documents from the DNC headquar-
ters, held by fingers in rubber gloves.[94]

When Liddy read the first logs, he realized "the interception was from a telephone" rather than the room bug he had ordered, and that "the telephone tapped was being used by a number of different people, none of whom appeared to be Larry O'Brien." McCord explained he still couldn't "intercept the signal from inside O'Brien's office." Baldwin described McCord as a "very close-mouthed person." McCord told him they were trying to bug Larry O'Brien but as they couldn't receive a signal from the bug on O'Brien's extension, the logs concerned "approximately 200 conversations" intercepted from incoming and outgoing calls on Oliver's telephone.[95]

There were a lot of conversations about "Spencer" and "Oliver" and for a while, Baldwin thought they were two different people. Even when he figured out it was one person, neither he or McCord knew if the name was Spencer Oliver or Oliver Spencer or who that person was.[96]

Two days after the second break-in, the US Supreme Court affirmed that US law prohibits electronic surveillance without a warrant, even in national security cases, and the District Court of Appeals subsequently ruled that Baldwin couldn't disclose the contents of the intercepted conversations during the Watergate trial. Baldwin did tell the FBI whose voices he'd been able to identify, however—Spencer Oliver and his secretary Maxie Wells; Robert Allen, the president of the Young Democrats, and his secretary, Marty Sampson; Barbara Kennedy, a secretary who worked across the hall from Maxie Wells; Robert Oliver, Spencer's father; and John Richardson from the State Department, whose Bureau of Cultural and Educational Affairs funded the American Council of Young Political Leaders.[97]

Baldwin later described some of the conversations he heard as "explicitly intimate" and prosecutors who interviewed Baldwin described them as "primarily sexual" and "extremely personal, intimate, and potentially embarrassing." Baldwin interpreted the conversations as "secretaries at the

DNC talking to their boyfriends, arranging dates . . . [and being] pretty explicit about what they were going to do on a given night." Hougan suggests the "boyfriends" Baldwin heard may have been the "johns" in Oliver's office and the "secretaries" were their "dates" at the Columbia Plaza. According to Lukas, some of the conversations were "so spicy . . . they have given rise to unconfirmed reports that the telephone was being used for some sort of call-girl service catering to congressmen and other prominent Washingtonians."[98]

Lead government prosecutor Earl Silbert initially put the spicy conversations and Oliver's alleged marital problems together to suggest the motive for the burglary was blackmail. "Hunt was trying to blackmail Spencer and I'm going to prove it!" he told Oliver's lawyer Charles Morgan. But Hunt and Oliver both later denied this.[99]

Baldwin gave the transcripts to McCord every day, with one exception. On June 6, McCord flew to Miami for three days and called Baldwin with instructions to leave the logs with the night guard in the CRP lobby.[100]

There were only two night guards at CRP who may have received the eavesdropping logs from Baldwin in early June, while McCord was in Miami—Lou Russell and Walter Edward Brayden. Brayden had worked as an intelligence officer for the Central Cover Staff's Operation Services branch until his retirement in October 1969. He had worked briefly for McCord's division before he retired. Frank O'Malley referred him to McCord Associates in early 1972 and McCord gave him a job. According to a later Office of Security interview, in April 1972, Brayden "served as a guard for Mrs. Martha Mitchell on a trip to Chicago, and he expected to work on a security survey of the Hotel Fontainebleau in Miami in late June 1972." He refused to carry a gun, even though McCord told him Attorney General Mitchell authorized him to do so. Brayden later told the FBI he had been "astounded" to read of McCord's arrest and claimed he had not seen McCord since April and had no knowledge of the Watergate incident.[101]

During the last two weeks in May, Lou Russell also worked as a guard at CRP and like Baldwin, he worked for CRP but was paid by McCord. Baldwin remembered the night guard as having "two first names" and Hougan suggests Lou Russell was the guard Baldwin delivered the logs to. As Hougan notes in later questioning before the Senate Watergate Committee, McCord "refused to identify the guard" who received the logs, "insisting he had nothing to do with Watergate . . . The Committee accepted that refusal and probed no further."[102]

On June 1, McCord put Russell on a retainer to investigate the source of classified information leaked to Jack Anderson and a week later, McCord submitted "an interim report on the association of Jack Anderson with Anna Chennault, Bobby Baker, Thomas G. Corcoran, the D.C. National Bank, the Washington Community Broadcasting Corporation, and other persons and organizations . . . one of a series of reports relating to Anderson and his activities." Another undated report tries to connect Anderson's leaks to his "ties to McGovern and Democratic hierarchy," principally through his links to the Ginsburg, Feldman, and Bress law firm, whose principals had represented John F. Kennedy, Lyndon Johnson, and McGovern and had close ties to Israel, lobbyist Irving Davidson, and Anna Chennault.[103]

After Gemstone was approved, Magruder claimed he didn't hear from Liddy again until he reported on the bugs installed and the photographs taken during the first Watergate break-in. Liddy asked his secretary Sally Harmony to type up synopses of the telephone conversations from Baldwin's logs on Gemstone stationery and these were delivered to Magruder with the photographs.

When Magruder showed Mitchell "the fruits of the break-in," Mitchell was underwhelmed, telling him they were "not worth the money" and summoning Liddy to express his displeasure. "One of the bugs isn't working and the other was put on the wrong phone," Liddy explained, "but I'll get everything straightened out right away."[104]

Mitchell later denied seeing any Gemstone documents or wiretap reports but in the weeks before the break-in, Magruder handed his assistant, Robert Reisner, documents printed on stationery with the letterhead "Gemstone" before a meeting with Mitchell, and Reisner subsequently saw Gemstone stationery and envelopes in the office, along with some photographs:

> *The Gemstone envelopes bore the words "Sensitive Material" in large red capital letters and the words "handle as code word material" in smaller letters . . . At the bottom of the Gemstone stationery, were the printed words "Warning, this information is for intelligence purposes only. Exploitation may compromise source and terminate flow of information."*[105]

On June 6, Rolando Martinez had his last meeting with his case officer, Robert Ritchie, before the break-in and James McCord arrived in Miami with members of White House staff. The Democratic and Republican National Conventions were due to be held in Miami in July and August and McCord had received warning from the Internal Security Division of the Justice Department that "some individuals in Florida planned to forge college press credentials to get into both . . . Convention sites, and blow up the communication centers of both parties there and cause havoc on the convention floor."[106]

McCord travelled to Miami "to survey and strengthen the security of the Doral Hotel," where both White House and CRP staff would be based during the conventions. McCord's post-survey report made thirty recommendations "to help protect against such violence." McGovern and his campaign would be based at the Doral Hotel during the Democratic Convention in mid-July, so McCord also recommended "thorough audio-countermeasures inspections" as soon as the convention was over, "since McGovern's family will occupy the same suite as Mr. Mitchell, and key personnel . . . will occupy the penthouse later in August."[107]

Curiously, "in the early summer of 1972," the Directorate of Operations (DDO) and Special Programs Division of the Office of Communications (OC-SPD) within the CIA tested audio surveillance equipment by placing receiving antennas on the roof of a hotel in Miami Beach, Florida. The Agency later claimed the location was chosen for its "similarity to the actual target site and environment in Saigon" but when a hotel employee asked why the antennas were on the roof, "a team member in effect told him that the group was an advance security segment for the Democratic National Convention." This clearly suggests the test was conducted on the roof of the Doral Hotel, the same hotel Hunt and Liddy were targeting ahead of the Democratic National Convention in mid-July, and by the same Agency component (DDO) Martinez reported to.[108]

On June 9, Hunt met Donald Segretti—another Nixon operative who specialized in "dirty tricks"—in Miami and asked him "to put together a group of peaceful demonstrators to picket the Doral Hotel during the Democratic Convention. Hunt explained that another group of unruly demonstrators was to join in the demonstration and attempt to disrupt it and that the bad conduct of the crowd would be blamed on Senator McGovern."[109]

Hunt had already asked Bernard Barker "to develop a network of informants along the Miami Beach hotel complex" who could report to him during the convention; to rent a houseboat "as a base for electronic surveillance" and to recruit "disreputable-looking . . . hippies to pose as McGovern supporters . . . [and] demonstrate in front of the Doral Hotel . . . and behave outrageously to . . . discredit [McGovern]." He also asked Barker to organize two safehouses near the convention hall as a base for "Miami Beach activities" and to "recruit Cuban employees at the Fontainebleau for possible intelligence activities within the hotel." McCord added that the Cubans would conduct "surveillance operations . . . against demonstrators and violence-oriented groups in Miami."[110]

The following day, Hunt met Barker for lunch and gave him two rolls of black-and-white film to develop—the film Martinez had shot during the first Watergate break-in. The two-week delay in developing the film was partly due to McCord, who had taken the film from Martinez to develop but then told Liddy "the photographer he knew . . . was on vacation or something," so the film was turned over to Hunt. It's hard to believe McCord didn't check the film while it was in his possession.[111]

Not realizing it was the film from the Watergate operation, Barker took it to Rich Photos, a camera shop in downtown Miami for processing on a "rush" basis. When Hunt told him what the film was, he panicked. Martinez was chatting to De Diego and Sturgis at the real estate office "when Barker burst in like a cyclone" and told them they needed to retrieve the film. They went straight to Rich Photos and Sturgis and Martinez covered the doors while a highly-excited Barker picked up the negatives and thirty-eight prints.

"It's real cloak-and-dagger stuff, isn't it?" said Michael Richardson, the owner's son behind the counter who had also developed the film. The 7x10 prints showed gloved hands holding typed documents with the letterhead "Chairman—Democratic National Committee" in front of the lens, many signed "Dick" or bearing O'Brien's name. When the Watergate scandal broke, the photo developer contacted the FBI and told them about the film. Barker gave the prints to Hunt at the airport and Hunt gave them to Liddy, who left them on Mitchell's desk. They seem to have been shredded in the days after the second break-in.[112]

According to Richardson, the documents were placed on a shag rug and four hands wearing rubber gloves were visible in the corners of each picture. The FBI were troubled when they found no such rug in the DNC offices but did find a similar carpet in Baldwin's hotel room. Hougan suggests McCord photographed a sanitized set of DNC documents in Baldwin's room, keeping the documents Martinez photographed away from Hunt's team.[113]

Martinez thought "it was crazy to have those important pictures developed in a common place in Miami." Barker had been Hunt's liaison to the Cubans at the Bay of Pigs and "trusted Eduardo totally" but for Martinez, "it was too much":

> *I talked it over with Felipe and Frank, and decided I could not continue. I was about to write a letter when Barker told me Eduardo wanted us to get ready for another operation in Washington.*

Not wanting to "jeopardize the operation," Martinez "agreed to go on this last mission."[114]

On Monday, June 12, Martinez and Sturgis purchased surgical gloves and on Tuesday, Martinez bought sixty rolls of Tri-X film. CIA records indicate that after Wednesday, June 14, for some unexplained reason, Martinez was "no longer able to be contacted."[115]

On June 9, a front-page story in the *Washington Star* with the headline "Capitol Hill Call Girl Ring Uncovered" reported that the FBI had "uncovered a high-priced call girl ring allegedly headed by a Washington attorney . . . involving at least one White House secretary" and that "a White House lawyer was a client." That morning, a grand jury had indicted Phillip Bailey on twenty-two counts, "including charges of blackmail, racketeering, procuring and pandering." John Dean summoned prosecutors John Rudy and Don Smith to the White House and asked to see the case file to determine who at the White House was involved. Dean blamed the Democrats for leaking the story and carefully studied the nude pictures of the Bailey raid. When the prosecutors refused Dean's request to keep the address book over the weekend, he had his secretary make a copy, so he could cross-reference the names against a White House staff directory. According to Rudy, the address book included the name of Dean's girlfriend Maureen

Biner, Bailley's codename for her ("Clout") and "Cathy Dieter," the alleged alias for Biner's friend Heidi Rikan. Dean identified a female attorney in the Office of Emergency Preparedness across the street as the "White House secretary" described in the story and shortly after Rudy and Smith left, called her boss Darrell Trent, who forced her to resign. She claimed she "had briefly been in love with Bailley" and "had no connection to any call-girl ring." A prosecutor told Hougan that Cathy Dieter's apartment at the Columbia Plaza "was rented in the name of Bailley's former girlfriend" (the fired female attorney) "without her knowledge."[116]

The ostensible purpose of the second Watergate break-in was to fix the bug on Larry O'Brien's phone, which was either faulty or being "shielded" by the steel structure of the building. Watergate testimony shows some disagreement as to who ordered the second break-in. John Dean testified that two days after the break-in, Liddy told him "the men arrested in the DNC were his men" and that "Magruder had pushed him into doing it" because "they were not getting good information from a bug that they had placed in the DNC earlier."[117]

Magruder told Ehrlichman the second break-in was Liddy's idea, and that neither he nor Mitchell "knew that another break-in was contemplated." But that's not what Liddy told McCord. Liddy said Mitchell had liked the "takes" from the first entry—the documents photographed—and "wanted a second photographic operation." As they were going in again, he also wanted to correct the second wiretap device, by repositioning it or replacing it if it was faulty.[118]

According to Liddy, Magruder ordered the second break-in on the Monday following Bailley's indictment. He wanted to repair the defective bug and to photograph O'Brien's files to find out what "derogatory" information he might use against the Nixon campaign. "I want to know what O'Brien has here!" said Magruder, slapping the desk drawer where "he kept his derogatory information on the Democrats."[119]

Later that day, McCord visited the listening post, gave Baldwin a crisp
new hundred-dollar bill, and asked him to "hang around" the Watergate
restaurant and cocktail lounge that week, monitoring and mingling with
DNC staff. McCord pointed out an office facing the Howard Johnson on
Virginia Avenue, which he believed was O'Brien's and asked Baldwin if he'd
seen O'Brien there. They had lunch at the Watergate restaurant and McCord
produced a glossy photo of O'Brien, hoping to spot him there. They sat with
their back to a stairwell down to a private restaurant and club for DNC staff
and politicians in the basement, not realising their backs were turned as their
targets of interest went downstairs to eat and socialize. It all struck Baldwin
as "kind of ridiculous."

"We've got to get you into the [DNC] for a tour," said McCord, intent on
penetrating Democratic headquarters and confirming the location of
O'Brien's office. McCord suggested the pretext of a "Coke repairman" but
Baldwin had a better idea. Posing as "Bill Johnson," he went upstairs and
asked for Spencer Oliver, knowing he was in Texas. He was introduced to
Oliver's secretary, "Maxine," "whose intimate phone conversations he had
been listening to with such interest." When he told her he was a law school
classmate of Spencer's and the nephew of Connecticut state chairman John
Bailey, she jumped up and gave him a "royal tour" of the DNC. Baldwin
asked to see Larry O'Brien's suite, so Wells introduced him to O'Brien's secretary, who showed him the chairman's office where his uncle used to work.
Baldwin suddenly realised John Bailey had been O'Brien's predecessor as
DNC chairman and that O'Brien's office was at the rear of the building,
facing the river and couldn't be seen from his balcony at the Howard Johnson. "Maxine" showed him the conference room next door and took him
downstairs to see the offices of Bob Allen on the first floor and the private
DNC club in the basement.

When Baldwin returned to room 723, he drew McCord a rough sketch
of where O'Brien's office was located and compared it to a sketch McCord
had of the office layout. McCord seemed genuinely surprised. From the

balcony, Baldwin pointed out the office facing Virginia Avenue they had been discussing earlier "as belonging to a Mr. Stewart," who was in Miami. O'Brien had also been in Miami for the past month, so McCord suggested Baldwin go down there. McCord told Baldwin to go back and get O'Brien's contact details in Miami, so Baldwin went back to "Maxine," told her he was on his way to Miami and wanted to contact O'Brien when he arrived. She took him back to O'Brien's secretary, who began giving him the number but then disappeared into an office to make a call. Thinking she was calling the police, Baldwin panicked, asked where the men's room was and fled. McCord berated him for not getting the number, so he went back to the lobby and called Maxine to apologise, saying he was on his way to the airport. "So glad you called," she said. "We called Miami and got O'Brien's number," which Baldwin gave to McCord. The next day, Spencer Oliver returned from Texas and Baldwin started monitoring his phone again.[120]

According to Wells, the tour lasted about an hour and at one point, Baldwin asked for O'Brien's contact number in Miami, so she "sat him in Mr. Oliver's office" and went to get some coffee, brought it back, then went off to get O'Brien's number for "quite some time." Her drawer would have been unlocked, and her key would have been on the desk or in the top drawer.[121]

In early June, Maxie Wells had left town for several days for a cousin's wedding, so she gave her spare desk key to another secretary, Barbara Kennedy, who worked across the hall. *Silent Coup* authors Colodny and Gettlin speculate that Baldwin targeted Oliver's office and "either somehow obtained a key from Wells, or stole one" during his visit.[122]

After the second break-in, Wells and Kennedy still had their keys, so it's possible Baldwin took a "clay impression" of them at this time. But if he had access to Wells' open drawer while alone in her office, why did Martinez have a key to it during the second break-in and why was he so keen to photograph documents in her desk?

Baldwin denies tampering with or removing anything during his tour of the DNC but what his story does confirm is that McCord had mistaken the office of Director of Communication John Stewart for O'Brien's office; had been trying to tap O'Brien's phone for two weeks in Washington while he was in Miami; and had been tapping the wrong phone with a bug that didn't work.[123]

On Wednesday afternoon, Liddy visited Hunt's office. "We've got to go into DNC headquarters again, Howard," he said.

"Why, for god's sake? Wasn't the photography sufficient?" replied Hunt.

"Oh, they liked the photos, and they want more. But McCord's screwed up somehow. Evidently he bugged the wrong telephone line. He was supposed to tap O'Brien's . . . . Have Macho [Barker] buy another camera and bring up a lot of film. They want everything in those file cabinets photographed."

Hunt was against it but reluctantly summoned Barker's team to Washington. According to Liddy, McCord told him the defective bug was a room microphone, only later did he learn it was "on another telephone."[124]

During the first or second weekend of June, McCord had tried again to install a bug in Mankiewicz's office in McGovern headquarters, while Tom Gregory distracted staff "but again he was thwarted—by guards and people working there at the weekend."[125]

On Wednesday, two days before the second break-in, Gregory asked to see Mullen Company president Bob Bennett. Gregory was a friend of Bennett's nephew and told Bennett that Hunt had planted him as a "spy" at McGovern headquarters while covering his living expenses in Washington. Gregory had now developed "moral uneasiness about the activity" and confided in Bennett as a fellow Mormon who understood the political scene.

Bennett thought Gregory's loyalties boiled down to his status within the McGovern campaign. If he was being paid or held "any position of trust in the McGovern campaign . . . you cannot morally discuss what you are doing with Howard Hunt and take money from him." But if he was simply a college student stuffing envelopes and licking stamps to experience a political campaign, he didn't see a problem.

"You have to draw the moral line and not step beyond it," he advised.

"Brother Bennett. I have gone way beyond that. I have long since crossed that line," replied Gregory, and Bennett advised him to quit. "Do you want me to tell you what they want me to do?" asked Gregory.

"No, Tommy, I don't. You have no need to confess everything to me unless it would make you feel better. Now, if you want to tell me something, I would be glad to listen to you, but I don't want to pry into everything that you have been doing on this assignment."

"Well, they want me to help them bug Frank Mankiewicz's office," said Gregory.

"Tommy, you cannot do that. You have got to get out," replied Bennett.

"I agree, but how? Mr. Hunt is a powerful man. He has a great deal of money and influence. I am afraid of what might happen to me if I should quit."

"Come on, Tommy, you are exaggerating things," replied Bennett. "This is just Howard. He works for me. This is not a great, powerful important man. Simply tell him you are quitting. If there is any problem, let me know and I will handle it."

Gregory was still upset, so Bennett asked him to write a letter of resignation to Hunt and he would handle it and he would never have to see Hunt again.

The next day, "concerned that he might be under surveillance," Gregory met Bennett in Lafayette Park and gave him the letter. Bennett read it and thought it was fine and advised Gregory to relax: "Don't go back to the McGovern headquarters. Don't go back to Howard. Don't take any more money from him. Don't have any more to do with him. Just get out."

Bennett left the letter on Hunt's desk but before they could discuss it, the break-in happened the next day. Days earlier, Hunt had told Bennett "he would see him on the following weekend if he was not in jail."[126]

On Thursday, the day before the break-in, Phillip Bailley was arraigned in federal court and pleaded guilty to a twenty-two-count indictment. According to author Phil Stanford, the charges involved "Bailley's alleged transgressions against four former girlfriends" rather than a "high-priced call girl ring." Bailley dated them, plied them with marijuana and wine, took compromising pictures and extorted them into prostitution. One of the victims, Astrid Leeflang, was blackmailed into having sex with a "train" of men at a party (who had all paid Bailley). Prosecutor John Rudy had no objection to Bailley's release, pending trial but in chambers, showed Judge Richey the sexually-perverted photographs and witness accounts of Bailley's behaviour ranging from "weird . . . to outright paranoia." Rudy asked Richey to consider ordering Bailley to undergo a medical examination at a local psychiatric hospital to determine if he was "competent to stand trial . . . [or] suffered some mental disease or defect." Richey remanded Bailley to the hospital as soon as a bed became available and placed a gag order on any public discussion of the case. Bailley continued to practice as an attorney until a bed became available in September but, as author Phil Stanford notes, "the one person who might be foolish enough to blow the whistle on the Columbia Plaza operation" had been silenced and discredited. Hougan argues that "concerns about the Bailley case" led to the second break-in the next day.[127]

CHAPTER 7

THE WATERGATE CAPER

Friday, June 16, 1972 was a bad day for Rolando Martinez. The day before, he had withdrawn what little money he had from his bank account. That morning, he attended court in Miami, where his second wife, Jean, was granted a divorce. The judge who heard their case died that evening. By now, he had a stepson in the Marines, a daughter, a son-in-law, a grandson and a new fiancée. After court, he drove to Miami airport, parked his car, and flew to Washington with the rest of Barker's team, equipped with surgical gloves and sixty rolls of film for more covert photography.[1]

About mid-afternoon, Peter Dailey, the head of the November Group office in New York, called McCord to report suspicious activity on their phone line. The November Group was Nixon's "personal advertising agency," a hand-picked team of advertising agency executives creating television and radio spots for his re-election campaign. Dailey reported that a secretary had her telephone conversation interrupted by a click on the other end of the line followed by "a tape recording . . . [of] an anti-Nixon and anti-war harangue." McCord and the telephone company thought the line was being "tapped" and there had been suspicious activity twice before, but neither McCord nor the telephone company could locate any device within the system.[2]

According to Jack Anderson, on an earlier visit to the November Group office in New York to "sweep their telephones for bugs," McCord "let slip that his next assignment was to bug [Larry] O'Brien's office." "We tap them, they tap us, it's routine," he said. One member of staff was a Democrat and "tipped off" former Kennedy advisor William Haddad. On March 23, Haddad wrote to Larry O'Brien, "warning of some very disturbing stories about GOP sophisticated surveillance techniques." He also alerted Anderson but the letter suggested the November Group was planning to bug O'Brien's office, "so [Anderson] missed the boat . . . [and] could not pin the story down." Anderson told Watergate investigators he "lost" the "packet of information" Haddad sent him and they never found the source of the "tip-off."[3]

Private investigator Arthur J. Woolston-Smith had also heard rumors in New York's intelligence community that "Gordon Liddy's November Group [sic]" were planning to bug the DNC and that "James McCord had bought a sophisticated scanner for monitoring bugs." On April 26, he met DNC Director of Communications John Stewart and Haddad, who had also heard from "intelligence sources" that "the Republicans were developing some kind of intelligence-gathering capability with the help of some anti-Castro Cubans," searching for proof the Democrats were taking money from Castro. Stewart recently claimed Woolston-Smith told him, "there was going to be a break-in, the Republicans were going to install listening devices, and wanted us to hire him . . . so he could monitor when the break-in happened, let them put the bug in, and then use the bug to feed false information . . . We never hired him because the whole thing seemed ridiculous at the time." But according to Woolston Smith, he kept up "a running commentary with Stewart by telephone" once or twice a week until the break-in, and in their last pre-Watergate call, they knew "something [was] about to happen."[4]

As Hougan notes, Woolston-Smith's secretary, Toni Shimon, was the daughter of Joseph Shimon, a "convicted wiretapper" who ran Allied Investigators Inc. with John Leon and employed Lou Russell part-time. According to Hougan, Russell was "freelancing as a tipster for Jack Anderson"—his job at GSS may have set him up as an "inside man" for McCord, "who may well have bragged to Leon and Shimon about the Republicans' plan to bug the Democrats." An acquaintance described Russell "as a Democrat extremely critical of Nixon."[5]

CIA Security Officer Ralph Orlando True visited McCord's office at CRP that day, just hours before the break-in, and later denied "any direct involvement in the incident." He claimed he met McCord because he was set to retire at the end of the month and "planned on assuming a position with McCord Associates or an affiliate security unit"—presumably CRP or the Institute for Protection and Safety Studies, which shared an office with McCord Associates.[6]

Harry Mahoney, a CIA operations officer in the Directorate of Plans, Western Hemisphere Division (WH/DDP) was also due to retire at the end of June and had been offered a position with McCord Associates. He was "a former polygraph examiner in the Office of Security" and knew Hunt, True, and McCord well. He had worked with Charles Anderson on mobile and photo surveillance of Soviet targets in Mexico City in the late fifties and Anderson subsequently coordinated phone taps and a mail intercept operation (LIFEAT) from the Latin American desk at headquarters. On May 10, 1972, McCord interviewed Mahoney at CRP offices but at the time of the break-in, Mahoney had "made no decision on taking the McCord offer."[7]

Late Friday afternoon, Barker's team arrived at National Airport in Washington and while Barker and Martinez picked up a rental car, Frank Sturgis ran into Jack Anderson in the lobby. They had known each other since the Bay of Pigs, when Anderson wrote a column about Sturgis. It was a strange coincidence, given Anderson already knew a break-in at the DNC was in the works.[8]

After finishing work at CRP, McCord arrived in room 723 around six-thirty that evening. He began preparing a "room bug" inside a smoke detector unit and sent Baldwin out to get some "speaker wire" and batteries. Later that evening, Hunt took the CIA disguise equipment down to the operations room in Room 214 of the Watergate and "the entry team helped themselves to whatever they wanted." Liddy, McCord, and Barker's team gathered for a final briefing on the two operations planned that night. Martinez was told "McGovern was receiving money from Cuba" and they were to search for documentary evidence. He would photograph documents at the DNC before another break-in would be attempted at McGovern headquarters. According to McCord, Hunt bought two typewriters that day. Their delivery to McGovern headquarters by two of his men at six the next morning would distract the guards while McCord installed "room bug devices" in the offices of Frank Mankiewicz—repeating the delivery man trick used for the Fielding entry.[9]

Before they left, Hunt took all the men's identification and put it in a briefcase in their room and gave each man two hundred dollars in cash to bribe their way out of trouble, if they got caught. He inexplicably told them to keep their room keys and gave Sturgis and McCord his own CIA-supplied identification for "Edward J. Hamilton" and "Edward J. Warren" respectively.[10]

Stephen Tingley Anderson had been working as a security officer for CRP under McCord's supervision and told the FBI about McCord's unusual behavior that evening:

McCord stayed at the CRP office much later than usual and instructed Anderson to get a key for each desk, file cabinet and office on the second floor of CRP (the Finance CRP floor). McCord told him the Finance CRP had some papers which they had ordered to be destroyed and the desks and

cabinets would have to be checked to verify this destruction. Anderson
assembled the keys and placed them on top of a file cabinet with written
instructions as to what was to be done with the keys.

Anderson was the twenty-seven-year-old son of Charles W. Anderson, a
Latin American specialist at the CIA who was stationed in Mexico from
1950 to 1958, and by the mid-sixties, was chief of political action against
Cuba. He was still employed by Western Hemisphere Division and would
have known Hunt well. His son Stephen had worked as a "summer employee"
at the Agency in the mid-sixties and met with an Office of Security representative before his FBI interview. Assisted by a CRP lawyer, he "furnished
negligible information" during the interview but called the interviewing
agents "late in the day" to confess what he knew.[11]

Just after nine o'clock, McCord left dinner with three of the Miami men
at the Watergate Hotel and said, "he was going to the Howard Johnson's,"
but CRP Security Officer Millicent "Penny" Gleason told the FBI that
"sometime between 9:30 and 10 p.m.," McCord came back to the CRP
office "to pick up his raincoat." His shirt sleeves were rolled up and he looked
unusually sloppy. As he left, he told her, "Penny, I want to thank you for
what you've done for our office." To Gleason, it felt "more like a 'goodbye'
than a 'thank you.'"[12]

Frank Sturgis had taped the doors during the first Watergate break-in but
this time McCord volunteered. He walked past the guard, took the elevator
to the Federal Reserve on the eighth floor and started taping the corridor
doors into the stairwell above and below DNC headquarters and three doors
providing access to the stairwell at the B-2 garage level. According to
Hougan, McCord stuffed the latches with "balled-up paper . . . [and] placed
strips of tape vertically along the edge of each door," covering the latches and
keeping the locks disengaged.[13]

McCord updated the command post and returned to the Howard Johnson, where he tested a "room bug" hidden in a smoke detector. At midnight, twenty-four-year-old security guard Frank Wills began his shift and the lights were still on in the DNC, as a summer intern stayed late to call his friends back home. McCord told Hunt they couldn't go in yet. At one o'clock, at the end of his first round of the building, Wills found masking tape over the latch on the edge of a door leading from the garage to the B-2 level, which prevented the door locking. He thought a building engineer had forgotten to remove it, so he took it off himself.[14]

Soon after, the lights went off in the DNC and the intern met Wills in the lobby and they went over to the Howard Johnson's restaurant for a late-night snack. McCord gave Baldwin his walkie-talkie and said: "I am going across the street, we have got some people over there, I want you to watch. If you see anything unusual, get on this unit and let us know."[15]

McCord met the rest of the team in room 214 and as they collected the equipment, Gonzalez (the locksmith) and Sturgis (his "lookout") proceeded to the garage door. As McCord recalls, "They returned with a stunned look on their face. The door was locked and the tape had been removed!" There was a sack of mail by the door, so McCord assumed it had been removed by the mailman, even though it was 2:00 a.m. Hunt and Barker wanted to abort the operation but McCord and Liddy were keen to continue and they went ahead.

Gonzalez picked the lock on the garage-level door and Sturgis let Barker and Martinez in. "McCord did not come in with us. He said he had to go someplace," Martinez later recalled. "We put tape on the doors for him and went upstairs." When McCord caught up a few minutes later, Martinez asked him if he had removed the tape and he said he did. As Gonzalez worked on the DNC door, Hunt and Liddy were monitoring the operation by walkie-talkie from room 214 in the Watergate Hotel and Baldwin was acting as a lookout at the Howard Johnson across the street. Barker's walkie-talkie had poor reception and was picking up static, so McCord eventually told him to turn it off.[16]

At 1:45 a.m., Frank Wills began his second round of the building. He soon found masking tape had been reapplied to the same basement level door and called the police. At 1:52 a.m., the police dispatcher issued a call to marked police cars in the area to respond to the Watergate. No one answered, so the dispatcher tried to locate a plainclothes tactical (TAC) unit in the area. Sergeant Paul Leeper and Officers John Barrett and Carl Shoffler were two minutes away and immediately responded in an unmarked car.[17]

Shoffler's regular hours were 4:00 p.m. to midnight but he worked overtime that night, a strange way to celebrate his twenty-seventh birthday. "We were experiencing a problem with office larceny and burglaries in the downtown area, and felt that working over may produce results," Shoffler testified. He had an interesting background, spending four years in the US Army Security Agency (part of the NSA), with "top secret crypto clearance," before joining the Metropolitan Police Department (MPD) in July 1969.[18]

Around this time, Gonzalez finally picked the lock to the DNC and the men gained entry. Barker turned on his walkie-talkie to tell Hunt. "Be advised that the guard is making his two o'clock rounds on the eighth floor," came the reply. Barker and Martinez got to work photographing documents as Gonzalez picked the lock on the glass door of Larry O'Brien's office.[19]

Shortly after two o'clock, from the balcony of room 723, Baldwin saw a guard (Frank Wills) standing in front of the Watergate complex, a car pull up, and three men enter the building. Wills led the officers down to the B-2 level and showed them the tape on the door and told them there had been burglaries recently on the sixth and eighth floors. They sent Wills back to the lobby and climbed the stairwell with Walter Hellams, a guard for the Federal Reserve Board on the eighth floor, where they also found tape on the

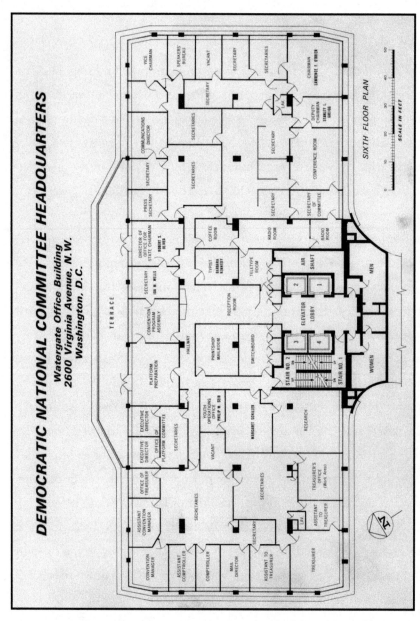

FIGURE 6: Chart showing layout of the DNC. Wells and Oliver offices adjoining terrace, O'Brien office bottom right (National Archives)

entry door. A search of the eighth floor found nothing, but curiously, none of Hellams' keys could open the offices. When Baldwin saw all eighth-floor lights go on, he informed Hunt by walkie-talkie. "That's the 2 o'clock guard check," came the reply. "Let us know if anything else happens."[20]

When the officers walked back down to the sixth-floor stairwell, they saw tape on the door and began searching the DNC offices. The door to the Platform Preparation room was propped open with a chair, which led them to believe they "might have surprised somebody and ran out on the balcony." As seen in Figure 6, Oliver's office was nearby and also led directly onto the terrace.[21]

Baldwin watched two casually-dressed men appear on the sixth-floor terrace of the DNC. One was wearing a cut-off army jacket and holding a pistol and flashlight. Baldwin didn't know Shoffler was a plainclothes cop. As Leeper searched the terrace, Shoffler "noticed a gentleman about our level" on the Howard Johnson balcony "observing us" and was worried he might call the police and "lights and sirens" would soon arrive.[22]

"Base 1, unit 1, are our people in suits or are they dressed casually?" Baldwin asked Hunt on his radio. "Our people are dressed in suits. Why?" "You have some trouble because there are some individuals out here who are dressed casually and have got their gun out," replied Baldwin. Liddy frantically tried to reach Barker but his radio was off.[23]

With guns drawn, the officers continued their search, turning on office lights and shouting, "Come Out! Police!" Officer Barrett walked past Oliver's office, turned right and found a door propped open. He stepped into a waiting room with a large column in the middle of it leading towards Larry O'Brien's office. There were secretarial cubicles, screened by frosted glass and wood partitions, along the right wall. A set of fluorescent lights were on in the far-right cubicle and he proceeded to that corner very cautiously, gun drawn. As he stopped by the end of the partition, he saw an arm move behind the frosted glass, inches from his face, and took cover behind a filing cabinet beside the column and yelled, "Hold it! Come out!"

"They have got us," whispered Barker into his walkie-talkie as the five intruders crouched down behind the partition slowly stood up with their hands raised. Hearing Barrett's shouts, Leeper and Shoffler ran to assist and the three officers ordered the men up against the wall for a pat-down. They were all wearing suits or sport coats, ties, and blue surgical gloves. Baldwin heard McCord say, "Are you gentlemen Metropolitan police?"[24]

According to Barrett's trial testimony, the burglars all had their hands up except Martinez, who was carrying a gym bag in his right hand and had a white trench coat draped over his left. At gunpoint, Barrett had to ask Martinez to drop the bag and then, the coat, several times. During the search, Martinez moved to reach inside his coat pocket and Shoffler wrested his arm away and discovered a notebook in the coat pocket with a key taped to the back. Shoffler testified that Martinez tried to hide the key from him and Martinez later admitted as much to Len Colodny and Robert Gettlin, the authors of *Silent Coup*. He also told them Hunt had given him the key. Ten days later, after trying numerous locks, the FBI discovered that key HL-311 fit the desk of Maxie Wells, suggesting whatever was inside her desk drawer was one of the targets of the break-in. What was inside the desk?[25]

Hunt soon appeared in room 723 as out on the balcony, Baldwin watched McCord and the burglars being led out of the Watergate building into waiting police cars. "Pack up all the equipment and get it the hell out of here," he said. "Take it to McCord's house." "Does this mean I'm not going to Miami?" Baldwin called after Hunt as he left.[26]

The final Senate Watergate Committee report concluded the second DNC break-in "was carried out with a sense of urgency by Liddy" but without the careful planning that went into the first "successful" break-in:

The burglars decided to proceed with the operation even though McCord found that the tape initially placed on the garage door leading to the stairwell had been removed making it necessary to pick the lock again. The risk of discovery was obvious to all the break-in team, yet, after hurried consultation with Liddy in the Watergate Hotel, the decision was made to continue. A second piece of tape was placed on the basement garage door, an action that was the burglars' undoing.[27]

McCord later blamed "a series of mistakes Liddy, Hunt, Barker, and I made" for the arrests. He admitted Liddy and Hunt should have aborted the operation when Barker told them the first tape on the door had been removed:

The second mistake was mine in not removing the ground floor tape, even though we had left three such tapes on that level in the first operation. The third mistake was Barker's in turning off the radio, while in the stairwell, which might have given us Baldwin's warnings that there were police in the building.

The fourth mistake was in Hunt's conveying a censored message that there was one guard making his two o'clock rounds, not four men [sic] with drawn guns, searching the floors above and below us, which Baldwin had reported.

Why the censored messages? I think it was Hunt and Liddy misreading what Baldwin saw. They could not see DNC from their view, Baldwin could. They were discounting what he saw and reported.

McCord didn't think there was a "double agent in the team" or that one of the men "had called the police to set us up." He later testified that he participated in the Watergate break-ins because he was told that Attorney General John Mitchell, and John Dean, counsel to the president, approved the plan.[28]

But as Lukas notes, McCord's blunders later led Hunt and Martinez to suggest "that the CIA's former head of physical security was either incompetent or a double agent." "I thought right away it was a set-up or something like that because it was so easy the first time," said Martinez.[29]

At the time of the arrests, burglary tools, a walkie-talkie, thirty-nine rolls of film, two Minolta cameras, three tear gas guns, three telephone tapping devices, and a portable receiver were found in the possession of the burglars. Two of the bugs were "operable for 150 yards;" the third unit had a faulty transmitter. None of them was set to the 118.9 frequency Baldwin was monitoring and no bugs were found on any of the telephones. The FBI speculated that the damaged bug may have been "taken off a phone" in the area where the men were arrested but McCord later denied doing "any work on the wiretaps" during the second break-in.[30]

Officer Barrett found a smoke detector with a device and wires inside it on the secretary's desk in the cubicle where the burglars were arrested. The MPD Mobile Crime Lab initially suspected "the men were planting a bomb" and the bomb squad was called but FBI agents soon identified the device as a room bug. When DNC deputy chairman Stan Greigg arrived, he noticed the glass door protecting his office and O'Brien's had been "jimmied" open. The FBI noted four ceiling tiles, a telephone jack and an air conditioning cover had been removed in the executive conference room next to Greigg's office, where strategy sessions were held, suggesting the room bug was being installed there. Carl Shoffler informed Greigg that screws had also been loosened on a telephone junction box in the conference room and gave the FBI case agent, Angelo Lano, the key taped to Martinez' yellow notebook. According to Lano, Shoffler told him Barker had tried to pass the key to Virgilio Gonzalez but Shoffler later insisted he took the key from Martinez. A page had been torn out of the notebook because an impression of what had been written on it was present on the first page—a room and telephone number for the Manger Hamilton hotel, where Martinez had stayed before the first break-in. Four documents seized from McCord had been taken from an unlocked file cabinet in Margaret Schiller's office, next to the rear door to the stairwell through which the burglars entered. Schiller handled college and press credentials applications for the convention.[31]

The burglars remained silent in custody. They refused to give their true names or call an attorney and the police officer in charge quickly realized "he had a political espionage team" on his hands. Two of the men were carrying their room keys, which led investigators directly to room 214 at the Watergate Hotel, the "command post" for the operation.[32]

Lou Russell told the FBI he had dinner at the Howard Johnson's restaurant across from the Watergate Hotel from eight thirty to ten thirty that evening and did not see McCord. They had dinner together the previous evening but claimed they didn't discuss the break-in and, when shown photographs, Russell picked out Hunt and Baldwin as men "he thinks he has seen . . . before but he cannot remember where." According to Hougan, after leaving the Howard Johnson, Russell drove to his daughter's home in Benedict, Maryland, forty-five minutes away. Just after midnight, Russell told his daughter he had to drive back to Washington to do "some work for McCord." Hougan believes Russell's presence near the Watergate that night accounts for some of McCord's unexplained delays and absences, and frames Russell as a possible saboteur who "was familiar with GSS methods and personnel."[33]

At three o'clock on Saturday morning, Hunt called Mullen Company attorney Douglas Caddy from his Mullen office and asked Caddy to represent him and the arrested men. He called Barker's house before signing out of the Mullen offices at three-thirty and driving over to Caddy's house. They recruited criminal lawyer Joseph Rafferty, who visited the five arrested men in the D.C. jail with Caddy that morning. Like the other burglars, Martinez had never met them before and he never paid them, but assumed things were being "taken care of."[34]

At four that morning, Baldwin put the radio receiver in McCord's panel truck and drove it to McCord's home. Mrs. McCord drove him back into Washington before he drove home to Connecticut.[35]

At 8:20 a.m., Gordon Liddy arrived at CRP offices and "asked to use the paper shredder." He proceeded to shred "the logs containing the data obtained from the wiretap." "My boys got caught last night," he told Hugh Sloan, the committee treasurer. "I made a mistake by using someone from here [McCord], which I told them I would never do. I will probably lose my job."[36]

Mitchell and Magruder had flown to Los Angeles the day before. At 11:30 that morning, Liddy reached Magruder and told him his Security Chief had been arrested at DNC headquarters. "You used McCord? Why, Gordon? Why?" cried Magruder, knowing McCord directly linked the burglary to CRP and the White House.

"That's incredible!" Mitchell exclaimed when he heard the news. They quickly dispatched Liddy to find Attorney General Kleindienst and secure McCord's release. An "agitated" Liddy found Kleindienst at his golf club. He told Kleindienst he had run the break-in as an intelligence operation for CRP and that Mitchell had sent him to secure the five men's release. Kleindienst couldn't believe his ears and "exploded":

What happens to the President if I try a fool thing like that? It's the God-damnedest thing I heard of! What the fuck did you people think you were doing in there? John Mitchell knows me well enough to call me himself if he has anything like that to say to me. Tell them I can't do it—won't do it. For the President's sake, I'm going to handle this one just like any other case.[37]

When police searched room 214 that afternoon, they found more electronic equipment, blue surgical gloves, and $4,200 in $100 bills—whose serials later matched the money Barker had laundered for Liddy. Barker and

Martinez had been staying in the room and the search located both of their address books. Barker's had a disguised listing for "HH"—Howard Hunt. The first number was prefaced with the initials "WH" [White House], under which was Hunt's home number and address at 11120 River Road, Potomac, MD; and the name, address and number of the Robert R. Mullen & Co, 1700 Pennsylvania Avenue. Martinez listed the same telephone numbers next to "Howard Hunt (W-House)," noting Hunt's Mullen office as Suite 770. Martinez later explained he worked in the same office as Barker, so he had copied all the numbers from Barker's book. In a dresser drawer, investigators also found a check written by Hunt and a statement in his name from Lakewood Country Club.[38]

Among the papers found in Martinez' briefcase was "a letter he was attempting to write requesting that he be permitted to remove himself from the activities which eventually led to his arrest. . . ." His probation officers interpreted this as a sign that age was catching up with him and he was "not as willing to take the risks that he did formerly . . . [now that] he had settled into a role of respectability as a real estate salesman." They concluded his role was "primarily that of a soldier under the command of Barker . . . [working] in the interest of Cuba":

> *[Martinez] lost all of his family's holdings when Cuba was nationalized and probably continues to have the dream of someday returning to again take over the hotel and factory . . . In Miami, he is listed as a registered Democrat, therefore, American politics . . . was not likely to have been a motivating influence.*[39]

Probation officer Frank Saunders later told Hougan "the Cubans were duped. They were told an assassination team was waiting in Spain, and that it would be sent to kill Castro if and when they broke into the [DNC]."[40]

• • •

In March 1972, McCord had contacted Gary Bittenbender in the Intelligence Division of MPD to establish a liaison with CRP regarding anti-war and anti-Nixon demonstrations. They had lunch in early April and met again in early June to discuss a prospective CRP employee who "had previously been arrested for assault with a deadly weapon." McCord gave Bittenbender a tour of headquarters, showing him "a close-circuit television operation used for security," receivers, anti-eavesdropping devices and radio scanners. He also invited Bittenbender to speak to CRP members of staff about security, "particularly involving demonstrations."

On June 17, Bittenbender was investigating the break-in when he saw McCord being processed following his arrest. That afternoon, he spoke to McCord in the cell block. McCord apologized and allegedly said the suspects arrested with him were "all former CIA men" and that the burglary was a "CIA operation." McCord would later vehemently deny this, accusing Bittenbender of either perjury or an "honest misunderstanding." McCord asked Bittenbender to notify his wife and tell her he was okay, but Bittenbender felt this would be improper and went over to CRP to ask Penny Gleason, a security officer there, to do it instead. Gleason had known McCord since taking his industrial security class at Montgomery College and "was extremely upset" and told Bittenbender "she looked to McCord as being her father."[41]

During the day, Mrs. McCord called, on the verge of tears, and asked Gleason to remove McCord's "personal pictures and plaques from the walls of the security office." Among them was a photograph showing CIA Director Helms presenting an award to McCord, with the inscription, "With deep appreciation, Dick Helms."[42]

According to "CIA cable traffic shortly after the Watergate break-in . . . Michael Mastrovito of the Secret Service . . . agreed to downplay McCord's Agency employment . . . was being pressured for information by a Democratic state chairman . . . [and] was advised by the CIA that the Agency was concerned with McCord's emotional stability prior to his retirement."[43]

By late afternoon, McCord and Hunt's identities and positions at CRP and as a White House consultant were known. FBI agents visited Hunt's home that evening, but he wouldn't talk without a lawyer.[44]

There is some controversy regarding when Richard Helms first learned of the Watergate arrests and the involvement of Hunt in the break-in. As the arrested men all used aliases, "initial name checks requested of the Agency by the Secret Service and others revealed no traces in Agency records." Helms testified that he first learned of the burglary and the arrests "through press or media coverage." According to CIA records, he was not officially informed until ten o'clock that evening, when Director of Security Howard Osborn called with "the true names of the five arrested individuals" and told him that "James McCord had in his possession a check from E. Howard Hunt."[45]

Special Agent Arnold Parham, at the Alexandria field office in Virginia, was the FBI liaison to the Agency and normally dealt with Osborn's office. He was first alerted to the break-in by a call from the Washington field office, asking him to call the CIA to request name traces on the arrested men. It was a Saturday, so Parham called the Agency's after-hours number and was called back by a duty officer around eight o'clock. According to CIA records, Osborn called Parham at nine forty five that evening and telephoned Helms fifteen minutes later.[46]

In his autobiography, Helms devotes the first chapter, "A Smoking Gun," to Watergate and "the telephone call that set in motion the events that would eventually end my intelligence career." He was preparing for bed when Osborn called to inform him that five men had been arrested at the Watergate building.

"Four Cubans and Jim McCord," said Osborn.

"McCord? Retired out of your shop?" replied Helms.

"Two years ago," replied Osborn. Helms recalled McCord "as a serious, straitlaced staff security and counter-audio specialist . . . [who] had retired with a good record." He told Osborn to get "the operations people" in Washington and Miami to do record checks on the Cubans to see if they had any Agency connection.

"Howard Hunt also seems to be involved in some way," added Osborn. Helms took a "deep breath."

"What in hell were they doing in the Democratic Party offices?" he asked.

"As of now, it looks as if they might have been trying to tap the phones and bug the place," said Osborn.

"Is there any indication that we could be involved in this?"

"None whatsoever," replied Osborn.[47]

Helms called Acting FBI director L. Patrick Gray—"I filled him in as much as I could and assured him that, despite the background of the apparent perpetrators, CIA had nothing to do with the break-in." He suggested Gray look at McCord and Hunt's ties to John Ehrlichman and their employment at the White House and CRP.[48]

Reflecting on Hunt's sensitive security appointment at the White House, Helms writes, "It struck me as peculiar that no one there had called to verify with me or the Agency his career and reputation." Helms admits Hunt was given "operational gear" and blames his deputy, General Cushman, for failing to ask what it was for and neglecting to inform him until Hunt's demands escalated and further assistance was cut off, with his approval, in late August 1971. "After almost a year of silence, we thought we had heard the last of Hunt," he writes, a model of misdirection and deceit.

• • •

In June 2014, the CIA released 208 pages to historian Luke Nichter concerning "Eugenio R. Martinez and the Watergate break-in of June 17, 1972, and his subsequent termination from the CIA." The release included a transcript of the "first call" between "Mr. O" [Osborn] and an FBI agent named "John."

At one point, Osborn says, "we're going to talk to Arnie Parham, who is our liaison over here with Jack's shop and we're going to give him what we have on McCord and Hunt . . . Mr. Helms, my Director, called Acting Director Gray in California, and Director Gray filled him in on what he knew and they're hand in hand on this." This places the call after Helms and Osborn spoke, between ten o'clock and midnight on June 17. "Jack" was probably John "Jack" McDermott, the special agent in charge at the Alexandria office.[49]

When Baker's staff reviewed this transcript while preparing to question Helms in August 1973, they were confused, as they were "aware of inquiries in both Miami and Washington much earlier . . . that day and [were] puzzled at Helms' ostensible lack of notice." The Secret Service representative at the Democratic convention hall in Miami heard about the break-in from the DNC and reported it to the FBI by three o'clock. He also notified the CIA's Miami chief of station Jake Esterline, who seems to have known seven hours before Helms.[50]

The second FBI teletype about the break-in was sent after ten o'clock that evening and is consistent with the Osborn call, noting the Alexandria office would immediately contact the Agency to determine if any of the men arrested "are actively employed by CIA."[51]

At 11:52 that evening, Alexandria confirmed Hunt and McCord's Agency employment but "CIA security checks [were] negative re Fred Frank Fiorini, Eugenio R. Martinez and Virgilio R. Gonzales, including their AKAs."[52]

It's very strange that the CIA claimed they had no record of Martinez. According to his case officer Robert Ritchie, on Sunday morning, Miami station chief Jake Esterline sent a cable to headquarters "regarding the activities of Martinez but deliberately omitting Martinez' prior reference to Hunt's activities."[53]

The Office of Security taped two calls between Osborn and "John"; and the MPD and the Office of Security Senior Duty Officer on the weekend of the break-in. Transcripts were given to Senator Baker's staff in March 1974 but they were denied access to the tapes.[54]

On Saturday night, Security Officer Penny Gleason was so upset, she was unable to sleep. At eight on Sunday morning, McCord's deputy security chief, Robert Houston, arrived at CRP, having read about McCord's arrest in the paper. He began removing McCord's files and tapes from the security office. She wasn't sure if he burned them or took them to McCord Associates. Houston admitted to removing some blank cassette tapes and personnel files to work on at home but denied the other allegations. He had just retired from the Army after twenty-eight years as a military policeman when McCord hired him, and terminated the FBI interview and asked not to be contacted again.[55]

On Sunday, John Leon suggested Carmine Bellino—a former Kennedy aide who would soon become chief investigator for the Senate Watergate Committee—call Lou Russell to find out more about the break-in. We don't know what they discussed but in August, Bellino's "close friend and longtime stockbroker," William Birely, moved Russell into a top-floor apartment in the Twin Towers complex in Silver Springs, Maryland, where Russell began living with "Cathy Dieter" and shortly thereafter got a job at McGovern headquarters. On the day of the break-in, DNC Communications Director John Stewart tried to reach Arthur J. Woolston-Smith, and when they spoke two days later, Stewart was "elated . . . that we had more or less called it the way it happened." They met at Bill Haddad's New York office the next day but Woolston-Smith had no further information. It's intriguing that Stewart's office was one of those targeted by the burglars.[56]

Following the break-in, Baldwin made no attempt "to conceal his activity," making several calls from his hotel room, including one to his attorney, Robert Mirto, in Connecticut. By Sunday, Baldwin was back in New Haven, meeting with his attorneys, Mirto and John Cassidento, who Baldwin later described as a "loyal Democrat" and "a close friend of former DNC Chairman John Bailey."[57]

On Monday, the FBI traced McCord and the others to the Howard Johnson motel room and traced Baldwin by his telephone calls. They also learned he was a former special agent. Later in the week, just after CRP attorney Paul O'Brien told Baldwin's lawyers their client "must not talk about what he knew," Baldwin recalled a curious conversation with Cassidento.[58]

"I've been in touch with very specific individuals on the Democratic side who are aware of what's happened," Cassidento said, "they are aware that you're a key player and that you have information. There's potentially a lawsuit by the Democrats and if it goes forward, you will be a main witness." According to Spencer Oliver, Cassidento called Connecticut state chairman John Bailley who told Senator Ted Kennedy (D—Massachusetts) and DNC chairman Larry O'Brien. Bailey was probably the state chairman who had contacted the Secret Service. In later years, Baldwin told the *Washington Post* he didn't object at the time to what seems a clear breach of legal ethics. On Tuesday, Larry O'Brien filed a $1 million civil action against CRP—whose head of security, James McCord, was one of those arrested—and told a press conference, "there is a clear line of direction to [CRP] and a developing clear line to the White House."[59]

On Monday morning, after visiting his safe in the Executive Office Building, Hunt stopped by Colson's office, where he left a message with Colson's secretary: "That safe of mine upstairs is loaded." The safe was drilled open and its contents were stored in two boxes for inspection by John Dean and associate counsel Fred Fielding the next day. Dean took a walk with Liddy that morning and debriefed him on what had gone wrong. Liddy apologized for using McCord—who directly linked the burglars to CRP—blaming Magruder for cutting his budget. Liddy said the Cubans that Hunt had recruited in Miami were "good soldiers" who would not talk. Two of them had been used in an earlier "national security" operation at the office of Daniel Ellsberg's psychiatrist in California. Jack Caulfield and Bud Krogh had already told Dean about the Ellsberg break-in several months earlier. Liddy told Dean the bungled operation was his fault and he accepted full responsibility: "If someone wants to shoot me, just tell me what corner to stand on and I'll be there, okay?" "I don't think we've gotten *there* yet," stammered Dean.[60]

The same morning, Carl Shoffler returned to the DNC to show FBI agents where the burglars had been arrested. He brought them to Maxie Wells' desk and described a camera clamp he had found set up there—presumably to photograph documents. The key found on Martinez had not yet been matched to Wells' desk drawer but when Wells overheard the discussion, she gave "a shocked look" and said something like, "My God, they haven't gone in there." According to Shoffler, Spencer Oliver was standing behind her and was "more calm" but "looked at her in a very stern way," saying, "Well, there's nothing in there of any importance anyway." "I can't tell you what she was covering up . . . [but] it was my impression, as a police officer, that I had been lied to," said Shoffler. Wells would later insist the only reason she kept the drawer locked at night was because summer interns working the phone banks in the evenings had pilfered a stapler, a pair of scissors and a jar of hand lotion from the drawer.[61]

Also on Monday morning, Martinez told attorney Douglas Caddy he "was worried about the papers in [his] car," some of which were "sensitive" and related to his "activities" and "the operation." According to a declassified CIA document, Martinez' wife or daughter "frantically" contacted a "Miami station maritime asset" (soon to be terminated) "requesting immediate assistance in getting Mr. Martinez' car out of the airport parking garage since it contained deeply compromising material which had to be removed before the FBI got to it."[62]

On Monday, the asset informed station chief Jake Esterline, who warned him not to get involved. Esterline claims he notified the Miami Field Office and CIA headquarters, who notified FBI headquarters. The asset gave Esterline a description of the car and its location but "a faulty description prevented immediate location of the car" and the FBI finally "found and impounded" it later that day. As noted in the Baker report, there are troubling discrepancies between this account and the FBI chronology, which as discussed shortly, places the call from the Agency and the search of the car two days later. Baker's staff never received a "satisfactory explanation . . . [for the] time lag and an accounting of Agency actions during the interim."[63]

At Helms' morning meeting at CIA headquarters, he noted the Watergate arrests and told senior staff McCord or Hunt "may be implicated." They should respond to press enquiries by stating "they are former employees who retired in August and April 1970 respectively." Osborn was to handle enquiries from government agencies and the Agency's only investigative role would be to respond to FBI requests for name traces.[64]

Helms asked senior officers if they knew of any Agency involvement and none did. Helms instructed them to quickly establish "rock-solid proof that despite its previous relations with the burglars, the Agency had nothing to do with the break-in." "Keep cool," he told them, "do not get lured into any speculation, don't volunteer any information, and just stay the hell away from the whole damned mess." In his memoir, he admits "Hunt's bizarre involvement was a major embarrassment" but aside from the Watergate chapter, he gives Hunt only the briefest mention.[65]

Also on Monday morning, Martinez' case officer Robert Ritchie was summoned to CIA headquarters from Miami:

> *His orders were that he was not to come by commercial airline but to drive his own car along the Interstate. He was not to stop, except to eat and purchase gas; and . . . when he did either, he was to telephone CIA headquarters to report upon his exact whereabouts.*[66]

As Hougan notes, the Agency wanted to debrief Ritchie quickly without leaving a paper trail of his trip. On arrival at Langley, Ritchie "had immediate and extensive briefings concerning his Martinez contacts, primarily by Colby and Osborn."[67]

Later that day, Helms wrote to all staff, directing "all inquiries from the FBI or others regarding Watergate" . . . [to] the Director's office." Colby also instructed all staff "to forward all information about Watergate . . . to the Director's office." Arnold Parham received an "initial written response" from the Agency that day, showing "only prior CIA association" with the Watergate burglars. They were still not admitting Martinez was on a retainer at the time of his arrest.[68]

Also on Monday, following Colby's instructions, Karl Wagner, General Cushman's executive assistant, "went directly into Helms' office and presented him with all his memoranda on the Hunt/TSD affair." Richard Krueger, deputy chief of TSD, "gave all notes and materials in his possession to Colby, including copies of the Hunt photographs." Wagner told Baker's staff that he first became aware of the content of the photographs "when [Chief of TSD Sidney] Gottlieb delivered Xerox copies to Colby in Wagner's presence at a time when all were trying to monitor post-Watergate activity . . ."[69]

2

From this, we can deduce that two days after the Watergate arrests, Helms, Colby, Gottlieb, Wagner, and Krueger had all seen the Xerox copies of the surveillance photographs taken by Hunt of Fielding's office building, and the photo enlargement identifying Dr. Fielding by name.

The same day, Ted Shackley, chief of the Western Hemisphere Division (C/WH), sent Jake Esterline guidelines on how to deal with the "great deal of publicity" generated by "the case of Sturgis, Martinez and Barker":

The case is a domestic political issue and we should stay out of it . . . we should not dig into the matter, for we have no jurisdiction to do so. On the other hand, we must be cooperative with those agencies that are charged by law with the responsibility of investigating the case.

All "legitimate requests for traces" were to be referred to the Director of Security in Washington:

If, in the normal pursuit of our operational tasks, we do find information that impacts on the case, please put it together and forward it to me personally in the electrical channel or courier it up to me by hand. . . .

Shackley prohibited off-the-record briefings to the press, so as "not to prejudice either the investigations or the arrested individuals' rights." Damage assessments were underway to check "what could be revealed about past activities . . . if in court the defense goes on a fishing expedition with the witnesses." He asked Esterline to do the same:

The Martinez case makes it mandatory that we get a better handle on what people are doing with their time. This is obviously a management and a motivational problem.[70]

We note the hypocrisy of this last statement, given Meyer and Shackley's admonishments to Esterline in April.

When Robert Bennett arrived at work on Monday morning, he went straight to Hunt's office and asked what was going on.

"I don't want to talk about it," replied Hunt. "Everything is under control. Everything will be taken care of. Those people will say nothing. There will be no damage done to the campaign. I just don't want to talk about it."

After a busy morning, Bennett rode down in the elevator with Hunt at lunchtime. "I have to get my glasses fixed," said Hunt. "The optometrist is out in Rockville [where McCord's office was]. I will be gone a long time and may not get back to the office."

When Bennett got back from lunch, two FBI agents were waiting in his office and wanted to speak to Hunt. Bennett told them he had gone to get his glasses fixed, so they left their details and a message for Hunt to call them.[71]

To Bennett's surprise, Hunt did come back that afternoon. He called him into his office and told him the FBI were looking for him. "I don't need to talk to them, I have spoken to counsel," Hunt replied, agitated. "They have nothing on me. I was nowhere near that place that night."

"At the time, I had no reason to disbelieve him," Bennett recalled. Hunt seemed to know a lot about the situation but he could have overheard conversations at the White House:

He told me that the purpose of the team was to photograph documents. He said that this was not the first time they had been in the Democratic National Committee . . . [and] they were so titillated by what the team had found the first time, they had sent them back for more.

Hunt repeated that he was "nowhere near that place" and left Bennett's office, but Bennett still felt Hunt was involved.[72]

By strange coincidence, James Everett, a CIA deep-cover officer assigned to the Mullen office in Amsterdam, was recalled to Washington and arrived in the capital on June 17, the day of the break-in. On Monday afternoon, Everett met Hunt for the first time at the Mullen office. By Everett's account, "Hunt met him like a long-lost brother, based on his own earlier CIA employment. Now they were both vice presidents of the same company."[73]

The Mullen office on Pennsylvania Avenue was right across the street from CRP headquarters. "They must be uneasy over there," said Everett, referring to "the stupidity of what had been done in view of the overwhelming strength of the President." Hunt didn't respond. A half-hour later, "there was a phone call, indicating the police had a lead." "My God, no!" said Hunt, and left. Hunt passed Everett on the street later that afternoon "but Hunt didn't even see him, he was so preoccupied . . . Everett never saw him again."[74]

The phone call above sounds remarkably like the call Bob Woodward made to Hunt that afternoon. In the early hours of Monday morning, Woodward's *Washington Post* colleague Carl Bernstein had been shown the address books of Barker and Martinez by a police source, and told about the signed check from Hunt found in room 214.[75]

Woodward called the White House that afternoon and confirmed Hunt was a consultant working for Colson. Colson's secretary told him Hunt wasn't there but gave him the number for Mullen and Company. When Hunt answered the phone, Woodward identified himself and asked him "why his name and phone number were in the address books of two of the men arrested at the Watergate." "Good God!" exclaimed Hunt. He refused further comment and hung up.[76]

Deputy director of White House communications, Ken Clawson—a former *Washington Post* reporter—checked on Hunt and told Woodward he "had worked as a White House consultant on declassification of the Pentagon Papers and, more recently, on a narcotics intelligence project. Hunt had last been paid as a consultant on March 29 . . . and had not done any work for the White House since."[77]

Woodward called Bennett, who said, "I guess it's no secret that Howard was with the CIA." It was news to Woodward.[78]

Late in the day, Hunt called Bennett into his office on the interoffice intercom and was "very, very nervous." "The White House wants me to get out of the country until all of this blows over," he said in a low voice, so the secretaries wouldn't hear. "John Dean will be in touch with you with some money for my wife. Will you please see that she gets it? I have to go. I am in a terrible hurry." Hunt left and Bennett assumed the money was back pay for his consultancy work. When Bennett went back to his office, Liddy called with a message for Hunt "to stay where he is until he gets further instructions." After consulting his wife Dorothy, who was on vacation in London, Hunt flew to Los Angeles and stayed with his attorney friend, Morton Jackson. He was soon joined by Liddy.[79]

Close to midnight, Jeb Magruder arrived home with the Gemstone file containing Baldwin's logs of the DNC intercept. The file "was about four or five inches thick, about half photographs and half transcripts of telephone conversations." He sat cross-legged by the fireplace and on the instructions of John Mitchell, tossed the papers into the fire, "chuckling . . . at the graphic details of the social lives of [DNC staff]."[80]

On Tuesday morning, "White House Consultant Tied to Suspect in Bugging Case" was a front-page story in the *Washington Post*. At Helms' morning meeting, Howard Osborn "highlighted developments over the past twenty-four hours with respect to the McCord/Hunt, et al., situation" and anticipated enquiries about former contract agent Bernard Barker. Helms maintained that, having acknowledged McCord and Hunt as former Agency employees, "we know nothing more about the case" and all future enquiries were to be referred to the FBI. He later disavowed Barker, saying he was "cut off" in the mid-sixties when "we found out he was involved in certain gambling and criminal elements and we didn't like the cut of his jib."[81]

At a staff meeting later that morning, Deputy Director of Support Jack Coffey told his team "the Agency has said all it intends to say on this subject and desires that there be no chitchat with friends and former employees about it . . . Any internal enquiries should be forwarded to Mr. Osborn. Oz would be interested in knowing of any present or former employees who might have been working with [one name redacted—probably Hunt]."[82]

Helms appeared in executive session before the Senate Foreign Relations Committee that day. "Do you want to volunteer any information on Mr. Jim McCord?" asked Senator Percy (R—Illinois). "Yes, I will volunteer anything you would like," replied Helms. "I would just like to distance myself from my alumnus . . . I can't conceive of what that caper was all about, I really can't conceive it."[83]

As the FBI began to investigate McCord, they discovered the bewildering network of current and retired Agency employees who had been offered employment with McCord Associates in the months before the operation. In a series of status reports in the weeks after the break-in, the CIA's Office of Security summarized its involvement in "protecting Agency equities arising from the 'Watergate Incident.'" Director of Security Howard Osborn kept a running inventory of all known current and former Agency staff employees, CIA connections and cover organizations subject to the FBI investigation.[84]

When Senator Wallace Foster Bennett (R—Utah) saw Hunt's name in the newspapers, he called his son Robert to ask what was going on. They met at his father's office and Robert told him everything he knew. By now, Bennett

Jr. was firmly convinced that Hunt and the White House were involved in the break-in, his "public statements to the contrary notwithstanding," but "we both agreed I had absolutely no proof of any of this." His father advised him to "suspend [Hunt] immediately until he gives a satisfactory explanation."

"Did you consider going to the FBI?" Congressman Lucien Nedzi later asked Bennett during the Nedzi hearings. "Yes," replied Bennett, "but I did not have anything to say to the FBI."

"Are you kidding?" replied Nedzi.

"Now, I realize that I did," said Bennett, "but at the time I did not feel that I did . . . I could not, at the time, put the pieces together in such a way as they added up to anything."

Bennett did consult a lawyer. "Do I have a responsibility to come forward?" he asked. "I am convinced that Howard is guilty. I am convinced that the White House is lying. I am convinced that there is an involvement here far, far deeper than anything that anybody is saying." After telling him the whole story, his lawyer told him it was hearsay evidence and he "could tear [him] to shreds under cross-examination." He followed his lawyer's advice to "cooperate fully with the prosecutor as they proceed to investigate this case."

Although Hunt never confessed anything to him and "pretended total innocence," Bennett felt "he was involved and probably guilty." The White House issued denials but he told friends in the administration what he knew and they were "absolutely shocked." "Somebody is misleading the President," he thought. "As a good Republican, I don't like this."[85]

On Tuesday morning, Jake Esterline finally sent a translated copy of Martinez' Spanish report to headquarters. In later testimony, he said he was "confounded as to why he was not told to terminate the Martinez relationship if the CIA headquarters suspected the involvement of Hunt in political activities." In later years, Esterline said Martinez' report and the case reports "disappeared" from his files and he didn't notice "until the case officer handling him [Gonzalez], who was a nice little fellow, but he wasn't the brightest man in the world, left":

I never saw him again. He was long gone someplace else. I think he left the Agency shortly after that . . . I was absolutely astounded, dumbfounded, when that whole [Watergate] thing broke and I realized that this poor guy Rolando Martinez had gotten himself into such a mess. He was a real good boat captain.[86]

Later in the day, when the FBI interviewed Martinez' estranged wife Jean, she refused to discuss the reason for their divorce but agreed to answer yes or no if the agent could identify the person involved. When the agent said "Howard," she laughed and asked why it wasn't a woman's name.[87]

The Agency sent the FBI separate memorandums on Frank Sturgis and the three Cubans on Tuesday. Though never recruited by the Agency, Sturgis was described as a soldier of fortune who had been associated with Martinez since the early sixties. Barker had worked for the Agency from 1960–66 while Martinez was recruited in 1961 and had been on a $100 a month retainer since 1969. Osborn's memo on Martinez notes "he was last met on 6 June 1972 and has been unable to be contacted since 14 June . . ." Begging the question, why were they trying to contact him?[88]

A few days after the break-in, journalist Carl Rowan attended a screening party at the MPAA and sat beside Helms and his wife, Cynthia:

The pre-film conversation turned to Watergate. "This Watergate thing is so ridiculous that if you wrote it as fiction the publisher would laugh you out of his office," Cynthia said. Helms laughed.[89]

On Tuesday afternoon, using transparent rubber gloves to avoid fingerprints, John Dean and Fred Fielding went through the contents of Hunt's safe in Dean's office, "item by item . . . like archeologists." The haul included a Colt automatic revolver, a black attaché case containing tear gas and microphones belonging to McCord, a "bogus" cable implicating the Kennedy administration "in the fall of the Diem regime in Vietnam," a file on Daniel Ellsberg including the CIA psychological profiles, and Hunt's operational notebooks. Dean claims Ehrlichman subsequently told him "to shred the documents and 'deep six' the briefcase."

"What do you mean by 'deep six'?" asked Dean.

"You drive across the river on your way home at night—don't you?" replied Ehrlichman. "When you cross over the bridge on your way home, just toss the briefcase into the river." Put on the spot, Dean pointed out that Ehrlichman crossed the river on his way home, too, and offered to bring the materials over.

"No, thank you," said Ehrlichman and Dean went back to his office.[90]

On Wednesday, the FBI tried to interview the burglars but they all refused to talk about the case. When asked why he was at the DNC that night, Martinez replied, "That's the $64,000 question, isn't it?" The same day, Ted Shackley sent a still-classified cable to Esterline, ordering the termination of Martinez, "effective 17 June 1972." A later Agency memo claims Martinez was "terminated in absentia on 17 June 1972 . . . as a result of his involvement in the Watergate break-in" but the four-day delay before Martinez was cut off is intriguing.[91]

That morning, after an unexplained two-day delay, a "deep cover" CIA officer called FBI agent Robert Wilson in Miami and told him a confidential source had reported that Martinez' car was at the airport. He gave Wilson a description of the car and added that "associates of Martinez" believed the car contained "incriminating documents and a gun . . . [and] were considering removing the car from the airport." Wilson later told Baker's staff "it was highly unusual for the CIA to voluntarily furnish the FBI with a lead of this kind." FBI agents located Martinez' Dodge Dart two-door sedan at the airport and noted "it was locked and showed no sign of previous entry." A notebook "bearing Spanish writing" was visible through the windscreen and when they obtained a warrant to search it that evening, the items included a heavy-duty knife, a matchbook from the Watergate Hotel, a Royal portable typewriter, a Marquette Page-a-Day calendar notebook, and a notebook containing various names and telephone numbers.[92]

As Hougan notes, the second notebook with Spanish writing and various names and numbers was allegedly Martinez' "operational diary." The FBI's Miami office finally sent it to Washington in September 1973, at the request of the Special Prosecutor, but it has never publicly surfaced. The parking inventory ticket beneath the windshield wiper was also dated June 17, the day after Martinez flew to Washington.[93]

According to a declassified CIA document, the car contained "a number of old documents relating to maritime operations in the early 1960's and a notebook, copies of which were made available to the Miami station by the FBI." Esterline confirmed that Martinez, "who was well known to the FBI to have been a CIA employee, was no longer an active employee but was maintained as an informant." He advised that there might be one or two emergency contact numbers for the Miami station in Martinez' notebook and assured them "the Station had been totally unaware of Mr. Martinez' secret relations with Mr. Hunt."[94]

Howard Liebengood, assistant minority counsel to Senator Baker on the Senate Watergate Committee, would later suggest the possibility that "Martinez told Caddy or some other CIA contact about this immediately after arrest and that they might have lifted the diary from the trunk before the FBI got to it."[95]

On Wednesday morning, John Ehrlichman called Acting FBI Director Pat Gray and asked him to call John Dean, who he had assigned to "handle" Watergate. The next day, Gray called Helms and said, "I think we've run right into the middle of a CIA operation."

"Why?" asked Helms.

"Well, because of the characters involved and the amount of money involved."[96]

The FBI had traced the serial numbers of the $6,500 in new $100 bills found on the burglars back to the five checks made out to Manuel Ogarrio and Kenneth Dahlberg deposited in Barker's bank account. The four Ogarrio checks drawn on an account in Mexico City raised suspicions.[97]

Helms assured Gray there was no Agency involvement in the break-in; that "none of the suspects . . . had worked for the Agency in the last two years"; and that his investigation into checks drawn on a Mexico City bank in the name of Manuel Ogarrio and deposited into the account of Barker Associates "was [not] touching any covert projects of the Agency, current or ongoing."[98]

When later asked about the call during televised hearings by the Senate Watergate Committee, Helms indulged in a classic piece of showmanship for the cameras:

I assured Mr. Gray that the CIA had no involvement in the break-in. No involvement whatever. And it was my preoccupation consistently from then to this time to make this point and to be sure that everybody understood that. It doesn't seem to get across very well for some reason but the Agency had nothing to do with the Watergate break-in. I hope all the newsmen in the room hear me clearly now.[99]

Despite Helms' assurances, Gray told Dean he was still concerned about CIA involvement and asked for guidance. Haldeman discussed Gray's request with the president, who ordered Haldeman to meet with Helms, his deputy, General Walters, and Ehrlichman "to find out whether the CIA was involved in Watergate" and whether the Agency was concerned about "possible exposure of past CIA or other national security activities of the ex-CIA people involved," including the Bay of Pigs operation.[100]

Haldeman briefed Nixon before the meeting on Friday morning and their "smoking gun" conversation described what Senator Baker later called "a plan to conspire to limit the original prosecutor's investigation of the Watergate to those already arrested." Haldeman said the FBI had already traced where the money came from (Mexico) "and it goes in some directions we don't want it to go." Haldeman, Mitchell, and Dean had decided that "the only way to solve this" was to play up the Cuban angle and have General Walters call FBI Acting Director Gray to stop the banking investigation in Mexico. Nixon advised them to say "the President believes it is going to open up the whole Bay of Pigs thing again . . . this fellow Hunt, he knows too damn much . . . If it gets out that this Cuba thing is all involved, it would be a fiasco. It would make the CIA look bad . . . Hunt look bad and it is likely to blow the whole Bay of Pigs thing." Haldeman said he'd proceed on that basis.

Later on Friday, Helms assured Haldeman the Agency was not involved and had "no concerns over exposing the Bay of Pigs or other covert operations." Helms claimed General Walters was asked to go see Gray "and talk to him about halting the FBI investigation in Mexico because it might run into CIA operations," even though Helms "had stated there were no such problems." Helms thought it "very odd" that Walters, his deputy and a presidential appointee, was asked to go and see Gray on such a serious matter, instead of him.[101]

Later that day, Walters met Gray and contradicted Helms by telling him that the FBI investigation in Mexico "could trespass upon some of our covert projects and . . . [as] the five men involved were under arrest, it would be best to taper the matter off there." Gray didn't know about the White House meeting earlier in the day and thought Walters was only speaking for the CIA. When Gray found out almost a year later, he couldn't understand why Helms and Walters agreed to send Walters to him with a message they knew to be false. On returning to the Agency that afternoon, Helms was told the investigation in Mexico "would not compromise any CIA clandestine assets" but he didn't tell Gray. Over the next two weeks, Dean contacted Gray twenty-five times, continuing to push CIA involvement while putting "tremendous pressure" on Gray to "frustrate the FBI investigation" into Mexican money laundering, insisting "there may be a conflict with CIA sources."[102]

On the Wednesday following the break-in, McCord called Baldwin in Connecticut and advised him to "say that he worked for McCord Associates, rather than CRP . . . use a CRP lawyer, not a lawyer of his own choosing . . . [and] plead the fifth amendment to questions." McCord promised money for attorney fees. When CRP attorney Paul O'Brien subsequently met Baldwin and his attorney, Robert Mirto, in Connecticut, it was clear to both men that O'Brien was just interested in the facts and "was not trying to be helpful."[103]

A couple of days later, Baldwin ran into CRP attorney Kenneth Parkinson, while at the US Attorney's office with Kenneth O'Grady, a lawyer O'Brien had recommended. According to Baldwin, Parkinson and O'Grady advised him to plead the fifth. In the last week of June, McCord called Baldwin again and told him "there was no money available in CRP" and that he "was in financial straits and would have to mortgage his home to pay his bills in connection with the case."[104]

On Thursday, there was a fire at McCord's home. Three days earlier, Mrs. McCord had received a bomb threat from a caller in Houston, Texas and told her imprisoned husband. Concerned that the papers in his office might catch fire if a bomb went off, McCord instructed his wife "to burn every piece of paper in his study."

CIA informant Lee Pennington later testified that when he visited the McCord home that day, he found Mrs. McCord throwing "books, magazines, files, photographs" into the living room fireplace with a couple called the Sweanys, and he joined in. The "Pennington incident" suggested McCord, Pennington, and their former secretaries had conspired to destroy evidence. Mrs. McCord had forgotten to open the flue, so the house "suffered considerable smoke damage and three rooms had to be repainted."[105]

Word of the incident—"considered fragmentary at the time"—spread back to Paul Gaynor on the Security Research Staff at Langley, who reported it to Howard Osborn and mentioned it to his colleague Edward Sayle. Sayle also discussed it with "Security Officer No. 1," an officer from the Personnel Security Division who had been assigned to assist Leo Dunn with the Office of Security's Watergate investigation.

"Is the name Pennington familiar to you?" Sayle asked.

"No," he replied.

"Pennington is a very, very sensitive source of the Office of Security. He is a person the director knows about, that Paul Gaynor knows about. He assisted the Office of Security after the Watergate incident." Sayle didn't say "what assistance had been provided" but said "Mr. Gaynor was aware of the incident" and had informed Osborn.[106]

At a CIA staff meeting a week after the break-in, an "old hand" suggested highlighting what a "tradecraft mess" the operation was, to rebut press allegations that the Agency was involved:

> The entry team had no cover for being in the building and no cover story for resisting interrogation. Their clothing hadn't been sanitized [Hunt's check and White House telephone number were soon found] . . . They all knew one another's true name, and . . . where everybody else worked. What's more, McCord actually went along with the entry team—it's unbelievable.

"No intelligence service worth the name would run an operation like that," agreed a colleague. In his memoir, Helms described the right way to run the operation:

> In the real world, a team undertaking an operation like this would have been recruited by a cutout—"Mr. Lopez"—who would say he was fronting for some well-heeled émigrés who wanted proof that the Democrats were taking money from Castro. It would have been a cash-and-carry event— all cash and no checks. None of the team would have anything to reveal but a sterile telephone number and a physical description of Señor Lopez, who would have vanished the moment the gong rang.[107]

The following Monday (June 26), Dean called Walters to the White House and continued to probe possible CIA involvement in Watergate. Dean said the FBI was investigating three theories: that either CRP, CIA, or "some other group" were responsible for the bugging. Walters reiterated that the Agency was not involved, "that none of the suspects had been on the Agency payroll for the last two years" and that the Agency had no objection to the FBI investigation in Mexico. According to the Nedzi report, Dean also "made the astonishing request that CIA provide bail money and salary for the CIA suspects using covert funds." Some of the arrested men were getting scared and "wobbling," said Dean. Walters said providing bail money and salaries was "out of the question" and the accused "could not implicate the Agency."[108]

As *Washington Post* reporter Walter Pincus notes, the same day, DNC attorney Edward Bennett Williams asked the judge handling the civil case "to hasten 'discovery,' the questioning under oath of potential witnesses." Williams told the judge he believed DNC headquarters had been under electronic surveillance "over a period of days and weeks" before June 17. As Pincus points out, "at the time, only the burglars and the Nixon campaign intelligence operation knew this information. It would be weeks before the FBI learned the same details." Baldwin's attorney John Cassidento was using him to keep the Democrats ahead of the game.[109]

On Wednesday, Dean met Walters again and "pressed [him] for ideas." Walters noted the "strong Cuban flavor" of the affair, suggesting Cuban anxiety to know future policy toward Castro provided a "plausible motive for attempting this amateurish job which any skilled technician would deplore." Dean "agreed that this was the best tack to take but it might cost half a million dollars"—presumably, to pay off the burglars. Walters felt Dean was "exploring the option" of blaming CIA for the operation and "covering something up." The same day, Assistant Attorney General Henry Petersen called the FBI's Charlie Bates to advise that:

> *A friend of his formerly with NSA . . . advanced the theory that Al Wong, a Secret Service official, directed "this whole thing" using Ralph True who had some CIA connections. Petersen advised it was probably one of many rumors around town but he passed it on for information.*

Bates sent a memo to Felt, advising that Ralph True "disclaimed any involvement in the case." Wong was in charge of the White House taping system and a former colleague told Jim Hougan that during Nixon's first term, "McCord was 'lending' CIA technicians to Wong to handle assignments at the White House." McCord later praised Wong as one of the heroes of Watergate.[110]

Also on Wednesday morning, Helms briefed Ted Shackley and Lawrence Sternfield (chief of the Cuban Operations Group) ahead of their planned meeting with Patrick Gray that afternoon and later summarized it in a memo to General Walters:

> I informed [them] that the Agency is attempting to "distance itself" from this investigation and that I wanted them along as "reference files" to participate in the conversation when requested. I told them that I wanted no free-wheeling . . . hypothesis or . . . conjecture about responsibility or likely objectives of the Watergate intrusion. In short, at such a meeting, it is up to the FBI to lay some cards on the table. Otherwise, we are unable to be of help. In addition, we still adhere to the request that they confine themselves to the personalities already arrested or directly under suspicion and that they desist from expanding this investigation into other areas which may well, eventually, run afoul of our operations.[111]

According to the Nedzi report, "in a cryptic call to Mr. Gray," Ehrlichman ordered him to cancel the meeting because "there is no reason at all to hold [it]." When Gray phoned Helms later that morning to cancel, Helms asked him not to interview Karl Wagner and John Caswell—two Agency employees whose names were found in Hunt's phone book. "They're active CIA agents," said Helms, "their names have to be kept secret." The Agency would conduct their own interviews with the men and share with the Bureau. It turned out Caswell had already been interviewed but Gray cancelled the planned interview with Wagner, whose knowledge of CIA support for Hunt was the key to unravelling the Fielding break-in.[112]

As Ray Locker notes: "Helms' misdirection enabled the CIA's role in the Pentagon Papers case to go undiscovered for 11 months amid a growing political scandal that would eventually force President Richard Nixon from office and lead to an extensive investigation into abuses by the CIA and other parts of the U.S. Intelligence community." Gray later accused Helms of "obstruction of justice."[113]

Meanwhile, the Agency ran damage assessments on "information the two former CIA employees, Bernard Barker and Eugenio Martinez, could reveal about their association with the Agency . . . [and] Frank Sturgis (Fiorini) could reveal as the result of his association with person(s) connected with the Agency."[114]

After ordering Gray to cancel his meeting with Helms, Ehrlichman met Gray with John Dean on Wednesday afternoon. Rather than "deep sixing" the material in Hunt's safe, Dean had persuaded Ehrlichman to turn it over to the FBI, except for two envelopes of "politically sensitive" material to be given directly to Gray. Dean also kept Hunt's notebooks to himself. They told Gray the documents in the envelopes were not related to Watergate but "should they leak out they would be political dynamite in an election year and thus should never be made public." The implication Gray took from the meeting was that he should destroy the material, which he did in the fireplace of his Connecticut home in December.[115]

As discussed in Chapter 4, according to Hunt, his detailed plan for the Fielding break-in "and the originals of the pictures he and Liddy had taken of Dr. Fielding's office" had been placed in his safe at the White House. When the FBI received the contents of Hunt's safe from Dean, "the memo and pictures were not there." It would have been crazy to give them to Gray, so presumably Dean retained them along with the Hunt notebooks. He already knew about the Fielding break-in and as the man in charge of the cover-up, now held key evidence for both the Fielding and Watergate operations. He would also prevail on Gray and Petersen to allow him to see raw FBI reports and interview summaries, tracking the progress of the case in real time—and sit in on interviews with White House staff. As FBI case agent Angelo Lano would later note, this helped Dean stay one step ahead of them during their initial investigation. "Making sure that the FBI did not surprise us was a key to protecting the White House," Dean later wrote. When the FBI requested an interview with the Plumbers' secretary,

Kathleen Chenow, Dean flew her back from vacation in England and told her "not to testify about 'national security' matters, like the Ellsberg break-in."[116]

The pressure of Dean's new role overseeing the cover-up took its toll on his personal life. He broke off his relationship with Maureen Biner and she flew home to California, just as John Rudy was serving subpoenas on witnesses to appear before the grand jury in the Bailley case.[117]

On Friday morning, June 30, Richard Helms gave his annual "State of the Agency" address to staff. To general laughter, he noted that "the latest notoriety that we've had, I suppose, is in connection with the Watergate caper":

> The other night, I was out at dinner and a lady and gentleman walked in, the gentleman being one of the senior officers in this Agency. His wife came up to me and said, "You know, the only thing about that Watergate caper I didn't like, was that it looked to me as though those people that have been identified with the Agency were a bunch of bumblers." And I said, "well, I couldn't agree with you more. It rather pained me, too, the impression it left. But let me just say something to you, that if we, as an organization, want to enter some building, or some apartment, we don't use your husband."

To loud laughter and applause, he continued, "There aren't many of you that I would entrust the job of entering some closed building. I don't think you'd know how to do it. And if you had picked up a little bit of information in one of the training courses about it, then I would certainly not let you do it . . . On the theory that a little knowledge is a dangerous thing":

> Obviously, in the Agency, we have those who know how to do these things. That's why you don't hear about them. In any event, to put your minds at rest, whatever was behind that caper—and I frankly don't know, so I'm not

holding out on you . . . Whatever the purpose of it was, for whatever reason
they went into the Watergate apartment of the Democratic National Com-
mittee. These individuals did indeed have Agency relationships but they've
not had them for some time. I don't know what's behind it, I don't know
who put up the money, I don't really know anything about it but I want to
put your mind at rest, the Agency had nothing whatever to do with it.[118]

The same day, Martinez was released on bail after his friends raised the bond
money and sent it to his attorney through his daughter.[119]

After his arrest, Martinez described his role in the operation "as an operative . . . [with] extreme trust in his superiors, particularly Barker, whom he
had known for more than 20 years and . . . Hunt who was known to him as
'Eduardo,' the commander of the Bay of Pigs Invasion." He believed it was
"an officially sanctioned government operation" and his task was to photograph documents:

> *The team was told to look for foreign contributors and possibly subversive*
> *contributions to the McGovern campaign, as the word had been given that*
> *the McGovern campaign as well as Senator Kennedy's campaign were*
> *financed by Communist organizations and by Castro himself.*

His defense lawyer "advised him to plead guilty, as he had been caught in the
act and there was no possible defense." He also felt bound not to reveal "any
of his instructions as this might cause the disclosure of classified information. He had always been told that, if arrested during a secret CIA operation,
the government would intervene to help him."[120]

By early July, Acting FBI Director Pat Gray had had enough of Dean's
"harassment" and insisted that the CIA confirm the Mexican investigation

would present a conflict before delaying it any longer. On July 6, he met Walters, who agreed to a memorandum confirming the Agency "had no interest in Ogarrio or Dahlberg" (whose names were on the checks deposited in Barker's account) and said he "wasn't going to let those kids [meaning Dean and colleagues] kick him around anymore." Gray called the president to confirm "there was no CIA objection to a full FBI investigation of the Mexican aspects of the Watergate case."

"Dick Walters and I feel that people on your staff are trying to mortally wound you by using the FBI and the CIA and by confusing the question of CIA interest in [Ogarrio and Dahlberg] . . . that the FBI wishes to interview," he said.

"Pat, you continue to conduct your thorough and aggressive investigation," the president replied.

According to Walters, Gray told Nixon "the case could not be covered up" and "the President should get rid of the people involved" but Gray denied this. His subsequent investigation of the Ogarrio checks uncovered the financing for the break-in, tying CRP to the operation.[121]

The Watergate controversy threatened to expose the CIA's long-standing relationship with the Mullen Company and posed immediate danger to the deep-cover officers in the two Mullen offices overseas. While Robert Bennett "denied the arrangement to the press," he shared what he knew with prosecutor Earl Silbert and explained the Agency cover arrangement. Silbert agreed "there was no purpose in exposing [it as it] had no bearing whatsoever on the Watergate break-in."[122]

A few days later, on July 10, Bennett met his case officer, Martin Lukoskie, in a cafeteria and briefed him on what he knew about the Watergate incident for the first time. Lukoskie's handwritten report of the meeting was "carried to Director Helms on or before July 14 . . . because of the sensitivity of the information":

Bennett said that when E. Howard Hunt was connected with the incident, reporters from the Washington Post *[among others] . . . tried to establish a "Seven Days in May" scenario with the Agency attempting to establish control over both the Republican and Democratic parties so as to be able to take over the country. Mr. Bennett said he was able to convince them that was nonsense. He asked them why they should want to ruin himself, his Company and other innocent persons because the Company has innocently hired Hunt following his retirement from CIA.*

Mr. Bennett said that the mission of the "Watergate Five" was to rejuvenate the bugging apparatus in the Democratic National Headquarters in the Watergate. Hunt had told Bennett that "THEY" had obtained such "great stuff" from the bug before it failed to function that McCord et al were instructed to install new batteries, mikes, et cetera, to make it work again. Hunt never identified "THEY" to Bennett who suspected that the order might have originated with Colson on a "I don't want to know about it, get it done" basis, or the money came from a "RIGHTIST" group, Caddy being "far, far right" and Hunt also "conservative and to the right."[123]

Two weeks later, Lukoskie convinced Robert Mullen to terminate Alfred Hochberg and close the Singapore office through an "agreed upon scenario" which included a "falsified Watergate publicity crisis." The real reason for Hochberg's withdrawal was a "WH flap" which "threatened to compromise Western Hemisphere operations" and which the CIA was loathe to share with Mullen.[124]

Hochberg was a CIA action officer stationed in Mullen's Singapore office. According to author Peter Levenda, who later worked with him, he was "debriefing Chinese defectors and running agents against . . . China." One day in August 1972, the office closed and Hochberg simply "vanished."

Under the cover of Watergate, he was "withdrawn for his safety" and moved to Manila.[125]

Given the timeframe, Phillip Agee later told Howard Liebengood he was "convinced that he was the 'WH flap'":

> *The Watergate occurred at the height of the Agency's efforts to stop [Agee] from publishing his book. He was meeting daily with Agency personnel in Paris and recalls telling them after Watergate that he noted that Howard Hunt was working with the Mullen Company, which he knew to be a CIA front organization which he had put in Mexico City himself. The Agency was most agitated about this. . . .*[126]

CIA documents confirm that the reference to a "Western Hemisphere flap, related to the Agee case" and according to David Corn, Ted Shackley was brought back from Vietnam in the Spring of 1972 to deal with the Agee problem as chief of the Western Hemisphere Division.[127]

James Everett had befriended Agee as a classmate on the CIA Career Training Program in the late fifties. Mullen opened an office in Stockholm in 1962 "staffed by two CIA men—James Everett and Jack Kindschi—who pretended to be working on a study for General Foods, one of Mullen's earliest clients, while they were actually debriefing Soviet and Chinese defectors." Everett was assigned to the LPGLOBE division, a CIA "proprietary" providing administrative support for "deep cover" operations officers abroad, using CCS cover. After a senior KGB official defected in 1967, the office was closed and Kindschi moved to Mexico and Everett set up shop in Amsterdam. Agee was reassigned to Mexico the same year "under Olympic cover" and became Kindschi's case officer. When Agee shared the manuscript for his *CIA Diary* with the Cubans, it blew Kindschi's cover and the Mullen office in Mexico was closed.[128]

Senator Baker's staff later confirmed that "Bennett was supplying information to the CIA about many aspects of the Watergate incident and . . .

serving as liaison between Hunt and Liddy," without disclosing these facts to the FBI.[129]

About a month after the Watergate break-in, Robert Oliver invited Bennett to his office "to compare notes on why Spencer Oliver Jr.'s telephone was bugged" with Oliver and his son. The Olivers suspected "the Hunt/ Mullen relationship was involved" and Spencer Oliver admitted "personally compromising information" had been obtained by the bug. When Bennett discussed the meeting with Robert Mullen, Mullen told him "that Spencer Oliver Jr. was a full-time CIA employee."[130]

On July 28, General Walters met Patrick Gray and disclosed that the Agency had given Hunt a tape recorder as well as "false documents and disguise[s] for himself and an associate." Walters told Gray the roll of film developed for Hunt showed "some unidentifiable place, possibly Rand Corporation. We had had no contact whatsoever with Mr. Hunt subsequent to 31 August, 1971."[131]

The following May, Helms' replacement as CIA director, James Schlesinger, admitted that Walters had been seriously "misinformed" and there had been additional contacts after that date "but they were all associated with the preparation of the Ellsberg profile." This statement wasn't true either. A later Watergate history compiled by the Inspector General's office notes several contacts "which seemingly have no relation to the Ellsberg profiles or the Watergate affair."[132]

In October 1971, after being cut off by Cushman, Hunt obtained unclassified material about a leak of French government documents from John Hart, chief of the European Division, where Hunt was once chief of Covert Action. John Caswell "received and filled Hunt's request" for the French documents and they were delivered to his office at the White House. As discussed, after Watergate, Helms tried to block an FBI interview with Caswell.[133]

In December 1971, Hunt requested a name trace on a Costa Rican through Elizabeth McIntosh, a "close personal friend" in the Agency's East

Asia Division he had known since his OSS days in China. Bill Broe, chief of the Western Hemisphere division, "agreed to service the request" but put it back in the proper White House channel by forwarding the report to Peter Jessup, the senior Agency officer with NSC staff at the White House. Jessup wrote a memo to Deputy National Security Advisor, General Haig, to alert him that Hunt had tried to go around him to trace foreign nationals.[134]

Hunt also requested various name traces on Latin Americans through Jessup during this period. Jessup forwarded the request to the Directorate of Plans, recommending "someone best check with Tom Karamessines as Hunt was no longer an Agency employee." Jessup didn't know what Hunt was doing or what the secret name trace material would be used for, and "was concerned that Hunt might make [it] available to outsiders."[135]

According to the Agency's draft Watergate history, Walters' remarks to Gray on July 28 were actually prepared by William Colby, and Colby later to wrote to Assistant Attorney General Henry Petersen, explaining that "the speculative identification of the building as Rand Corporation was his, based on "the Agency's understanding" that the White House investigation of Ellsberg "could have focused on Rand property and activities."[136]

Yet, as discussed above, two days after the second Watergate break-in, Helms, Colby, Gottlieb, Wagner, and Krueger had all seen the Xerox copies of the surveillance photographs taken by Hunt of Fielding's office building, and the photo enlargement identifying Dr. Fielding by name. Helms later claimed this was the first time "senior officers in the Agency" had seen the pictures:

At that time, even though Dr. Fielding's name was discernible on a wall that was photographed, no one in the Agency who had seen the pictures had identified Dr. Fielding or was aware that his office had been broken into.

Even in the latter part of 1972, when Mr. William Colby took copies of the photographs to the Department of Justice, neither he nor I knew why Hunt had taken them.[137]

Helms' lack of curiosity on this point is completely implausible. A telephone call to Dr. Malloy would have instantly identified who Dr. Fielding was and his relationship to Ellsberg and, by that point, he knew of Martinez' association with Hunt around the time the photographs were taken. He would sit on the photographs for six months until the Justice Department started asking about them.

CHAPTER 8

THE COVER-UP

In the late afternoon of July 5, Alfred Baldwin agreed to cooperate with prosecutors to avoid an indictment. Earlier in the day, CRP attorney Paul O'Brien had "disavowed" him. Although Baldwin worked for CRP, he was employed by McCord Associates, so there would be no money or help forthcoming from O'Brien. Baker's staff later noted "O'Brien conduct re: Baldwin is incredible"—he made no attempt to stop Baldwin from telling prosecutors what he knew. O'Brien knew Baldwin could tie Hunt and Liddy into the break-in, but nobody higher up the chain. O'Brien had worked for the CIA in the early fifties, and after meeting the defendants' attorneys on June 24, he told co-counsel Robert Mardian "he thought the CIA was involved in the Watergate break-in . . . [and] would stake his life on it." Mardian testified O'Brien was still "in the employ of the CIA" but the Agency denied it. As we shall see, O'Brien's law firm, Hanson, O'Brien, Birney, and Stickle, had close ties to the CIA.[1]

Baldwin confessed to the FBI and prosecutors that he had monitored telephone calls to Spencer Oliver's phone in DNC headquarters and that "there had been a tap on Oliver's phone, which as far as he knew, they had missed." Curiously, the FBI don't seem to have gone back to Oliver's office to check this until September. Baldwin told them he worked for McCord but had contact with Hunt and Liddy, "who were in the immediate vicinity of the break-in" but had escaped.[2]

In his first FBI interview on July 5, Baldwin said "the taps were on at least three lines, because whenever Oliver would talk on one line, a second call would come in. Oliver would tell the first person to hold and switch to the second. Baldwin said he would also pick up that conversation. The third conversation was mainly by the secretary [Maxie Wells] to Oliver. He said he received the transmissions on about 118 megacycles [on his receiver]."[3]

In a second interview five days later, Baldwin went into more detail. He recalled monitoring the first conversation between Mr. and Mrs. Oliver on either Thursday or Saturday evening (May 25 or 27). When McCord tuned the receiver to 118.9 megacycles, he picked up Oliver's phone but when McCord turned a second receiver to 135 megacycles, hoping to pick up the second bug, he only picked up a radio station. "We'll have to move to a higher level," McCord said. But as Jim Hougan points out, there's an obvious problem with Baldwin's dates here. Even if the monitoring started on Saturday night, the break-in didn't happen until late Sunday evening. Had McCord gone in before the break-in team?

It's also curious that Baldwin didn't mention the first break-in during either of his FBI interviews. In his next detailed interview with DNC attorney Alan Galbraith in late August, Baldwin's "best recollection" was that when he arrived back in Room 419 on Thursday evening, McCord told him bugs had already been installed "on two phones across the way . . . in the 'Chairman's office and the office of his first assistant.'" On October 3, Baldwin gave separate but consistent interviews to two Los Angeles Times reporters and two DNC attorneys. On Thursday evening, McCord told him he was "going to put some units across the street." Baldwin watched McCord turn on the light in Oliver's office, come to the window, wave at him, pull the drapery shut and turn off the light. He monitored the first conversation the next day. The FBI soon discovered Baldwin had picked up his car from a garage in New Haven at ten minutes past nine on Thursday evening and didn't return to Washington until Friday afternoon, so this was reflected in his trial testimony three months later. But by now, the story had changed.

Baldwin recalled seeing McCord draw the blinds in Oliver's office at sunset one evening, a day or two after he had started monitoring Oliver's phone. McCord told him he was going across the street because "there was trouble with his shielded unit"—he still couldn't pick up the second bug on O'Brien's phone. This again suggests an earlier break-in by McCord, but nobody picked up on the discrepancy during the trial.

On Monday afternoon, May 29, Baldwin and McCord moved to room 723, hoping to get better reception. Baldwin told the FBI that after a couple of days listening, he identified Spencer Oliver as the head of the American Young Political Leaders Conference, a tax-exempt organisation. Oliver spoke to John Richardson at the State Department about its exchange programs and asked his father, an "influential lobbyist," to lobby Congress for more funding, but knew if his potentially illegal efforts to solicit funds were discovered by Congress, "the shit would hit the fan." As executive director of the Association of State Democratic Chairmen, Oliver was supposed to remain impartial but he was secretly "attempting to pull delegates away from [Senator] McGovern in favour of former North Carolina governor Terry Sanford." According to Baldwin, "all political conversations monitored were related to the policy of getting rid of McGovern" and the Sanford Committee paid for Oliver's trip to Texas for the state's Democratic convention. Oliver was worried DNC Treasurer Bob Strauss would find out about his "back-door politics." Oliver left Washington on June 8 and was not due to return from Texas until Tuesday, June 13. Baldwin told the FBI he also monitored calls from Oliver's secretary, Maxie, Bob Allen, Barbara Kennedy (another secretary) and "that many of these conversations had to do with extramarital affairs." McCord subsequently prepared background material on Oliver and briefed Baldwin.[4]

After interviewing Baldwin with the FBI, Earl Silbert wrote in his diary: "The principal target of conversation really was girls and this was Baldwin's interest . . . Here he was . . . sitting ten to twelve hours a day monitoring a phone, had no social life of his own and [it was] just driving him crazy having to listen to these conversations. But he listened to every single one and remembered every one of them virtually in detail." Before and during the trial, Baldwin told lead prosecutors Earl Silbert and Seymour Glanzer that "McCord knew a lot and should be granted immunity," but they insisted "McCord had nothing to give and that they were not interested in making any deals . . . the case did not go any higher than Hunt and Liddy."[5]

In developing his defense, McCord wrote a note to his attorney on July 21, citing "self-defense as Security Coordinator" as his prime reason for the break-in. He claimed he had "used non-deadly force to obtain evidence of DNC and others in conspiracy with violence-oriented groups to commit violence and battery against" the Republican National Committee and CRP, the two organizations he was employed to protect. He argued "the obtaining of such hard evidence was only possible by methods used."

He sketched in the background to his mission and responsibilities as security coordinator: the "history of prior political espionage against GOP"; "volunteer penetration"; "threats to kill the Mitchells [and] bomb threats against the Committee"; Baldwin's intelligence-gathering "among violence-oriented groups during May demonstrations in Washington . . . [and] their links to Democratic leadership"; and evidence that the Democrats were funding such groups to subvert the Republican Convention in August through violent demonstrations and using forged credentials to access and blow up the communications center at the Miami convention.

McCord also pointed to the bugging of the November Group office in New York on June 16 "by elements believed associated with the Democratic Party." He wanted Democratic leaders to be questioned under oath "about this and other activities in political espionage against the GOP this year."[6]

McCord explained to his lawyer, Gerald Alch, that he believed there was "a direct relationship between these potentially violent antiwar groups and the Democratic Party and that his participation in the Watergate burglary

was [motivated] in the hope of obtaining advance evidence of planned potentially violent demonstrations." Alch explained that this best fit "the legal
defense of duress, wherein the perpetrator felt compelled to break a law in
order to prevent a greater evil" and they agreed that this was "the only defense
available" and prepared the case on this basis.[7]

A week later, McCord sent a letter to Helms. The envelope was marked "Personal" in McCord's handwriting and postmarked July 30, with no return
address and the cover note:

> *From time to time I'll send along things you may be interested in from an*
> *info standpoint. This is a copy of a letter that went to my lawyer.*

The letter noted that "when Paul O'Brien was engaged by [CRP] as their
lawyer in this case, the Committee told him that the operation was a CIA
operation." When "one of the defendants" later told O'Brien "the facts, [he]
says he blew up over it." McCord noted that "leaks this week by the prosecution and/or the FBI to the *New York Times* still are trying to infer that this
was a CIA operation":

> *Now that the CIA story has not held water, or more correctly, will not be*
> *allowed to stand by CIA, the prosecution is now planning to charge that Liddy*
> *"stole the money for the operation from the Committee and in turn bribed*
> *McCord and Hunt to participate, giving McCord a $16,000 bribe on one*
> *occasion witnessed by a participant [Baldwin] who has turned state's*
> *evidence."*

> *Rest assured that I will not be a patsy to this latest ploy. They will have to*
> *dream up a better one than this latest story . . . Liddy may sit still for this;*
> *I will not.*

McCord didn't feel he could get a fair trial in Washington due to "prejudicial press coverage [and] the high percentage of registered Democratic voters [and government employees] from whom the jury would be picked."[8]

On August 2 or 3, the director's office routed the envelope to Howard Osborn "as a routine piece of 'crank mail'":

> *The envelope contained a carbon copy of a typewritten letter signed "Jim" with the name in the salutary address excised—"Dear _____". After dismissing the letter as a piece of crank mail, I had second thoughts and recognized the handwriting on the envelope and the signature "Jim" on the latter as being similar to that of McCord, who formerly worked for me as a security officer before his retirement from the Agency.*[9]

The draft CIA Watergate History mistakenly states this letter "was signed only with the initial "J" . . . Osborn thought he recognized the initial and guessed that the writer might be James McCord." After discussing the letter with Helms and Houston, "it was decided that Osborn would hold the letter in a secure file in his office and not turn it over to the FBI as he had initially suggested."[10]

The reference to CRP lawyer Paul O'Brien in McCord's letter is interesting. On August 2, 1972, the chief of the Central Cover Staff (CCS) informed Helms, via Karamessines, that "Mr. Arthur Briggs Hanson, head of the law firm, Hanson, O'Brien, Birney and Stickle of Washington, D.C., has cut short his vacation plans and returned to Washington to assist in the defense of E. Howard Hunt in the Watergate 5 case." The next three lines are redacted but notes from Baker's staff confirm that Hanson was "active in the Agency [and] runs cover for overseas agent, a project with which O'Brien is familiar." The firm's overseas office provided cover "for a CIA operation in Europe," involving an attorney "who is in fact a CIA man."[11]

The memo continued: "CCS has no information that Howard Hunt knows of Mr. Hanson's [redacted]." In other words, CIA was trying to set Hunt up with an Agency lawyer without his knowledge. It didn't work and he retained William Bittman, a former assistant US attorney in Bobby Kennedy's Justice Department, who had successfully prosecuted Teamsters president Jimmy Hoffa for stealing from the Teamsters pension fund.[12]

In late August, in a letter to his attorney Gerald Alch, McCord noted a petition filed by Daniel Ellsberg's attorneys to disclose a government wiretap on the Chilean embassy in Washington, which had intercepted conversations with Ellsberg's attorney Leonard Boudin: "Petitioners are making a pitch of course for government dismissal of the case, rather than disclose the Chilean Embassy foreign wiretap."[13]

McCord saw three ways the "wiretap defense" could be applied to his own case. He believed the telephone lines of the Chilean embassy were being tapped by the government on national security grounds and his young Chilean employee, Rigoberto Ruiz, had called the Chilean military attaché's residence from his office phone the previous spring. Ruiz had also received calls on McCord's phone from his family in Chile at night. After his arrest, McCord was also convinced that the Attorney General had authorized wiretaps on his home and office phones on "domestic security grounds" and continued to suspect they were tapped until the end of the year.[14]

One name conspicuously missing from the CIA's internal Watergate history and the "Family Jewels" is Lee R. Pennington, Jr. His name would probably have remained buried in Office of Security files, were it not for the courage and integrity of two whistleblowing CIA security officers who refused to suppress it. As serving Agency employees, they were identified as "Security Officer No.1" and "Security Officer No. 2" in the Nedzi report but now, their identities can be revealed for the first time as Frederick N. Evans (No.1) and Lawrence J. Howe (No. 2).[15]

Evans and Howe worked in the Personnel Security Division under Deputy Director of Security Steven L. Kuhn and Assistant Deputy Director Hollis Whitaker. There were two other Office of Security divisions—Physical and Technical Security; and Investigations, which included the Security Research Staff, headed by Paul Gaynor, who oversaw Edward Sayle and Louis Vasaly (see Office of Security organizational chart, Figure 7).[16]

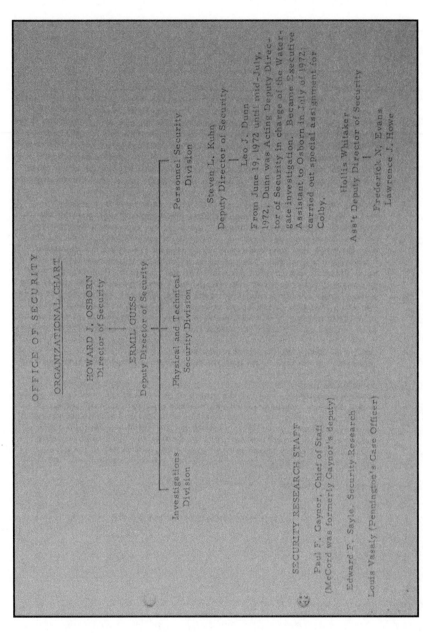

FIGURE 7: CIA Office of Security organizational chart (Library of Congress)

Lee Pennington retired from the FBI in 1953 and became the director of the American Legion's National Americanism Commission. His extensive personal library and the files of the commission became a valuable tool to intelligence agencies in checking subversives. Informants within the Communist Party were feeding him information, which he would channel to the Internal Security Subcommittee of the House Committee on Un-American Activities and other government agencies. James McCord was the first CIA officer to visit the American Legion headquarters to research the files and they soon became friends. Pennington's secretary, Donald Sweany, was married to Lucille Sweany, McCord's former secretary in the Security Research Staff.[17]

By 1972, Pennington was being paid $250 a month as a CIA consultant. His case officer was Louis Vasaly of Gaynor's Security Research Staff and Pennington was the only paid source of information in Gaynor's office. McCord had initially recruited Pennington while Gaynor's deputy. During "the late summer and fall of 1972," Gaynor prepared "about half a dozen" memoranda "relating information Pennington would relay to us." He confirmed these were kept "in the Pennington file, pertaining to McCord."[18]

On August 18, Special Agent Parham, the CIA liaison at the FBI's Alexandria office, requested a trace on "a [Mr.] Pennington, who was supposed to have been Mr. McCord's supervisor." When Evans received Parham's request, he recalled his conversation with Edward Sayle "and checked with [him] concerning the circumstances of Mr. Pennington's possible post-Watergate involvement":

Mr. Sayle told [Evans] that Mr. Lee Pennington was a (former) Federal Bureau of Investigation Agent who had assisted the Office of Security at the time of the Watergate incident. Specifically, Mr. Pennington had, according to Mr. Sayle, entered Mr. McCord's office and home destroying any indication of connections between the Agency and Mr. McCord. In burning documents the McCord home suffered considerable smoke damage and, according to Mr. Sayle, three rooms had to be repainted.[19]

In later testimony, Evans said he documented what Sayle told him about Pennington in a series of memoranda for Kuhn and Osborn in August 1972, which remain sealed. Evans later wrote a memorandum for the Inspector General on the "Pennington materials," which was published in the testimony of the Nedzi hearings and helps us track how the "Pennington file" gradually surfaced. The Agency responded to the FBI trace request by throwing Parham a "red herring":

> *After a check of Office of Security files, Mr. Parham was provided with the name of Cecil Harold Pennington, a former Office of Security employee who had not been Mr. McCord's supervisor and who had been retired for a number of years.*

Three days later, Parham requested Cecil Pennington's date of birth and Evans evidently realized what had happened and wrote his memo. Three days after that, Sayle told Evans that Lucille and Donald Sweany had repainted three rooms in the McCord home "after Mr. Lee Pennington burned documents there."

On August 25, Special Agent Parham called to request Pennington's Personal History Statement and mentioned that the Bureau was trying to identify "the individual who picked up Mr. McCord following his release from jail" and did not believe it was Cecil Harold Pennington. Three days later, the Office of Security continued to give Parham the runaround, advising that Pennington's personnel file "contained no [further] pertinent information . . . if the Bureau receives additional information . . . we would be glad to conduct further checks." The same day, seventy-two-year-old Cecil Pennington was interviewed and "emphatically denied" any involvement.[20]

According to investigator Gordon Freedman, the two lawyers in New Haven, Robert Mirto and John Cassidento, "were representing Baldwin out of friendship, getting very little money for their services." Cassidento was a Democrat who was very involved in New Haven politics and "was after a judgeship in the city." In late July, Cassidento called Edward Bennett Williams, whose law firm were representing the DNC in the civil action against CRP, with Joseph Califano as general counsel. Cassidento told Williams he had a client who has "a lot to say about Watergate . . . and wants to get it out." Williams told Califano, who sent his associate J. Alan Galbraith—son of the economist and diplomat John Kenneth Galbraith—to New Haven to meet a man named "Al" and his attorneys on August 26.[21]

According to Baldwin's attorneys, certain "ground rules were established to give Baldwin the ability to deny that he had talked to the DNC lawyers":

> Baldwin was not to be talked to directly by the DNC lawyers and Baldwin was not to know the identity of the DNC lawyers and they were not to know his identity . . . To this day, Baldwin does not know if he met with them.

Galbraith's impressive twenty-six-page memo of the meeting casts doubt on this. Galbraith was there alone and noted, "Al learned my name (when he insisted on making my return flight reservation)." After an hour, Baldwin started answering his questions directly: "Al was anxious to tell his story . . . as accurately as possible" and Baldwin's detailed account was consistent with his earlier FBI interviews and later testimony. As Hougan notes, Baldwin later "vehemently denied" providing the DNC or its attorneys with information about Watergate but in a recent interview, Alan Galbraith insisted Baldwin knew who he was. Galbraith is now seventy-seven years old and the mayor of St. Helena in California. He recalled the meeting took "about five hours" and revealed the earlier break-in in May; the frequency of the bug Baldwin was listening to; and how Baldwin had posed as a nephew of John Bailey to get a tour of the DNC. Baldwin identified himself as "Al" but showed Galbraith the check numbers and amounts he was paid by CRP, so within days, Galbraith discovered his real name by checking declared campaign expenditure at the Federal Election Commission. When I sent Galbraith a copy of his memo, he was surprised at its length and proud of its detail: "I was writing for an audience of one [Ed Bennett Williams]—and viewed [it] as the most important audience in the world!"[22]

Williams shared the memo with Larry O'Brien and had also briefed him in advance—on August 15, O'Brien told reporters he had new evidence that showed DNC headquarters had been "bugged for a period of time." In a later oral history interview, O'Brien recalled Williams briefing him after the Baldwin meeting. He said "Al" had been hired by Hunt and Liddy and stationed in the Howard Johnson Motel to monitor O'Brien's telephone:

> The [second] break-in that night was for two purposes: one, to correct a malfunction of the bug on my phone. They weren't getting clear and total signals at all times. James McCord would correct that. In addition, they were to install an additional or a new ceiling bug to monitor conversations in my office and take additional files of mine to supplement their prior burglary.[23]

In return for the information, Cassidento shook hands with O'Brien at the state Democratic dinner and hoped he would "look kindly upon him for his service to the party" if a future judgeship came up. Cassidento got his judgeship but died during heart surgery before Nixon left office.[24]

In 2009, Max Holland interviewed Galbraith and noted that Williams, Connolly, and Califano had also represented the *Washington Post*. After receiving a detailed report on the Baldwin meeting from Galbraith, Williams had told him to leak the information to Bob Woodward and Carl Bernstein. On September 11, Woodward and Bernstein reported that a "self-described participant has [given] Democratic investigators . . . a detailed account of wiretapping of Democratic headquarters at the Watergate."[25]

Fred Thompson later described an early theory among Baker's staff that Baldwin was a "double agent." He struck them as "unusually inept in not alerting the [burglars] when a group of men left a car and ran into the Watergate." When they heard of his collaboration with Califano, their suspicions grew, as did Howard Hunt's. Baldwin denied "being a double agent," saying he had always been a registered Republican.[26]

On September 6, Henry Rothblatt, the attorney for the Watergate Five, subpoenaed ten "top Democratic officials for questioning under oath" in pretrial depositions in the $1 million civil suit brought by the DNC. They included Larry O'Brien and Spencer Oliver. The day before, John Mitchell had told DNC lawyers, "I'm afraid I don't know who Mr. Spencer Oliver is." At two o'clock on September 7, O'Brien held a press conference to announce that his phone and Spencer Oliver's had been bugged but did not indicate that the bug on his phone had not worked. Earl Silbert wasn't telling the DNC anything about his investigation of the bugging, so O'Brien's sole, unwitting source was Alfred Baldwin.[27]

O'Brien had known Oliver's phone was bugged for weeks but didn't tell him until the morning of his press conference. In a recent interview, Oliver told me he wanted his name kept out of a potentially career-damaging scandal and asked O'Brien's deputy to change the press release to say O'Brien's phone "and one other." But the release had already gone out and the DNC attorneys then told him Rothblatt had summoned him for a deposition the next morning. In his testimony, Oliver revealed that shortly after the FBI matched the key found on Martinez to Maxie Wells' desk, DNC Deputy Chairman Stan Greigg told him, which "came as a complete surprise." When he asked Wells about it, she didn't know if anything was missing from her desk and showed him both keys (having presumably taken back the one she loaned Barbara Kennedy). Rothblatt suggested Oliver had abused his neutral position by favouring certain presidential candidates and asked: "Who is Terry Sanford?"

The next day, Ida Wells was subpoenaed to appear before the grand jury in Washington. "Unnerved by the Watergate scandal," she had resigned from the DNC shortly after the convention in July and flown home to Mississippi. She returned to Washington on Monday, September 11, "to talk to Spencer and the DNC lawyers, plus to get one of my own, maybe."[28]

By then, Spencer Oliver had a new secretary, Marie Elise Haldane—who had worked downstairs for Bob Allen at the Young Democrats—and in the days after the bugging revelations, she was "at the peak of paranoia." Wells' former office was now being used as a press room, so Haldane sat at a desk in Oliver's office, where two new phones had been recently installed. The following Tuesday afternoon, Haldane reported a fault on her phone—the light "would not go out," the bell kept ringing after she picked up an extension and she heard clicking sounds on the line. A repairman couldn't find anything wrong with the phone but made minor adjustments to her extension in a phone box in a closet off the lobby. Haldane then asked him to check the phones for bugs after the newspaper reports that Oliver's phone had been intercepted. He referred her to the telephone company's security office and with Oliver's approval, she called in a request for a security check.[29]

On Wednesday morning, Wells and Oliver met Earl Silbert for the first time and gave sworn grand jury depositions. Oliver was "astonished to learn" that Silbert had "detailed information on some of the conversations which had been illegally overheard by the wiretappers" and thought Silbert was breaking the law by even discussing them with him.[30]

Around ten o'clock the same morning, two telephone company security officers checked the phone on Oliver's desk, Haldane's phone and another phone on an adjacent desk. Roger Fewell found a device on Oliver's phone but didn't tell Haldane and notified the chief of the security office, Earl Connor. At two o'clock, Fewell returned with Connor and checked the phones. As they were leaving, Connor told Haldane he hadn't found anything and she seemed surprised. Shortly after Spencer Oliver arrived at the DNC that afternoon, Connor returned with three FBI agents, removed the cover from Oliver's phone and showed them a black device inside it—just over an inch long and three quarters of an inch wide, with three black wires. They checked the device on the line but it was not transmitting due to a defective transistor. Oliver summoned a photographer from McGovern headquarters and posed with the mysterious bug in a photo that made the London *Times* the next morning. The press was tipped off and when reporters arrived, the FBI agents packaged up the phone and the bug and left the DNC, with newsmen in hot pursuit.[31]

DNC attorney Alan Galbraith was also present when the FBI examined the bug on Oliver's phone. He remembered meeting Maxie Wells on the day the bug was discovered and believed it was Maxie who suggested her successor, Marie Elise Haldane, check the phones for bugs—"if they did it to you once, they could do it to you again," she said. He also thought it was Maxie who called to tell him about the bug and summon him to the DNC that afternoon. In her nineties deposition, Wells claimed she was in the office when the FBI "discovered" the bug and Galbraith has a vivid memory of her sitting on the couch in his office that day or close to it.

The following day, Spencer Oliver had his home phone checked for bugs and that evening, Pat Gray instructed Charlie Bates to "go all-out" on the investigation of the bug. The next morning, a new case file was opened, reflecting the FBI stance that "no connection has been proven between [this] matter and previous incident." It was soon dubbed "Watergate II" and ordered interviews with everyone at the DNC and telephone company with any possible information.

Oliver, Haldane and Wells were interviewed by the FBI that day and Haldane "constantly smiled and laughed" throughout her interview (she later blamed this on nerves). FBI investigators were troubled by Haldane's "inappropriate reaction" and the homemade, unsophisticated nature of the bug, which was inoperative due to a defective transistor "but when activated, operated within the general range that Baldwin stated he was monitoring." One expert told them he "cannot believe anyone serious about intercepting conversations would use such an outdated piece of equipment." They doubted Haldane's story and suspected the device had been planted in her phone as a "throwaway," intended to be found.[32]

According to office manager Harold Wolff, the DNC had "no security officer as such" and relied on building security. Stranger still, six days before the bug was found, on the day of Larry O'Brien's press conference, private detective Nick Beltrante was contracted to handle security at McGovern headquarters, debug all phones and rooms, and do a weekly telephone sweep. He found himself working alongside Lou Russell, but didn't trust him because of his connection to McCord. In the first week of September, Beltrante conducted a survey of DNC offices to prepare a quote for a similar sweep there but was told "the cost was too high." Former Pentagon employee Gerald Lamm did the audio counter-measures work for Beltrante and Baker's staff suspected Beltrante had the expertise and access to "plant" the September bug.[33]

On September 15, 1972, Hunt, Liddy, and the five Watergate burglars were indicted on charges of conspiracy, burglary, and violation of wiretapping laws. The indictment noted that the telephone bugged was "used primarily . . . by Robert Spencer Oliver and Ida M. Wells."[34]

That evening, Dean, Haldeman and Nixon were pleased that after three months' work, they had limited the indictments to two "low-level" White House aides and the scandal had "been kept away from the White House almost completely and from the President totally."

"What's happened on the bug?" Haldeman asked Dean. "On the what?" asked Nixon. "The second bug," replied Dean. "There was a bug found in the phone of . . ." "You don't think it was left over from the other time?" Nixon interrupted. "Absolutely not," said Dean. "The Bureau has checked and re-checked. The man who checked the phone first said that his first check was thorough . . . it had to be planted after . . ." "What the hell do you think is involved? What's your guess?" asked Nixon. "I think the DNC planted it, quite clearly," replied Dean. "Did they get anything on the finger prints?" asked Haldeman. "[None] at all—either on the telephone or on the bug," replied Dean. "The FBI has unleashed a full blast investigation over at the DNC starting with O'Brien right now . . . O'Brien has charged the Bureau with failing to find all the bugs." "Good, that will make them mad," said Haldeman. "I think that's a good development because it makes it look so God damned phony . . . It looks silly," said Nixon. "Absolutely," replied Dean. "If we can find that the DNC planted that, the whole story will reverse . . . they are trying to ascertain who made the bug . . . who he sold it to and how it came down through the chain."[35]

Dean also told Nixon that Henry Rothblatt, the lawyer for the burglars, had started taking sealed depositions in the civil suit brought by the DNC: "He's quite a character. He's been getting into the sex life of some of the members of the DNC." "Why? What's his justification?" asked Nixon. "Well, he's working on an entrapment theory that they were hiding something or had secret information, affairs to hide and they could somehow conspire to bring this thing about themselves. It's a way-out theory . . ." Six days later, to avoid prejudicing a fair trial in the criminal case, Judge Richey halted the taking of depositions in the civil suit until after the criminal trial. The Democrats were furious, in the knowledge that neither trial would now take place before the election.[36]

The FBI's Laboratory Division was perplexed. On the night of the arrests, three telephone bugs, a room bug and one transceiver had been recovered from the burglars but FBI agents found no "hidden electronic surveillance equipment" in the offices of O'Brien, deputy chairman Stan Greigg and DNC general secretary Dorothy Bush, or in the executive conference room. Earl Connor, chief of Security of the telephone company, conducted a survey of all telephones in the DNC that afternoon and was "positive" all telephones, including Oliver's, were taken apart and checked and no bugs were found. He dismantled all "handsets, terminal boxes, speakers and wiring in the frame room" which received and rerouted incoming calls and detected "nothing unusual." The office of press secretary Joe Mohbat was locked and Connor "was advised by [DNC] officials . . . that this room need not be checked." As the FBI noted, Mohbat's office was "adjacent to R. Spencer Oliver's office but has no interconnecting door . . . and has no telephone service in common with Oliver's."[37]

On June 29 and 30, Special Agent Wilbur Stevens, chief of Electronic Countermeasures at the FBI laboratory, conducted a "security survey" of the DNC with his team. They conducted an electronic "sweep" of DNC headquarters and "opened and inspected" all phones. but no bugs were found. On September 14, the day after the new bug was discovered, Stevens confirmed all phones had been checked, including those in Oliver's office: "I state positively and categorically that this additional device was not present in any of the telephones at the time of the security survey." Later that day, the telephone company confirmed that Oliver's phone had not been changed since June, so Stevens concluded the bug had been installed since the end of June and noted the new device was of a different design to the three identical devices recovered on June 17. In a television interview on September 21, Attorney General Richard Kleindienst said FBI agents had made "a thorough sweep" of the DNC offices after the break-in and concluded, "somebody put something on that phone after the FBI was there." Vice President Spiro Agnew and Acting FBI Director Pat Gray made similar statements. It's important to note that the FBI didn't know Spencer Oliver's phone had been bugged until they interviewed Alfred Baldwin on July 5, the week after their search. There is no indication in FBI files that they went back to check Oliver's phone once they discovered this, which is odd.[38]

On September 25, in an interview with the *New York Post*, Spencer Oliver complained that four FBI agents had spent the past week interviewing eighty DNC staff members about him. "It is kind of frightening," he said, "I'm the victim of a crime, but now they're investigating me and not the [CRP] . . . They're asking the staff here what kind of person I am, do I come in here late, if I have marital problems . . . who are my enemies, who are my rivals. . . ." Oliver suspected the FBI had not checked his phone and the "September bug" was the one Baldwin overheard, either "placed on his phone by mistake or the intruders thought his dealings with state party leaders would give them advance knowledge about who would get the nomination . . . The questions being asked by the FBI now are intended to find out if someone here did it," he said.[39]

Lead prosecutor Earl Silbert was skeptical. He concluded the newly discovered bug was "the original device which permitted Baldwin to overhear the conversations he did" and told his boss, Henry Petersen, the FBI had "goofed" by missing the bug on Oliver's telephone in June and was now "compounding the goof" by treating the recently discovered device as "newly installed," without any evidence of who put it there.[40]

Silbert outlined five reasons for his view, which FBI technicians quickly dismantled. While Silbert questioned why the burglars would remove a bug that was producing useful information, "the absence of a device in Oliver's phone at the time of the [FBI] security check" did not necessarily mean the burglars had removed it and it was one of the three devices recovered on the night of the arrests. Silbert was also rather naïve in thinking the idea of "anyone planting a device in the Democratic headquarters after Watergate" was "too ludicrous." The Bureau noted:

> Democrats, or sympathisers . . . could have decided to make a more recent "installation" and call attention to it in order to keep the pot boiling. Baldwin had previously disclosed approximate frequency and fact Oliver's phone was involved . . . Oliver's office cognizant of [this]. Moreover, O'Brien has recently publicly alleged his office was bugged.

On September 21, Robert Kunkel (SAC, WFO) had passed on information from a reporter to Mark Felt about Larry O'Brien's previous role as a lobbyist for Howard Hughes; how he was replaced by Robert Oliver and the Mullen

Company; and Oliver was pushing his son's political ambitions within the DNC: "O'Brien has felt that Oliver is part of the 'Palace Guard' of the Democratic Party, which when McGovern fails in his attempt to obtain the Presidency, will attempt to take over the Democratic Party." O'Brien had allegedly asked two assistants to gauge Oliver's support among state chairmen and "the story goes that these two assistants, in the fashion of Hunt and Liddy, hired a local wiretapper to place a transmitter on Oliver's phone, which could in fact be monitored on a slightly modified FM radio within the confines of the [DNC]."

Silbert thought the FBI missed the bug because "Oliver's office . . . [was] almost the last place one would expect a tap to be placed—nowhere near O'Brien's office or anywhere else of importance." The FBI called this a "totally erroneous reason," noting that laboratory technical personnel "considered [the] possibility Democrat sympathizers might make additional installations to exacerbate the situation, and therefore all rooms and all phones were considered highly suspect and were thoroughly searched."

In mid-October, the FBI conducted tests to determine how well radio signals from the miniature transmitters recovered in June and September could be received by the receiver system in rooms 419 and 723 of the Howard Johnson. The transmitters were placed in the offices of Spencer Oliver and the office formerly occupied by Director of Communications John Stewart and the tests were closely observed by Oliver and Galbraith. All signals "could be satisfactorily received" and as expected, the signal in room 419 was weaker than room 723. For the purposes of the tests, the defective September bug was replaced by an identical model and the signal from this later device was noticeably weaker than the output from the transmitters recovered in June. Prosecutor Donald Campbell requested the test in Stewart's office, presumably in the belief that McCord had initially mistaken it for O'Brien's.[41]

Alan Galbraith told me he was "absolutely sure" the FBI missed the bug in their electronic "sweep" because this was a new type of bug which was only activated when a phone was in use. When I told him the phone company and FBI had physically checked the phones in June, he replied, "I don't believe that at all." During the FBI tests in October, the technicians were happy to tell him the frequency the September bug was transmitting at and it matched the frequency Baldwin told him he was monitoring "perfectly," but the FBI lab reports do not reflect this. For a detailed analysis of the FBI Laboratory testing of the bugs, see Appendix 2.[42]

After an extensive investigation, the FBI found no evidence that "any other party" had placed the bug in Oliver's phone and concluded: "It appears fruitless to debate the issue further." Spencer Oliver condemned the FBI's "intensive investigation of [his] personal and political life with what appeared to be a motive of digging up some other reason for someone to have tapped [his] telephone." He complained to the Justice Department, considering this "an unwarranted invasion of . . . privacy," and later called it "a very intrusive and obnoxious assault on my private life . . . [trying to] tie me to radical groups . . . [find out] whether I was an alcoholic, whether I had a broken marriage, whether I had had any affairs."[43]

Jim Hougan suspects that Lou Russell planted the bug in Oliver's telephone in September "to shore up Baldwin's story and . . . prevent investigators from pursuing the 'loose ends' implied by the absence of a bug on Oliver's phone . . . not only was he a co-conspirator of McCord's, but he was also responsible for bugging the Columbia Plaza." As discussed in Chapter 6, Russell was an informant for McCord during his investigation of journalist Jack Anderson. McCord has always refused to discuss Russell and threatened Hougan with lawsuits from himself, Alfred Baldwin, and "the Pennington family" if he wrote about him. As Hougan notes:

> Russell performed a number of tasks for McCord, patrolling the offices of CRP at night, infiltrating the Jack Anderson apparat by day, and eavesdropping on the Columbia Plaza in between.[44]

In September and October, James McCord tested out the "wiretap defense" on his own case by making calls to the Israeli and Chilean embassies, on the assumption both calls were monitored. In his memoir *Undercover,* Howard Hunt refers to McCord's call to the Chilean embassy on October 10:

> *He identified himself as a Watergate defendant and requested a visa. McCord's assumption was that the embassy's phones were tapped and that when he filed a motion for government disclosure of any wiretaps on his line, the government would drop its case against him rather than reveal that the Chilean Embassy phone was tapped.*[45]

McCord would later note that "several cases have been dismissed on these grounds recently, rather than disclose in adversary proceedings the contents of such calls and conversations, and the names of the parties involved." McCord's attorney, Gerald Alch, said McCord was "very, very cryptic" about his calls to the embassies and listed the CIA, FBI, and NSA as the agencies involved in the electronic monitoring. Alch was skeptical the "wiretap defense" would work but in a pre-trial motion, he petitioned the government "to reveal any electronic surveillance" on those lines. The government said there was none.[46]

Charles Colson later confirmed to Senator Lowell Weicker (R—Connecticut) that "the CIA broke into the Chilean Embassy in the fall of 1971 to install wiretaps. The taps were shut off during the elections but resumed afterward to monitor information relating to trade delegations coming to the United States. The taps were removed in May of 1973 because the CIA thought Dean knew of their existence." It's no coincidence that May 1973 was when Schlesinger and Colby began investigating CIA misdeeds. If McCord knew the CIA was tapping the Chilean embassy, his letter suggests the Agency was tapping the Israeli embassy as well.[47]

• • •

On September 21, after fifteen days in St. Elizabeth's mental hospital and forty-five minutes of psychiatric consultation, Phillip Bailley was judged sane and brought to court for pre-trial discussions. To avert a damaging trial that would focus press attention on his address book and potentially call John Dean as a witness, Bailley was pressured into pleaded guilty to one count and given a five-year sentence. As Hougan notes, "he was bundled off to a federal prison in Connecticut where, ironically, he served on the Inmates Committee with Howard Hunt and other Watergaters."[48]

While Earl Silbert admitted that "at the very start of the investigation, because of the CIA association of a number of the defendants and their ties to Cuba, we did speculate as to whether the Watergate break-in had some connection with the CIA . . . we had not the slightest evidence at the time of the trial to believe or suspect that the CIA was involved in the Watergate matter."[49]

Concerned that Hunt and the accused might mount a "phony CIA defense . . . [and] falsely claim that the Watergate break-in was a CIA sponsored operation," the three prosecutors, Silbert, Glanzer and Campbell, met the CIA's deputy general counsel, John Warner, on October 11 to ask questions about CIA connections to the principals in the Watergate indictment, which repeated the FBI enquiries of late June. Silbert's questions primarily related to Hunt's knowledge of the Mullen Company cover; alias documentation and equipment provided to Hunt by the CIA in July and August 1971; and Martinez' last contact with the Agency.

The questions were answered and a package of supporting documents were delivered to Attorney General Richard Kleindienst by Helms and his General Counsel Larry Houston on October 24. Assistant Attorney General Henry Petersen joined the meeting late and retired to his office with Houston to discuss the materials in further detail. Petersen called Silbert to confirm receipt of the package and tell him "there was no need for [him] to see it . . . [as] it simply revealed no information relevant to the break-in," but Silbert felt it was "vitally important" he see it, and Petersen let him bring the documents back to the US attorney's office where he "reviewed them very carefully" with Glanzer and Campbell.[50]

Silbert and the FBI had suspected the phony IDs of Edward Warren and George Leonard were Hunt and Liddy and the CIA packet of materials received in December now confirmed the false IDs had been supplied by the CIA.[51]

Silbert later admitted, "we never were able to determine the precise motivation for the burglary and wiretapping, particularly on the phone of a relative unknown—Spencer Oliver. Baldwin had told us that McCord wanted *all* telephone calls recorded, including personal calls . . . Many of them [were] extremely personal, intimate and potentially embarrassing. We also learned that Hunt had sometime previously met Spencer Oliver at Robert R. Mullen & Co. and opposed his joining the firm because he was a liberal Democrat. Therefore, one motive we thought possible was an attempt to compromise Oliver and others . . . for political reasons . . . [but] we never had any direct proof of this since neither Hunt or Liddy . . . would talk to us."[52]

On November 7, Richard Nixon was re-elected president in a landslide, taking sixty percent of the popular vote—eighteen million more than Senator McGovern—and every state except Massachusetts and the District of Columbia. The next day, Howard Hunt was allowed to examine material seized from his White House safe and found his "operational notebook, files and telephone list" were missing—evidence, he later argued, that would have shown he was acting on orders and "in good faith."[53]

By November 14, Hunt was desperate. He drafted a memo titled "Review and Statement of Problem" on behalf of the seven defendants, who had "bugged DNC offices against their better judgment, knowing that Larry O'Brien was seldom there, and that many items of interest were being moved to Florida." Their sponsors had "compounded the fiasco" by "failure to quash the investigation while that option was still open, allowing Hunt's safe to be opened and selected contents given to the FBI," permitting the FBI to humiliate them and their families, "granting immunity to Baldwin," permitting them "to fall into the hands of a paranoid judge and three self-admitted liberal Democrat prosecutors"; and "an apparent wash-hands attitude now that the Election has been won," leading the defendants to feel "they are being offered up as scapegoats ultimately to be abandoned."

The memo gave CRP a deadline of November 27 to abandon its "continued indifference" and meet and renew its financial commitments to men who had lost their jobs, futures and "reputations as honorable men" acting on their behalf—"half-measures will be unacceptable."

Hunt suggested John Mitchell had already perjured himself in his deposition, "immunity from prosecution . . . for cooperating defendants" was on the table, the media were "offering huge sums for defendants' stories" and made veiled reference to the Fielding break-in:

> *The Watergate bugging is only one of a number of highly illegal conspiracies engaged in by one or more of the defendants at the behest of senior White House officials. These as yet undisclosed crimes can be proved.*

The defendants had followed all instructions meticulously and maintained their silence. Now they expected the Administration to "live up to its commitments": financial support, legal defense fees, pardons and rehabilitation:

> *The foregoing should not be misinterpreted as a threat. It is among other things a reminder that loyalty has always been a two-way street.*

Hunt telephoned Charles Colson at noon that day and summarized his key demands. Promises made in July and August had not been honored, legal bills and living expenses were outstanding. Through silence, "we are protecting the guys who are really responsible," said Hunt, "this thing must not break apart for foolish reasons." He asked Colson if he would "receive a memorandum from [him] . . . read it and destroy it." "Nope," replied Colson, so Hunt said he would "lay" the memo on CRP attorney Kenneth Parkinson instead. Colson gave a tape of the call to Dean, who played it to Haldeman, Ehrlichman and Mitchell. On November 20, Hunt's attorney William Bittman read the memo to Parkinson and eight days later, a $50,000 cash payment was made but Hunt's demands would continue.

Two weeks after the election, Nixon called Richard Helms to Camp David and told him he was being replaced. Helms knew Nixon and his aides disliked and distrusted him and regarded the Agency as an Ivy League elite. He later concluded, "President Nixon himself called the shots in the Watergate cover-up," in league with Mitchell and Haldeman. "The arrest of former CIA employees and agents at the scene handed Nixon a weapon that he thought would serve his cover-up."[54]

On November 27, Petersen and Silbert met CIA Executive Director William Colby and Acting General Counsel Warner and posed additional questions to the Agency. According to Warner's memo on the meeting, the prosecutors stressed they did not intend "to use any of the information relating to the Agency in its case in chief . . . [but] simply wished to know all the facts wherein CIA might be involved in order to avoid surprise moves by the defense."

Silbert quizzed Colby about the Agency support for Hunt and wanted to interview CIA staff who had contact with Hunt and Liddy, raising fears that Agency witnesses might be called to testify at trial. The support had been provided in response to a "duly-authorized extra-Agency request" but the Agency had not yet told the FBI who had given the authorization. Colby recalled that he "danced around the room several times for ten minutes to try to avoid becoming specific on this, finally naming the White House, and was then phoned by Silbert with a demand for the name." Colby informed Silbert that John Ehrlichman had initiated the support for Hunt the previous July.[55]

Silbert moved on to James McCord. "Can you confirm that McCord had no other contacts with the Agency after his retirement other than referrals of names and résumés from the retirement placement people?" he asked.

"That's correct, and I can testify to that effect," said Colby, who later confirmed it in writing: "Our records reflect that all official Agency contact with McCord, following his departure from the organization, centered on retirement matters." According to the Rockefeller Commission report, Colby's calculated lie was based on the legal opinion of Larry Houston: "Helms obtained advice from the CIA's General Counsel that he was under no obligation voluntarily to turn the [McCord] letters over to the FBI (which did not know of them) and on the strength of that advice retained them in the Agency's files."[56]

Colby clarified Hunt's correspondence with Houston about his annuity and they also discussed Martinez. Two days later, Silbert telephoned Warner with further questions.[57]

As acting deputy director of Security in the Personnel Security Division, Leo J. Dunn oversaw the first month of the Watergate investigation until he was appointed executive assistant to the Director of Security, Howard Osborn. From December 1, Dunn began working with Colby to "coordinate CIA's response to Watergate inquiries" from the Justice Department. This seems to be the "secret investigation of the Watergate matter" referred to in the Baker report, in which Dunn "was instructed to make no copies of his reports, to utilize no secretaries, and to tell no one but Colby [and Helms] what his findings were." In December, Dunn interviewed Martinez' two case officers and wrote a report for Colby and Helms.[58]

In late November or early December, James McCord sent Lee Pennington a memorandum on Jack Anderson and Pennington gave it to his case officer,

Louis Vasaly, of the Security Research Staff. On December 4, 1972, after showing the memorandum to Osborn, Steven Kuhn wrote a memo to Evans:[59]

At the request of the Director of Security, I advised Mr. Vasaly that he is not to ever discuss Mr. McCord with Mr. Pennington nor is he to accept any more items from Mr. Pennington which concern Mr. McCord or which come from Mr. McCord. Mr. Vasaly agreed and stated that, in all of his future contacts with Mr. Pennington, Mr. Paul F. Gaynor, chief, security research staff, would be present.[60]

On December 8, a mistrial was declared in the Ellsberg case and Dorothy Hunt died in a plane crash in Chicago. Since early July, Hunt's wife had been the conduit for CRP money to cover living expenses and attorneys' fees for Hunt, Liddy, and the Watergate Five through a "Mr. Rivers," who would call her at pay phones and left the first payment in a locker at Washington's National Airport. Dean later identified Rivers as Nixon intelligence operative Tony Ulasewicz. When $10,000 in hundred-dollar bills was found in Dorothy Hunt's purse in the plane wreckage, a "barrage of innuendo and insinuation" followed, but the serial numbers did not correspond to the checks lodged in Barker's bank account and the CRP payments "had been in untraceable bills." Hunt claimed the money was for a hotel investment (according to Baker's staff, a proposed Holiday Inn in Nicaragua). Curiously, before boarding the plane, Dorothy bought $250,000 in flight insurance, payable to her husband. As Hunt flew back to Washington after the funeral, facing "the stress of a four-to-six-week trial now less than a month away, and convinced that the government was concealing the only documentary evidence [his notebooks] . . . that I had been acting in good faith, I decided to plead guilty. . . ."[61]

On December 13, the CIA completed preparation of its answers to Silbert's questions. By now, Ehrlichman had heard about Colby's revelation (perhaps Peterson had mentioned it to Dean) and two days later, he met with Colby, Helms, and Dean to hear how his name had been reluctantly surfaced. While Helms and Colby had provided the material to allow Silbert to prepare for a possible "phony" CIA defence, they worried Silbert "was now talking in somewhat different terms." Dean thought Silbert probably wanted to use CIA testimony "to prove that Hunt and Liddy operated in alias . . . [but] it was agreed all around this would be a mistake, as the entire matter was totally irrelevant to the main trial and would be a red herring." Dean asked Colby to sit on the package prepared for Silbert for a few days.[62]

Finally, on December 20, as Silbert chased him for a response, Colby called Dean, who agreed to release the second package of documents. Colby reminded Dean that the CIA objected to being actively involved in the trial, as it "could create the misunderstanding of our having been involved in the Watergate itself" and were prepared to "go to the Attorney General, if necessary." The package was sent to the Justice Department the next day, with a cover memorandum from Warner to Petersen, reminding him that Silbert had agreed "these matters are solely for the background information of Mr. Silbert in preparing appropriate contingency responses to matters or contentions which might possibly be raised by the defendants."[63]

On Friday, December 22, the last working day before Christmas, Silbert lined up meetings with the CIA, John Dean and DNC attorney Charles Morgan amid frantic preparations for the trial in early January. Petersen and Silbert reviewed the second package of CIA documents with Warner, which included a summary of Hunt's contacts with Cleo Gephart, John Caswell, and Stephen Carter Greenwood; Karl Wagner and General Cushman's knowledge of assistance to Hunt; and Hunt's involvement in dealings between the Agency and the Mullen Company.

As discussed in Chapter 3, on December 5, Leo Dunn had written a memo on the photographs the Agency had developed for Hunt. After seeing this document, the prosecutors asked Warner whether the Agency had copies of the photographs. Warner said he would check. On returning to

Langley later that day, Warner learned "that the Agency did have Xerox copies of these photographs and . . . Xerox copies of the ten photographs were delivered by Mr. Goldin of [the Office of General Counsel] to Mr. Petersen on 3 January 1973."[64]

Also on December 22, Dean met Silbert and Petersen about a motion from Hunt's attorney to suppress evidence "based on what he contended was an illegal search of the Hunt office at the White House" and concealing exculpatory evidence in the form of two Hermès notebooks missing from the seized inventory. Dean lied and told Silbert he knew nothing about the notebooks but later, in the corridor, he claims he told Petersen he had given documents that "were politically very embarrassing" to Acting FBI Director Pat Gray. "Oh shit!" exclaimed Petersen. When they returned to the conference room, Petersen quickly brought the meeting to a close. Word soon spread to Gray, who told Dean he had destroyed the documents.[65]

The same day, ACLU attorney, Charles Morgan, acting for Spencer Oliver and the DNC, met Silbert for lunch. In mid-December, the prosecutors had told Oliver and Maxie Wells they planned to put them on the witness stand, so Oliver hired Morgan to exclude the contents of the intercepted conversations from trial testimony and protect the "primary users of the tapped telephone"—Oliver; Wells; Robert Vance and Severin Beliveau, the state chairmen for Alabama and Maine respectively; and Robert Allen, national president of the Young Democrats. As Morgan later noted, the prosecutors had granted Baldwin immunity in exchange for telling them the "whole truth," but there were no recordings and all written evidence of the wiretaps had been destroyed, so they were relying entirely on Baldwin's memory of the calls. "The Democrats felt trapped," Morgan writes in his memoir. "Oliver asked me to represent them. . . . My task was to keep the Democratic victims of the crime from becoming victims of the trial. To do that, I had to cover up—to suppress Baldwin's testified 'recollection' of the conversation—and keep his version of the 'whole truth' from public view."[66]

Silbert wanted Oliver to discuss the intercepted conversations at trial but Morgan insisted this was against the law. Silbert angrily told him, "Hunt was trying the blackmail Spencer, and I am going to prove it!" Oliver thought Silbert's claims were "preposterous" and Morgan thought Silbert wanted to "characterize the most sensitive personal and political conversations as potentially suited for blackmail." They would soon meet in court to decide the issue.[67]

On December 21, the defense counsels met to discuss trial strategy and Alch explained "the defense of duress" McCord was planning to use. The "security motivation" was only applicable to McCord as chief of Security for CRP, so in trying to find a common defense, the question of possible CIA involvement arose, given the connections of many of the defendants to the Agency and the fact that two of them were carrying "CIA-forged documents." Each lawyer agreed to ask his client "whether or not he had any knowledge of any CIA involvement."[68]

Alch met McCord and "local counsel" Bernard Shankman for lunch at the Monocle Restaurant after the meeting. During pre-trial discovery procedure, Alch had just received a statement from MPD intelligence officer Gary Bittenbender, who alleged that, at the time of his arrest, McCord referred to the Cuban Americans as "all good former CIA men." McCord had also sent Alch "various memorandums pertaining to telephone calls made by him to various foreign embassies, relevant to the case, which he believed has been the subject of electronic surveillance."[69]

During lunch, Alch asked McCord if the Watergate break-in was a CIA operation. "This suggestion so unsettled McCord," writes Hougan, that he became "in effect . . . a double agent within the defense team, reporting secretly by letter to the CIA's General Gaynor."[70]

Over the following two weeks, Paul Gaynor, chief of the Security Research Staff at the CIA's Office of Security, received five letters from McCord.

Gaynor had served in his role since 1951, except for a two-year assignment in Germany in the late fifties. He was responsible for "counterintelligence as it applies to staff employees of the Agency." McCord had served on his staff from 1955 to 1962 before a two-year posting in Europe. McCord returned to a different section of the Office of Security but Gaynor said they had a "close working relationship" and had lunch occasionally.[71]

Osborn's order that Gaynor should be present at all future meetings between Vasaly and Pennington establishes a clear reason for the timing of McCord's letters. No longer able to communicate with Vasaly via Pennington, he would now write to Gaynor directly himself.[72]

The first letter was dated December 22—the day after the lunch at the Monocle—and sent to the apartment of Gaynor's son in Arlington. Gaynor speculated that "Mr. McCord may have been in a hurry when he did this, because my son was listed ahead of me in the telephone directory." Gaynor received the letter on Christmas Eve:

> Dear Paul —
>
> There is tremendous pressure to put the operation off on the company [CIA]. Don't worry about me no matter what you hear. The way to head this off is to flood the newspapers with leaks or anonymous letters that the plan is to place the blame on the company for the operation. This is of immediate importance because the plans are in the formative stage now, and can be preempted now, if the story is leaked so that the press is alerted. It may not be headed off later when it is too late.
>
> The fix is on one of the police officers in the MPD intelligence department [Bittenbender], to testify that one of the defendants [McCord] told him the defendants were company people and it was a company operation. He has probably been promised a promotion for changing his story to

this effect. Be careful in your dealing with them. I will do all I can to keep you informed. Keep the faith.[73]

On December 28, McCord sent the White House a message through his contact Jack Caulfield:

Jack —

Sorry to have to write you this letter but felt you had to know.

If Helms goes, and if the WG operation is laid at CIA's feat [sic], where it does not belong, every tree in the forest will fall. It will be a scorched desert. The whole matter is at the precipice right now. Just pass the message that if they want it to blow, they are on exactly the right course. I'm sorry that you will get hurt in the fallout.[74]

As the final report of the Senate Watergate Committee notes, "McCord had become increasingly alarmed over what he considered efforts by his attorney and persons at CRP and the White House to have him falsely assert as a defense to the criminal charges against him, that the break-in was part of a CIA mission." The letter was unsigned but Caulfield recognized the sender and immediately briefed John Dean's assistant Fred Fielding and "the problem" went up the chain from Dean to CRP attorney Paul O'Brien to John Mitchell, "who directed O'Brien to have Caulfield determine McCord's intentions."[75]

McCord also wrote Gaynor that day, from that point sending letters to his home address. The second envelope was received on December 29 and contained a list of five names—"J. Mitchell, J. Dean, J. Magruder, Colson, Liddy"; a copy of his letter to Caulfield, addressed to "Jack" but with the full name handwritten in the top right-hand corner; and a page with three sentences typed on it:

> The MPD officer's name is Carl Bittenbender.
> The pressure is still on. They can go to hell.
> Anytime you need me to testify before a
> Congressional committee in your behalf just yell.

Gaynor took "in your behalf" to mean "the Agency" and later said he didn't know Jack Caulfield.[76]

On Friday, December 29, as Gaynor received the second envelope, McCord sent a third. It contained a page of "notes" and a letter he had just given to his local counsel Bernard Shankman.

In the notes, McCord wrote that he was "convinced that the fix is on Gerry Alch and Bernie Shankman, too many things don't add up." They planned to call Richard Helms to testify and to get CIA whistleblower Victor Marchetti "to lay the background re CIA employees once caught in the act, refusing to admit it." He was suspicious of "their persistence in trying to find out how much I know about Mitchell's involvement" and their efforts to downplay it; and their "failure to really debrief me on my whole participation and knowledge . . . to let time run out before the trial starts."

He attacked "the fixed police officer's report" [Bittenbender's statement] as "absolutely false" and said it can be read as either an admission by him "that this was a CIA operation" or an operation which McCord and the Cubans "cooked up on our own":

> *They are trying to put the blame for the operation on CIA and/or McCord, or both, shifting the focus away from the White House (Liddy*

*and Hunt). They appear willing to get McCord off but only on the con-
dition that he place the blame for the operation on CIA—or take the
blame himself. No go.*[77]

The letter to Shankman announced he was firing Alch as his defense attorney in the Watergate case because of his insistence that "the Watergate operation was a CIA operation . . . [or] that the 4 Cubans and I cooked up the
bugging operation on our own." He called these claims "flatly untrue" and
said they would prejudice a fair trial:

> *The implications inherent in these two proposals imply the deepest corrup-
> tion and perversion of the criminal justice system in recent history . . . Never
> in our nation's history has the integrity of the national intelligence system
> and especially of the FBI been in such jeopardy.*

He claimed, "the hundreds of dedicated fine men and women of CIA" now
feared "political recrimination" after seeing "their fine director [Helms] . . .
summarily discharged . . . to make way for a politician [Schlesinger] who
will write or rewrite intelligence reports the way the politicians want them
written":

> *Nazi Germany rose and fell under exactly the same philosophy of govern-
> mental operation. This nation is truly in the deepest trouble it has been in
> in 200 years. I fully expect the most intense character assassination cam-
> paign and harassment to be mounted against me. So be it. The integrity of
> the CIA and of the FBI and of the whole Federal Criminal Justice System
> is far more important than one man's future or life.*[78]

He had "the evidence of the involvement of Mitchell and others, sufficient to
convince a jury, the Congress and the Press." What he needed now was evidence of perjury by Bittenbender ("I know he is lying"); and "evidence of

illegal [government] wiretapping of our telephones, either on national security grounds or domestic security grounds, both of which are done on authority of the attorney general's signature alone."[79]

McCord wanted to release the letter to the press that day but Shankman asked him to hold off until he could speak to Alch after the New Year holiday. At the time, Gaynor was "baffled" by the reference to the "national security calls" to the embassies and "couldn't figure out what [McCord] was driving at." Later, it became clear that McCord thought his phone was tapped and he was calling the embassies "to prove an illegal tap to set the ground for a dismissal of the trial."[80]

On New Year's Eve, Howard Hunt sent a letter to Colson, complaining that he had ignored his attorney's request for a meeting:

> *My wife's death, the imminent trial, my present mental depression and my inability to get any relief from my present situation all contribute to a sense of abandonment by friends on whom I had in good faith relied . . . There is a limit to the endurance of any man trapped in a hostile situation and mine was reached on December 8.*

On January 2, Colson sent a copy of the letter to Dean, with the note: "Now, what the hell do I do?" That evening, CRP attorney Paul O'Brien told Dean that Hunt wanted a White House assurance of executive clemency before changing his plea to guilty. On January 5, after consulting Ehrlichman and Nixon, Colson gave Hunt's attorney, Bill Bittman, a "general assurance . . . that clemency generally came up around Christmas and that a year was a long time."[81]

On January 3, McCord sent another letter to Gaynor which began, "It would appear that we have headed them off at the pass. The crisis appears to be over."

He had delivered his letter to Judge Sirica the day before, who then called a meeting of defense and prosecuting attorneys to sort out the problem. He cleared the air with Alch, who "assured [him] the issue was dead, that he would not try it again, nor would anyone else." The issue was discussed briefly in court "without disclosing exactly what was at stake . . . [and] we advised [Sirica] that we were going to give it a new try at working together":

> *Bittman was shook and has obviously taken the heat on this because of my violent reaction. He should because he had transmitted to Alch the original idea. We know of course who passed the idea to Bittman. We took them up to the brink on this, and I don't believe they will try it again. Breaking it to the press could have gotten some of them disbarred and broken the whole mess wide open . . . Now we'll work on the other problems at hand. Keep the faith.*[82]

Gaynor told Nedzi he had no idea "who passed the idea to Bittman." [83]

The same day, "an envelope containing Xerox copies of 10 pictures . . . taken by Hunt and developed by CIA" were hand carried to Petersen, who examined the pictures with Silbert. They knew Hunt had been in California but "could not ascertain any relevancy to the Watergate investigation," so they took no further action.

Silbert was later questioned about this by Senator Gary Hart (D—Colorado) during lengthy nomination hearings before his appointment as US attorney for the District of Columbia:

> *I remember poring over those photos with Mr. Petersen and we just couldn't figure [them] out . . . I took the whole packet, including the photographs, back and showed them to Mr. Glanzer and Mr. Campbell and again we*

went over them and tried to figure out what was going on . . . We had
airplane records and hotel reservations of Edward Warren and George
Leonard in California and a lot of our inquiry to the White House
witnesses . . . was trying to find out what the purpose of this travel was . . .
The CIA . . . claimed not to know the purpose the Ed Warren and George
Leonard phony identifications had been given.[84]

When Hunt pleaded guilty and Liddy refused to talk, the CIA part of the
case lost importance and Silbert didn't pursue the issue further.[85]

During the same hearings in June 1974, Henry Petersen was questioned separately about the Fielding photos by Senate Watergate Committee chairman,
Senator Sam Ervin (D—North Carolina), and Senator Tunney (D—California). Petersen acknowledged that neither he or Silbert knew who Fielding was
but they didn't find anything in the photos to "arouse [their] suspicions." "Neither the parking lot, the picture, or the names suggested any degree of relevance, and we simply did not make a name check," Petersen told Ervin.

"But here was Liddy, one of the people indicted for Watergate," said a
baffled Ervin. "Here was Hunt, another one of the people indicated in connection with Watergate. Here you have information that the CIA had loaned
the disguises and false identifications not only to Hunt but to Hunt for
somebody else, and a clandestine camera. You had evidence that Hunt had
sent certain negatives to the CIA to develop, and that one of these negatives
revealed the pictures of George [sic] Liddy, another person under indictment
in the same case, being present before a building obviously occupied by doctors. You had all of that information, didn't you?"

"Yes, sir," Petersen replied. The file on the Ellsberg burglary had been closed
after Elmer Davis' false confession, so Petersen claimed if he had investigated
further, "the only thing I would have learned is . . . that Dr. Fielding was a
psychiatrist who treated Dr. Ellsberg . . . we would have come up with zero."

Ervin wasn't convinced. "You can never tell whether you are going to
catch fish until you go fishing."

"It's hard to catch a burglar that's confessed," replied Petersen, betraying his ignorance. As discussed in Chapter 5, a check of Elmer Davis' police records would have revealed he had been in jail at the time of the Fielding break-in and maintained his innocence.[86]

Two days later, after a briefing from Charles Morgan, Senator Tunney was also mystified why Silbert, who was investigating Hunt and Liddy's use of false identification and trips to California, would see a photograph of Liddy standing outside Fielding's office and not find out who Dr. Fielding was.

"I have asked myself a hundred times why in the world did you not ask somebody to check out Fielding's name," Petersen finally admitted. "It was a faux pas, I should have done it, even if it did turn out to be negative, but I did not . . . I am not prepared to criticize Mr. Silbert for what I did not have sense enough to tell him to do. I saw the documents as well as he did."

Tunney pointed out that Judge Byrne had issued an exculpatory order in in the Ellsberg trial (*US v. Russo*) in September 1972, requiring the Justice Department to turn over all relevant information that they had. If the FBI had interviewed Dr. Fielding in December or early January, the prosecutors would have found out about the burglary and Fielding could have identified his office and apartment building.[87]

During later nomination hearings in May 1975, Senator Tunney of California took Silbert to task for overlooking the importance of these photographs and established the following:

The prosecutors knew that Hunt's responsibilities at the White House involved investigating and "plugging" leaks, particularly the Ellsberg case . . . [and] that Hunt and Liddy had used the same aliases and false identification in California as in the Watergate break-in.

When the contents of Hunt's safe were turned over to prosecutors in early July 1972, they included a twenty-eight-page chronology of Ellsberg which noted Ellsberg underwent psychoanalysis from October 1968 to October 1970, and mentioned a call to "Dr. Lewis Fielding (psychiatrist)" the following January and "two FBI memos on Dr. Lewis Fielding . . . [from late July 1971], trying to establish that Dr. Fielding was Daniel Ellsberg's psychiatrist."[88]

As McCord later pointed out, Silbert and Petersen had access to the "TSD photographs" memo which identified the license plate as Dr. Fielding's and a check of FBI files would have immediately connected him to the Ellsberg case. The trial started five days later and McCord concluded "Silbert and Petersen wanted to conceal this information from the Watergate jury." At this point, the implication of the photos to Helms, Colby, Dunn, and Warner should also have been clear.[89]

In early February, Petersen discussed the CIA material regarding Hunt with White House counsel John Dean and showed him the pictures the Agency had processed, which "included a picture of Liddy standing in front of Ellsberg's psychiatrist's office." Dean had heard rumours of the Fielding break-in in April or May of 1972. Now here was proof and the FBI director and Watergate prosecutors had it:

It was inevitable that the burglary of Ellsberg's psychiatrist's office would be discovered. I felt that any investigator worth his salt would certainly be able to look at the pictures in the files at the Department of Justice and immediately determine the location and from there discover the fact that there had been a burglary of the office that was in the picture.

Dean told Ehrlichman, "Peterson has got the pictures" and they both just shook their heads. Ehrlichman requested that CIA retrieve all materials sent to the Justice Department on the grounds of national security, before Senate investigators could receive copies of the material, but the Agency refused.

Dean knew the exposure of the Fielding break-in was now just a matter of time.[90]

On January 5, McCord sent Gaynor further "Notes":

> *The outfit tried to lay this operation at the feet of CIA this week and that failed.*
>
> *Yesterday they tried to get all of the defendants to plead guilty, thus protecting those higher up from involvement, and that failed. Barker and Hunt allegedly were willing to plead, so it is said. McCord and Liddy refused.*
>
> *In revenge, now the prosecution is planning to state that the motives of at least some of the defendants was blackmail . . . It was anticipated that when I refused to implicate CIA they would undertake a massive character assassination attempt.*
>
> *The judge is not buying this ploy . . . referring to it as a "cover story" and indicating that the world was watching this case . . . and that the jury was going to get to the bottom of it . . . Some of the newsmen say we are scapegoats. They are right.*[91]

Gaynor claimed he hand-carried the letters to Osborn as soon as he received them. The letters were unsigned but from the context, and the use of the words "company" and "operation," Gaynor immediately realized they were from McCord. Gaynor never acknowledged receipt and said he had not seen or spoken to McCord since the summer of 1970 "when he was retired and he came into my office to say goodbye."[92]

Gaynor said he was in routine, monthly contact with "a close personal friend" of McCord, "who serves as an intermittent source for my staff." In the fall, he commented on "how Mrs. McCord was bearing the strain of Mr. McCord's difficulties in attempting to raise bail [and] of the bad effect his absence from the home was having on their retarded daughter." They discussed McCord again in early January, just before the start of McCord's trial.[93]

Howard Osborn's testimony before the Nedzi Committee confirms this "close personal friend" was Lee Pennington. Osborn "was informed McCord and Pennington were close personal friends. What Pennington was telling Mr. Gaynor and Mr. Vasaly was that Ruth McCord was in dire straits, needed money, that Pennington had loaned her some money . . . that he was helping out, that he was going over to see her, trying to console her, guide her, advise her. I had no reason to believe that Pennington was in any way involved in the Watergate affair. I have no real reason to believe that he is now."[94]

In mid-January, as Richard Helms prepared to leave the Agency, Osborn requested three copies of the McCord letters from Gaynor and took them to Helms "and asked for guidance as to what he should do with them":

> *DCI Helms reviewed the file, directed Osborn to check with General Counsel Houston, and if the latter had no objection, Osborn was to continue secure retention of the letters. Osborn proceeded as directed and, Houston having no objection, returned the letters to his safe.*[95]

Osborn returned the letters to Gaynor and he "placed them in the drawer of [his] safe in [his] office." Gaynor couldn't say why the flow of letters stopped at that point or why, thinking they had stopped, Osborn copied all the letters.[96]

"Why do you think these letters were addressed to you?" he was later asked.

"Because of the fact we had worked together some years back, and I imagine McCord was assuming I was still in the same position I had when he left, and that he knew I would have direct channel of communications directly with the Director of Security, I would report to him, I would see these letters would get somebody's attention. I think he could have sent them to other people he knew. I don't know why he didn't."[97]

During the Nedzi hearings, Gaynor was asked, "What kind of a man was McCord?"

"He is a quiet, religious man, deeply devoted to his family, totally patriotic, and I know, had a very high regard for the Agency. I think this is why he took this course of action, these letters . . . I believe he was under tremendous pressure, sir, at that time, and I think that would have covered his language.[98]

On January 8, worried that Hunt was telling the Watergate Five about the assurance of executive clemency, CRP attorney Paul O'Brien and John Mitchell advised Dean to give a similar assurance to McCord. John Dean asked O'Brien to tell McCord's lawyer that he would receive a call that evening from a White House "friend." After midnight, McCord received a call and was told "to go to a nearby phone booth to receive a message." When he answered the phone, a voice he didn't recognize said:

> *Plead guilty. One year is a long time. You will get Executive clemency. Your family will be taken care of and when you get out, you will be rehabilitated and a job will be found for you. Don't take immunity when called before the grand jury.*

Nixon intelligence operative Tony Ulasewicz made the call for his boss, Jack Caulfield and reported back "McCord's apparent satisfaction" but McCord wanted to meet Caulfield in person. Through another call to the pay phone, Ulasewicz set up the first of several meetings between Caulfield and McCord on the George Washington Parkway in Virginia on January 12. Caulfield urged McCord to "plead guilty, receive clemency and be rehabilitated," saying his message came "from the very highest levels of the White House" and the president knew of the meeting. The next day, "when Caulfield asked if the offer came from the President, Dean replied it came 'from the top.'"

On January 14, Caulfield met McCord again and told him "his efforts to develop as a defense . . . his claims of Government wiretaps of certain phone calls he had made to foreign embassies would not be successful. McCord became very concerned and was assured that he would receive clemency after 10 or 11 months' imprisonment." Caulfield told McCord, "The President's ability to govern is at stake" and that impending scandal could bring down the Government:

> *Everybody else is on track but you, you are not following the game plan, get closer to your attorney.*

In two phone calls over the next two days, McCord told Caulfield that "he had no desire to talk to him further and suggested that if the White House wanted to be honest it should look into McCord's perjury charges against Magruder, and his claims as to the tapping of his two embassy calls."

At a final meeting on January 25, "Caulfield repeated the offers of clemency, financial support and rehabilitation" and warned McCord that if pursued "his wiretap defense" against "high administration officials, the administration would undoubtedly defend itself. McCord interpreted this as a 'personal threat' to his safety but stated his willingness to take the risk."

Caulfield concluded "that McCord was definitely going to speak out on the Watergate burglary and would probably make allegations against White House and other high officials." He told McCord:

> *Jim, I have worked with these people and I know them to be as tough-minded as you and I. When you make your statement, don't underestimate them, If I were in your shoes, I would probably be doing the same thing.* [99]

McCord continued to receive his CRP salary of $3,000 a month through January 1973, as well as $25,000 to cover legal fees.[100]

On January 7, 1973, a story appeared in the *Washington Post* about Martinez' operational diary. The next day, Leo Dunn interviewed Robert Ritchie, who knew nothing about a diary and had not asked Martinez to keep one. Two days later, Ramon Gonzalez also knew nothing about a diary and said, "Martinez did not like written reports . . . Gonzalez had 'to draw out information for a written contact report.'"[101]

A week later, in a lengthy article for the *New York Times*, Seymour Hersh reported that Martinez was "an active [CIA] employee . . . at the time of the break-in and kept a diary. He was stricken from the Agency's payroll within a day of his arrest and his diary was subsequently found by Federal investigators in the trunk of his car [at Miami airport]."[102]

The next morning, Hunt, Martinez and the other burglars—who had initially pleaded "not guilty"—changed their pleas to "guilty" and were sent to jail. In his six months out on bail, Martinez had received a couple of thousand dollars from Barker but he denied it was an inducement to change his plea, or that anyone had induced him to remain silent or plead guilty through threats or promises of executive clemency.[103]

In the *Washington Post* that morning, Martin Schram claimed "the Watergate burglary and espionage mission . . . was part of a widespread project in which documents were photographed in the Embassy of Chile and several liberal Democratic senators [Mansfield, Church, and Fulbright] were kept under electronic surveillance, according to a source close to the defendants." A three-man team had broken into the Chilean embassy—one pulled documents, one photographed them, and one refiled them. They also tapped the phone of Sol Linowitz, former US ambassador to the Organization of American States (OAS). The story also claimed the existence of Martinez' diary, "written without the knowledge of the codefendants, indicates that the [CIA]—or at least a CIA case officer—may have been monitoring the activities of the Watergate team."[104]

The flurry of press stories prompted the CIA to promptly gather all its material on Martinez. Four days later, Chief of the Western Hemisphere Division Ted Shackley wrote to Helms, confirming receipt of "all of the information pertinent to Martinez" from the Miami station, including "correspondence between headquarters and [Esterline], and contact reports of meetings with Martinez going back as far as June 1971. We also have the report written by Martinez which was taken in a sealed envelope to the chief of station (the Spanish report)."[105]

The source of these articles was Andrew St. George, who had known Frank Sturgis since 1958, when Sturgis (then known as Frank Fiorini) was a guerrilla fighter in Castro's revolutionary force before splitting with Castro when he embraced Communism. Fiorini later adopted the name Sturgis after a character in one of Hunt's novels, *Bimini Run*. In September 1972, St. George approached Sturgis to write an "adventure biography" of his life and Sturgis made "fragmentary revelations" about his role in the Watergate break-in and other operations. Sturgis described his role as stealing or copying documents with Felipe De Diego and Rolando Martinez.[106]

Sturgis alleged that Sol Linowitz, a Washington, D.C. attorney and "important McGovern advisor," had brokered a deal for Allende's government to "funnel money into the Presidential campaign of candidate George

McGovern in return for certain concessions" if McGovern was elected. Sturgis claimed he had broken into the attorney's office with Martinez, intending "to publish any embarrassing information" he found. Linowitz confirmed to St. George that his office had been searched but he had chosen not to publicise the incident. Sturgis also claimed he had broken into the Chilean embassy with Martinez and Felipe De Diego and "had been in and checked out the Chileans twice."[107]

St. George's book outline was leaked to Seymour Hersh, who published some of its claims on January 14, which Sturgis vehemently denied. On March 8, Ted Shackley reviewed a Jack Anderson column titled "Chilean Break-Ins Reflect Watergate" that appeared that morning in the *Washington Post*. There was "no foundation to the allegation that E. Howard Hunt was engaged on behalf of ITT in breaking into Chilean diplomatic installations in Washington and New York," he wrote. ITT called the allegations "completely inaccurate and untrue" and denied any link to the break-ins at the embassy or Chilean diplomats' residences: "ITT never hired E. Howard Hunt or any so-called 'Mission Impossible team.'"[108]

"One weekend during the trial," Dean writes in his memoir, he located the "two Hermès notebooks and a metal pop-up address book" from Hunt's safe he had kept to himself in a safe at home since late June. Hunt had pleaded guilty, so Dean figured "they were no longer relevant for the trial . . . [but] were certainly dangerous to the cover-up. He decided to feed them into his new shredder but failed to mention this in his Senate Watergate testimony and withheld it "until after he pleaded guilty to a conspiracy to obstruct justice charge."[109]

On Sunday evening, January 16, Charles Morgan read the transcript of an interview Alfred Baldwin gave to the *Los Angeles Times* in October 1972 and was intrigued by several references to the CIA. Baldwin described how McCord "talked CIA-style" and how the CIA were permitted to mount a wiretap operation against a subversive group without a warrant until the

Supreme Court ruled against it shortly after the break-in. They may have regarded McGovern as a subversive but why Spencer Oliver?[110]

Asked if the motive for the break-in was "mostly to find out what the Democratic strategy was," Baldwin replied, "I wouldn't put it that way. They could have political blackmail over somebody very easy . . . there was a tremendous feeling on the part of the US attorneys that . . . this might have been CIA." Baldwin's attorney John Cassidento thought it was a CIA operation and Baldwin agreed it was a possibility.[111]

Morgan raised Baldwin's frequent mentions of the CIA at an in-camera hearing with Sirica, Silbert, and Glanzer at five thirty the next day. As Baldwin thought he might have been working for the CIA, Morgan proposed a motion requiring the prosecution to prove "they were not Governmental wire taps."

"I don't think this is an issue in the case, is it?" asked Sirica. "I have never heard that before."

"I would deny it absolutely," replied Silbert, pointing to a legitimate correction Glanzer had made that morning. While McCord was in Miami, the transcript stated Baldwin delivered a "particular capsule" to the CIA. Silbert said this was a misprint. A few lines later, it's clear Baldwin meant he had given the logs to CRP, not CIA. But Silbert glossed over the other references to the CIA in the transcript and as Morgan's aim was to "protect the conversations [and] keep the transcript secret" on behalf of his clients, he stayed quiet.

The next morning, Sirica ruled that Baldwin's conversations were admissible during the trial but he was overruled the next day by the District Court of Appeals, which concluded that the intercepted conversations Baldwin heard were "not required to prove the charge for which the defendants are on trial" and "would frustrate the purpose of Congress in making wiretapping a crime."[112]

On that same Monday, just weeks before he retired, Richard Helms received a letter from Senator Mansfield (D—Montana), "requesting that the Agency retain any records or documents which have a bearing on the Senate's forth-coming investigation into the Watergate break-in." A week later, "Helms' secretary asked him what should be done about the voluminous tapes and transcripts which were then in storage." The central taping system allowed Helms to record telephone calls and room conversations and he sometimes used it as an aide-mémoire for subsequent memos. The tapes were routinely transcribed. Helms and his secretary "made a cursory review" of "three file drawers of transcripts . . . and recalled none to have related to Watergate." Helms then ordered the tapes, transcripts, and logs destroyed and the taping system was removed. Helms later described the destruction of "his personal notes to be a routine part of vacating his office . . . he assumed that anything of permanent value had been transferred from the tapes to the Agency's records, and he felt obligated that records of confidential conversations between him and others should not become part of Agency files." The Rockefeller Commission later criticised his "poor judgement." The Office of Security had its own taping system but shared only two transcripts judged to be Watergate-related with Baker's staff.[113]

Among the questions Senator Baker's staff prepared for Richard Helms in February 1973 were: Why was Helms not informed of the Martinez–Hunt conversations among senior staff in March 1972? Cord Meyer testified "he checked with Karamessines prior to his cryptic response to Esterline that he knew that Hunt's activities at the time were of concern to the CIA." Why didn't Karamessines tell Helms? Would Helms not have been "concerned that Hunt was in contact with a current Agency operative? Would not Hunt's contact with Martinez pose a security problem for the Agency that would justify inquiry . . . and would not the Nicaraguan aspect of Hunt's Miami contacts justify CIA action?"

They also wanted to know when Helms saw "the Miami correspondence regarding Martinez/Hunt? Why was Martinez not used to report on Hunt or, as an alternative, dismissed to avoid Agency taint in the area of concern?" Why were these conversations not shared with the FBI "in a timely fashion"?

And could Helms explain the two-day delay in notifying the FBI about Martinez' car?[114]

On February 7, Helms testified that Martinez had been on a one hundred dollar a month retainer at the time of the break-in. It was "a very loose kind of arrangement in which he reported in from time to time [to his case officer] . . . on individuals coming in from Cuba . . . either legally or illegally, whom he thought might have some information that would be useful to the U.S. Government . . . As soon as it was found out he was involved in the Watergate thing, we simply turned him off and have not talked to him since."[115]

On February 17, 1973, after confirmation hearings for Pat Gray's permanent appointment as FBI director were announced, Hunt wrote Gray a caustic letter, noting he had been criticized for "the Bureau's alleged failure fully to investigate the Watergate Case":

From my own experience I am able fully and freely to testify that the Bureau left no grain of sand unturned in its investigation. My late wife and children were interrogated, blackmailed, threatened and harassed by Special Agents of the Bureau . . . Threats and intimidation were not the least of the investigative tools employed . . . under your direction . . . During my projected appearance before the [Senate Watergate] Committee, I will be eager to make the thoroughness and savagery of the FBI's Watergate investigation a matter of public record.

A month later, six days before the burglars were due to be sentenced, John Dean began discussing Watergate with Nixon and told him about the Fielding break-in for the first time.[116]

Two days later, McCord cracked and wrote his famous letter to Judge Sirica, after his probation officer had questioned him about "details of the case, motivations, intent and mitigating circumstances" for his presentence report. McCord wrote that he felt himself "whipsawed in a variety of legalities," fearing certain testimony could be used against him in future litigation but failure to cooperate might result in a much harsher sentence. While his family feared for his life if he disclosed what he knew, he feared "retaliatory measures will be taken against me, my family, and my friends should I disclose such facts. Such retaliation could destroy careers, income, and reputations of persons who are innocent of any guilt whatever."

"Be that as he may," he continued, "in the interests of justice, and in the interests of restoring faith in the criminal justice system," he had decided to step forward, alleging:

1. *There was political pressure applied to the defendants to plead guilty and remain silent.*
2. *Perjury occurred during the trial in matters highly material to . . . the motivation and intent of the defendants.*
3. *Others involved in the Watergate operation were not identified during the trial, when they could have been by those testifying.*
4. *The Watergate operation was not a CIA operation. The Cubans may have been misled by others into believing that it was a CIA operation. I know for a fact that it was not.*
5. *My motivations were different than those of the others involved. . . .*

Following sentence, I would appreciate the opportunity to talk with you privately in chambers. Since I cannot feel confident in talking with an FBI agent, in testifying before a Grand Jury whose U.S. Attorneys work for the Department of Justice, or in talking with other government representatives, such a discussion with you would be of assistance to me.[117]

McCord testified "that at the time of the Watergate trial, pressure was brought on himself and other defendants to claim for purposes of a defense that Watergate was a CIA operation" but he saw no evidence to support that:[118]

> *Quite the contrary . . . it was an operation which involved the Attorney General of the United States at that point in time. Subsequently he became the director of the Committee to Re-Elect the President, involved the counsel to the White House, involved Mr. Jeb Magruder and Mr. Liddy . . . Therefore, in my mind, there was an absolute certainty that the CIA was not involved, neither did I ever receive any statement from any of the other co-defendants at any point in time . . . that this was a CIA operation.*[119]

During grand jury proceedings on April 6, 1973, James McCord revealed the location of the second bug, and believed it was still installed on a phone at the DNC. The FBI conducted a search of the office McCord identified that afternoon, and after clearing "the pertinent office space . . . of its personnel," found no bugs on the telephone "in question . . . and every other telephone in that room." According to the telephone company, two or three phones had been removed from "the area in question" one month before, with six-button telephones replacing the seventeen-button call director telephones present on June 17. The "area in question" was described as "adjacent to Spencer Oliver's room . . . to the east of Mr. Oliver's office." As seen in Figure 6, the offices directly east of Oliver's office and facing Virginia Avenue belonged to Press Secretary Joseph Mohbat, Communications Director John Stewart and Stewart's personal secretary Susan Davis Cantril. While both the FBI reports and McCord's book don't identify the precise location, the clues above strongly suggest it was the space adjoining Spencer Oliver's office and marked "Secretaries" in Figure 6. According to Davis Cantril, three secretaries worked in this room: Gretel Uhl, Fleurette LeBow and Susan Meushaw.

All seventy-seven phones in the DNC were physically checked by the FBI that afternoon and "no bugging devices were found." An electronic sweep was also negative. The two regular installers who serviced the DNC for the telephone company told the FBI they had examined every phone in the DNC on September 13, 1972, after the bug was discovered in Oliver's office and no other devices were found. Any phones which had been replaced at the DNC since June 17 were routinely sent to the Western Electric plant in Arlington for servicing and reissue to another customer but no bugs had been found in those either. It remains a mystery why the bug in the second office was never found. The bugs were only activated and could only be picked up in an electronic sweep if the receiver was off the hook but no second bug was found during at least four complete physical checks of the DNC offices. McCord also denied doing "any work on the wiretaps"—removing or installing—during the second break-in.

The following Monday, in further grand jury testimony, McCord examined the device discovered in September and claimed it was identical to the bug he had installed in Oliver's phone. The FBI Laboratory insisted "the device removed from Oliver's telephone was not there in June 1972" and telephone company personnel agreed. But as noted in Appendix 2, McCord's identification of various bugs presented at trial and in grand jury testimony make little sense.[120]

Three weeks later, during a deposition in the civil case brought by the DNC against him and the burglars, McCord described entering the DNC through the rear door to the stairwell during the first break-in with two telephone bugs. Barker met him inside, "pointed to the room at the end of the hall on the left, and said, 'This is the room you want.'" While Barker "was working in the room," McCord checked a call director phone to see if it carried Larry O'Brien's extension number. The window was so full of books, it was impossible to close the curtains, so McCord decided to check another office, where he couldn't be observed from the Howard Johnson, to look for a phone with O'Brien's extension. He also discussed where to install the second bug with Barker:

> *We agreed that Oliver's phone . . . seemed to a logical one because of his position as Chairman of the Association of State Democratic Chairmen [sic]. So while Barker was working in the first office . . . I went into Oliver's office, pulled the curtains, took the telephone cover off of the telephone and made that installation, came back, went into the secretary's office that I have referred to [previously], took the cover off of the call director which had about 18 lines . . . and checked the telephone.*

The color coding on the wiring had been changed, so rather than risk a faulty installation, McCord checked another phone in the room with two or three lines, one of which "appeared to come off the same call director" and carry O'Brien's extension: "I took the cover off of that . . . [and] made the second installation . . . [on] the extension of the call director that was sitting on the secretary's desk." This seems to confirm the identification of the "Secretaries" office above.[121]

A month later, at the Watergate hearings, McCord told Senator Baker that Liddy's instructions from Mitchell were to install devices in "O'Brien's offices" and "another senior official's office." He was vague on why Oliver's phone was chosen and didn't know it was Oliver's phone until Baldwin began listening to the intercepts. He said he planted both bugs "in offices that face Virginia Avenue." O'Brien's office was on the opposite side of the building from Virginia Avenue.

"One of them was on Mr. O'Brien's telephone?" asked Baker.

"That was an extension of a call director that was identified as Mr. O'Brien's," replied McCord. "The second was . . . in a telephone that belonged to Mr. Spencer Oliver."

McCord's choice of words here and the location he describes clearly indicate he realized, in retrospect, it was not O'Brien's phone or office but Baker didn't notice. In McCord's book, he makes clear that he did not plant a bug in O'Brien's office:

> *Barker pointed out the area of interest for the electronic work, and I began checking the telephone call director arrangement. I had been asked to install only one device but had brought a second "for insurance" in case needed.*

He planted bugs in "an office with a direct view across the street at the Howard Johnson Motel" and on an extension "off a telephone call director in an adjoining room." While McCord may have been instructed to plant a bug on Larry O'Brien's phone, he clearly didn't know where O'Brien's office was during the first break-in and bugged what he thought was O'Brien's extension in an office on the other side of the building with a device which wasn't received by Baldwin in any case. Or at least, that's his story.[122]

On Sunday, April 15, Dean told Silbert that Hunt and Liddy had "burglarized the offices of a psychiatrist of Daniel Ellsberg to obtain the psychiatrist's files relating to Ellsberg." Silbert wrote a memorandum to Petersen the next day. While the prosecutors in the Ellsberg trial knew nothing about the burglary, a check of FBI files turned up the Bureau's interview with Dr. Fielding "and that," said Petersen, "led us to the photographs and then we made the connection."[123]

Dean also told Petersen he had given the FBI's Pat Gray two files from Hunt's safe. That same Monday morning, when confronted by Petersen, Gray initially denied it, but the following morning, he admitted he had accepted the files from Dean. John Ehrlichman had suggested dumping them in the Potomac River but he had burned them in his fireplace without reading them.[124]

On Wednesday, Petersen informed Nixon about the Fielding break-in: "The President replied that he knew of it, that it was a national security matter, and that the Department of Justice was not to investigate it. The President also ordered the Watergate prosecutors not to question E. Howard Hunt about these activities . . . He said it would blow the Ellsberg case."[125]

A week later, "with clear evidence that Mr. Hunt was involved in the [Fielding] break-in," Nixon agreed with Attorney General Kleindienst "that the information be transmitted to Judge Byrne immediately."[126]

On Wednesday, April 25, Pat Gray went to see Senator Lowell Weicker to make a partial confession. He claimed he had thrown Hunt's files in the burn wastebasket in his office on July 3 without reading them. It later emerged he burned them at home six months later after reading them.[127]

On Thursday, the Justice Department sent the Silbert–Petersen memorandum to Judge Matthew Byrne, who was presiding over the Ellsberg trial. He disclosed it to the defense and read it out in open court the next day, angering the government.[128]

The following day, Acting FBI Director L. Patrick Gray resigned. Later that day, Ellsberg called Dr. Fielding to inform him of the break-in, and Fielding met Ellsberg and his attorney the next day and prepared his affidavit.[129]

On Monday, April 30, as the cover-up began to unravel, Nixon accepted the resignations of Ehrlichman, Haldeman, Dean, and Attorney General Kleindienst and made his first televised address to the nation about the Watergate investigations, which had ensnared "some of [his] closest friends and most trusted aides":

> *I was appalled at this senseless, illegal action, and I was shocked to learn that employees of the Re-Election Committee were apparently among those guilty . . . Some people, quite properly appalled at the abuses that occurred, will say that Watergate demonstrates the bankruptcy of the American*

*political system. I believe precisely the opposite is true. Watergate repre-
sented a series of illegal acts and bad judgments by a number of individuals. It was the system that has brought the facts to light and that will bring
those guilty to justice . . . We must maintain the integrity of the White
House . . . There can be no whitewash at the White House.*

He pledged to reform the political process, ridding it of "inexcusable campaign tactics that have been . . . too readily accepted in the past, including
those that may have been a response by one side to the excesses or expected
excesses of the other side. Two wrongs do not make a right."[130]

Two days later, Hunt disclosed the Ellsberg psychological profiles and
CIA equipment used in the Fielding burglary to the Watergate grand jury.[131]

On May 11, Judge Byrne declared a mistrial in the Ellsberg case and dismissed all charges against the defendants, "based on the government's gross
misconduct." "The bizarre events" undertaken by the White House special
unit while Ellsberg was under indictment—the Fielding break-in conducted
with CIA disguises and equipment, the psychological profiles and the wiretapping of Ellsberg—"offend a sense of justice," wrote Byrne in his order of
dismissal, "and incurably infected the prosecution of the case."[132]

"The sonofabitching thief [Ellsberg] is made a national hero and is going
to get off on a mistrial," Nixon raged at Haldeman. "And the *New York
Times* gets a Pulitzer Prize for stealing documents . . . They're trying to get
at us with thieves. *What in the name of God have we come to?*"[133]

Carl Rowan, who had made light of Watergate with Helms at the MPAA
screening party, turned on Helms and the Agency in a piece that day, titled
"CIA's Involvement Appalling":

*I can only conclude that the CIA was up to its armpits in the dirty work
masterminded by Hunt and Liddy, in the Ellsberg case but also in the*

Watergate crime. I can only conclude that this vast organization with all its secret money, all its capacity for eavesdropping and other dirty tricks, was turned into an apparatus for perpetuating the power of Richard Nixon and his cronies.[134]

Ehrlichman and Young argued "there were legitimate national security considerations for obtaining Ellsberg's psychiatric file" and that a profile would help determine "whether we were dealing here with a spy ring or just an individual kook, or whether we were dealing with a serious penetration of the Nation's military and other secrets." But Hunt assumed any derogatory information would be leaked to the press through Colson as part of a politically-motivated smear campaign and Senate Watergate Committee Chairman Sam Ervin could not see any connection "between Dr. Fielding's notions of the mental state of Daniel Ellsberg and foreign intelligence activities." Ehrlichman, Liddy, Colson, and Krogh were given prison terms for violating Ellsberg's civil rights; Martinez and Barker received suspended sentences; and De Diego was granted immunity for testifying and his indictment was dismissed.[135]

President John F. Kennedy with Anna Chennault, chairwoman of
Chinese Refugee Relief, June 1962 (photo by Abbie Rowe, JFK
Library)

June 28, 1968

PERSONAL & CONFIDENTIAL

Hon. Richard M. Nixon
810 Fifth Avenue
New York, N. Y. 10021

Dear Mr. Nixon:

I was in New York day before yesterday and had a very pleasant
meeting with your secretary, Miss Scarney. I assume by now she
has already relayed to you my message and I am confident of your
judgment of this most important and serious issue at this time.
In my humble opinion, the Johnson Administration owes to the American
public to tell them what to expect of the Paris peace talks and what
position the Administration plans to take if the peace talks should
fail.

I had a long talk with Ambassador Robert Hill this morning and I
depend on him to relay to you some of the information I have received
the last few days.

President Thieu of South Vietnam's visit to Washington was canceled
after Senator Bob Kennedy's assassination but now it has been re-
scheduled. He will be in Washington for two days. After talking
with Ambassador Hill, if you should decide to meet with President Thieu,
please let me know and I will work out the detail and make the arrangement.

One final note: Remember my prediction on March 25th when I wrote you
and predicted the eventual pull out of Khesanh. There is so much going
on in Southeast Asia and so few of us really know the truth.

Please take good care.

With warmest regards to you and Mrs. Nixon.

Sincerely,

Anna Chennault

[Handwritten annotations: "NO! NO!"; "A.C. = melody"; "TO RN — Allen recommends this not be done for any reason and under no circumstances. Proposal dangerous in the extreme and injurious to our VN position, i.e. to US nat. interests. rva"]

Chennault letter to Nixon, June 28, 1968, with annotations by Richard
Allen (photo by author at Hoover Institution Archives)

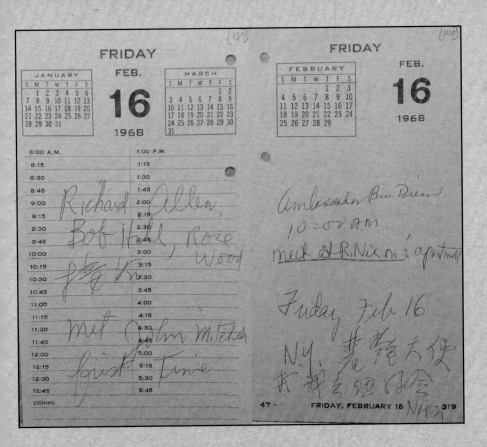

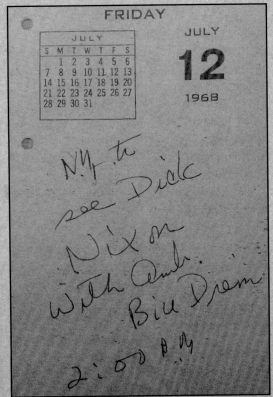

ABOVE: Chennault calendar entry, February 16, 1968, including the Chinese words "contact" and "ambassador" (photo by author at Schlesinger Library)

LEFT: Chennault calendar entry, July 12, 1968 (photo by author at Schlesinger Library)

ABOVE: President-Elect
Richard Nixon and
President Lyndon B.
Johnson in a White House
elevator, December 12,
m1968 (photo by Yoichi
Okamoto, LBJ Library)

RIGHT: President Richard
Nixon with U.S. Army 1st
Infantry Division troops
in South Vietnam, July 30,
1969 (National Archives)

ABOVE: President Nixon with Henry Kissinger and Anna Chennault, vice president of the Flying Tiger Line, in the Oval Office, April 12, 1971 (photo by Oliver Atkins, Nixon Library)

BELOW: President Richard Nixon greets a crowd of Air Force servicemen at Homestead AFB in Florida, August 24, 1972 (National Archives)

Richard Helms with Richard Nixon (National Archives)

WARNING—ALTERATION, ADDITION OR MUTILATION OF ENTRIES IS PROHIBITED.
ANY UNOFFICIAL CHANGE WILL RENDER THIS PASSPORT INVALID.

NAME
E. HOWARD HUNT

BIRTH DATE
OCT. 9, 1918

BIRTHPLACE
NEW YORK, U.S.A.

HEIGHT
5 FEET 9 INCHES

HAIR
BROWN

EYES
BLUE

WIFE
X X X

ISSUE DATE
JULY 21, 1971

MINORS
X X X

EXPIRATION DATE ➤ JULY 20, 1976

SIGNATURE OF BEARER

IMPORTANT: THIS PASSPORT IS NOT VALID UNTIL SIGNED BY THE BEARER.

ABOVE: Hunt passport,
1972 (National Archives)

RIGHT: Howard Hunt
(date unknown) (National
Archives)

HUNT, E. Howard Jr.
23500

Dr. Lewis J. Fielding, Daniel Ellsberg's psychiatrist, arrives at Los Angeles Criminal Court during the Ellsberg trial, 1973 (photo by John Malmin, Los Angeles Times Photographic Archive, Special Collections, Charles E. Young Research Library, UCLA)

Some of the president's men (clockwise from top left: John Ehrlichman, Charles Colson, H.R. Haldeman, John Dean, Jeb Magruder, John Mitchell)
(National Archives)

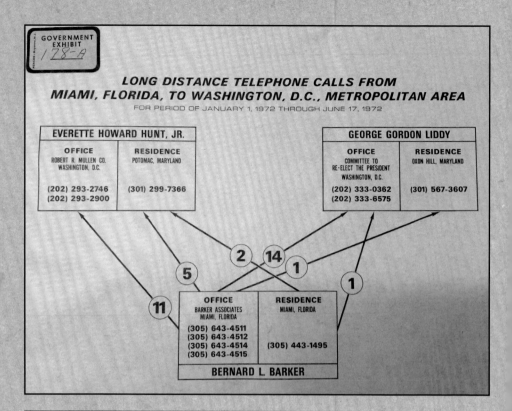

ABOVE: Chart prepared by Watergate prosecutor Earl Silbert for the trial (photo by author at National Archives)

BELOW: Police mugshot of James McCord, June 17, 1972 (National Archives

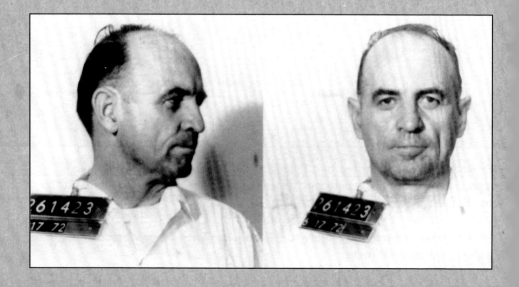

The Howard Johnson motel (bottom left) across the street from the Watergate complex. The Columbia Plaza apartment complex can be seen in the distance, top left (National Archives)

TOP: Photo of gym bag and contents, June 17, 1972, including two cameras, a clamp stand, rolls of film and three bugging devices (National Archives)

BOTTOM: Property seized from "Jean Valdes" (Martinez), including the key to room 214 at the Watergate Hotel, and the key to Maxie Wells' desk taped to a notebook (National Archives)

TOP: Police photo of the waiting room in which the burglars were arrested. They
were found hiding behind the partition in the far-right corner (National Archives)

BOTTOM: Photo from inside the secretarial cubicle where the burglars were caught
hiding behind this partition (National Archives)

A recent photo of the key to Maxie Wells' desk and Martinez' yellow notebook, inscribed with the initials of Carl M. Shoffler (photo by author at National Archives

CHAPTER 9

THE INVESTIGATIONS

In January 1974, Rob Roy Ratliff, the Agency liaison to the National Security Council (NSC) at the White House, made an extraordinary statement to the CIA's Inspector General, later published by the House Judiciary Committee:

> *My secretary, Mrs. Evelyn DePue, and I frequently speculated about the possible involvement of Howard Hunt in the Watergate Affair and the possible involvement of the Agency.*

In the months before Watergate, Ratliff was the senior CIA officer in the Executive Office Building, working in close proximity to the Plumbers. His predecessors as Agency liaison to the NSC included Peter Jessup, who held the role from 1963 until the late sixties, and Frank Chapin, a former assistant to Allen Dulles who held the position until 1971, when he became ill and Jessup returned to cover for him. In the spring of 1972, Jessup trained up Peter Ferguson for the role but he only lasted a month and Ratliff took over in April or May. Evelyn DePue had served at the White House since the Kennedy administration and was secretary to Jessup, Chapin, and Ratliff.[1]

Ratliff said he was "aware that Hunt had frequently transmitted sealed envelopes via our office to the Agency. We had receipts for these envelopes but were unaware of the contents." While Peter Jessup was covering for

Chapin and "breaking in" Ferguson, "he had opened one of the packages one day to see what Hunt was sending to the Agency":

> *The envelope was addressed to Dr. [Bernard] Malloy [Chief, Psychological Services Branch] and appeared to contain "gossip" information about an unknown person—[Jessup] assumed that it had something to do with a psychological study of that person. Mrs. DePue subsequently confirmed this information.*

Clearly, these were materials for the Ellsberg psychological profile. At this point in his typed statement, Ratliff added a handwritten note: "We were also aware that Hunt passed 'gossip' items to Helms."[2]

"As the news of the Watergate and Hunt's involvement spread," he continued, "we . . . decided that it was not prudent nor necessary to retain the receipts for envelopes which we had transmitted from him to CIA and we destroyed these receipts." When press reports linking Hunt to the psychological studies appeared, Ratliff decided to raise the alarm. He didn't know if Helms had authorized the profiles, or whether Hunt "had prevailed upon Dr. Malloy" to do them or Malloy was doing them unofficially on a "freelance" basis. "But I felt strongly that the Agency should be aware of this Hunt–Malloy connection, in case it did not already know."[3]

On May 2, 1973, Hunt's explosive grand jury testimony about the Fielding break-in at the Ellsberg trial in Los Angeles prompted the Agency to publicly state:

> *The Central Intelligence Agency had no advance notice of any sort whatsoever of the break in by Mr. Hunt of the office of Mr. Ellsberg's psychiatrist or of the Watergate incident. The newspaper reports of these two events were the first notice to anyone in the agency: all agency information on our*

contacts with any persons involved in these incidents has been reported fully
to the Department of Justice.[4]

Well, not quite. The same day, Ratliff called Helms' successor as CIA Director, James Schlesinger, and said he had "a confidential matter to discuss with
him." They met at six thirty that evening and Ratliff told the director what
he knew "about envelopes from Hunt to the Agency" and "transmittal of
information to Dr. Malloy." Schlesinger seemed surprised by the revelations
and Ratliff recommended he speak to Dr. Malloy to "get his side of the
story":

> *I found it hard to believe that an individual of the Agency would*
> *become involved in something like this without some approval from*
> *higher authority within the Agency, also, that I was sure that someone*
> *had compiled the facts about the Agency's involvement with Hunt and*
> *the Watergate and that it should be available somewhere in the Agency*
> *if he had not already seen it. He seemed dismayed and bewildered that*
> *something like this could have happened and that he did not know*
> *about it.*

The next day, Tom Latimer, Schlesinger's assistant and a former colleague of
Ratliff's on the NSC staff, called to say Schlesinger was "very upset and had
asked him to look into this right away." Ratliff stopped by his office and
remembered another detail his secretary, Mrs. DePue, had told him:

> *One day, Hunt had come to see [Ferguson] and they had talked behind*
> *closed doors. After the talk, [Ferguson] came out and remarked to [Mrs.*
> *DePue] that he was amazed, shocked and bewildered by the things that*
> *Hunt told him he was doing. He scratched and shook his head, remarked*
> *what an interesting job Hunt had, but revealed none of the details of his*
> *conversation.*

Ratliff felt sure "that Mr. Helms was probably aware of some of Hunt's activities and might have authorized the use of Dr. Malloy" and assumed Schlesinger didn't know about it because of "his newness on the job." Ferguson was interviewed but claimed no knowledge of Hunt's activities. Ratliff suggested interviewing Jessup who had opened at least one envelope Hunt sent to Malloy and might know more "from his personal talks with Hunt":

> *Latimer told me sometime later that Schlesinger was awarding a medal to General Walters for his role in the Watergate affair and remarked again that my report had triggered the revelation of the iceberg. We joked about how the Generals always get the medals!*[5]

Ratliff gave his typed statement to John Richards of the Inspector General's office, who had just written the Agency's draft internal history of Watergate. Inspector General Donald Chamberlain sent Ratliff's statement to William Colby, who had recently replaced Karamessines as Deputy Director for Operations and was also the executive secretary of the Agency's Management Committee. Chamberlain added the following handwritten remarks on the routing slip:

> *Rob Roy Ratliff has just typed this up and given to John Richards. It infers a series of messages over a period of time from Hunt to Mr. Helms, who, of course, has not admitted anything of this sort. The Ferguson–Hunt conversation is also disturbing. Ferguson, when interviewed by Latimer, said he knew nothing. John Richards believes Ferguson would have told Tom K/ Helms about the conversation. If Hunt has told [Senator] Baker about these things, it may account for [Baker's] persistence. Should Richards try to see Ferguson?*

A list of still-classified documents indicates Ferguson was interviewed the following day and Mrs. Evelyn DePue provided a statement a week later. These interviews and reports were cross-referenced with cables to and from Peter Jessup, who was stationed abroad during this period. Apart from Ratcliff's statement, none of this material has ever surfaced publicly.[6]

John Richards investigated Ratliff's allegations but died after a short illness in 1974. The internal draft history of Watergate he left behind ends with an entry for November 26, 1973 "concerning Ambassador Helms meeting with Special Prosecutor [Leon] Jaworski"—who had by then replaced Archibald Cox—and a tentative conclusion:

> *This is not to say that the Watergate affair is ended; or that the Agency will not continue to be questioned by the media, by the Special Prosecutor's office and by the Congress. However, the Agency's pattern of cooperation and responsiveness has been set and will undoubtedly continue.*

> *It is believed, however, that there remain no significant unknown facts concerning the Agency's connection with the whole range of events that have become known popularly as "Watergate." If there are aspects of the matter that have not been developed, we doubt that they would add significantly to an understanding of what did and did not happen. If some such information is developed, the significance is more likely to lie in the interpretations placed on it than in the facts themselves.[7]*

On January 20, 1975, the imprisoned Charles Colson told Senator Baker and Senator Weicker that "Hunt delivered sealed envelopes and packages to Richard Ober, a CIA counterintelligence officer, who forwarded them to . . . Richard Helms. Colson said he suspected that the envelopes contained tapes and other material relating to operations of the White House Plumbers unit. Colson said Hunt continued to pass the material to Ober until late May 1972." Questioned about the story two days later, Helms "didn't recall any such thing." Richard Ober famously headed up Operation CHAOS, the Agency's illegal domestic spying program.[8]

In 1982, Ratliff told author Jim Hougan that "Hunt's packages were routinely received and hand-carried to the CIA until shortly before the Watergate arrests in mid-June 1972." Ratliff believed the practice started almost as soon as Hunt was hired by the White House and the packages contained "gossip" about "White House officials and others in the administration," but not about Daniel Ellsberg. Charles Colson told Hougan he had seen "the CIA's Watergate file" and that "Hunt's White House packages contained tape-recordings *as well as* written information." As Hougan notes, Hunt "continued to send his secret packages to the CIA long after the Ellsberg profile had been abandoned, and way beyond the alleged cut-off of CIA assistance at the end of August 1971." A source on the House Judiciary Committee told Hougan the gossip was "almost entirely of a sexual nature. It was very graphic. Some of it concerned people who worked in the White House."[9]

But two declassified files suggest these packages did contain "gossip" on Daniel Ellsberg, and of a primarily sexual nature. In the week following their October 27 meeting, Liddy sent at least two "addendums" to Malloy, based on FBI reports and consistent with the material Ratliff describes. They did not mention Ellsberg by name (one mentioned his wife, Pat Marx) and concerned "gossip" of a sexual nature.[10]

One describes the couple visiting the "Sandstone Club" in California the previous summer: "The club caters to individuals interested in sexual orgies . . ." reads the report, "persons present at the club are in a complete state of undress and perform various forms of sexual activity in front of each other."[11]

Hunt later criticised this report as an example of "FBI lassitude—and inexactitude—in its coverage of Daniel Ellsberg." The Bureau provided no follow-up information about the club, which a later magazine article described "as a reputable and legitimate institution for group treatment of sexual dysfunction."[12]

In later testimony, Hunt admitted sending "occasional things over to the CIA" in sealed envelopes regarding his "annuity problem" but denied sending envelopes to Helms: "Mr. Colson has in the past adverted to a supposed continuing intelligence liaison between then-Director Helms and myself, which, in fact, did not exist."[13]

On May 7, 1973, the CIA launched an internal inquiry into the support for Hunt and three Senate and Congressional committees announced plans to investigate allegations of CIA involvement in the Fielding break-in. The next day, James Schlesinger confirmed CIA equipment had been given to Hunt and Liddy and used in the Fielding break-in.[14]

On May 9, in Washington, Schlesinger summarized his investigation into Hunt's activities before the Senate Committee on Appropriations and concluded the Agency was not aware of the Fielding or Watergate break-ins at the time. He agreed the Agency had been "insufficiently cautious" in assisting Hunt:

> Later, when the nature of Mr. Hunt's requests for assistance began to indicate a possible active involvement by the Agency in activities beyond its charter, the Agency terminated the relationship and refused further assistance.

He accepted the "preparation of a profile on an American citizen under these circumstances lies beyond the normal activity of the Agency . . . [and] shall not be repeated":

> As Director, I have called for a review of all Agency activities and the termination of any which might be considered outside its legitimate charter. . . .

I have directed each employee . . . to submit to me any cases which they may question. I am determined that the Agency will not engage in activities outside of its charter but will concentrate its energies on its important intelligence mission.[15]

Bizarrely, he revealed that CIA staff who had prepared initial documents for the Department of Justice in October 1972 were still not aware of the Ellsberg profiles. Later that day, Schlesinger called on all current and former staff to report to him directly on any past "activities outside CIA's charter" and any future instructions "which in any way appear inconsistent with [it]." The Inspector General's Office also began an investigation "to see if there was any further contact or information re Watergate and the arrested suspects."[16]

Two days later, Schlesinger appeared before the Special Subcommittee on Intelligence of the House Committee on Armed Services, as it began an inquiry, chaired by Democratic Congressman Lucien Nedzi, into "the alleged involvement of the Central Intelligence Agency in the Watergate and Ellsberg Matters." Ambassador Helms was called back from Iran to testify and on May 17, he told the Nedzi Committee he had not known Hunt was involved in the Ellsberg profiles. Yet Dr. Malloy later told Baker's staff that he was so concerned about Hunt's involvement, "he had insisted that Helms be advised" and he was assured "Helms had been informed of Hunt's participation."[17]

Four days later, Helms appeared before the Senate Foreign Relations Committee. Facing prosecution for his role in the Ellsberg break-in, Bud Krogh's recent affidavit in that case had stated that "a psychological profile could be put together with information derived from Dr. Fielding's files." "Did the CIA inform Krogh that to put together a profile it would be necessary to have the Fielding data?" asked Senator Fulbright (D—Arkansas), who chaired the hearing.

"The first time I ever heard that Dr. Ellsberg had a psychiatrist was when I was in Shiraz, Iran, a week ago Sunday, when I read an English language newspaper that a break-in had been made in the office of the psychiatrist of Dr. Ellsberg," replied Helms.

Fulbright asked if the film from Hunt's trip to California was processed by the CIA. "I have learned since that the film was processed, and I have also learned that the photograph was of an unidentified building," Helms said.

"One day after this film was delivered to the CIA for processing, the cooperative arrangement between the Agency and Hunt was terminated. Was it the discovery of the contents of the film that led to the termination of the relationship with Hunt?"

Helms said he didn't know "what the contents of the film were" at the time.

"Were you aware on August 27 that Liddy was casing the premises of Dr. Fielding's office?"

"I was not, Mr. Chairman."

"The Agency was aware that Liddy and Hunt were preparing to commit a crime, were they not?"

"They were not . . . I never heard anybody in the Agency mention any such thing . . . To the best of our knowledge, no crimes were contemplated, nobody had given us the slightest indication that anything underhanded was afoot."

Helms said he hand-delivered a package of materials including the photographs to Kleindienst and Petersen on October 24, 1972 and by that time, he knew "what was in the film."

"By that time, is it then fair to conclude that you knew or suspected that Hunt and Liddy were involved in a domestic crime?" Fulbright asked.

"Sir, you would have to look at the photographs . . . to the best of my knowledge, those photographs were of an unidentified building and I did not know what it was and nobody was ever able to identify it."

Senator Stuart Symington (D—Missouri)—a close friend of Helms— interrupted and let him off the hook: "In sworn testimony before the

[Senate] Armed Services Committee, nobody thought they could find out what the photographs really actually showed."[18]

The CIA's Office of General Counsel later corrected Helms' testimony. The Xerox copies of the Fielding photos were not included in the first "Justice package" in October but hand-delivered as a supplement to the second package on January 3, 1973.[19]

On May 14, when Chamberlain's predecessor as inspector general, Bill Broe, and his deputy checked with Howard Osborn about any further skeletons in the closet, "Osborn recalled the existence of seven letters, which were presumed to be from James McCord that were in a special file in his safe." The next day, Osborn gave copies of the letters to Broe, containing "veiled allegations that an attempt was being made in the White House to pin the blame for Watergate on the Agency." They were shared with lead prosecutor Earl Silbert and included in a report sent to Colby and Director James Schlesinger on May 21. The next day, General Counsel Larry Houston wrote to J. Fred Buzhardt, special counsel to the president, "setting forth how the McCord letters were brought to light and why this had not happened before."[20]

On May 23, Colby wrote a follow-up letter to staff, asking them to report "any connection or contact with individuals on the attached list" to the inspector general or director's office. The names on the list were Hunt, Liddy, and the Watergate burglars; Haldeman, Ehrlichman, Dean, Krogh, Young, Colson, Caulfield and, curiously, McCord's former student, Juan Rigoberto Ruiz Villegas. As Colby noted, their activities spanned "not only the Watergate affair, but any investigative work on the Pentagon Papers/Ellsberg case and . . . efforts to locate and stem leaks of classified information to the press starting as early as July 1970 . . .":

It is imperative that every piece of information bearing on these matters be reported immediately for evaluation by the senior management of the

Agency. The public interest requires that all information be produced and reported to our oversight committees (on a classified basis if necessary) so that the Agency's actual role will be clarified with respect to various charges and speculation.[21]

The same day, Deputy Director of Operations Colby and Inspector General Bill Broe met Congressman Lucien Nedzi to review material submitted by the various CIA directorates describing "Agency activities that had flap potential." When told of the McCord letters, Nedzi "expressed astonishment that the material took so long to be surfaced and when surfaced took so long to get to the Director. He was very outspoken in his criticism of the people involved."[22]

Ahead of an appearance at the Nedzi hearings the next day, Director of Security Howard Osborn signed a five-page affidavit recording his knowledge of the Agency's receipt and handling of the unsigned letters from McCord. CIA reports note that the following day, Chairman Nedzi and Chief Counsel Frank Slatinshek criticized General Counsel Larry Houston "rather severely for the Agency's not reporting the existence of the McCord letters to the FBI at the time they were received":

Representative Wilson said he wondered if the Agency had actually gone along with "McCord's game plan." He said this would explain why these letters were just now being surfaced. Mr. Houston had a conversation with Nedzi and Slatinshek after the hearing and it seemed he was able to dispel some of their concern.[23]

Gaynor, Osborn and Broe also testified and Nedzi told the press afterwards: "One of the reasons they gave was the familiar 'I forgot.' They also said it was a matter of turning it over to someone else and assuming he would pass it on."[24]

In a highly dubious comment in the CIA Watergate History, Richards states: "The Agency had no reason to suppress the letters, as they tended, if anything, to defend the Agency. The failure to report them earlier can simply be attributed to the relatively minor significance attributed to them and the resulting loss of their existence from the memories of extremely busy men."[25]

On May 16, Nixon discussed the events of a year earlier with White House counsel J. Fred Buzhardt in the Oval Office.

"When you get down, for example, to the break-in at the Chilean Embassy. That thing was part of the burglars' plan. . . ."

"That's right," said Buzhardt.

"As a cover . . ." continued Nixon, "Those assholes are trying to have a cover—or a CIA cover. I don't know. I think Dean concocted that." Nixon connected the two break-ins and suggested Dean was behind it. In 1999, when the tape was released, Dean called Nixon's accusation "laughable."[26]

Two years later, Assistant Special Prosecutor Nick Akerman investigated allegations that some of the Watergate burglars "may have also broken into the Chilean Embassy." While he found no "hard evidence," he concluded there were "four circumstantial factors which strongly indicate" they did:

First are Sturgis' admissions of his involvement to reporters. Second is the fact that on June 21, 1972, four days after the arrests at the Watergate, the FBI received information that Barker's men had broken into the Chilean Embassy in mid-May. Third is the information from former CIA Director Schlesinger that someone in the CIA told him that Hunt had been involved in this burglary. Fourth, there is nothing to disprove that Barker or any members of his group were not in Washington, D.C. when the burglary occurred.[27]

Baker's staff compiled a list of forty-five unsolved burglaries during this period, at the homes and offices of Chilean diplomats and of "persons or organizations that might be deemed hostile to the Nixon Administration" or be on its "Enemies List."[28]

When I interviewed Rolando Martinez in April 2017, he warned me that he would not talk about anything that "hadn't come out yet." The only point in the interview where he turned serious and refused to answer was when I asked if he had been involved in the Chilean embassy break-in.[29]

The FBI source mentioned by Akerman was Cuban exile leader José Elias de la Torriente, whose Torriente Plan to invade Cuba in the early seventies never materialized. In April 1974, Torriente was shot in the back of the head by a sniper while watching television at home one evening. A note signed with a zero was left at the scene and a letter signed with a zero was sent to a local Hispanic newspaper, claiming "Torriente was executed as a traitor to his country." "Zero" threatened further executions, creating "an atmosphere of terror in Miami" and the FBI speculated "Torriente's assassin may have been a political enemy among Cuban exile groups, such as Cuban Power and Accion Cubana [led by Orlando Bosch], since Torriente opposed terrorist tactics of such groups." Bosch was identified as an early suspect but fled the United States when he was subpoenaed.[30]

On May 17, the Senate Watergate Committee began televised hearings, gripping the nation over the months that followed. The resignation of Nixon's top aides and the Attorney General led to public concern about "assumed interference from Justice Department and White House officials" in the Watergate affair. During confirmation hearings, Nixon's nominee for Attorney General, Elliott Richardson, pledged to appoint a Special Prosecutor and on May 25, Archibald Cox was named to lead a new task force to investigate Watergate and "all offenses arising out of the 1972 presidential election," including the Fielding break-in. The three federal prosecutors (Silbert, Glanzer, and Campbell) stayed on for a month but resigned at the end of June.[31]

On June 25, in televised Senate Watergate Committee testimony, former White House counsel John Dean read a 245-page statement into the record: "The Watergate matter was an inevitable outgrowth of a climate of excessive concern over the political impact of demonstrators, excessive concern over leaks, an insatiable appetite for political intelligence, all coupled with a do-it-yourself White House staff, regardless of the law." Dean's "whistleblowing" testimony made no mention of his destruction of Howard Hunt's notebooks back in January.[32]

On July 16, in further televised testimony, Alexander Butterfield, a former deputy assistant to the president, revealed the existence of White House tapes of the president's conversations in the Oval Office for the first time. A week later, investigators subpoenaed key tapes, but the president refused to hand them over, citing executive privilege, so the Committee began legal action to enforce the subpoenas and secure the tapes that eventually led to Nixon's resignation.[33]

After sentencing, Howard Hunt and the Miami burglars were sent to a federal prison in Danbury, Connecticut. A prison staff evaluation completed on June 28, 1973 noted that this was Martinez' first arrest and that he was led to believe the burglaries of Dr. Fielding's office and the DNC "were a matter of national security" and sanctioned by the government. He admitted that some of his previous operations for the CIA "had been essentially illegal but had the backing of the government and were thus sanctioned."

The evaluation was effusive in its support of Martinez, praising his "very high intelligence" and "outgoing and friendly" manner:

He is extremely patriotic and is very aggressive. In addition, his long history of heroic activity makes him a natural leader in his Cuban-American community of Miami. This man is a Cuban patriot and is also an

American patriot. . . . He migrated to the United States, was recruited by
the CIA, and became a leader in the Bay of Pigs Invasion, as captain of a
small boat having made several hundred heroic missions. He was seen as a
hero in the Cuban district of Miami and is referred to as 'Muscalito' [sic]—
meaning muscle man. Martinez believed that this offense was part of a
mission sanctioned and ordered by the government, and states that he was
not aware of the illegality of the mission until after his arrest when some of
the facts became known. As a CIA agent, he learned early never to ask
questions, and thus did not question Barker and Hunt.

While he was "definitely not seen as having criminal intentions," it was noted
that "his unquestioning loyalty to his superiors . . . led him into the current
offense." He was engaged to be married but his health was deteriorating.[34]

On the same day that the prison evaluation was written, explosive testimony given by Howard Hunt resuscitated the matter of Martinez' diary. Questioned by Nedzi, Hunt claimed he hadn't known Martinez was a paid "employee or informant" of the Agency before the break-in, but Frank Sturgis had recently told him in prison that Martinez "had been keeping the CIA posted of our plans and our activities . . . by means of the diary or journal . . . seized by the FBI."

"Mr. Hunt, this is very dramatic testimony," said a stunned Nedzi, checking that Hunt realized the gravity of his statement.

"I understood, sir, that a diary had been seized in the car Mr. Martinez left behind at the Miami airport when he flew up here for the second entry operation, and that diary was sort of a shorthand report . . . through which he reported to his current CIA case officer. This came as quite a shock to me when I found out that he had been maintaining any diary at all. I have understood subsequently, I believe through Mr. Sturgis . . . that such a record was in fact seized and that there was a case officer in charge of Mr. Martinez at that time to whom he was reporting our activities."

While admitting that "some of this is conjecture on Mr. Sturgis' part," Hunt said, "everyone was shocked to find out . . . Martinez had maintained a diary; the fact it had been seized was even worse." Sturgis thought Martinez "was being used by the [CIA] as an informant on the Latin American community in the Miami area, with some emphasis on [the] collection of narcotics information" but he had also "been so indiscreet as to include in [the diary] references to . . . [his trip to] Hoover's lying in state at the Capitol, [and] operational situations like that, which you really should not have reported to anyone. . . .":

> I have heard frequent references to Martinez' notebook that was seized in his car at the time . . . at the Miami Airport. It was traced there, that there was such a notebook. I don't know that it was ever entered into evidence.

But "without the evidence of the diary itself," Hunt admitted he couldn't confirm "whether or not Martinez did in fact report [Hunt's] activities to the case officer. . . ." If an operational diary did exist, according to Silbert, it was never found.[35]

William Merrill had been appointed as head of the Plumbers Task Force at the Watergate Special Prosecutor's Office and oversaw the Fielding investigation. In July, he interviewed General Cushman, who insisted that before cutting off further support for Hunt in a call to John Ehrlichman on August 27, "he had not seen or heard about the pictures Hunt had taken of Dr. Fielding's office . . . [and] did not know of Young's request to the CIA for a psychological profile on Ellsberg at the time":

> Even to us amateurs on the Special Prosecutor's staff, the pictures of the building and Fielding's car looked like surveillance for surreptitious entry. It would have been easy for the CIA to have checked the ownership of the car from the license numbers in one of the pictures, and by August a check

of the FBI indexes would have revealed that Dr. Fielding had been inter-
viewed in connection with Daniel Ellsberg. I did not believe Cushman was
telling me the truth. . . .[36]

On August 2, in a televised Senate Watergate Committee hearing, Senator
Baker confronted Ambassador Helms about the burglars' CIA connections
and the forged identity documents, voice alteration device, wig, camera,
tobacco pouch, and film processing service provided to Hunt and Liddy and
discussed by the White House and CIA staff. When these men were caught,
wasn't it reasonable to suggest the Agency may have been involved?[37]

Helms held firm and said he had first read about the Fielding break-in
in an English-language newspaper in Iran in May 1973: "That was the first
time I had ever heard of Dr. Fielding, a burglar, or the fact that Dr. Ellsberg
had had a psychiatrist." Helms was subsequently "assured by members of
the Agency" that "the equipment given to Hunt was not used in the
Fielding burglary" but he didn't know at the time what it was used for.[38]

According to Howard Liebengood's notes of his testimony, Helms did
admit to hearing about the camera at the time but could not recall "film
being developed for Hunt."

According to Helms' public testimony, only Xerox prints were retained by
the Agency but that "at the time, nobody knew what the films represented":

If we go to July and August of 1971, I certainly was totally unaware of any
illegal activity, any improper activity, or anything that would have raised
a question about the type of thing that Mr. Hunt was involved in. I assure
you there hadn't been any intimation whatever that there was any question
of a burglary . . . of stealing anything . . . of his having committed any ille-
gal or improper acts.[39]

According to Liebengood's notes, Helms claimed he "blew the whistle
on Hunt as soon as he found out that something improper might be

happening . . . [but] didn't investigate the use of equipment because that would be the FBI's responsibility. Likewise, he didn't investigate Watergate because CIA cannot concern itself with internal security. The only in-house investigation which the CIA conducted after the break-in was to check the records of the defendants."[40]

Helms called the second Watergate break-in "amateurish in the extreme . . . breaking and entering and not getting caught is a very difficult activity and for it to be done properly, one has to have trained individuals who do nothing else and who are used to doing this frequently and are trained right up to the minute in how to do it."

"Was McCord in that category?" asked Baker.

"Obviously not," chuckled Helms.[41]

General Cushman—the former deputy director who initially met Hunt and approved the alias documentation and disguises—followed Helms. He claimed he didn't know about the development of the film for Hunt until May of 1973; and that Hunt returned the camera because it was "not suited to whatever it was he wanted to use it for." Wagner's memo to Cushman on August 26, 1971 noted that Hunt requested a camera for a "new assignment" and that the camera was needed to photograph persons in a poorly-lighted area." Cushman said he had "no idea" what the camera was used for and didn't know if the film developed had come from the tobacco pouch camera. Why did the Agency show no interest in the Dr. Fielding at the center of Hunt's "new assignment"?[42]

The day after questioning Helms and Cushman, Senator Baker received three bound volumes of CIA documents, including several letters from McCord, but the "Pennington file" was not among them. While preparing the package for Baker, Leo Dunn had asked the Office of Security and other Agency components to send him "Watergate materials which had not been previously sent to the Seventh Floor." Frederick Evans reviewed the Office of

Security files and found several items which he "had prepared as background materials for Mr. Kuhn [deputy director of Security] and Mr. Osborn." He forwarded them to Kuhn and mentioned the "Pennington material" but the file was not included in the package sent to Dunn. Evans expressed his concern to Kuhn's secretary about this but he didn't raise it with Kuhn in person, or "argue the point strongly enough with Mr. Kuhn to achieve a reversal of the decision." The Pennington material remained suppressed.[43]

In mid-September, former CIA officer Miles Copeland published a provocative article in William Buckley's *National Review*. At this point, Hunt was in jail and Buckley was guardian to two of his children. Under the subheading "A Set-Up?" Copeland asked:

> *So how did one fine operator like McCord get himself involved in the Watergate mess? Do you know how long it takes for a CIA-trained operator to get into an office like the one in Watergate, install a microphone, and get the hell out? It takes less than one minute, and it requires a team of exactly two persons, the operator and a lookout. But at Watergate, Jim McCord, who had undergone the training and knew the procedure, had entered the Democratic offices with Abbott, Costello, the four Marx brothers, and the Keystone Cops, and had horsed around for almost half an hour without a lookout.*

When Copeland asked former colleagues at Langley, "What *really* happened at Watergate?" their reaction convinced him that "with or without explicit instructions from someone in the Agency, McCord took Hunt and Liddy into a trap." He argued CIA specialists in "dirty tricks" "had a lot to gain from putting the White House's clowns out of business."[44]

On September 25, in televised hearings before the Senate Watergate Committee, Howard Hunt said his missing "operational notebooks" contained "the names, figures and the positions of those who, in fact, had authorized the creation of the Gemstone plan." One notebook contained "a large number of CIA names and telephone extensions, but also several names of Gemstone personnel," the other was an "address and telephone book which contained the names, addresses, pseudonyms and phone numbers of every person [Hunt] dealt with in the Gemstone context." Asked by Senator Baker to explain the disappearance of the notebooks and why they were "so sensitive," Hunt said, "they would provide a ready handbook by which any investigator with any resources at all could quickly determine the parameters of the Gemstone operation. And other operations in which I was involved, and contemplated." According to Hunt's memoir, the notebooks identified "Liddy's principals by name: Mitchell, Magruder and Dean," and he later told Len Colodny, the notebooks contained "the full operational story of Watergate as he knew it. . . . [and] would have implicated Dean long before the Watergate cover-up."[45]

On Friday, October 19, as the court battle over the White House tapes dragged on, Nixon proposed that Senator John Stennis (D—Mississippi), who was famously hard of hearing, could listen to the tapes and provide Special Prosecutor Archibald Cox with summaries. Cox rejected the "Stennis compromise" and the next day, Nixon ordered Attorney General Elliot Richardson to fire him. On Saturday evening, Richardson refused and resigned, as did his deputy, William Ruckelshaus, in what became known as the "Saturday Night Massacre." Public opinion quickly turned against the president and in favor of impeachment.[46]

The following Tuesday (October 23), the Nedzi report on the "alleged involvement of the Central Intelligence Agency in the Ellsberg and Watergate matters" was published. The report criticized the propensity of Haldeman, Ehrlichman, Young, and Dean to "dip directly into the CIA for improper purposes" beyond its charter and called the White House commissioning of the Ellsberg profiles by CIA technical personnel "an abuse of CIA facilities."

While "convinced that the CIA did not know of the improper purposes for which the technical materials were to be used," the report noted continued CIA contact with Hunt after Helms and Cushman terminated further assistance in late August 1971. Had the Agency demanded the return of the equipment then, its use in the Fielding and Watergate break-ins "would have been prevented."

The report took an extremely lenient line on the Agency in a section titled *The Ellsberg Psychiatrist Caper*, which seems to make light of the situation:

> While the timing would indicate some known connection between CIA and the Ellsberg break-in, the testimony shows a coincidence rather than any suggestion that CIA had any prior knowledge of the illicit entry into Dr. Fielding's office . . . In all fairness, it must be repeated that the CIA was not aware of the true purpose for which the camera and equipment was to be used.

The report criticized the efforts of Haldeman, Ehrlichman, and Dean "to deflect the FBI investigation of the Watergate break-in by invoking non-existing conflicts with the CIA" and the "substantial efforts" made by Dean "to involve CIA in the Watergate break-in without any foundation" and to "use the CIA to provide assistance to the Watergate defendants," in violation of its charter:

> There was a clear picture of White House aides avoiding former Director Helms and looking to career military officers, Cushman and later Walters, for unquestioned compliance.

While Dean "was handling the Watergate case, nonetheless, he was exerting personal pressure on the CIA to involve itself in a matter that was clearly illegal."

The report recommended new legislation "to expressly prohibit the Director of Central Intelligence from performing any acts [outside its charter] without the express authorization of the President" and to "prohibit transactions between former CIA employees and the Agency above and beyond purely routine administrative matters."[47]

On November 2, two weeks after Dean secured a guilty plea agreement, he disclosed to members of the Special Prosecution Force the destruction of Hunt's notebooks for the first time. He claimed he hadn't looked through them but "assumed [they] related to the Ellsberg break-in" and that he had forgotten to tell the Senate Watergate Committee about them in his testimony the previous summer. In his memoir, *Blind Ambition*, Dean finally admitted, "I leafed through them. [CRP attorney] Paul O'Brien had told me they contained the names of people Hunt had recruited for the Ellsberg break-in and his "other White House operations."[48]

Senators J. William Fulbright and Howard Baker were not convinced by the Nedzi report and wrote to Colby in response to an article by Andrew St. George in the November issue of *Harper's* magazine which threw the focus back on Martinez. St. George claimed, "the CIA had infiltrated [the Hunt-Liddy team] with a confidential informant . . . an old Company operative named Eugenio Martinez, code-named 'Rolando' . . . [who] reported in advance on the Watergate project."[49]

On November 20, CIA Legislative Counsel John Maury signed an affidavit, noting that only three Agency officers (Esterline, Gonzalez, and Ritchie) had contact with Martinez "during the period of Mr. Martinez' part-time retainer of $100 a month, from 1 July 1971 to 17 June 1972" and none spoke to Helms about Martinez. Gonzalez estimated he had "32 contacts" with Martinez during this period, Esterline met him three times and Ritchie met him twice.[50]

In a letter to Fulbright, responding to the St. George allegations, Colby confirmed that when "the project to which [Martinez] was assigned was terminated in 1969 . . . he was held on a part-time retainer to report on individuals coming from Cuba to the Miami area whom he thought could provide information on Cuba useful to the United States. The last meeting with Mr. Martinez occurred on 6 June 1972, and the relationship was terminated by the Agency as a result of his involvement in the Watergate break-in."[51]

In answer to seven questions posed by Baker, Colby noted that aside from the assistance to Hunt and Liddy already outlined in Helms' testimony—disguises, alias documents and material for the Ellsberg profiles—the Agency "had no information or reports prior to 17 June 1972 which might have suggested or referred to domestic clandestine operations by those individuals associated with or who took part in the Watergate break-in or the break-in of Dr. Fielding's office."

Colby admitted that Martinez, "in late 1971 and again in March 1972 brought Mr. Hunt's presence in Miami to the attention of an agency field representative [Esterline] [who] reported this to CIA headquarters and was advised that he should concern himself with the travel of Mr. Hunt, who was an employee of the White House, undoubtedly on domestic White House business of no interest to CIA. Mr. Martinez made no mention of what have become known as the Watergate and Ellsberg break-ins."

When questioned twice by the Senate Armed Services Committee in mid-November, St. George alleged that Martinez "had been instructed by his CIA case officer in Miami to join the Hunt/Liddy team when asked to do so by Hunt but on the condition that Martinez systematically report to CIA on the activities of the group as if this were a regular intelligence project." His source for the Martinez allegation was Frank Sturgis, "who claims that Martinez confessed to his cohorts on his CIA role immediately after his arrest, including the maintenance of a 'contact diary.'" St. George had struck "a confidential agreement" with Sturgis shortly after the Watergate arrests for "a book, a magazine article, and a television program."[52]

CIA officials told the Senate Armed Services Committee they had no foreknowledge of the break-in, refuted St. George's allegations and denied the Agency had "led the burglars into a trap."[53]

In his November 8 letter to Colby, Baker also asked if "any of the individuals associated with these break-ins" had discussed them with the CIA after the Watergate arrests, "other than Mr. McCord?" The Agency admitted one contact, on July 10, 1972, with "an officer of a commercial concern [Robert Bennett of the Mullen Company]," regarding the "Watergate Five." While "the relationship of this informant and his company to the Agency was and is classified," Lukoskie's handwritten memo gave Baker and his colleagues new insight into "the scope of the CIA's dealings with Robert Bennett, and Mullen and Company, and led to a further intensification of the staff's investigative efforts in other CIA-related areas." Over the next several months, Baker's investigators—Fred Thompson, Michael Madigan, and Howard Liebengood—would seek unprecedented access to Agency files.[54]

In a memo headed "Potential CIA involvement," they summarized their key suspicions about McCord, as follows:

1. Botched break-in. Tape on door, walkie talkies
2. Relies on dummy Baldwin when most former associates referred by CIA
3. Mary McGillan theory [McGillan was McCord's former secretary at CIA]
4. Career CIA type
5. Post-break-in correspondence with Agency which CIA not forthcoming about
6. Pico says appeared to know Watergate security people—signed register etc.

7. Exposed cover-up
8. Mysterious bail money[55]

On November 16, Howard Liebengood wrote Fred Thompson about the Martinez diary: "While we have the Martinez address book in the [security] cage, it's clearly not the Martinez counter-diary that we are looking for." WSPF investigator Bill Merrill, advised "that they had heard of the Martinez diary, supposedly in the trunk of his car at the Miami airport, from several sources" but had not been able to find it. They had "some indication that Barker's people had access to it but Barker denies it." Strangely, Merrill did not seem to know about the second notebook and other materials from Martinez' car which had been sent to Washington, at the Special Prosecutor's request, back in September; or the FBI investigation Deputy Special Prosecutor Henry Ruth had commissioned in mid-October, based on information that an unknown individual had removed a diary from Martinez' car before the FBI "located and impounded" it. For more detail on that investigation, see Appendix 1.[56]

Four days later, Thompson interviewed Reinaldo Pico, a "close friend" of Martinez, who had participated in the first Watergate break-in. Pico told Thompson, "I am almost certain that everything we were doing was known to the CIA through Martinez." He remembered Martinez would take notes in a diary, to report to an American friend in the CIA. A few days before the first break-in, Martinez told him he was invited to go to Santo Domingo with the friend (his case officer Ramon Gonzalez). CIA-sponsored Cuban groups were preparing to invade Cuba from Costa Rica at the time. Mrs. Barker told Pico the FBI took the diary—"where Martinez had written everything down that was going on"—from Martinez' car after his arrest. In jail, Barker scolded Martinez for writing everything down.[57]

On November 28, Henry Kissinger met Richard Helms and reported a call from White House Chief of Staff Alexander Haig a few days before. Haig proposed to Kissinger "that Senator Baker be permitted to make a statement to the effect that the Agency knew about the Watergate burglary 30 minutes before it occurred and therefore had some relationship to it." "To do this would be wildly irresponsible," Kissinger protested, and Haig seemed to drop the idea, but in a cable to CIA headquarters a week later, Helms thought "it indicated a kind of desperation on the part of the White House, with Senator Baker prepared to play a helpful role. It is still not clear to me whether he would be basing his allegation on information from Martinez or just what." Since July, Senator Baker had stored classified material relating to the Senate Watergate investigation in the secure vault of the Joint Committee on Atomic Energy, whose deputy director George Murphy was a former Agency case officer. In response to Baker's November letter, Colby sent him four volumes of secret documents. On December 7, he examined Volume IV with Murphy and Agency lawyers while assistant minority counsel Michael Madigan was attempting to summarize the first three. Later that day, Liebengood briefed Baker after viewing the Page-a-Day calendar notebook found in Martinez' car. It contained a few names, phone numbers and receipts but it still wasn't the operational diary they were looking for. Baker still felt "the real case officer diary may have been lifted by CIA before FBI got to the Martinez car. He noted that CIA Legislative Liaison people got up-tight when the diary was brought up":

> *The Senator remains perplexed and intrigued by what we do not know about the break-in, i.e. What were they looking for? What was the break-in plan? How did they really get caught, etc.*[58]

After testifying in executive session in May, Martinez was called back for further questioning on December 10 and I am the first author to access transcripts of this testimony. Martinez was good-humoured if a little perplexed by the fact that the country he secretly worked for was now prosecuting him. In what he called "the United States against Rolando Martinez," the court was asking him to speak about classified operations by a government agency. If that agency refused to supply his records, what was he supposed to say? He was torn between his oath of loyalty to the CIA and his obligation as a citizen to tell the truth.[59]

To "general laughter," Martinez pointed to the letter the CIA had given him, clearing him to testify about his activities since July 1, 1971 and said:

> *That doesn't clear anything, it is just a letter to comply with you, that doesn't clear a thing. They are the ones that I am going to meet later on . . . I have nothing. I have to live with the same community, with the Cubans, Cuba's Fidel Castro, and we are still working [to defeat him] . . . If I lose this little thing I have [his relationship with the Agency], I have nothing left.*[60]

"If, assuming for a moment that he was acting as a double agent in some capacity . . ." his lawyer added, "you gave him that letter with the CIA having publicly maintained that it had no information, it would mean nothing to him."

"He would have to comply with his agreement . . . not [to] talk about that," added Fred Thompson, "regardless of what letters we produced."

"But this is not the case," interjected Martinez, adding, to general laughter: "Go ahead, I really enjoy the conversation. In jail, I do not have a chance to talk to articulate people like you."

"Here you are, a loyal Company man, used to working through channels . . . through your CO or through your Station Chief," said Thompson. "And you have Barker, who does not even know that you have this relationship with the CIA, and you have Hunt, who you only know by reputation and the fact that he claims some White House relationship. And you are requested to do something through your ordinary channels to tell them what is going on. And instead of complying on that, you rely on some belief that there is more to it than what you are being told. In other words, you rely upon your out-of-channel people's belief, Hunt and Barker, as opposed to your CO, who you say you were very close to."[61]

"Let me tell you one thing," Martinez replied. "We have been working out a project, and someone is working in a project opposite to us, and my CO is telling me the wrong thing . . . and later on, I have found out that they have been produced by the same outfit . . . so I have been talking against this, and later on I have been fighting with these people, and these people have been working with us . . . So the only thing you try to learn is to keep yourself out of trouble . . . not to relay information that is not required . . . I know Hunt is there [in Miami], so it has to be known by the Company that Hunt is there in Miami, so I just say Hunt is here and Hunt has been in the office. I have clear myself . . . So it is up to them to tell me not to be with Hunt or not to do this or the other."[62]

Asked if his CO was deceiving him about Hunt not working for the White House, Martinez replied: "He was not deceiving me, he was not [giving me the] information . . . I thought I did not need to know."

Thompson suggested he was being deceived and given "false information" but Martinez insisted he had no "need to know" and to ask why would have been "ridiculous." He was just given a plan and expected to follow orders, do what he was told, and not ask questions.[63]

Martinez considered it "a privilege . . . to speak to a Senator from the United States [or] to anyone from the CIA":

You see the people watching Mission Impossible, Mannix . . . *I was able to do this thing in real life. What is wrong with that? I was serving United States. I was risking my life. I was doing a lot of things for what I believed was a true cause. I believed that Ellsberg is wrong . . . to give those Pentagon Papers . . . To see the Viet Cong flag in the street, is that good for you people? . . . So, I don't intend to protect myself, or try to protect the*

Company . . . In ten years, I might not be alive. I am 51, so I am not trying to live that long . . . I am indebted to the United States. I was given my part, I am very proud of this past. . . ."[64]

By mid-December, as Baker's staff kept probing, there was growing concern within the CIA about Baker's intentions. Charles Colson was promoting Baker's CIA investigation to the press, but reporters reacted with suspicion and Agency allies began to counter-attack, suggesting "Baker's pursuit of the CIA was really an attempt to protect the White House." Robert Bennett fed stories to *Newsweek* and Bob Woodward at the *Washington Post* and on December 11, former CIA covert action officer Tom Braden published a syndicated column in support of Helms, titled "Can He Blame it on CIA?"[65]

The last turn in the defense of Richard Nixon will be to blame the Watergate on the Central Intelligence Agency. Such is the view of former CIA Director Richard Helms, and such is the direction in which Sen. Howard Baker (R-Tenn.) and his minority staff on the Senate Watergate committee are now proceeding. It is not a very salable theory, but it's about all that's left; and if it could be made salable, it might get Richard Nixon off the hook.

Consider: If CIA accomplished the break-in, the subsequent White House cover-up might be excused on the grounds that the President had to protect his secret intelligence service. . . .

The Copeland and St. George magazine articles suggested "the President's last stand," according to Braden. Senator Baker's staff were analyzing a twenty-eight-page memorandum prepared by George Murphy (who according to the Agency, "had served as a staff assistant to Senator Baker in the

Andrew St. George matter") and, Braden wrote, "Murphy's findings, Baker hints, implicate the CIA":

> *From the time he first learned of the Watergate break-in, Helms has been afraid that it would be blamed on him. Put yourself for a moment in his shoes . . . First, an old friend of the President, Patrick Gray, is appointed to be chief of your major rival agency. One month later, you are told by H. R. Haldeman that the President has appointed another old friend, Gen. Vernon Walters, to be your deputy. Another month later, and just after the break-in, you and your new deputy are summoned to the White House. You listen while Haldeman tells your deputy that "it has been decided" that he should go to Gray and ask him not to investigate the money found on the burglars because it might expose your operations. For the next few days, the White House calls to discuss the break-in and to suggest that you pay money to the families of those arrested. Eleven days after the break-in and on the eve of your departure for a long-scheduled trip, Gray calls to cancel an appointment you had made with him. With this sequence of events in mind, what would you suppose? That people at the White House might be trying to blame the Watergate on you? That's what Helms supposed and supposes still.*[66]

In a December 17 cable to Helms, Agency lawyer John Maury wrote that he had asked Tom Korologos, deputy assistant to the president for Legislative Affairs, to "throw light on [the] Baker problem" by discussing the "Agency/Watergate matter" with Baker. Korologos told Maury "in confidence . . . that Baker's central hang-up is [the] thesis advanced by Copeland and St. George that [the] Agency staged Watergate in order to entrap [the] plumbers. Korologos indicated Baker may have been particularly influenced by [the] Copeland allegations."

In his executive session testimony, Martinez said Sturgis had denied making the allegations attributed to him in the St. George article:

However, Martinez did state to Baker that he considered [the] tradecraft of [the] plumbers unbelievably faulty. From this, Baker apparently infers that this faulty tradecraft was deliberate on the part of at least one of the participants who sought thereby to lead other participants into [a] trap. Martinez flatly denied St. George allegation that he was "anyone's double agent."

Maury also reported on a meeting between Baker and Robert Bennett of the Mullen Company and his father, Senator Wallace Bennett, "to review agency memos covering our relations with Mullen Company." After the meeting, Baker told Lyle Miller (of the Agency's Office of Legislative Counsel) "that everything Bennett said was consistent with what [the CIA] had told Baker and it was becoming clearer that [the] Agency [was] not involved [in] Watergate but Baker reserves [the] option to pursue [the] matter further since he doesn't want to go to his grave without having gotten to the bottom of it."[67]

Until January 21, 1974, Frederick Evans had "no really conclusive evidence to indicate . . . that the Pennington situation was not known to the Director of Security or to the Seventh Floor [Director]." That day, John Richards—the man from the inspector general's office who had by now completed the extant draft of the Agency's Watergate report—phoned Evans to say that he and Lyle Miller "would be down in ten minutes to begin a review of Office of Security Watergate holdings," as approved by Mr. Osborn.[68]

Evans remembered his reaction to the earlier Pennington decision and reviewed Osborn and Gaynor's testimony from May 1973 "regarding the unnamed Office of Security source (who was Mr. Pennington)." He was troubled by contradictions between their testimony and his 1972 memoranda. On his way to another office, he passed Richards and Miller in the hallway, and by the time he returned, Lawrence Howe—who had been working with him on the "Watergate matter" since late October—had let them into the small office where the main Watergate files were kept. "They were reviewing and extracting certain documents," Evans recalled. "I believe these pertained to an attorney named [Paul] O'Brien and Robert Spencer Oliver, as well as A. J. Woolston-Smith."[69]

Late that afternoon, Evans briefed Osborn's deputy, Steven Kuhn, on the situation, and Kuhn went to see Osborn. A few minutes later, Kuhn returned to his office and started putting away his files and closing his safes for the night. "Remove the [Pennington] materials from the [Watergate] files and maintain them separately," he declared. "We'll see about that," snapped Evans, as he left Kuhn's office. Evans went to Howe's office and told him what had happened and they quickly "concluded that we simply could not tamper with the files."[70]

The next morning, Evans and Howe made copies of the Pennington materials. At eight fifteen, they visited Kuhn's office with "the Watergate volume containing the intact Pennington materials and explained to Mr. Kuhn what [they] thought would be the consequences of separating pertinent information from the file." Kuhn took the file and brought them into the adjoining office of his boss, Stanley Ense, the deputy director of Personnel Security and Investigations, and the four of them discussed the situation at length:

> I took from the file the memoranda I had written in August 1972 which outlined the development of the Pennington matter. These memoranda were passed to Mr. Ense, who then read them for the first time. Mr. Ense stated that there was no question that these materials would have to be included in the Inspector General's review of the Office of Security Watergate holdings, and all four of us agreed.[71]

"I don't cross the Potomac on my way to work in the morning. The Agency can do without its own L. Patrick Gray," remarked Evans at the end of the meeting. Kuhn brought the Pennington memoranda back to his office and put them on his desk, alongside the volume where they were normally kept. As Evans left, Ense took him aside and asked quietly, "You haven't destroyed any documents, have you?"

"No, and it's not about to happen on my watch," replied Evans.

"Good, we Musketeers have to stick together," said Ense with a smile (they had gone to the same university).

A half-hour later, Howe collected the Pennington memoranda from Kuhn's desk and restored them to the main volume with Evans. Over the next four weeks, Richards continued to review the Office of Security Watergate files but "did not reach that portion of the flies containing the Pennington materials." Meanwhile, Evans and Howe interviewed Gaynor, Rocca, and Pforzheimer regarding the David St. John novels.[72]

After interviewing Martinez and Hunt in December, Baker's staff began intensive interviews with CIA staff in the first week of February. According to Colby, "24 Agency witnesses" voluntarily testified under oath. Most of the executive session interviews took place in Thompson's office, which was swept for electronic listening devices by CIA technicians each day before the interviews began. It seemed to Thompson that Baker's position on the Senate Watergate Committee allowed himself, Liebengood, and Madigan to see "more CIA agents, [review] more classified Agency material, and [delve] deeper into CIA affairs than any outsiders in the history of the Agency."[73]

While I managed to access the transcript of Martinez' executive session testimony at the National Archives, the testimony of other CIA staff is still classified. I have been able to decode the names of those interviewed by cross-referencing footnotes in the Baker report identifying officers by job title with the files of Baker's staff and recently released CIA documents.

In the first week of February, Baker's staff interviewed Martinez' second case officer, Robert Ritchie, and Miami station chief Jake Esterline; Robert Bennett, Robert Mullen, and their case officer, Martin Lukoskie, about the Mullen Company; and Krueger, Gottlieb, Karamessines, and Greenwood about the support provided to Hunt.

The Agency never produced Martinez' first case officer, Ramon Gonzalez. According to Ritchie, Gonzalez was still in Miami at the time of the break-in:

> *According to the CIA, however, the case officer had left the United States at the end of May [1972] to go on "an African safari." While abroad he was reassigned to Indochina and, despite Senate requests, was never made available for questioning.*[74]

By early February, Liebengood and Madigan had seen excerpts from the "CIA/Martinez Contact Reports." In a report to Senator Baker dated February 20, Fred Thompson expressed frustration with the CIA's slow compliance to his requests:

> *Lyle Miller [Agent X in Thompson's book] insists you contact Colby directly in order to get Gonzalez (Martinez' case officer) back from Vietnam for an interview. Note: Almost everyone connected with this affair is either retired or has been transferred.*[75]

He also requested "originals of all Martinez contact reports by Ritchie or Gonzalez and not the 'cut and paste' jobs of portions of certain reports that we have received," noting:

> *The CIA is hopelessly confused as to when Gonzalez left Miami and when Ritchie took over. The evidence is conflicting and it is certain that they have this information.*[76]

Curiously enough, in 1992, without knowing his Agency background, the *New York Times* reported Ramon Gonzalez was a "safari specialist." An African safari may have been a convenient excuse to get him out of town.[77]

On February 19, Fred Thompson writes in his memoir, "the CIA evidently determined it was time to halt our efforts." That morning, a final package of documents arrived in the Office of Security with "a covering statement to the effect that the Agency had furnished to appropriate Committees all materials in Agency files pertaining to the Watergate matter." The statement had been drafted by Lyle Miller for Director William Colby to sign but first, it arrived in the Office of Security "for review and concurrence."[78]

Kuhn was off sick that day, so Evans and Howe discussed Miller's statement while driving to an interview and decided over an ice-cream cone that "the all-inclusive nature of Mr. Miller's covering statement . . . did not jibe with . . . what we now knew of the Pennington matter."[79]

Evans phoned Miller that evening and learned that Colby had told Miller to use the "all-inclusive" phrasing. Evans alerted Miller to the material which the inspector general had not reviewed, and went with Howe to brief Ense. The Office of Security finally "surfaced" the Pennington materials to the Inspector General's Office the next day and all relevant Office of Security personnel were interviewed.[80]

Pennington's case officer, Louis Vasaly, admitted Pennington had "made a passing reference to having entered the home and office of Mr. McCord after the Watergate break-in to search for documents which might link the Agency with Mr. McCord . . . Pennington had told him nothing about destroying any documents or . . . any other items." Vasaly assumed Mrs. McCord had requested the research and confirmed Pennington had been "under contract as a Confidential Informant . . . [on] a salary of $250 a week" until he was terminated on December 31, 1973.[81]

• • •

On Friday, February 22, Howard Osborn finally wrote a memorandum admitting that the Office of Security "has in its files unconfirmed information reflecting that shortly after the Watergate break-in":

> *Mr. Lee R. Pennington, Jr., who is a former confidential source of the Office of Security's Security Research Staff, is believed to have entered the home and possibly the office of Mr. James W. Mc Cord, Jr., for the purpose of destroying documents which might establish a link between Mr. McCord and the Central Intelligence Agency. There is no indication that this activity was undertaken at the initiative of any representative of this Agency.*

Osborn claimed this information had not "been established" until two days earlier, when Evans and Howe bridled at Miller's draft memorandum, in the knowledge that "memoranda pertaining to aspects of the Pennington incident" had probably not been "disseminated beyond the Office of Security."[82]

On Saturday, Lyle Miller asked to see Senator Baker and gave him a draft memo from Evans, outlining the Pennington story and naming the individuals who had suppressed it. Baker's staff "realized that the CIA might have its own John Dean." They interviewed Lee Pennington that evening and scheduled interviews with Osborn, Evans, Gaynor, and Sayle early the following week.[83]

On Sunday, the "Pennington file" was "submitted under seal" to John Richards, anticipating questions from Nedzi and Baker at committee hearings the next day. That night, Evans prepared his memo for the inspector general and submitted copies of his August 1972 memoranda for Kuhn and Osborn as a sealed exhibit. Summaries of these had been included in the Osborn memo two days before. Having unburdened himself, Evans concluded his memo with the belief that "there is now nothing pertinent to Watergate in Office of Security holdings which has not been disclosed to the appropriate Agency officials . . . [or] were ever destroyed."[84]

• • •

The next day, after hearing testimony from Colby, Osborn, Kuhn, Evans, Howe, Sayle, and Vasaly, Lee Pennington was questioned by Lucien Nedzi, the Michigan Democrat who chaired the Nedzi hearings. "It has been alleged that you had gone to Mr. McCord's home after his arrest, and to his office, and destroyed certain documents pertaining to the Central Intelligence Agency," began Nedzi, "Will you give us your version?"

Pennington said he was sitting at home with his wife on Thursday morning (June 22) and they were feeling sorry for Mrs. McCord, who had "one daughter with somewhat arrested development." Mrs. Pennington suggested he visit Mrs. McCord to see if he could help, so he drove over there:

Things were in quite a turmoil when I got there . . . Apparently, they had started to burn whatever they had without opening the flue, and as a result everything was black all the way around, and up on the second floor, and they said that Jim wanted the material in his house burned.

A couple of days after McCord's arrest, his wife had a bomb threat and during a prison visit, her husband asked her to burn the papers, newspaper clippings, and magazines kept in his "office," in an alcove of the living room.

Pennington insisted McCord didn't ask him to go up there and when he arrived, Mr. and Mrs. Sweany were helping Mrs. McCord to "burn everything." Lucille Sweany had been McCord's secretary and McCord "got very well acquainted" with Donald Sweany while he was Pennington's assistant at the national headquarters of the American Legion. According to Pennington, after Sweany left the House Committee on Un-American Activities, he worked in the Chicago office of the American Security Council, where Pennington also worked for "a considerable period."

As Mrs. McCord "was throwing stuff in the fire," Pennington picked up a file or envelope with "a few loose papers in it . . . that had CIA on it . . . [and] threw it back on the pile of that material that she was burning." He stayed about an hour and by the time he left, McCord's office had been cleaned out and everything burned. When he got home, he telephoned Gaynor—who he met for lunch regularly and used to give material on subversive and right-wing groups—and reported what he had done.

When questioned by Baker's staff on Saturday evening, they had read him excerpts from what he called a "twisted and distorted seven-page so-called secret memorandum":

> *And, gentlemen, the last paragraph in there made me feel like I wanted to go swinging on somebody. There was an inference that the Central Intelligence Agency had sent me up to McCord's to go through whatever files he had and remove anything relating to the Central Intelligence Agency. They never at any time requested that I go up and get files, or look for files.*

After being questioned about the folder he had burned, Pennington called McCord, who said "he had a small folder there containing correspondence [about] his anticipated retirement . . . [and] a letter of commendation which he had received from the Central Intelligence Agency [because] he had gone out and made an address for them after his retirement." McCord said he kept no classified Agency material at his house.

When McCord was released on bail, he told Pennington that his attorney was trying to "get him to involve the Central Intelligence Agency" in his case:

> *He told me that the Central Intelligence Agency had nothing to do with it, he was no longer employed by them, but he did write a series of five or six letters to Mr. Gaynor, which went on into their files . . . He came to me after he thought his attorney was trying to put him on the spot.*

"Was he aware of your association with the Agency?" asked Nedzi.

"Yes, because he was responsible for it in the first place."

"Did he ever ask you to convey this kind of information to the Agency?"

"Yes. He suggested that I inform the Agency that he thoroughly distrusted his own attorney, and I implied from that . . . perhaps he thought the attorney and the prosecuting attorney were playing ball together . . . As I recall it, I just reported what he told me . . . Frankly, I am sorry I got mixed up in it, but due to our friendship with the McCords we were trying to help."

"Do you remember to whom you reported that?" asked Nedzi.

"I don't know whether it was Gaynor or Vasaly. I am not sure."[85]

As Fred Thompson notes in his memoir, the Pennington file was made available to Nedzi but not to Baker. The CIA used its allies on the House and Senate Armed Services Committees—Senators Nedzi, Stennis and Symington—to allay press fears and accept their word "that the Agency's activities were proper and lawful."[86]

While Helms repeatedly claimed the Agency did no serious investigation of Watergate, the testimony of Evans and the Security Research Staff made clear the Agency began "a vigorous internal investigation . . . almost immediately after the break-in." One SRS officer described it as a state of "panic."[87]

One of most intriguing memos in Howard Liebengood's papers concerns Cord Meyer, the senior CIA officer who dictated the message to Miami station chief Jake Esterline that Hunt "undoubtedly is on domestic White House business, no interest to us, in essence, cool it"; and who later told Esterline the Agency "became uneasy about what Hunt seemed to be doing in March or May 1972." On February 6, in an informal interview, Howard Hunt told Baker's staff that, if the CIA were monitoring his activities, Cord Meyer and counterintelligence chief Jim Angleton were probably behind it. According to the memo, "Meyer met with Mullen and Hunt regarding possible cover arrangements in India on an unknown date." Baker's staff wanted to interview Meyer to find out how aware he was of the Plumbers' operations or the Ellsberg profiles: "Did Meyer see, or was he told about, the reconnaissance photographs of Hunt?" On February 28, Meyer was finally questioned about what he knew of Hunt's activities but there is no report of what he said.[88]

In the first week of March, final interviews were conducted with Leo Dunn, Karl Wagner, Dr. Bernard Malloy, and General Cushman. According to the executive session testimony of Karamessines and others, General Cushman's executive assistant, Karl Wagner, initially called Sam Halpern, executive assistant to Karamessines, about the support given to Hunt and later called Karamessines directly, but Karamessines denied any knowledge of the Ellsberg profiles.[89]

Wagner told Baker's staff that he was not told of the content of the photographs until June 1972, "when Gottlieb delivered Xerox copies to Colby in Wagner's presence at a time when all were trying to monitor post-Watergate activity . . . On June 19, 1972, the Monday following the break-in, Wagner went directly into Helms' office and presented him with all his memoranda on the Hunt/TSD affair." Krueger's affidavit states that "he gave all notes and materials in his possession to Colby, including copies of the Hunt photographs."[90]

On Friday, March 8, the Baker investigation culminated with a final encounter between Baker, Thompson, and Richard Helms, summoned home from Iran again by the State Department to testify. He had asked his "close friend," Senator Symington, to accompany him to "see what Mr. Thompson wants" and apparently feared an indictment. Baker asked if the tapes Helms had ordered destroyed when he left office included conversations with Nixon, Haldeman, and Ehrlichman? "No!" shouted Helms, contradicting his secretary's testimony two weeks before.[91]

As Thompson described the "Pennington matter," Hunt's post-August 1971 request for a lock-picker and specialist in "entry operations"; "the mysterious relations that Martinez had with the Agency before the Watergate break-in . . . [and] the way the CIA had maneuvered its case officers after the break-in . . . Helms stared straight ahead and did not speak." He took a "hard line" and stuck to what he'd told the Senate Watergate Committee.[92]

On the same day, Colby wrote to Baker, refusing to release key outstanding documents, like the Ellsberg profiles, the Pennington file, the Agency's Watergate file and the "Mr. Edward" file kept on Hunt. Colby agreed to make these "completely available to inspection by any member of the CIA Subcommittee of the Senate Armed Services Committee," chaired by Helms' friend, Symington. In Baker's view, this effectively terminated his "CIA investigation" and he asked his staff to begin writing their report.[93]

During March, CIA General Counsel John Warner wrote twice to Hunt, based on information that he was "planning to publish a book about [his] experiences as a case officer with CIA." He enclosed the secrecy oath that Hunt signed before leaving the Agency, promising to seek written consent before publication; and two secrecy agreements signed in 1950 and 1966. Warner asked Hunt to submit his manuscript for review "to determine whether it contains any classified information." Shortly after receiving the second letter, Hunt acknowledged Warner's "admonitory communications" with a note that he had referred them to his attorney.[94]

The following month, Warner "bumped into James McCord on the street" in Washington and they discussed recent press stories about McCord's plans to publish a book. McCord reassured Warner the manuscript "would not discuss his activities with the Agency" and "that he would never reveal any classified information." He offered to send Warner a copy and told him he had "done everything in his power to help the Agency . . . [counter] efforts to link the Agency with this 'awful mess.'"

Later that day, Warner reminded McCord of his obligations in writing and McCord wrote back a week later, promising to comply and affirming that aside from biographical details discussed in public testimony, *A Piece of Tape: The Watergate Story—Fact and Fiction* would be limited to his post-retirement activity. *A Piece of Tape* was published shortly thereafter and begins with an eccentric epigraph, invoking the Creator:[95]

> *A piece of masking tape opened a door that shook a nation to its very foundations. A measuring tape that was Watergate plumbed the depths of the most powerful nation in the world. A piece of magnetic tape may impeach the most powerful man in the world. Is a nation's will and character now being measured with yet another piece of tape in the hands of Him who created all that is?*[96]

CIA Director William Colby had hoped that supplying twenty-four staff interviews, "over 700 documents and 2,000 pages of testimony" to Baker would provide "sufficient concrete evidence . . . that CIA had no prior knowledge of the Watergate or Ellsberg break-ins or cover-ups." After reading the first draft of the Baker Report on April 1, he was disappointed. Two days later, he sent Baker 160 comments on the draft but "practically none" of them made the final revised report which, Colby felt, "implies that . . . the Agency and its officers and employees had prior knowledge of and were wittingly involved in the break-ins and the cover-up."[97]

The Baker Report was published on July 2, 1974, not in the main body of the Senate Watergate Committee's formal report, but as an appendix to Senator Baker's individual views, summarizing his "investigation of CIA activity in [the] Watergate incident." Twenty-one of the CIA's comments appear as an appendix to the Baker report and the three examples discussed below toe the well-worn Company line.[98]

Baker notes that, after reviewing the Hunt photographs, Krueger "immediately reported their content to Cushman and [Wagner] . . . With a degree of incredulity, however, he denies telling his superiors that he blew up one of the photographs and that it revealed the name of Dr. Fielding. Moreover, both Cushman and [Wagner] denied ever having been told about the content of the photographs by [Krueger] or anyone else." The CIA responds: "At that time, the name Dr. Fielding had no meaning to the Agency personnel involved. . . ."[99]

Baker notes that, "it was only after these photographs were developed and examined that the CIA technician dealing with Hunt [Greenwood] was ordered to cut off all support for Hunt"—a decision made by Cushman and/ or Helms. The CIA responds: "The decision to cut off support to Hunt was made in the face of escalating demands and was not based upon the development of the photographs."[100]

In executive session, Dr. Malloy told Baker's staff he was assured that "Director Helms was advised of his concerns regarding Hunt's participation and comments" yet Helms "denied that he was ever told that Hunt was involved in the CIA's Ellsberg profile project." The CIA response confirmed that Helms and Osborn were never advised of Hunt's role in the profiles: "Further, there is no other Agency official who had knowledge of both the provisioning of Hunt and Hunt's involvement in the preparation of the Ellsberg profile."[101]

The report concluded that "the recently curtailed investigation . . . would appear to raise many unanswered questions as to the involvement of the CIA in matters outside its legislative parameters." Baker also felt it "raised a number of questions regarding the CIA's contacts with the participants of both the Watergate and Fielding break-ins."[102]

The final "Action Required" section of the report sought further interviews and documents to resolve outstanding questions. "To determine the extent of the CIA's knowledge of Hunt's activities," Baker wanted to interview Bill Broe, chief of the Western Hemisphere Division (1971–April 1972) and his successor, Ted Shackley; Lawrence Sternfield, Sam Halpern, Meyer's executive assistant, and Martinez' case officer, Ramon Gonzalez. The two-day delay in the CIA notifying the FBI of Martinez' car still bothered Baker and he wanted to interview the chief of the Office of Security in Miami, the informant who called Esterline about the car and the informant's source.

He also wanted all unabridged case officer contact reports for Martinez from 1971 to July 1972; all CIA correspondence regarding Martinez' car "to resolve conflicting evidence supplied by the FBI"; and "all reports or memoranda relating to the debriefing of Martinez' last case officer [Ritchie] upon his return to Washington, D.C.," after the Watergate break-in, "to determine whether [Martinez] provided any Watergate-related information to his case officer."

Baker also wanted to interview Dr. Tietjen, "who supervised . . . the preparation of the Ellsberg profiles" and his supervisor, John Coffey, who oversaw the Office of Medical Services and served as the liaison with Helms; and to obtain copies of the Ellsberg profiles and the data on which they were based, which included FBI reports on Dr. Fielding. He also wanted to interview Ronald James, the CIA technician who had developed Hunt's film, to determine "what was done with [the] blow-up and whether it was subsequently used for briefing others at CIA."[103]

In its year-end assessment of the Watergate investigation, the CIA's Office of Legislative Counsel noted that, "In the opinion of most observers, Baker's report was long on innuendo but short on facts and conclusions. As the *Washington Post* put it: 'Senator Baker has done a difficult task unsatisfactorily.'"[104]

• • •

On August 8, Nixon resigned. At the end of the month, the Office of General Counsel received the manuscript for Hunt's autobiography, *Undercover*, from attorney William Snyder. The Directorate of Operations identified six "hard core" items in the manuscript among thirty-two "proposed security deletions and revisions": "the Agency should insist on their deletion or revision and be prepared to obtain an injunction and engage in litigation should Hunt refuse to cooperate."[105]

In late September, Ray Rocca, deputy chief of the CI Staff, and Acting General Counsel John Morrison met Hunt, Snyder, and his assistant in the CIA's Washington Field Office. "As the meeting began, Hunt asked if it was being tape-recorded," reported Rocca, "I assured him that it was not." They proceeded to review the thirty-two items, including three non-negotiable "classified items," which Hunt and his lawyers agreed to revise. One of these concerned a "surreptitious entry" into the Guatemalan embassy in Mexico City.[106]

Hunt felt most of the other changes "should not be considered sensitive since they had been publicized extensively . . . [or] the principals involved were dead" but he agreed to four further changes. At first, Hunt hoped the meeting and Agency review wouldn't be publicized, fearing perceived collusion would lead to accusations of a "whitewash." But according to Morrison, he was persuaded that the Director's decision to issue a press release, acknowledging "the fact that we had reviewed the manuscript would be in his interest as well as ours":

> *I would note here, however, that both Mr. Rocca and I felt that Hunt and his lawyers were genuinely cooperative and that a press release which is too harsh or denigrates the book or Hunt's motives might be unfair and considered by him to be in bad faith. Hunt appears to retain admiration and respect for the Agency and seems convinced that nothing in his book will harm our operations or personnel.*[107]

Three days later, Hunt's attorney William Snyder wrote to confirm that Hunt and his publisher had reluctantly agreed to the required changes and *Undercover: Memoirs of An American Secret Agent* was published the following month. In late October, Hunt testified in *U.S. v. Mitchell*—the trial of Mitchell, Haldeman and Ehrlichman. Appalled at how Nixon and his co-conspirators had disparaged him on the White House tapes, he no longer felt any loyalty to his "principals" and decided to come clean. He admitted some of his previous testimony and parts of his book were "selectively untruthful" and that his Hermès notebook had not, in fact, recorded "the actual progress of Gemstone from its inception, mentioning Liddy's three principals by name: Mitchell, Magruder and Dean."[108]

As discussed in Chapter 6, during the Agency's internal investigations after Watergate, Howard Osborn sent Colby a "catalogue of potential violations of the CIA's legislative charter" which became known as the "Family Jewels." As one State Department history notes, the catalog "was referred to by Colby as 'the skeletons in the closet.'" Its 693 pages covered "domestic operations against the anti-war movement, a mail intercept program conducted by CIA counterintelligence, experiments involving LSD, surveillance and bugging of U.S. journalists, involvement in the assassination or attempted assassination of foreign leaders, and connections to the Watergate break-in." On December 22, 1974, many of these illegal activities were first exposed in a *New York Times* article by Seymour Hersh and in the ensuing fallout, counterintelligence chief James Angleton was forced into retirement and President Ford launched a broader investigation into past CIA illegal activities.[109]

"A press and political firestorm immediately erupted," recalled Colby in his memoir. "All the tensions and suspicions and hostilities that had been building about the CIA since the Bay of Pigs and had risen to a combustible level during the Vietnam and Watergate years, now exploded." As the State

Department history of the incident notes, "the story came as a surprise to the White House, which had never been briefed on the existence of the catalogue of CIA misdeeds, the so-called 'Family Jewels,' that Schlesinger had commissioned the year before." Colby reassured President Ford that none of Hersh's allegations were currently "going on in the Agency" and Kissinger asked Colby and Helms for a full report on what he privately referred to as the "Helms matter."

On Christmas Eve, Colby sent the President a detailed response, which became known as the Colby Report and formed the basis for the investigations which followed. From Tehran, Ambassador Helms cabled his response to Kissinger before flying back to Washington:

> *I remember no illegal or unauthorized quote break-ins, telephone taps, or inspections. I do not know what Schlesinger and Colby have done to dredge up material designed, if not carefully explained, to hurt me. I still feel I had a lot of unnecessary grief over Watergate. In any event, someone or some group seems to have it in for me and does not want to give up.*[110]

In January 1975, Secretary of Defense (and former CIA Director) James Schlesinger discussed alleged "CIA domestic activities" with President Ford. "Was the CIA involved in Watergate?" asked Ford.

"Not as an organization," replied Schlesinger. "Some paraphernalia was given to Hunt and a psychological profile of Ellsberg was given to the Plumbers. There may have been an old boy net at work, but in my judgment CIA was not involved as an agency. There is a layer in the Agency which you can never really find out what is going on. So you don't ever want to give them a clean bill of health. I am not sure that Bill [Colby] knows all, nor that I did. You should defend it and call for clean actions, but not give them a wholesale acceptance."[111]

The next day, Ford established a "Commission on CIA Activities within the United States" to investigate Agency activities within the United States which exceeded its charter and to make recommendations to the president to prevent further violations. Vice President Nelson Rockefeller was appointed to chair the commission and the Justice Department would investigate any criminal wrongdoing.[112]

The same day, Ford met Ambassador Helms. "Dick, you and I have known each other a long time. I have only the most admiration for you and for your work," said the president. "Frankly, we are in a mess. I want you to tell me whatever you want. I believe the CIA is essential to the country. It has to exist and perform its functions." Ford hoped the Rockefeller Commission would "stay within their charter, but in this climate, we can't guarantee it. It would be tragic if it went beyond it, because the CIA needs to remain a strong and viable agency. It would be a shame if the public uproar forced us to go beyond and to damage the integrity of the CIA. I automatically assume what you did was right, unless it's proved otherwise."

"I have been in the service 32 years," replied Helms. "At the end, all one has is a small pension and a reputation—if any. I testified in Watergate. I didn't dump on President Nixon and I stuck to the truth. I intend to fight this matter":

> The CIA is the President's creature. If allegations have been made to Justice, a lot of dead cats will come out. I intend to defend myself. I don't know everything which went on in the Agency; maybe no one really does. But I know enough to say that if the dead cats come out, I will participate. I think the mood of the country is ghastly. I feel deeply for you, Mr. President. I am a member of your team and I don't intend to foul the nest if I can avoid it.

"I have no doubt about your total integrity," replied Ford. "I plan no witch hunt, but, in this environment, I don't know if I can control it."[113]

• • •

Three days later, Helms reported to Henry Kissinger's executive assistant (Lawrence Eagleburger) on a meeting with William Colby. Helms said Colby was "very up tight" and "close to a basket case."

"First I had Phoenix, then Watergate, and now this," he complained.

After tense discussion, Helms asked, "All right, Bill, what do you want to do, save the Agency?"

Colby—"flushing and pursing his lips," according to Helms—replied, "Yes, but I will not do anything illegal or lie in order to do so."

"I never suggested you do and I do not appreciate the intimation," snapped Helms, "in some agitation."

Colby showed Helms the "Family Jewels," but after speaking to people in the Agency and retirees, Helms told Eagleburger he was not convinced that Colby "knows what the facts are" and he found Colby's report very thin:

Apparently, Colby, in an attempt to marshal his facts, has sent some of his Agency people to talk to retirees or people no longer on active duty. The Attorney General has told Colby that he should focus his investigation solely on those now on active duty in the Agency.[114]

On January 22, 1975, Richard Helms testified before the Senate Committee on Foreign Relations on CIA activities and was asked by Senator McGovern to provide a written response to a "very damaging" *New York Times* article by Walter Pincus from the previous October, titled "Helms, the CIA and Public Trust." The article compared Helms' testimony before the same committee in May 1973 (discussed earlier in the chapter) to material released on the CIA's role in the Ellsberg break-in almost a year later by the House Judiciary Committee. "Sworn statements from agency personnel along with other testimony indicate that Mr. Helms did not tell the true story," Pincus wrote:

According to a Cushman aide, C.I.A. technical personnel had determined that the assistance already given to Mr. Hunt, "appeared to involve the agency in clandestine operations," a finding confirmed, if not initiated, by the C.I.A. general counsel's office, which also had reviewed the pictures. The decision was made to end further assistance to Mr. Hunt unless Mr. Helms ordered it continued. . . . In 1971, Mr. Helms in a public speech asked the American people to recognize that in the case of autonomous secret agencies such as the C.I.A. "the nation must to a degree take it on faith that we too are honorable men devoted to her service." Mr. Helms appears to have broken that faith and in a matter that involves corrupt activities at the highest Government level. If he and his former agency are ever to again gain the public trust they need, they must make a full public accounting of past Watergate-related conduct.

"This is simply not true that I knew about . . . the break-in of Dr. Fielding's office," Helms responded. "I had seen some photographs, but nobody had ever identified to me what buildings those photographs were of." He hadn't heard of Dr. Fielding until the newspapers first reported the break-in in May 1973.

"Apparently, members of the CIA knew about this," replied Senator McGovern. "They were supplying material to Hunt. They developed the film apparently, and saw the name Fielding on the part in the parking lot. Members of the Agency knew about that. The thing that puzzles me is why as Director of the Agency something that sensitive wouldn't have been called to your attention."

Senator Symington, who had chaired the previous hearings, interrupted before Helms could answer, again letting him off the hook.

Helms concluded: "No one had ever intimated to me until that date in 1973 when I read in Shiraz that Mr. Ellsberg had a psychiatrist, that it was a man named Dr. Fielding and his office had been broken into. I put my hand up, sir."

• • •

Helms subsequently responded to Pincus' charge of false testimony in writing:

> *The implication of the Pincus article is that since photographs developed by the Agency for Mr. Hunt in August 1971 showed Dr. Fielding's name on the wall of a building, I must have had knowledge at that time of Hunt's intended break-in of Dr. Fielding's office. He states it was because of these photographs that I terminated further aid to Hunt and contends that in my testimony on May 21, 1973, I was apparently covering up information relevant to a criminal investigation then under way.*

> *When an Agency employee developed some film for Mr. Hunt in August of 1971, I was not aware at that time that this had been done or that the Agency had copies. I had no idea of what Mr. Hunt's objective was except that he told General Robert Cushman that he wanted disguise material "to elicit information from an individual." Since I did not know of the existence of the photographs, they did not have anything to do with cutting off aid to Hunt.*

As discussed earlier, Helms claimed the pictures "were not seen by senior officers in the Agency" until after the second Watergate break-in.[115]

In 1977, Helms was convicted of lying about trying to overthrow the government of Chile during the same confirmation hearings. He escaped with a $2,000 fine and a two-year suspended jail sentence and wore the conviction "like a badge of honor," claiming his secrecy oath superseded his obligation to tell the truth to senators who had not been cleared to question him on CIA activity.[116]

• • •

On January 27, the US Senate established a Select Committee to Study Governmental Operations with Respect to Intelligence Activities across a range of government agencies and the extent to which certain intelligence activities were "illegal, improper or unethical." It was chaired by Senator Frank Church (D—Idaho), Senator Tower was vice chairman and Senator Howard Baker also sat on the committee.[117]

Among the subjects investigated by the Rockefeller Commission—whose files are still classified—was possible CIA foreknowledge of or involvement in the break-ins targeting Dr. Fielding's office in Los Angeles and the DNC headquarters at the Watergate. In its report, published in June 1975, the Commission concluded there was no evidence of CIA foreknowledge or participation in either case.

The Commission took an incredibly lenient view of the Fielding break-in. The Xerox copies of the surveillance photographs taken by Hunt of Dr. Fielding's office building and the blow-up identifying Fielding's name above his parking space were placed in a folder in the safe of Richard Krueger, the acting chief of TSD on August 27, 1971. The report concluded that they "appear to have been examined only by him and his technician":

> *The medical staff working on the Ellsberg profile evidently was not aware of them. The pictures were discovered after the Watergate break-in and turned over to the Department of Justice in January 1973. There is no evidence that anyone in the Agency was aware of their significance until the Fielding break-in was disclosed to the Watergate Grand Jury in April 1973.*[118]

This is a very crude and misleading statement, and on the evidence presented in this book, completely implausible. The report continued:

> *Martinez testified that late in 1971 he casually mentioned to his case officer that Hunt had been in Miami and was working for the White House.*

The case officer later told him that he had run a name check on Hunt at the Station (as indeed he had) and that there was no information respecting Hunt's being employed by the White House. Martinez took that response to mean that Hunt was on a secret CIA mission of which the Miami Station was not to know. On the strength of his past experience with maintaining the secrecy of CIA operations, he therefore disclosed none of the Hunt-related activities to his case officer.[119]

Only Director Helms knew that the Agency was preparing the Ellsberg profile at the time when it was also providing certain technical support to Hunt. The Commission has found no evidence, however, that either the Director or any other Agency employee had knowledge of facts sufficient to disclose the plans for or the carrying out of the Fielding break-in.[120]

In providing "the disguise and alias materials, tape recorder and camera to Hunt, as well as in providing the Ellsberg profile," the Commission concluded the Agency exceeded its charter "and failed to comply with its own internal control procedures." While the Agency was a victim of misuse by the White House and apparently unaware of the "intended improper purposes" of the equipment supplied to Hunt, it failed, "after public disclosure of the improper White House activities, to undertake a thorough investigation of its own and to respond promptly and fully to the investigations conducted by other departments of the government."

The Commission found no evidence of CIA advance knowledge or involvement "in the planning or execution of the Watergate break-in":

Although Martinez was the one person in regular contact with the CIA who had knowledge of Hunt's improper activities, the Commission has found no evidence to indicate that he provided the Agency with information about those activities.[121]

But it seriously criticized the Agency for failing to provide information "which it should have known could be relevant to the ongoing investigation and preparation for the first Watergate trial in January 1973," especially as it concerned possible crimes "by employees or ex-employees with whom it had had recent contacts":

> *The basis for the Agency's action appears to have been the Director's opinion that since the Agency was not involved in Watergate, it should not become involved in the Watergate investigation.*

The Commission found no evidence that Agency officers "actively joined in the cover-up conspiracy formed by the White House staff . . . [or] sought to block the FBI investigation" and General Walters "firmly rejected . . . subsequent cover-up overtures by the White House."[122]

The report criticized Office of Security staff for deliberately withholding "sensitive" information about Lee Pennington from the FBI but limited blame to "officers at the operational level, apparently acting without direction from above." It found "no evidence that this decision was intended to cover-up any possible connection between the CIA and Watergate" or that Pennington was directed by anyone at the Agency to destroy "files of McCord having possible relevance to Watergate."

It recommended "a single and exclusive high-level channel should be established for transmission of all White House staff requests to the CIA . . . [from] an officer of the National Security Council staff designated by the President and the office of the Director or his Deputy"; and that "any direction or request reaching [Agency staff] . . . outside of regularly established channels should be immediately reported to the Director."[123]

●   ●   ●

The publication of the Church Committee Report in April 1976 led to the creation of a permanent Senate Select Committee on Intelligence a few months later, to "provide vigilant legislative oversight over the intelligence activities of the United States." Senator Baker was vice chairman, Howard Liebengood was deputy staff director and Michael Madigan was minority counsel.[124]

Around this time, Baker drafted a fifteen-page "sequel" to his report, reflecting on further investigation he and his staff had done, using the investigative powers of the Church Committee to request materials previously denied by the CIA to the minority staff of the Senate Watergate Committee. Liebengood and Madigan could finally access "the materials referenced in the 'Action Required' section of the Baker Report" from the CIA and examined "some 50-plus files" in the Inspector General's "Watergate File" and twenty-four files held by the Office of Security in their entirety.

Where they once had been denied access to Martinez' original contact reports, now they could read them in secure facilities at Langley and confirm they contained "no references to Watergate-related information."

"No notes were taken of sensitive information contained in the reports which was not related to Hunt or in some other way relevant to the Committee's inquiry," Baker reported, showing that "Congress can responsibly safeguard access to vital secrets necessary to meaningful intelligence community oversight."

While "a feeling of . . . distrust" permeated the Agency's initial relationship with the Church Committee—with some feeling the Committee "was an enemy out to destroy the CIA or . . . to pry into areas where he had no business prying"—Baker thanked former CIA Director Colby, then-Director George Bush, and former CI chief James Angleton, for dispelling that notion. He was now satisfied that his investigation into CIA involvement was complete and that "the major questions that arose have been answered so far as humanly possible."[125]

• • •

Baker reached four conclusions. He could find no "conclusive" or "substantial" evidence "that elements of the [CIA] were wittingly involved in the planning or the execution of either the Watergate break-in or the break-in of Dr. Fielding's office."

He observed that, "for much of the post-Watergate period, the CIA itself, while proclaiming publicly no institutional association with the Watergate break-in, was really not sure of all of the possible connections itself . . . [and] underwent extensive internal scrutiny" on the issue.

He felt the "concepts of compartmentalization, circumlocution and plausible deniability" used in the intelligence world "precludes a definitive resolution of the central issue . . . [and] important and intriguing questions remain."

He also criticized the Agency for withholding information from the Senate Watergate Committee by stating there was "no Watergate-related information" in requested documents, or only responding to "particular questions." He felt this "frustrated meaningful investigative efforts and did great harm to the CIA by unnecessarily creating an aura of suspicion and ambiguity."

While Baker was satisfied his investigation had now run its course, he still felt "Watergate is an event that remains clouded in mystery":

> *I am still not satisfied that we know all that needs to be known about the reason for the Watergate burglary and the scope of participation in that infamous effort. Thus, nagging pieces of evidence and gnawing questions unfortunately remain. . . .*[126]

Author Jim Hougan discussed the case extensively with Baker and Liebengood in the early eighties for his book *Secret Agenda*. At that point, they remained convinced that the CIA was "deeply involved" and "deeply implicated" in the Watergate break-in. I get that sense that *The Baker Report: A Sequel* was a pragmatic move on Baker's part to draw a line under an investigation that could go no further and build bridges between the nascent Senate Select Committee on Intelligence and the agencies it would oversee.[127]

In May 1976, former CIA Director William Colby—who had been replaced by George Bush—met James McCord and his attorney, and McCord subsequently wrote two letters to Colby. After the Agency's "previous unpleasant experience regarding letters from Mr. McCord," the letters were shown to the special prosecutor, who noted a reference to Mr. Pennington and requested material on him.[128]

The meeting and letters seem to be connected to McCord's interest in the *R. Spencer Oliver v. CRP* civil action and a motion filed by Daniel Schultz, the attorney representing the Miami burglars, in November 1976. McCord submitted a sworn declaration that his CIA retirement was genuine and not a cover for any subsequent "covert (or overt) CIA assignment." He denied that anyone—including "any CIA friend, acquaintance, or agent"—destroyed "CIA documents" at his home after his arrest.[129]

A supporting nine-page affidavit laid out his charges against CRP attorney Paul O'Brien, who "was named as an unindicted co-conspirator" for his role in the Watergate cover-up, while Haldeman, Ehrlichman, Mitchell, and his co-counsel Kenneth Parkinson were indicted.[130]

After serving his time for the Watergate affair, Howard Hunt was then accused of involvement in the JFK assassination, which he later strongly denied:

It is very hard to prove a negative, you know. I didn't have anything to do with the assassination, didn't know anything about it. It is unfortunate everything I went through in Watergate has bled over into a great national tragedy, and that was the assassination of President Kennedy, and I think that the nation is willing to forgive Watergate now. I certainly think I have paid my penalty for being involved in it, but to have this new stain attached to me . . . in the last two or three years, this assassination of the President is something really that the nation is never going to forgive. I am afraid I will be forever stained with some kind of suspicion that I had something to do with it. It is very, very unfair. I did my time for Watergate. I shouldn't have to do additional time and suffer additional losses for something I had nothing to do with.[131]

CHAPTER 10

THE CUBAN MISSION

Rolando Martinez spent more than fifteen months in jail, what he later called a "tragedy." In an article for *Harper's* magazine in 1974, Martinez couldn't "help seeing the whole Watergate affair as a repetition of the Bay of Pigs":

> *The invasion was a fiasco for the United States and a tragedy for the Cubans. All of the agencies of the U.S. government were involved, and they carried out their plans in so ill a manner that everyone landed in the hands of Castro—like a present.*[1]

After leaving prison that year, Martinez returned to Miami and was warned by former CIA colleagues he would be a target for Cuban intelligence. According to Doug Valentine, Barker and Martinez were then recruited for a clandestine intelligence unit of the Drug Enforcement Administration (DEACON 1), which operated through a front company in Miami, "designed to improve relations between Cuban and American businessmen." At the time of the Watergate arrests, FBI agents in Miami already knew of Martinez' association with the Agency and he seems to have had a long-standing relationship with the Bureau in the Miami area. He is named as an informant in a 1964 report into "Anti-Fidel Castro Activities" shared with the

CIA's Miami station, all branches of military intelligence, the Coast Guard, Border Patrol and Customs:

> *On January 3 1964 [MM T-1] advised he is a member of the action section of the MRR and has been going on clandestine missions to Cuba for the past year. MM T-1 stated that the MRR continues to send men from the United States to Central America and it is hoped that MRR military training facilities will be established in the near future in Central America. [MM T-1] explained that the activities of the MRR are compartmentalized and that a person in the action group would not necessarily know what operations are being carried on in Central America.*[2]

A later memo, dated October 1975, identifies him as a "well-placed source" and refers to information provided on Aldo Vera Serafin of Accion Cubana, "a small Cuban exile terrorist group in Miami." The memo was shared with the 902nd Military Intelligence Group at Homestead Air Force Base, Florida; the Office of Special Investigations at Patrick Air Force Base, Florida; and the Secret Service, Naval Investigative Service and INS.[3]

According to declassified CIA documents, on May 23, 1977, "a former source" contacted the Agency with a detailed message from Martinez, "another former source of this agency and convicted Watergate burglar":

> *Martinez was contacted in Miami, Florida by Salvador Aldereguia, a.k.a. "El Gallego" and asked to meet with a Cuban intelligence officer in Montego Bay, Jamaica on 24 May. Aldereguia told Martinez that in view of Martinez' imprisonment and mistreatment by the U.S. government following the Watergate affair, that Martinez might be interested in meeting with the Cuban IS officer.*

Martinez, accompanied by Aldereguia, plans to fly to Montego Bay at 1100 hours, 24 May. The Cuban IS officer who is to meet with them is supposedly flying from Cuba and not stationed in Jamaica.

Martinez is prepared to be debriefed after his return to Miami.

According to Martinez, the FBI is aware that he has been approached previously in Miami.

Martinez said that Aldereguia is a Cuban exile who works for World Finance Company in Miami, Florida.[4]

When the CIA's internal history of Watergate was released in August 2016, former CIA officer Felix Rodriguez revealed he was the source who passed the information to both agencies. Martinez called him up and said, "Felix, I have a problem. I've been asked to go to Cuba, and I'm trying to contact the CIA but I can't reach anyone." Rodriguez called a contact in "agency operations" and told him what Martinez had said. His contact said, "We can't touch Rolando with a ten-foot pole. Tell him to go to the FBI." Martinez told Rodriguez the FBI didn't want him to go on the mission because they thought he would be arrested, given his anti-Castro background and CIA connections, but like a good soldier, he went.[5]

On May 26, 1977, Rodriguez reported to the Agency on Martinez' meeting with Cuban intelligence officers in Montego Bay the day before. Martinez and Aldereguia-Ors had met with Juan Carbonell—a Cuban consular official who was the head of the Kingston station for the DGI, the main Cuban intelligence agency— and "another Cuban, who was introduced as 'Mario.'" It was a rapport-building exercise and Martinez was told, "We know we have been enemies in the past, but we are willing to forget that and begin a new friendship." Castro "had sent word that he would like to meet Martinez in Cuba" and Martinez was invited "to return to Jamaica on 28 May to meet a Cuban officer, a Colonel and veteran of the Angola fighting who was referred to as 'Jorge.'"

The Cubans had also told him they would execute Luis Posada, then in jail in Venezuela, charged with the bombing of a Cubana airliner the year before. Martinez felt Aldereguia-Ors was "definitely working for Cuban intelligence" and asked the government for "guidance regarding the proposed 28 May meeting in Jamaica."[6]

Sure enough, "senior officials in Cuban Security" invited him to meet in Jamaica and he subsequently met Colonel Antonio de la Guardia, of the Interior Ministry, in Mexico. "The guys prepared well," he recalled. "They knew almost everything about my life and show solidarity with my situation. As a proof of good faith, in just three days they relocated my father-in-law in the United States. Then, I accepted to visit Cuba." According to Rodriguez, Colonel Antonio de la Guardia picked Martinez up on a beach in Ocho Rios, Jamaica and took him by landing craft to Fidel Castro's Bluebird yacht, where he met Interior Minister José Abrantes and they went on to Santiago de Cuba. After hundreds of CIA infiltration raids into Cuba, this final trip was made "together with officers of the Castro regime and aboard the yacht of Fidel."[7]

From there, he flew to Havana and was questioned for several days by one of Castro's generals but not Fidel himself. The highest leader he met was José Abrantes, the minister of the Interior (MININT). He was then taken to his native province and by the end of the trip, the Cubans "were sure of having a new agent for the Castro regime." According to Martinez, they wanted to turn him into a "double agent" and he "made them believe that [he] was going to cooperate with them."

According to Rodriguez, "they did not ask him to be a spy for Cuban intelligence" but wanted him to use his heroic reputation "to lobby to lift the embargo [and] to re-establish negotiations with Cuba." They saw him as a figure who could reunite Cubans in Miami and Havana and gave him "plans to develop how I should get more influence, how I should infiltrate" and he turned them over to US authorities.[8]

An intriguing CIA memo dated June 2, 1977 and published here for the first time, confirms Martinez' story:

> *DGI officers also contacted the convicted Watergate burglar, Roland Martinez, met him in Jamaica in a rapport building session, and asked him to meet them again.*

The memo also notes that the FBI was preparing a memo for high-level officials concerning:

> *A recent DGI meeting with a FBI double agent who is also in contact with the Cuban exile Antonio VECIANA, who has claimed (falsely according to his file) that he and his CIA case officer met Lee Harvey OSWALD a month before President Kennedy's assassination. At the meeting the DGI officers had the double agent prepare a video tape in which he discussed, among other things, VECIANA and CIA's alleged involvement in President Kennedy's assassination and the double agent and VECIANA's involvement in attempts to assassinate CASTRO in Havana in 1961 and Chile in 1971.*

The memo concluded:

> *These two DGI contacts suggest the possibility that the DGI is preparing a propaganda campaign attempting to prove that CIA was involved in President Kennedy's assassination and the Watergate burglary.*[9]

The double agent was Felix Zabala Mas, a business partner of Veciana, whom he regarded as a brother. They had unsuccessfully tried to kill Castro with a bazooka and a gun hidden in a camera in Havana and Chile respectively. Veciana's CIA case officer Maurice Bishop had been involved in the Chilean plot and Veciana had recently testified before the House Select Committee on Assassinations (HSCA) about a meeting with Lee Harvey Oswald and Bishop in Dallas two months before the JFK assassination. In late 1976, hoping to sabotage Jimmy Carter's attempts to soften relations with Cuba, Veciana gave Zabala a letter addressed to Castro from his supposedly disgruntled secretary, spilling the beans on the previous assassination attempts and his meeting with Oswald. Veciana hoped Castro would publicly rail against the CIA assassination plots, damage US relations and establish his name as a CIA agent, strengthening his credentials during further testimony. Zabala sent the letter to Castro through his sister in Cuba and was soon recruited by Cuban intelligence, who debriefed him in Jamaica, Panama and Mexico City about his knowledge of the assassination plots and anti-Castro terrorist activity. By April, Veciana suggested he contact the CIA and get them involved but instead, the FBI were tipped off and interviewed Zabala on suspicion of consorting with foreign agents. He was debriefed about his meetings with Cuban intelligence over the previous five months and turned into a double agent.

The FBI briefed him before the April 9 meeting in Mexico referred to above, where he produced a photograph which allegedly showed Oswald at an Alpha 66 meeting in Dallas in 1963, where Veciana spoke. His video interview lasted ninety minutes and was intended for Castro: "In the last segment of videotaping in Mexico, [he] was confronted with enlarged photographs of the alleged Alpha 66 meeting and was asked to point out the individual similar in description to Oswald." The FBI concluded it wasn't Oswald but were pleased with their new spy within Cuban intelligence.[10]

• • •

The cast of characters in the Cuban pitch to Martinez is worth exploring. Salvador Aldereguia-Ors was a Bay of Pigs veteran and "a former captain in Fidel Castro's rebel army who later broke with Castro and came to Miami vowing to help overthrow the premier."[11]

On March 3, 1978, he was on his way to Kingston, Jamaica to meet DGI station chief Jose Carbonell when he was arrested at Miami airport, on suspicion of spying for a foreign power. A letter from "a Cuban secret police agent" was found in his briefcase, directing "Samuel," "a Cuban spy in Miami," to return to Cuba.[12]

Aldereguia-Ors told the FBI that over the past year, "he travelled to Jamaica numerous times . . . to arrange for visas to reunite Cuban families. Juan Carbonell, the Cuban consul in Jamaica, was an old-time friend from revolutionary days, he said, adding that he had lodged petitions for the freedom of key political prisoners in Cuba with Carbonell".[13]

He said he ignored earlier FBI suggestions that he should register as a foreign agent in connection to his trips to Jamaica because he had not been instructed to do so by either the U.S. State or Justice departments.[14]

The letter in the briefcase "caused investigators to doubt his explanation" and speculate that "Samuel" (Aldereguia-Ors) "was headed for the Cuban consulate in Jamaica to protest [his] reassignment":

Special Agent Willis Walton of the FBI testified . . . that the briefcase also contained "operational instructions from a foreign country," directives for activities in the United States, and other papers.[15]

Sources said the FBI knew "who hand-delivered the letters to Aldereguia" and "the letters also furnished 'Samuel' with names of persons who would be helpful in setting up a business 'front' in Miami and explained how to get visas to bring people into Miami who could help with the company."[16]

The timing of Aldereguia-Ors' arrest was interesting. Four days later, his former boss at WFC Corp., banker Guillermo Hernandez-Cartaya, was arrested and charged with "using a passport borrowed from a fellow Bay of Pigs veteran [Aldereguia-Ors] to escape from the Persian Gulf Emirate of Ajman," where officials had confiscated his passport, "demanding he account for $37 million in Arab funds allegedly channelled by . . . [his] investment banking firm."[17]

Sources said the pair had been charged with passport violations the previous summer but the passport charge "may have been simply a means of keeping Aldereguia in the country."[18]

In response to the charges, Salvador Aldereguia-Ors came out fighting. He accused the FBI of fabricating the letters and framing him "in an attempt to discredit" Hernandez-Cartaya:

Aldereguia denied there were any letters to a Cuban spy in his briefcase . . . "I am not Samuel . . . I don't know such a Samuel and there were no such letters," Aldereguia has said.

Aldereguia said the briefcase contained some 100 visa applications.

Some, he added, were applications for permits to leave the island temporarily; some were applications for permits to leave the island permanently and others were visa applications for exiles to visit their relatives in Cuba.

FBI agents testified in court that they also found in the briefcase pictures of Hernandez-Cartaya, identical to one pasted on a passport belonging to Aldereguia.

"He [Hernandez-Cartaya] is my friend . . . I am not going to soil his name or reputation," Aldereguia said.[19]

• • •

Three weeks after Aldereguia-Ors' arrest, his friends in the US intelligence community started coming out of the woodwork. The *Miami News* reported that, according to federal officials, the "46-year-old Bay of Pigs veteran . . . [had] a long-standing relationship" with the FBI and the Bureau of Narcotics and Dangerous Drugs, "volunteering information on drug traffic and other matters" from the late sixties "until at least 1974," which helped solve some drug cases in New York. He was described as the "former right-hand man of Guillermo Hernandez-Cartaya, president of the Coral Gables-based financial conglomerate, WFC Corp," having been hired as Hernandez-Cartaya's assistant in 1971.[20]

"No one has to defend me. My actions speak for themselves," Aldereguia-Ors told reporters. "I don't know how I can be accused of working against the national security of the country when I have worked for the national security of this country." Aldereguia-Ors said he was introduced to federal agencies ten to twelve years earlier by Jack Cogswell, a retired US naval officer. Cogswell was initially suspicious of his motives "because Aldereguia wanted to talk about the need to fight drug trafficking":

> *I always thought there might have been a connection between Castro people and drugs . . . He said he knew something about narcotics so I told him, "Why don't you do something about it?"*[21]

Cogswell introduced Aldereguia-Ors to Frank O'Brien, an FBI agent based in New Jersey, who specialized in Cuban affairs. According to Cogswell, "Aldereguia's information concerned narcotics traffic." O'Brien confirmed Cogswell's story and admitted meeting Aldereguia-Ors "for about 20 minutes" in Miami, while there "on other business after the arrest," at the invitation of the arresting agent, Willis Walton. According to the *Miami News*, "federal investigators said Aldereguia's background with U.S. government agencies 'will probably help him in court.'"[22]

• • •

In the early seventies, the FBI warned Antonio Veciana that they had information that Castro was targeting him for a possible kidnapping. "If anyone
invites you to leave the country with whatever excuse be wary of it," they told
him. Sure enough, "a few months later, one of Castro's agents . . . his sur-
name is Aldereguia, invited me to go to a sporting event in Panama," recalled
Veciana. Aldereguia offered him a free ticket and Veciana "immediately realized that what they wanted was to kidnap me in Panama." Later on, Castro
"played another trick" on Veciana:

> Apparently, Aldereguia, who had been one of Castro's agents, had been
> recruited by the FBI, so then someone called Rolando Balance, one of Cas-
> tro's agents, came from Cuba and visited me in my office and proposed me
> to kill Aldereguia.

He told Veciana he worked for the Cuban government but thought they were
unjustly persecuting him—"I had the right to dissent from the Cuban government and that I was a family man and that they shouldn't try to kill me":

> He said that Aldereguia had received a large amount of money to find a
> killer for me and that he was there to warn me about it. Then he suggested
> that I kill Aldereguia. He was going to set him up and take him to a house
> where I would be able to kill him. I realized that this was an ambush set
> up by the Cuban government. I reported it to the FBI and they said to me:
> "Look, we are going to set up an ambush for Rolando Balance to arrest him
> because he is one of Castro's agents." I refused to do it because this man had
> at least come to warn me and I didn't want to go ahead with the ambush.[23]

After that, Veciana's relationship with the FBI deteriorated and Cuban agents
unsuccessfully tried to assassinate him in September 1979. Aldereguia-Ors

was never prosecuted and in 1984, he was again arrested by Miami police for carrying a briefcase containing "what appeared to be sensitive documents tying him with Communist Cuba." By now, he had retrained as a veterinarian and his license was suspended five years later when investigators found he had purchased "large amounts of anabolic steroids and other drugs," which he couldn't account for.

For years, Martinez' Cuban mission remained classified but he worried that, one day, details of the operation might leak: "Imagine how it would look if I were accused of being a double agent, a Cuban infiltrator in Watergate."[24]

In 1999, that's what happened when the exiled Cuban writer Norberto Fuentes, a famed biographer of Ernest Hemingway and Fidel Castro, revealed the episode in his Spanish-language book *Sweet Cuban Warriors* and suggested Martinez had been a spy for Castro. Fuentes' source was a letter from Antonio de la Guardia, who told him "he directed the operation that brought the Watergate burglar to Cuba."[25]

According to the *Miami Herald*, Fuentes had grown close to Antonio and Patricio de La Guardia, and Arnaldo Ochoa, during the Cuban intervention in Angola in the eighties. All three were senior military and intelligence officers, later convicted of drug smuggling and treason "in a controversial 1989 trial":

> *Amid widespread suspicion that they were framed by Castro because he saw them as potential rivals, Ochoa and Antonio de la Guardia were executed, while Patricio de la Guardia remains imprisoned.*[26]

In the letter, de la Guardia confessed that "Musculito was really a Cuban agent."

"Those are your lies, Tony," replied Fuentes.

"There is nobody more blind than he who does not want to see."

"Our man at Watergate?"

"Watergate. In the CIA. And the White House."[27]

The book gave few details but reportedly "caused something of a stir in Cuban exile circles."[28]

Sensing his life was in danger and he could be "in big trouble" with some of the more "hot-headed" members of the Cuban exile community in Miami, Martinez was grateful when his "American friends" convened a press conference at a local Cuban restaurant to publicly dispel the charges. Former CIA colleagues advised Martinez to come clean at the press conference and he was relieved to get it off his chest.

What Fuentes didn't know was that Martinez' contacts with Cuban officers and infiltration into Cuba "had been authorized and supervised operations by the American intelligence agencies." Martinez sat with "distressed friends, relatives and supporters," including a pair of retired FBI agents and legendary exile CIA operative Felix Rodriguez.

Martinez denied the charges: "Every time I left the country—and it is documented that I participated in 354 clandestine missions in Cuba—it was with the full knowledge of the security agencies of the American government. Since leaving Cuba, I have never met or worked for Castro. This book is just a novel."

After Fuentes' book was published, Martinez refused to discuss the details of the Cuban mission, "or whether he continued to work with the CIA after Watergate or whether he is now retired." "Classified," he said.[29]

Former CIA officer Felix Rodriguez sat beside Martinez and said the trip to Cuba was authorized and "of great benefit to this country. Martinez went as a "guest"—"at that time, Martinez contacted me, and I contacted the CIA and the FBI. What he has done was honorable."[30]

Former FBI agents, Vincent Warger and Frank Gibbons, turned up to support Martinez as "a good fellow" and longtime friend, but wouldn't confirm if they'd ever worked with him. "There was a Fidel man in Watergate," said Fuentes, standing by his book. "You might have to rewrite the whole history of Watergate."[31]

In 2015, Martinez appeared on a Spanish-language television program in Miami and confirmed his trip to Cuba but denied he was a Cuban agent:

> *He said the Cubans contacted him because they thought that after serving his sentence for Watergate, he would be upset with the United States and would be willing to change his colors. "They were sure that because I had been sentenced to 40 years in jail, I had to be very upset with the Americans, and that was the point they used to get me."*

He assumed the information gleaned from the mission "was useful to the CIA . . . because then they gave me a presidential pardon for that operation." Around the same time, Patricio de la Guardia was released from jail in Cuba and sent Martinez an apology "to dissociate himself from the trick against me. I was amazed."[32]

When the CIA's internal history of Watergate was released in August 2016, Felix Rodriguez was interviewed by a Spanish newspaper about Martinez and the Cuban mission. He said the Cuban officials gave Martinez a sum of money, which he turned over to the FBI on his return, along with information concerning his trip—how the Cubans made the pitch, "what Cuban officials told him and what tactics they used to take him to Cuba," where he stayed, who he met—all of great interest to the intelligence community. The FBI report on Martinez' debriefing after his return from Cuba "convinced President Ronald Reagan to grant him a presidential pardon for his role in Watergate."[33]

Reagan granted Martinez a presidential pardon on May 11, 1983 as "one of the least culpable of those involved in Watergate-related crimes" while pardon applications from E. Howard Hunt and Jeb Magruder were rejected. Martinez joined Richard Nixon as the only other figure granted executive clemency in the Watergate scandal but at the time, nobody quite knew why.[34]

CHAPTER 11
THE CALL-GIRL THEORY

In 1998, in ruling on a defamation suit brought by Ida Wells against Gordon Liddy, US District Court Judge J. Frederick Motz outlined the background to the case:

> *Liddy is among a group of persons who dispute the conventional wisdom that the purpose of the break-in was to repair a tap on the telephone of then-DNC chairman Larry O'Brien that had been installed during an earlier burglary. Instead, Liddy and his fellow revisionists theorize that the goal of the break-in was to obtain information about a call-girl ring that was connected to the DNC. Plaintiff Wells was a secretary at the DNC. Liddy has alleged that Wells' telephone and desk were used in making assignations between visitors to the DNC and prostitutes who were members of the ring, thereby implying that Wells had a connection to the call-girl operation.*[1]

First mentioned by Lukas in 1976, the "call-girl theory" of the break-in was further developed in *Secret Agenda* (1984) by Jim Hougan:

> *Hougan discovered and publicized, for the first time, the fact that one of the burglars, Eugenio Rolando Martinez, had been captured holding the key to Wells' desk. Hougan suggested that the actual targets of the bugging*

operation were the clients of the prostitutes in the Columbia Plaza Apartments, and that the actual target of the break-in was Wells' desk.[2]

Carl Shoffler, John Rudy, and Phillip Bailley were Hougan's sources on the call-girl operation and in 1986, Bailley drafted a book proposal with Phil Stanford on the Columbia Plaza operation and its connection to Watergate. Bailley claimed Nixon speechwriter and later ABC News anchor Diane Sawyer, Deborah Sloan (the wife of CRP treasurer Hugh Sloan), Maureen Biner, DNC staffer Sheila Ellis Hixson, and "one of John Mitchell's former secretaries" were involved in the ring but didn't find a publisher.[3]

Two years later, after guest appearances as a covert operations officer in *Miami Vice*, Liddy began "extensive conversations" with author Len Colodny. According to author James Rosen, when Colodny showed Liddy the floor plan of the DNC, he realized that Spencer Oliver's office faced the Howard Johnson Motel across the street where Baldwin was monitoring his telephone, and that "the wiretap could transmit only to a receiver in the line of sight, meaning that Mr. O'Brien's office could not have been the target."[4]

In May 1991, *Silent Coup* by Len Colodny and Robert Gettlin was published and fleshed out the "call-girl theory" by identifying Heidi Rikan as the "Tess" in Hougan's book and claiming Rikan's close friend and roommate Maureen "Mo" Biner knew Bailley and was listed as "Clout" in his address books. *Silent Coup* suggests the burglars were looking for a compromising photo of Biner in Maxie Wells' desk drawer, establishing a motive for John Dean's interest in the Bailley indictment and Dean's role in changing the target for the second break-in. The authors conducted extensive interviews with major players in the Watergate story in the late eighties and early nineties and I gained access to the transcripts of many of these interviews, in which key witnesses address the main elements of the call-girl theory for the first time.

In 1990, Rolando Martinez had lunch with Benton Becker—the attorney who negotiated Nixon's pardon and was now representing Colodny—and a follow-up interview with Becker and Colodny. He remembered a short briefing from Hunt and Liddy on the day of the second break-in, when one of them gave him the key. Liddy denied it, so by a process of elimination, Martinez accepted it must have been Hunt. He was also given a "DNC floor plan . . . [with] an X mark on Spencer Oliver's desk and on the desks near Spencer Oliver's desk . . . [and] told to photograph the records and papers in the X-marked desks designated on the DNC floor plan." Martinez believed the floor plan information came from McCord, who "was sent down inside those offices to go coordinate all the floor plans . . . [and was] involved in the direct casing of the building." Spencer Oliver's name was never mentioned and Martinez never had time to take any pictures or open Wells' drawer before his arrest. If he had found the alleged nude photos in Wells' desk, he said he would have taken them. Liddy claimed he never saw a floor plan, so it may have come from McCord, whom Martinez always felt was a "mole" in the operation.[5]

Eight months later, when Colodny questioned Howard Hunt about the key, Hunt seemed genuinely bewildered: "This is the first I've heard of a key to a desk and a floor plan . . . I don't know where [Martinez] got the key from. . . ." Hunt didn't appear to know about Baldwin's visit to the DNC five days before the second break-in and suggested, "the logical route for that key would be Baldwin, McCord, Martinez, if there was a key."[6]

"The target was a file safe . . . [in] Larry O'Brien's office," claimed Hunt. "We were looking for account books . . . to reflect any unexplained donations that might have come from Castro's Cuba or the Vietnamese." Contrary to what's published in *Silent Coup*, Hunt did not "confirm that the target of the first break-in was a phone . . . used by Wells and Oliver." Hunt said McCord was in charge of the electronic surveillance and he believed the bugging of Oliver's phone had been a "mistake."[7]

Hunt denied seeing "transcripts of any Oliver conversations" and only heard from Liddy "that they were calls between Oliver and a girlfriend at a time when Oliver was involved in divorce proceedings." In a later deposition, Hunt seemed equally bemused when asked if he was ever questioned about attempts to blackmail Spencer Oliver (he wasn't) and added:

> All I ever heard was that Liddy said that the tape is not what they want, it turns out Oliver's calling some bimbo, there's some, he implied, salacious exchanges being made over it, and in the meantime the guy is trying to divorce his wife or he's in the middle of a messy divorce.[8]

During extensive research interviews for *Silent Coup*, Phillip Bailley told author Len Colodny he first met Mo Biner in Nathan's bar in Georgetown in the spring or summer of 1971. Cathy Dieter gave him Mo's number and he added it to his pocket address book and called her several times. Bailley wasn't aware of Mo's connection to John Dean and claimed she got the nickname "Clout" in December 1971 "from her ability to get herself and others invited to parties [and] on invitation lists."[9]

After spotting an opportunity to drum up business at the DNC, Bailley telephoned Maxie Wells and pitched her a way to tell visitors "where a sharp party was . . . [with] real high class women . . . not prostitution." He introduced Wells to Dieter, who took her out to lunch and pitched her what sounded "like an escort service" without telling her it was illegal. Wells allegedly signed on and the "telephone located in [Oliver's] seldom-used office . . . was used to arrange dates with Cathy Dieter's Columbia Plaza call girls." Bailley thought Biner "probably knew about [his] arrangement with the DNC" and he, Dieter and Biner "joked about it." Wells and Maureen Dean both deny any connection to Bailley or any call girl operation.[10]

Shortly after *Silent Coup* was published, Gordon Liddy interviewed Bailey about his involvement in the call-girl ring and subsequently endorsed *Silent Coup* in an updated edition of his autobiography. In the Wells case, Judge Motz summarized the Liddy version of the "call-girl theory" as follows:

> *Members of the DNC allegedly used the Columbia Plaza call-girl ring to entertain important visitors. According to Liddy, Wells kept a "brochure" containing about twelve photographs of the call-girls in her desk. Visitors to the DNC allegedly would stop at Wells' desk to consult the brochure and use Wells' phone to arrange assignations with the call-girls . . . Liddy suggests that the break-in took place because John Dean learned of the photographs in Wells' desk and wanted to remove the pictures to protect his girlfriend. As a result, Liddy asserts, Dean told some of the Watergate burglars to break into Wells' desk to remove the envelope containing the pictures. Liddy contends that he personally was not informed of this reason for the burglary at the time and that he operated under the assumption that the goals of the break-in were political espionage and repair of the O'Brien wiretap.[11]*

Bailey told Liddy he took the photographs of the call-girls in see-through negligees and the DNC secretaries were paid a commission for each customer referred.[12]

After initially stating Liddy and Mitchell ordered the second break-in, Jeb Magruder now told Colodny and Gettlin it was Dean. Liddy, Hougan and *Silent Coup* all suggested that Dean did so because "he'd learned of the relationship between the Columbia Plaza call-girl ring and the DNC."[13]

In 1992, John and Maureen Dean filed a defamation suit against the authors of *Silent Coup*, their publisher St. Martin's Press, Gordon Liddy, Phillip

Bailley, Jim Hougan, Phil Stanford and others, accusing them of malice for claiming Dean was "guilty of criminal conduct in planning, aiding, abetting and directing the Watergate break-ins, and gave perjured testimony." They also denied any involvement with Phillip Bailley or an alleged call-girl ring. Dean was represented by the former Senate Watergate Committee attorney David Dorsen, and later dropped his claims against Stanford, Hougan, and Liddy and agreed an undisclosed out of court settlement with the *Silent Coup* authors and publisher before the case went to trial. According to James Rosen, "*Silent Coup* author Colodny, was, like the Deans, paid by Colodny's insurance company to let the matter die . . . [and] not one word of *Silent Coup* had to be retracted."

"Eight of years of litigation," Dean later wrote, "established . . . no admissible evidence whatsoever" to support his "false claims" and "bogus hearsay" about Watergate and "Bailley's fantasies." Dean attacked Bailley's credibility as the only admissible witness "who claimed first-hand knowledge" of the operation, claiming Bailley had "bipolar disorder" and "had been under psychiatric care, on and off, his entire adult life."[14]

As I was completing this book, I managed to access many of the pre-trial depositions taken in the *Dean v. St. Martin's Press* case, where questions about the call-girl theory were posed under oath to key characters in the Watergate story for the first time, providing a fresh and valuable perspective on the continuing mysteries surrounding Watergate.

When deposed in 1993, Lt. Jeannine Bailley Ball was a registered nurse in the US Air Force. As a teenager, she had worked as her brother's secretary for two years until the FBI raid in April 1972 and recalled receiving numerous calls from Maxie Wells and Mo Biner. She recalled both names were listed in her brother's address book but she never met them in person. When Jeannine saw Biner's name next to the nickname "Clout" in the address book, she asked her brother what "Clout" meant, and he explained "she had political connections and . . . was an important person." When Biner telephoned the office, she used her real name but once referred to herself as "Clout." Jeannine also remembered calls from "Candy Cane" and "Champagne"—women who would call and leave messages for Phillip using codenames—but her brother never told her anything about a call-girl ring; she just knew them as clients. According to Jeannine Bailley, on the day of the FBI raid, her brother had his telephone book in his pocket, so the two address books seized from his office were hers—one a chronological telephone log, the other an alphabetical address book she had been transcribing from her brother's. She insisted the name "Maureen Biner" and "Clout" appeared in both address books. She also remembered receiving between "ten and thirty" calls from Maxie Wells, and claimed they spoke five times. At the end of May 1972, she left on a trip to Europe and was told FBI agents had travelled to Milan to look for her, to subpoena her to appear before the grand jury in her brother's case.[15]

The most authoritative witness on the call-girl ring should have been John Rudy, the assistant US attorney in charge of the grand jury investigation of Phillip Bailley, but his 1,139-page deposition in the Dean case was clouded by a dispute with Len Colodny. Rudy had agreed to speak to Colodny "on background" for *Silent Coup* but was quoted at length and later supported the prosecution of Colodny for illegally taping their calls. Rudy disputed much of what he told Colodny on tape in his 1996 deposition, leading the defendants to believe he was taking Dean's side.

At the time of the FBI raid on Bailley's office in April 1972, Rudy was investigating a bordello at Dupont Circle, where informant Lou Russell had told him hidden cameras were documenting "the sadomasochistic proclivities" of local judges, who either were blackmailed or granted acquittals or light sentences in return for sexual favors.[16]

According to Rudy, two notebooks were seized from Bailley's office—one with names and addresses, the other with code names—and four from his apartment. Rudy brought the book with names and addresses to his meeting with Dean at the White House while the FBI were trying to decipher the names in the code book. Rudy initially thought the code book was "evidence of a deranged mind" but came to realize it "had to do with the Columbia Plaza operation." Lou Russell helped him identify some of the girls in the code book who were working at the Columbia Plaza, including the alleged madam of the operation who used the alias "Cathy Dieter" and the code-name "Erika." Rudy thought Russell may have introduced him to Dieter and told him her real name but he couldn't remember what it was.[17]

In return for immunity from prosecution, Cathy Dieter became an informant and helped him identify further names in the code book. Rudy remembered the codenames "Clout 18" and "Green House Nymph" and Dieter later identified "Clout 18" as a woman with the initials M. B. Rudy referred to her by the military code "Mike Bravo" during his investigation and remembered her full name as "Maureen Biner, Binner or Bowmer."[18]

Rudy issued subpoenas to girls identified in Bailley's address books and asked the FBI to track them down. More than a hundred people were interviewed. "We had them coming up and down the back elevator to my office," Rudy recalled, "so no one would see them. They were beautiful girls and they were terrified of being connected [in public] to Bailley's activities."[19]

While there were no names in the address book of any DNC employees, Rudy testified that "one of the FBI agents identified one of the coded names [in Bailley's address book] as being a person who worked either at or with the DNC." Rudy believed she was a secretary, "who arranged for liaisons . . . [as] kind of a go-between." According to Rudy's deposition, Cathy Dieter "mentioned Spencer Oliver in the sense that he either knew of or had been involved in some way in the Columbia Plaza operation . . . That he had been seen at the Columbia Plaza operation." But Rudy's memory was vague and he subsequently denied any "personal knowledge of any call girl related activities being carried on at the [DNC]." There is no evidence of Oliver's involvement and he denies any knowledge of or connection to such operations.[20]

Rudy said he began to look at possible connections between the Columbia Plaza and the DNC but the investigation "never really got off the ground" before it was "iced" by Principal Assistant US Attorney Harold Titus in early August 1972, for fear that it might be "construed or interpreted as being politically motivated":

The directions that I received were that the DNC should not be pursued. That it was a political timebomb. It was very politically sensitive because of the Watergate break-in . . .

What we would have investigated was whether there were women at the DNC who were participating in prostitution operations, whether they were putting their employers together with prostitutes at the Columbia Plaza or whether they, themselves, were participating at the Columbia Plaza in prostitution operations that may not have been associated with the DNC.[21]

Cathy Dieter told Rudy that tricks were being filmed and tape-recorded at the Columbia Plaza, often at the request of the johns. Rudy also heard the Metropolitan police had placed "one or more bugs" in the apartments: "There were a lot of people doing a lot of things over in those apartments who had different motivations and interests. Some were known and some were unknown and I think that may have been one of the reasons why our side of it was shut down. Too many people involved. I mean, people were bugging the buggers, tape recording buggers."

"What do you mean, 'people were bugging the buggers?'" Rudy was asked.

"I believe there were phone taps that were being conducted pursuant to a court order. There were people [doing] illegal taps . . . There were perhaps other agencies involved . . . in some type of intelligence operations. I mean, it was a ball of wax."[22]

During his deposition, Rudy could not disclose evidence revealed to him in grand jury testimony—evidence of connections between the Columbia Plaza and the DNC which he was stopped from pursuing when the investigation was "iced." Following his at-times acrimonious testimony, Rudy submitted an affidavit stating that he had "no personal knowledge of any call-girl related activities being carried on at the [DNC] during 1971 or 1972."[23]

Heidi Rikan was the alleged madam at the center of the Columbia Plaza call-girl ring, using the nicknames "Cathy Dieter" and "Erika." The Deans have confirmed that Rikan was a "close friend" and bridesmaid of Maureen Dean but was she the same woman as the "Cathy Dieter" described by Rudy?

In a 1995 deposition, Carl Shoffler was convinced she was but admitted he had no conclusive proof. Working closely with the vice squad as an MPD intelligence officer, Shoffler had well-placed sources on prostitution and organized crime. They told him Heidi Rikan, Carolyn Rainear, and Mo Biner had a reputation as "party girls," looking for a Mr. Big, who would finance their lifestyle in exchange for sexual favors. Rikan was "kept" by mobster Joe Nesline and allegedly interceded with Dean on behalf of Jimmy Hoffa before Nixon pardoned Hoffa in December 1971. Her "close friend" Carolyn Rainear was the long-term mistress of another prominent organized crime figure in the city, Emmitt Warring. Nesline ran an illegal betting operation and was involved in high-class call girl operations, not as a pimp but for information: "Primarily, he liked to have females involved with football players. That gave him an edge on becoming a better rather than a bookie." Ed Bennett Williams, whose firm represented the DNC and the *Washington Post*, was also Nesline's attorney. Lawrence Higby, a former aide to H. R. Haldeman, claimed Cartha DeLoach told him "the FBI file on Maureen Dean was incredible . . . she was listed as a public relations specialist for the New Orleans Saints but in fact was a call girl down there." Dean's former husband George Owen was a football scout for the Saints and had first introduced her to Heidi Rikan in the late sixties. Maureen Dean denies the allegations.[24]

Shoffler and Bailley were convinced Rikan used the alias "Cathy Dieter" and was a madam and "high priced call girl." In a court filing, Len Colodny produced a detailed and persuasive comparison of the physical characteristics and life histories of Rikan and Dieter—both had blonde hair, a voluptuous figure, a German accent, were prostitutes, were friends with Maureen Biner Dean, used the name "Erika" and drove a Corvette.[25]

In the early eighties, Rikan told her longtime maid, "I was a call girl at the White House." After her death in 1990, her sister Kathie found a "little black book" in her belongings, some of which was later published in Phil Stanford's biography *White House Call Girl*. Her personal phone directory contained the names of the Deans (including John's private White House number and unlisted home number), Jeb Magruder, Maurice Stans, Mitchell aide Fred LaRue, Senator Lowell Weicker (a neighbor of the Deans), Sam Dash (chief counsel for the Senate Watergate Committee), Joe Nesline and Irving Davidson, the Washington lobbyist for Jimmy Hoffa and Carlos Marcello, who shared an office with Jack Anderson. Rikan's sister Kathie and close friend Josephine Alvarez confirmed Heidi used the alias "Kathie Dieter."[26]

In the late nineties, author Anthony Summers contacted "Lil Lori," a madam who, according to police records, operated call girl operations out of two apartments at the Columbia Plaza. However, as John Dean later noted, "she did not know Heidi Rikan or any of the women Bailley and Stanford had claimed were involved." She told Summers her clients included both Republicans and Democrats and "a lot of business was done" at the DNC: "these people were good to me, trusted me." She admitted she "knew people involved with the Watergate break-in" and received a visit from a senior Democrat "at the height of the Watergate crisis," seeking assurance she wouldn't talk, if questioned. Researcher Bob Fink told Shoffler that Lil Lori suggested to him she was helping McCord with an intelligence-gathering operation.[27]

During his deposition, Carl Shoffler admitted he had never met Phillip Bailley and had no personal knowledge that Bailley managed a call-girl ring at the Columbia Plaza or what apartment it was run out of. But he testified that the Watergate Lounge was deemed "a chronic prostitution spot" at the time and admitted using electronic surveillance, raising the possibility that Shoffler or McCord (or both) were "bugging the buggers" at the Columbia Plaza.

In the years since *Secret Agenda*, Jim Hougan has changed his view on Shoffler and now thinks he "cut him too much slack": "He was clearly tipped off to the break-in—of that I have no doubt. The Joe Nesline business was also more important than I'd imagined." Strangely, Shoffler wasn't asked about a possible tip-off in his deposition. He confirmed he recovered the key from Martinez but not the floorplan or the page apparently torn out of Martinez' yellow notebook. Shoffler thought he remembered "some sort of chart or little diagram" in the notebook but it's not there today.[28]

A week after John Rudy's main testimony in July 1996, Alfred Baldwin gave one of most important depositions in the *Dean v. St. Martin's Press* case. At the time, Baldwin was an Assistant State Attorney in the Criminal Justice Division in Connecticut, often dealing with cases of prostitution. After the break-in, Silbert, the FBI and Senator Weicker had asked Baldwin if the sexual nature of the calls he overheard related to prostitution:

> *The conversations [were of] a sexual nature, but they weren't asking for money, they weren't the type I would classify as prostitution or call girl or escort service, dating service . . . They were people who knew each other, conversing to arrange dates or rendezvous or dinners, whatever, and sexual relationships to follow . . . I had never heard any type of a conversation that would specifically lead to a call girl ring or prostitution ring. . . .*

He heard no evidence of a call-girl ring or prostitutes operating out of the DNC, no reference to the Columbia Plaza apartments and none of the code names in Bailley's address book. He knew from his FBI days how prostitutes had to be discreet on the phone but he heard "none of those type of conversations." The sexual conversations he heard were between "single . . . or even married people, making a rendezvous . . . but not, quote, a sexual prostitution-type ring." These people generally knew each other and weren't arranging first dates but were discussing "very intimate" details of ongoing affairs, "describing certain things that happened the night before, [what they] would like to happen the next night" and so on.

Baldwin could identify some of the intercepted voices but most he could not. It was hard to keep track of the voices, day by day—was the female voice the same one as yesterday? He didn't know "if you had one very active secretary or you had ten . . . if you had one very active male or you had ten."

McCord told him to record all political calls and all personal calls of a private and confidential nature and to call him the minute he received that kind of material. McCord was interested in both calls relating to political strategy and calls of a sexual nature:

> There seemed to be a little bit more priority to the sexual, to be honest, then the political, but the political would be there. . . . "When you hear anything involving McGovern, let's hear that. . . . call us immediately, if you hear anything involving any [strategy] plan book . . . [If] two people are talking about sex they had, if there is any names, I want to know about it."[29]

Baldwin's deposition is very damaging to the "call girl theory" and while what Bailley initially told Jim Hougan was intriguing, Hougan shares my skepticism about Bailley's evolving story: "Since *Secret Agenda's* publication, Bailley has made a number of statements that, in my opinion, exaggerate his role and importance in the affair. I am very skeptical of his description of the operation at the Columbia Plaza as recounted in Phil Stanford's otherwise excellent book." Carl Shoffler had no direct knowledge of the call girl ring at the Columbia Plaza and John Rudy couldn't discuss relevant grand jury testimony, so as Dean notes, Phillip Bailey is the primary source for the "call-girl theory" and his later allegation that eight DNC staff members (including Larry O'Brien's secretary) were "runners" for the Columbia Plaza call-girl operation, paid a commission to solicit clients, strains credibility.[30]

It's clear from Rudy's testimony that Phillip Bailey kept a code book of girls, some of whom were involved in the Columbia Plaza call-girl ring, but the address books are missing from Justice Department files, so we can only rely on the memories and testimony of those who admit to seeing them—Phillip and Jeannine Bailey, and John Rudy—as to what they contained. In his 1995 deposition, John Dean denied looking at or making a copy of Bailey's address book during his White House meeting with Rudy and Smith, but given Dean's record of suppressing key evidence in this case, I don't believe him. Putting the testimony of Rudy and Jeannine Bailey together, it seems Mo Biner's name and nickname "Clout" were in Bailey's address books. Otherwise, why would Dean ask for a copy? *Silent Coup* suggests that after seeing the Bailey address book, Dean ordered the second break-in, targeting Maxie Wells' desk drawer without Liddy's knowledge, but how would Dean have known photos of Biner were allegedly kept in Wells' desk drawer? It's clear from Baldwin's testimony that there was no discussion of call girls on the intercepted conversations, so if they were involved, only Maureen Dean or Cathy Dieter/Heidi Rikan could have tipped off Dean about where the alleged trick book was located. And how could Dean have changed the target without Liddy knowing? There's no evidence that Dean had a direct line to Hunt or McCord, and Dean claimed he met Hunt only once with Colson before Watergate.[31]

While depositions were being taken in his lawsuit with John Dean, Gordon Liddy was not shy about publicly airing his alternative theory of Watergate, drawing on his interview with Bailley and the claims of *Secret Agenda* and *Silent Coup*. Dean's attorney, David Dorsen, was present when Liddy spoke at James Madison University in April 1996:

> *[Baldwin's lookout post] looked directly down at a desk of a secretary, named Maxine Wells, and her telephone. And they had a telescopic lens camera pointed at that. And that is where the wiretap was subsequently found by the Democrats on that phone. Now why was there a wiretap on there? And why did they go back in?*

Liddy described a manila envelope in Wells' desk containing photographs of twelve girls and "one group photograph of them." As DNC customers looked at the brochure and called to arrange their date, they were being "wiretapped, recorded and photographed."

A year later, with Dean's encouragement, Ida Maxwell Wells filed a five-million-dollar defamation suit against Gordon Liddy through David Dorsen, citing four occasions on which Liddy had cast her as a "procurer of prostitutes" while discussing the "call-girl theory" of the break-in, including his appearance at James Madison University.[32]

In her deposition in the *Dean v. St. Martin's Press* case, Wells had denied any knowledge of "any call-girl ring operation linked in any way to the DNC." She said she didn't know Cathy Dieter but may have known Bailley as "a sort of hanger on of the Young Democrats, somebody who appeared at parties and things like that." During her six months at the DNC, she dated five men, including Severin Beliveau, president of the Association of State Democratic Chairmen and State chairman for Maine, who visited Washington once a month "because I was single [and] it was a great, great time"; Joe Farmer, who worked for the Young Democrats; Peter Range, a *Time* magazine reporter in Atlanta; and James York, a D.C. narcotics officer she met when her car was broken into on June 14. Beliveau used Oliver's phone when he was in town and Wells was also his secretary:

> *It was her desk that had been rifled through. They were allegedly looking for evidence . . . that she was providing prostitutes for the party chairs, which is of course absolutely untrue . . . the listening device on our phone worked, they taped [sic] all our conversations.*[33]

During discovery in her own lawsuit, Maxie Wells produced a box of Watergate-related materials which included an unsent letter written to a friend before her grand jury testimony in September 1972 and an impending "crisis." She lived in a house with five men and she was worried:

> *I was subpoenoed (sp?) on Saturday to appear before the Grand Jury in Washington on Wednesday. I'm flying up tomorrow to talk to Spencer & the DNC lawyers, plus to get one of my own maybe . . . . It appears that the Republicans are going to try to discredit Demo. witnesses on moral grounds. They've got the makings for a good scandal in my case because I've lived with those guys, Joe, etc. and they apparently know a lot of it. Spencer & I both feel (hope, really) that I probably won't be important enough for them to bother, but I am really upset & nervous & will really be glad when it's all over. The FBI has a file on me a mile long now, which isn't any big deal, & I may have to bare (or bear) all in court, which also isn't so terrible but I am really afraid the press will take off & run with all of this when they smell gossip. The other records will be private, & I don't think I've broken any laws, but you can understand my nerves.*

At the end of the letter, she referred to herself as a friend "who needs help keeping her nose clean."[34]

During her defamation trial, Wells testified her life "was pretty wild" at the DNC, given her small-town Mississippi background: "Living in a house with five men, dating several different people, working for a man who was rumoured to have numerous affairs, and gossiping on the phone about it with my friend. . . ." She was "kind of appalled" by the culture of casual sex, adultery, and one-night stands and gossiped about it on the phone with her friend Marty Sampson, who worked a few floors below. Other secretaries also used Oliver's office to "[talk] to their sweeties on the phone," she said. In his memoir, Alex Ray, the former executive director of the Republican Party in Maine, writes about a reference in Baldwin's logs to "two men from Maine . . . discussing the women with whom they had slept." "That conversation was between Severin [Beliveau] and me," he writes, and it "made it into the Watergate tapes [sic]."[35]

In his 1998 opinion dismissing Wells' suit, Judge Motz determined that Phillip Bailley was Liddy's sole source of information with "personal knowledge of Wells' alleged role" and acknowledged he had "a long history of mental illness and drug and alcohol addictions." He also noted that Bailley's "story about his own involvement in Watergate has changed several times since 1972." Bailley told Hougan that Wells was referring DNC customers to a Washington madam whom Hougan calls "Tess." In his book proposal with Stanford, Bailley claimed he managed "four full-time prostitutes and six part-time prostitutes (including Maureen Biner and several other well-known women) . . . [and] Wells was only one of eight 'runners' working for Bailley at the DNC":

His final version, about Wells having in her desk photographs of approximately twelve prostitutes who worked for Cathy Dieter/Heidi Rikan at the Columbia Plaza, first surfaced after Bailley's conversation with Liddy and Colodny in 1990 or 1991.

While acknowledging Bailley's deficiencies as a witness, Motz ruled there was sufficient circumstantial evidence to corroborate the "call-girl theory" and to justify its publication.[36]

The appeals court reinstated the suit, finding that while circumstantial evidence presented "may tend to corroborate the overall *Silent Coup* theory of the break-in," it did not "sufficiently corroborate the central issue in this case—whether Wells was personally involved in prostitution activities."[37]

In January 2001, the case was reheard by Motz in Baltimore. Liddy's attorney John Williams portrayed his client as a man hired by Dean to bug O'Brien's office and duped into thinking the purpose of the break-in was "political espionage." Instead, the burglars planted a bug on Spencer Oliver's phone to collect "sexual dirt" on the Democrats "to use as blackmail." He proclaimed Liddy's first-amendment rights, saying, "This is a part of American history; if Liddy can't talk about it, nobody can talk about it."[38]

Liddy had refused to testify against his "principals" in the Watergate trial, saying, "My father didn't raise a rat and a snitch." Twenty-eight years later, in his first public testimony about Watergate, he claimed he was duped about which phone was bugged. Martinez had been given a map, on which the location of Wells' desk in the DNC was marked with an X "and it was nowhere near the office of Mr. O'Brien. That's the same desk that that wired telephone was on and when he was caught he had a key with him." "This was a John Dean op," he said, calling Dean "a serial perjurer." He said his "big mistake" was telling his men to tape the locks on the doors.[39]

During the trial, Wells again admitted using Oliver's phone "to gossip with friends about married DNC staff members who were having affairs during a period that she called the 'height of the sexual revolution' . . . [but] adamantly denied Liddy's claims that she was involved in a prostitution ring and said she knew of no such operation." Before her grand jury testimony, Spencer Oliver had warned her "the Republican prosecutor was going to try to dig up . . . immoral dirt on the Democrats to embarrass them . . . the dirt that had been uncovered through the phone books and you know, I guess anything they got at the burglary . . . [to] put that all over the papers and embarrass the Democrats and take the heat off the White House." In his original manuscript for *The Strong Man*, author James Rosen suggests this "verbal slip" by Wells alluded to the phone books kept by Phillip Bailley and may have "revealed the true purpose of the Watergate break-in" but nobody picked up on it in court that day. [40]

The jury found seven to two in Liddy's favour but couldn't reach a verdict, so the judge declared a mistrial and then dismissed the case, a decision again overturned on appeal. "I'm not saying the conventional theory is wrong," Motz said, "but certain portions of it have been brought into question in this case." Maureen Dean told the Associated Press, "It's been extremely hurtful and humiliating to be linked to this imaginary call girl ring."[41]

Six weeks later, Judge Motz issued a detailed opinion, which largely upheld his verdict from three years earlier. He argued that "while the placing of a tap on Spencer Oliver's telephone line that was accessible through an extension on Wells' desk may only support the call girl theory generally, the fact that one of the burglars had a key to the desk specifically ties the desk to that theory . . . [and] Carl Shoffler, the same arresting officer who seized the key from Martinez, had testified on deposition in the *Dean* case that a camera placed by the burglars was found on Wells' desk." But as discussed in Chapter 7, a camera was not found on Wells' desk—Shoffler referred to "photographic equipment," in the form of a camera clamp.[42]

Judge Motz noted that Carl Shoffler was also present when Wells was told that "a piece of photographic equipment" had been found on her desk. She looked shocked and said, "'My God, they haven't gone in there,' or something to that effect."[43]

In his second opinion, Motz cites eight facts that Liddy "could reasonably believe support Bailley's statements about the contents of Wells' desk": the key found on Martinez which unlocked her desk; the camera equipment found by the arresting officers on her desk; the "conversations of a sexual nature . . . intercepted over Oliver's tapped telephone line"; the mystery about the motive for the break-in; Rudy and Jeannine Bailley's statements;

Wells' reaction to finding out the burglars had targeted her desk; and the unsent letter she had written to her friend.[44]

The appeals court again found Bailley an unreliable witness. The court agreed the evidence presented "tends to corroborate the call-girl theory generally" but felt it failed "to corroborate Bailley's [specific] statements concerning Wells' personal participation in the call-girl ring."[45]

In June 2002, a new trial began in Baltimore and Liddy introduced FBI documentation inferring the bug found on Oliver's phone in September 1972 was a "plant." Carl Shoffler had died in 1997 but the jury were shown a 1992 documentary, *The Key to Watergate*, in which he said, "We wouldn't be sitting around again with all the puzzling and all the mysteries had we taken the time to find out what that key was about." According to the *Baltimore Sun*, the federal judge said Liddy "had built a strong circumstantial case" linking the break-in to a call-girl ring and the jury returned a unanimous verdict in Liddy's favor.[46]

In 2013, shortly before the publication of Phil Stanford's biography of Heidi Rikan, *White House Call Girl*, John Dean threatened Stanford's publisher with a defamation suit for the false suggestion that the Deans knew about or were involved with the so-called "White House call-girl operation." After a robust reply from Stanford's attorney, *White House Call Girl* was published later that year and included pages from Rikan's address books. According to Stanford, one of Heidi's girls, "Candy Cane," worked with Maureen Biner "on the federal anti-drug task force." This seems to be a reference to an attorney at the BNDD whose name was Candy, is listed in Rikan's address book and appears on John Dean's White House telephone log for June 8, 1972, the day before Bailley's indictment and John Rudy's meeting with Dean at the White House. In June 1972, when Maureen Biner called John Dean from New York after returning from a vacation trip to Europe, he broke off their relationship. Biner returned to Washington and stayed with Candy, who she describes as a "very close friend." In her memoir, Biner writes, "John knew I would be going to Candy's—I had no place else in Washington to go. That night, he telephoned and then came over." Was Dean tipped off that the indictment was coming or was he just calling to talk things through with Maureen? Was news of the incident the reason for the break-up and for her leaving town?[47]

Bailley told Stanford he once saw "Candy Cane" standing outside her apartment building with a man he later recognized as Jeb Magruder. As Magruder was driven away in a chauffeur-driven black sedan, "Candy" told Bailley, "You weren't supposed to see that, that's the boss of bosses. You should forget what you saw." When Stanford spoke to the real Candy, she admitted she knew Mo and Heidi but denied knowing Bailley and Magruder, or anything about a call-girl ring.[48]

In a 2011 blog post, Hougan considers the key to Maxie Wells' desk central to the mystery behind Watergate, alongside another little-known fact:

> The only bugging device ever recovered from the headquarters of the DNC was a broken "toy" that the FBI believed had been planted in order that it might be found. And it was found, but not until nearly three months after the Watergate arrests, and not until Alfred Baldwin had gone public with his testimony about eavesdropping on the DNC . . . Did James McCord lie about bugging Larry O'Brien and Spencer Oliver? And if he did, why did he? And if Alfred Baldwin wasn't listening to telephone conversations being broadcast by a transmitter inside the DNC, what was he listening to? Because the burglars ultimately pleaded guilty, obviating a need for a trial at which the evidence would be presented and contested, the discrepancy never came to the public's attention.[49]

As a witness during the *Wells v. Liddy* trial, Hougan saw only two possible explanations: "either the bugs were removed from the DNC prior to the break-in on June 17—or Baldwin was listening to telephone conversations emanating from a bugging device at another location. The most likely place . . . was the call-girls' apartment in the Columbia Plaza, a block from the Watergate and in line-of-sight of Baldwin's motel room."[50]

The original prosecutors entered the key into evidence and had an FBI report matching the key to Maxie Wells' desk, but the FBI never probed why the burglars had the key and what was in Wells' desk. Wells and Oliver were called to testify at trial but, in an astonishing lapse, Silbert never asked either Wells or Rolando Martinez about the key. Arresting officer Carl Shoffler took the key from Martinez, but did not mention it in his Senate Watergate testimony and Jim Hougan was the first to highlight its importance in his 1984 book. Martinez denied knowledge of the key to Hougan but later told Benton Becker that Hunt gave him the key at a briefing on the day of the break-in, along with a floor plan of the DNC offices with "an X mark on Spencer Oliver's desk and on the desks near Spencer Oliver's desk."[51]

The key and the floor plan can both be traced to Alfred Baldwin and the June 12 tour he was given by Maxie Wells. Baldwin sketched out a floor plan of the DNC offices for McCord that day and when Wells left him alone in Spencer Oliver's office, he would have had time to make a "clay impression" of her key and to remove the bugs McCord had placed in the immediate vicinity. Baldwin denies both accusations but he testified that almost nothing was coming from the bugs he was monitoring on the Thursday and Friday before the break-in. It's also possible that one of the three bugs recovered from the burglars at the crime scene had been removed from Oliver's phone during the short time between their entry and their arrest. While McCord denies touching any of the bugs installed at the DNC that night, if his main purpose was to replace a faulty, misplaced bug, it seems reasonable to suggest he would have immediately tried to remove it.[52]

Baker's staff didn't know that a key to Maxie Wells' desk was found on Martinez at the time of his arrest. Their focus was on the desk of Larry O'Brien. Howard Liebengood told Colodny, "The focus of inquiry as to the essence of Watergate might have shifted significantly had we been advised of the key." As the minority investigation wound down, Liebengood had interviewed Wells on June 20, 1974 and asked her why the FBI suspected her desk "had been tampered with." The FBI had told Maxie Wells a key to her desk was found in the possession of one of the burglars but she chose not to share this with Liebengood.

Liebengood concluded the Senate Watergate Committee "rushed to the issue of cover-up and what the president knew and when he knew it etc. . . . [and] gave short shrift [to] examining the genuine motives for the break-in thoroughly. They sort of accepted the story that this was a political operation that was designed to target Larry O'Brien, etc., and didn't focus on the details of the actual break-in and its motives." The key was overlooked.[53]

Why was Spencer Oliver's phone targeted in the first break-in? Before the trial, Earl Silbert suspected Howard Hunt was trying to blackmail Oliver, who threatened his position at the Mullen Company and whose father was a Mullen Company consultant, handling the Hughes Tool account. McCord claimed Barker told him where to plant the bug, presumably on the instructions of Hunt, so it's possible Hunt used the first entry to serve his own "hidden agenda," but Hunt insisted he didn't even know Oliver was at the DNC until Liddy told him they were bugging him. Baldwin was convinced McCord did not know where O'Brien's office was located at the time of the first break-in and that McCord didn't know who Spencer Oliver was. Baldwin subsequently overheard evidence of extramarital affairs on the wiretap which could be used for blackmail but, bizarrely, the calls were not taped and Hunt claims he never saw copies of Baldwin's logs.

Beyond his Mullen Company connections, Spencer Oliver's work with the American Council of Young Political Leaders international exchange program may have attracted the interest of the CIA's Security Research Staff. The CIA reported that on August 5, he was with a delegation in Moscow when he "left unexpectedly to return to Washington." Tom Eagleton had just resigned as George McGovern's running mate after eighteen days and the DNC called a special meeting to replace him. When Howard Liebengood subsequently asked Maxie Wells if her former boss was a CIA agent, Oliver was "outraged" and called Liebengood and told him to stop. Liebengood was "very snotty" and said, "We have it under oath." Oliver subsequently sued the *Village Voice* for an article making similar allegations, which he called "totally absurd and completely false." From 1971 to 1974, Oliver served as president of the NATO Young Political Leaders and from 1976 to 1985, he served as the first chief of staff and general counsel of the US government's Commission on Security and Cooperation in Europe, which "advances American national security and national interests by promoting human rights, military security, and economic cooperation in 57 countries." While it's possible that McCord, with his staunch anti-Communist views, may have been spying on Oliver for his old colleagues at the Special Research Staff, Oliver says the exchange program was a bipartisan effort with Republicans like Pat Buchanan and doubts this. After McCord's release on bail, he was picked up by SRS informant Lee Pennington, who burned CIA-related papers at McCord's house and later gave the reports McCord had commissioned Lou Russell to prepare on Jack Anderson to SRS.[54]

In an interview with Robert Parry in 2004, Spencer Oliver had his own theory. Oliver thought the nomination of anti-war candidate George McGovern would be catastrophic for the party and he connected the tap on his phone to his covert attempts to block McGovern's nomination in favor of a "compromise candidate" like Duke University President Terry Sanford. This was precisely what Baldwin had told the FBI in his second interview: "all political conversations monitored were related to the policy of getting rid of McGovern." In April 1972, Pat Buchanan identified McGovern as the candidate "we want to run against"—"he could be painted as a left-radical candidate," whose campaign pledge "to chop 32 billion out of defense" would horrify Wallace, Daley, and Meany Democrats. When Muskie withdrew from the race at the end of April, Buchanan wrote, "we must do as little as possible . . . to impede McGovern's rise." After McGovern won the California primary, the last chance to stop him was at the Texas Democratic convention on June 13, 1972. McGovern had the support of only 30 percent of Texas delegates and Oliver hoped the majority could be mobilized to shut him out of the delegates completely and derail his campaign.[55]

Oliver told Parry he used his phone to call "every state chairman or party executive director to find out where their uncommitted delegates would go . . . to see whether McGovern's nomination could be stopped." Baldwin heard all this activity and reported it to CRP through McCord. Texas Democrat John Connally had joined Nixon's cabinet as treasury secretary in 1971 but mysteriously resigned in May 1972, leaving office on June 12, the day before the Texas convention. Though not publicly announced until July, he would head up Democrats for Nixon, a campaign to stop a radical McGovern presidency and Oliver believes Connally was mobilized to ensure McGovern got his fair share of the delegates in Texas and Nixon had an easier opponent to beat.

After McGovern's resounding defeat in December, Connally protégé Robert Strauss was elected DNC chairman and wanted to put Watergate behind him. When Oliver refused to drop his civil suit against the burglars, Strauss cut off his pay as executive director and help with the suit from DNC lawyers. Oliver was suspicious of Strauss' political allegiance to John Connally and Parry suggests Strauss was, effectively, a "Republican mole" within the DNC.[56]

Oliver's theory and the timing of the Texas convention make a lot of sense. Oliver's covert attempts to stop McGovern through Sanford were reported to the FBI by Baldwin in July 1972, but have been strangely overlooked by Watergate historians. The wiretap delivered important political intelligence as well as evidence of marital difficulties that could be used against someone like Oliver, if he later took a leading role in Sanford's campaign. On June 16, Colson sent a memo to Dean asking if "anyone had run any [background] checks or investigations on the key McGovern staffers," so they were clearly digging for dirt on the key staff of all potential contenders. The national delegate count Oliver describes matches Ida Wells' account of the work she did at the DNC and the burglars may have thought her drawer contained reports on the delegate count, indicating Oliver's projection of who would take the nomination. The involvement of Connally and Strauss on either side of the political aisle ensured a cover-up.[57]

But how to explain the sexual nature of some of the calls? On April 14, 1973, Jeb Magruder told John Ehrlichman the Baldwin logs included "a young Democrat politician . . . calling girls in Mississippi, saying, 'Honey, I'll be down there for the weekend.'" Magruder told Fred LaRue the young Democrat was Oliver. The same afternoon, Ehrlichman told Nixon: "What they were getting was mostly this fellow Oliver phoning his girlfriends all over the country lining up assignations." All this innuendo can be traced back to one call Baldwin reported Oliver making to "a female in Greenville, Mississippi," planning to spend the night there en route to Texas. Greenville was home to Oliver's best friend and political ally, Hodding Carter. Oliver told me "the stopover in Greenville was to ask Carter to agree to place Terry Sanford's name in nomination at the Convention as well as to try to pick up a few Sanford votes in the Mississippi delegation."[58]

After Strauss stopped paying Oliver's salary, Barbara Rhoden Kennedy recalled "there was a rumor . . . that the reason that Spencer Oliver was fired was due to a call girl ring. And we all laughed about it. No one took it seriously." In fact, Oliver wasn't fired and remained executive director until 1975, with the state chairmen paying his salary. Kennedy went on to get a job at the Senate Watergate Committee, where she came face-to-face with Alfred Baldwin, who recognized her voice from the wiretaps. Sometimes, the secretaries had lunch in Oliver's office and she was told she had been taped arguing with her children on the intercepted conversations.[59]

In a 1996 deposition, Robert Strauss admitted there were rumors around the time of Watergate "that some of the state chairmen would come into

[Oliver's] office and use the phone to make dates for that night. Now, whether they were with call girls or with their fiancées or their grandmothers, I have no knowledge . . . some of the calls . . . could have been embarrassing to some of the people who made them . . . because it could have been a married man who was calling an old flame of his or it could have been a prostitute. . . ."[60]

Author James Rosen claimed Strauss went further in an interview, telling him "Democrats in from out of town for a night would want to be entertained." "It wasn't any organized thing," said Strauss, "but I could have made the call, that lady [Maxie Wells] could have made the call and these people were willing to pay for sex."[61]

Spencer Oliver has avoided interviews about Watergate over the years but recently retired and has time to finally read the books published by "all the president's men," with a view to telling his own story. As I was completing this book, we spoke for two hours and he confirmed that what he told Parry was still his "take" on Watergate.

One evening after the Watergate trial in 1973, ACLU attorney Charles Morgan—who was representing Oliver and the DNC in their civil suit against CRP—invited him over to his office for a drink. When Oliver arrived, he was surprised to find none other than James McCord sitting there alongside Morgan. "Why my phone?" asked Oliver. "We knew who you were, we knew what you did and we thought we could get political information," replied McCord. At a meeting with Hunt, Liddy, and the Cubans before the first break-in, McCord said, they had selected the targets. They had all the names and the floorplan. O'Brien was number one, treasurer Bob Strauss was number two, and Oliver was number three. The burglars couldn't get into Strauss' office because the door was locked, so they bugged Oliver's phone instead. While what McCord told Oliver is consistent with his testimony, it conflicts with Baldwin's claim that McCord didn't have a floorplan or know where Larry O'Brien's office was at the time of the first break-in.[62]

On September 13, 1972, Maxie Wells visited the DNC after her grand jury deposition and was present when the bug was found in Oliver's phone. Wells and Oliver were interviewed by the FBI in Washington two days later. According to Oliver, on one of those days, Maxie and Marty Sampson came into his office. Sampson was the executive secretary to Robert Allen at the Young Democrats and Wells' closest friend at the DNC. They were both single, attractive young women and they told him the "sex talk" Baldwin had overheard was them gossiping to each other on the phone. Marty's office was downstairs and "they talked to each other all the time and compared notes about their dates." "If you thought guys' locker room talk was bad, we were much worse," they said.

Oliver denied there was a culture of "entertaining" visiting chairmen at the time and told me there were no visits from state chairmen in June anyway, as everyone was busy in their home state or preparing for the convention in Miami. Oliver had a wife and three kids at the time and was close to a "very unpleasant divorce" but undergoing marriage counselling. He denied any affairs and said there was nothing of any political importance in Wells' desk drawer. The hard delegate count he discussed on the phone was being done by Don Fowler, the state chairman in South Carolina, and his secretary. He dismisses the call-girl theory as "a nasty part of the Republican effort to discredit the whole Watergate thing—like we planted the bug ourselves, it was a CIA operation etc. . . . Imagine for a moment that the Republicans had any information about something like that based on the wiretap. Wouldn't they have used it in the campaign to damage the Democrats? All of that stuff was pure propaganda, vicious lies, and absolute baloney."[63]

In his recent memoir, Pat Buchanan reveals he grew up in the same neighbourhood as Spencer Oliver and they had been friends since they were teenagers. Oliver and Buchanan conducted a thirteen-day tour of the Soviet Union with the American Council of Young Political Leaders in November

1971 and on September 13, when news broke of the bug discovered on Oliver's phone, Buchanan called and invited Oliver over to his Watergate East apartment for a drink (Buchanan lived "right next" to John Mitchell). Both men were "shaken up" and Buchanan couldn't figure it out: "Why was the CRP bugging Spencer?"

According to Oliver, before the trial, Silbert would call him at home at night, trying to eke out what was in the intercepted conversations. Oliver was also a lawyer and found it unethical. Today, he thinks Silbert and Glanzer were "part of a criminal cover-up." Despite protests from Oliver and Morgan at lengthy nomination hearings, Silbert became US attorney and Glanzer got a job at Charles Colson's law firm.[64]

Why was Maxie Wells' desk targeted in the June 17 break-in? After the publication of *Silent Coup*, John Dean's role in the commissioning of the second break-in became clear to Mitchell, Ehrlichman, Liddy and others. Liddy, Hougan, and Colodny believe Dean ordered the second break-in after reviewing Phillip Bailley's phone books on Friday, June 9 with John Rudy and learning "of the relationship between the Columbia Plaza call-girl ring and the DNC." The following Monday, Magruder told Liddy his team had to go in again, ostensibly to fix the bug on Larry O'Brien's phone that wasn't working and to photograph whatever damaging information about the Nixon campaign O'Brien kept in his desk drawer.

The theory goes that Dean was trying to retrieve a "compromising" picture of his girlfriend but Hougan suggests "the instigator of the break-in (whether Dean, Magruder or someone else)" may have been looking for more than pictures—a log of clients who had used the call-girl scheme. Baldwin met Maxie Wells on June 12 and "cased" O'Brien's office. Wells left Baldwin alone in Oliver's office, so why didn't he just access her desk drawer then? Baldwin denies touching the key or removing anything from Wells' office.[65]

After reading the Baldwin and Wells depositions, I'm not convinced that Wells had anything to do with a call-girl ring. Several of the men she was seeing were often out of town and Baldwin's description of the calls fits her personal circumstances at the time. In 1976, Maxie Wells became Jimmy Carter's personal secretary during his presidential campaign. She worked in the White House for two years as his social assistant and had a top-security clearance and access to the President's Daily Briefs. If there had been any evidence of her connection to a call-girl ring, how could she have been cleared for such a job in the White House?[66]

Phillip Mackin Bailley moved to the Philippines and was active on social media before his death in 2015. In October 2013, he was promoting a planned book titled "National Secrets" and tweeted: "I recanted the Columbia Plaza Call Girl Ring Hoax to John and Mo Dean." The LinkedIn profile he left behind claims he was National Campaign Manager for the National President of the Young Democrats, R. Spencer Oliver, from October 1970 to June 1972 and that CRP "illegally obtained the private office phone number of R. Spencer Oliver" from his private address book and planned to use the tapped conversations to "blackmail the Democrats." Oliver was president of the Young Democrats from 1967–69 and denies Bailley held any position with them, so this seems baseless, like many of Bailley's claims.[67]

How do we explain the apparent incompetence of McCord? He did not know where the target office was during the first break-in, bugged Spencer Oliver's phone but didn't appear to know who he was, sat on the photos of documents taken by Martinez for weeks and may have tampered with the film, left the tape on the doors that led to the burglars being discovered during the second break-in, and refused to tell Baldwin the nature of the mission. In a revealing interview with James Rosen in 1995, Baldwin, an ex-Marine and FBI agent, remembered McCord as a deeply religious, conservative Texan with an innate "fear of Richard Nixon": "Richard Nixon wasn't a team player, wasn't an American, wasn't, you know, 'one of us' . . .":

> *I believe that everything that happened that night was well-planned and well- calculated . . . and that the resulting events would take place the way they've taken place . . . Jim McCord is not a bungling electronics man . . . He's very intelligent, he's very precise in what he does . . . Jim McCord knew what he was doing and it was very purposeful . . . You had to have wanted that tape to be discovered . . . he turned his radio off. Jim knows it, I know it . . . he wanted to be caught.*

After his arrest, McCord's first impulse was to protect the Agency, but from what?

Did McCord sabotage the operation, did he have a "secret agenda" or was he simply incompetent?[68]

The role of McCord's close associate Lou Russell is also fascinating. Russell worked part-time for General Security Services, Inc. (which managed security at the Watergate) from December 1971 to March 1972 but not at the Watergate complex. William Birely had known Russell for two years and employed him as a part-time researcher. Birely was friends with Lee Pennington and had two apartments in the Twin Towers complex in Silver Springs. He used one as an office and let Russell stay in the other in return for cleaning his apartment. He described Russell as a Democrat "who was extremely critical of Nixon."

Russell didn't have a bank account, so Warren Love at the First National Bank, directly below the CRP offices, cashed several checks made out to Russell through McCord's personal account. Shortly after McCord's arrest, Russell told Love, "I guess you're wondering who 'the sixth man' was. Well, it wasn't me."[69] As Hougan observes:

> *In November 1972, three days after Nixon's election, Russell purchased more than $4,000 in stock of the Thurmont Bank, a bank in which*

[Russell's patron, William] Birely was then a director. Five months later, on March 23, 1973, Russell purchased . . . [additional] shares . . . with a check in the amount of $20,745.

As Hougan notes, March 23 was the day McCord's letter to Judge Sirica was read out in open court and a few days later, Russell sold the shares for a $2,445 profit.[70]

Nine days after Baker's staff subpoenaed Russell for questioning, and on the day McCord began his public testimony before the Senate Watergate Committee, Russell had a massive heart attack. He suspected he'd been poisoned and died six weeks later of a second heart attack at the age of sixty-one.[71]

Russell may have been the "sixth man" on the night of the second break-in and was also well-placed to plant a bug on Spencer Oliver's phone in September, by which time he was working at for the Democrats at McGovern headquarters. Birely's characterization of Russell as an anti-Nixon Democrat suggests a trap or sabotage followed by a reward. The role of senior figures at the DNC in all this is just as intriguing. They had advance warning of the break-in; Baldwin's attorney fed them privileged information within days of the arrests; DNC attorneys interviewed Baldwin without his knowledge; and the FBI suspected the DNC had planted the bug found in September. Today, Jim Hougan regrets he failed to dig deeper into Bill Haddad's foreknowledge of the break-in "and the plotting that took place in Edward Bennett Williams' office" on behalf of the DNC.[72]

What was the CIA's role in the Watergate break-in? In *Secret Agenda*, Hougan concludes:

The evidence is overwhelming that the retirements of Hunt and McCord had been fabricated by the CIA. Hiring the Cubans under false flags, they conducted domestic operations on behalf of the CIA's Security Research Staff, using the White House as a deniable cover in the event of the operation's exposure. That this was an institutional commitment of the CIA, rather than some "runaway" operation conducted by rogue agents, is plain.[73]

With the benefit of recently-released CIA records, I don't think Hunt and McCord's retirements were fabricated. Hunt's Agency career was petering out and he was in dire financial straits, so Helms got him a job with Mullen and Company and they remained close. While Paul Gaynor thought he'd simply assumed another cover with the Mullen Company, Hunt's troubles with his annuity suggest his retirement was real. McCord's retirement is more complicated. It's surprising, given his experience and responsibility for physical security, that he was involuntarily retired at a time of unprecedented revolutionary protest and anti-war activity. And Alfred Baldwin was convinced McCord was still with the CIA. In any case, after officially leaving the Agency, Hunt and McCord recruited old boy networks to build their own intelligence and covert action capabilities with new sponsors within the White House and CRP respectively. Colson and Ehrlichman were mobilized to get the Agency to do Hunt's bidding while Hunt was very conscious of not letting his former colleagues know what he was up to, except for Karamessines and Helms at the top.

Hougan also suggests the Columbia Plaza call-girl ring was "either a CIA operation or the target of a CIA operation . . . for [intelligence] or counter-intelligence purposes":[74]

CIA agents working under cover of the CRP came to be targeted against their own operation by the very organization that unwittingly provided them with cover. All that the agents could do was to stall, and when all else failed, blow their own cover. Whereupon the White House, lacking deniability, attempted to cover up—with the result that it was soon buried.[75]

While Lil Lori's possible association with McCord is the only evidence I can see that the Columbia Plaza call-girl ring was a CIA operation, the ring's alleged clientele at the DNC were ripe for political blackmail and as Hougan notes, "all of the photos taken and all of the documents stolen by the Plumbers were diverted to the CIA—with the White House receiving either nothing at all, or adulterated versions of the take." The Fielding photos were developed by the Agency and given to Hunt. McCord sat on the photos of the first break-in and the authenticity of the subsequent photos developed by Barker in Miami is questionable.[76]

The CIA's handling of the photographs developed for Hunt tells a story of Agency denial and deception, blaming its compartmentalized ethos for the fact that the left hand didn't know what the right hand was doing within the organization. I share Senator Baker's incredulity that Richard Krueger commissioned a blow-up of the photograph showing Dr. Fielding's name on his parking space but did not share Fielding's name with deputy director General Cushman and his assistant, Karl Wagner, in subsequent discussions. They clearly looked like casing photographs and the timing of the decision to cut off Hunt on the morning the photographs were studied is damning.

Hunt's behavior in his dealings with CIA support staff while at the White House is very odd. At the end of their meeting about the Ellsberg profile on August 12, 1971, Hunt asked Dr. Malloy not to divulge "his presence and participation in the meeting" to his Agency colleagues because, Hunt claimed, his house was being repainted by Osborn's son, and "[Osborn] has been trying all summer to find out what I was doing." If Hunt wanted to hide what he was doing from Osborn and former Agency colleagues, why did he ask CIA technicians to develop the film of Dr. Fielding's office and why did he ask Osborn's son to paint his house? On top of this, Hunt played tennis every Sunday morning with a "previous supervisor" of his at the CIA.[77]

Dr. Malloy immediately reported his concerns about Hunt's involvement in the Ellsberg profile and was assured they were passed to director Helms, but despite conversations with Malloy's superior, deputy director of support John Coffey, Helms and Osborn denied knowledge of Hunt's involvement. It is inconceivable that Coffey did not share Malloy's concerns with Osborn, who would have shared them with Helms. The Agency claimed, "no other Agency official . . . [knew] of both the provisioning of Hunt and Hunt's involvement in the preparation of the Ellsberg profile," so they couldn't put two and two together. In the weeks following the Ellsberg break-in, it's hard to believe Helms and Osborn didn't put the Hunt photos and the Ellsberg profiles together. Their testimony on this matter is simply not credible.

It's now clear that Richard Helms' relationship with Hunt was much closer than previously disclosed. Hunt was in touch with CIA General Counsel Lawrence Houston about his annuity weeks before the first break-in and Helms was actively pitching Hunt's novels to film executives until questioned about it on May 19, the week before.

According to General Cushman's executive assistant Karl Wagner, two days after the Watergate arrests, he gave Helms the "Mr. Edward file" containing the Xerox copies of the Fielding photos. So, within days of the "Watergate caper," Helms knew exactly what Hunt had been doing in California and went into damage limitation mode, withholding evidence, obscuring his links to Hunt, and deceiving prosecutors. When the McCord letters finally surfaced, he feared an indictment.

I'm not convinced Helms had advance knowledge of the Watergate break-in or that the gossip in Hunt's packages to Helms were directly connected. But the CIA's own records indicate Helms, Osborn, and Cord Meyer were closely monitoring Hunt's activities and they were causing unease. The original prosecutors also failed miserably to connect the Hunt photographs with an operation targeting Dr. Fielding, to properly investigate the key to Maxie Wells' drawer and to question why no bugs were found at the crime scene much earlier in the process.

• • •

Jim Hougan calls the conventional wisdom about Watergate "a counterfeit history," enshrined in the mythology around "Deep Throat"—the anonymous source for Woodward and Bernstein's *Washington Post* reporting, later revealed to be the FBI's number two man, Mark Felt, but more likely to be a composite figure drawn from several sources. Hougan is also critical of the narrow focus of Woodward and Bernstein's book, *All the President's Men*:

> *There is little or nothing about the CIA's role (which was comprehensive), the sexual nature of the intercepted telephone calls, the fact that after repeated and targeted physical and electronic searches, the FBI was unable to find a [bug] anywhere in the DNC. McCord's sabotage of the break-in is similarly ignored (as is the role of McCord's henchman, Lou Russell) and . . . well, the omissions are so many and egregious that one can only wonder at his intent.*[78]

FBI case agent Angelo Lano has always thought "it was a set-up." He knew two of the arresting officers, Carl Shoffler and Paul Leeper, a sergeant in the burglary unit, and on the morning of the arrests, asked himself, "What's Leeper doing out at 2 a.m.?" In the Watergate hotel rooms, the neat arrangement of the evidence the burglars left behind felt "planted"—"everything [was] arranged like somebody knew it was gonna happen." On the night of the break-in, McCord disappeared for two hours in search of batteries which were never going to fit the smoke detector and Lano still can't understand why the doors were retaped:

> *You've got a guy who's expert in key entry, burglary [Virgilio Gonzalez]. Why did they have to put the tape back on? You put the tape on one door, it wasn't necessary to put it on six doors. There's always been a question in my mind [about] the response of the police department—2:30 in the morning—the placement of the items [in the hotel room], the tape. To this*

day, I still think that one of those guys tipped off the police department and it was either Hunt or McCord . . . .It was time for all this activity to come to an end. Was it McCord or was it Hunt? My gut feeling, I always thought it was Hunt.[79]

Before his death in 2007, Howard Hunt videotaped a confession for his son, St. John, detailing his involvement with Cord Meyer in the JFK assassination but Hunt made no deathbed revelations about Watergate. In his interview with James Rosen, Alfred Baldwin claimed McCord told him he was in Dallas on November 22, 1963. When asked what Watergate was all about, Baldwin deferred to McCord to "break the code of silence," but based on his conversations with McCord in that motel room, he felt McCord "inserted himself into that operation for a reason." McCord gave him the impression he was "a soldier going down for God and country . . . He was going to be a prisoner of war for . . . what he believed the United States to be . . ." By which he meant the removal of the president: "If you do a psychological profile on Nixon, and you know what a son-of-a-bitch liar he's gonna be . . . you know things are gonna happen a certain way, why not set him up? . . . That's what I would ask Jim McCord . . . Was Richard Nixon set up?" James McCord passed away in June 2017—his family wanted no obituary—so the secrets of Watergate may have died with him. Baldwin refused to speak to me and is reportedly working on a book.[80]

For the record, Rolando Martinez still thinks the burglars were set-up by McCord. After doubting how much longer he would live in executive session testimony in 1973, he's still a heroic figure in Miami at the age of ninety-six—the only one of the Watergate burglars ever pardoned, and we now know why. His covert operations failed to free Cuba and resulted in the "loss of two presidents"—the assassination of President Kennedy, which he believes was an act of revenge by Fidel Castro; and the resignation of Richard Nixon. As I finished this book, I asked him why he had the key that night and he told me with a chuckle, "I don't remember and I don't want to remember. I want to be consistent with what I said before. I don't want it to come out, I'm sorry." His first case officer, Ramon Esteban Gonzalez III, went on to a successful career as a stock broker with Merrill Lynch and is still an avid safari buff.[81]

MARTINEZ' CAR

On October 15, 1973, Deputy Special Prosecutor Henry Ruth asked the FBI to investigate information that an unknown individual had removed a diary from Rolando Martinez' car before the FBI "located and impounded" it on Monday, June 19 and to locate the diary. According to the source, on June 18, Manolo Villamanan had been contacted by "the daughter, wife or girl friend of [Martinez]" to help remove the car from the airport parking garage "as it contained deeply compromising material." Ruth's request seems to have been inspired by a declassified CIA memo which states the FBI impounded the car on June 19, two days earlier than they actually did.[1]

When the FBI impounded and searched the car on June 21, they found two notebooks—a Marquette Page-a-Day calendar notebook, containing five names and addresses and another notebook "without cover containing over 100 names and telephone numbers." The Page-a-Day notebook was sent to Washington on December 22, 1972, with instructions to interview all persons named therein as soon as possible. The second notebook languished in Miami with the other materials from Martinez' car until they were forwarded to Washington in mid-September 1973.[2]

On January 15, 1973, the Miami burglars pleaded guilty and lead prosecutor Earl Silbert sought to quell media speculation about Martinez' alleged operational diary by entering the Page-a-Day calendar notebook into evidence as the purported diary: "There are very few pages in it that have any writing. It is almost totally blank and whatever information that is in there was run down." No evidence of value had been found in the search of Martinez' car, Silbert told Judge Sirica, "nor were there any leads developed from that search at that time." But Silbert had never seen the second notebook in Miami and there's no indication in FBI files that the "100 names and telephone numbers" in it were ever run down.[3]

The following October, the FBI investigation revealed that Clara Barker (Bernard's wife) had spearheaded efforts to secure Martinez' car, calling on Manuel Villamanan and Martinez' daughter Yolanda Toscano for help.[4]

Villamanan was a sales manager at Anthony Abraham Chevrolet and had known Martinez since 1961 when they were both active in the MRR. On the Monday or Tuesday after the second break-in, Clara Barker contacted him to say Martinez' daughter would be calling him for help in securing her father's car from the airport parking lot. For the previous three months, during divorce proceedings, Martinez had been staying with his daughter Yolanda and her husband Antonio Toscano. Martinez called Toscano from prison and asked him to get his car out of the airport "to avoid a continuing storage charge." Martinez suggested Toscano ask Manuel Villamanan for help and on Tuesday, June 18, Villamanan invited Toscano and his wife down to his showroom to discuss the situation. Villamanan told the FBI they didn't show any urgency about securing the car or concern about "compromising material" and Villamanan suggested they contact the airport police department. That evening, he drove with them to the airport parking lot and they located the car. Martinez had the only key for the burglar alarm, so rather than cause a scene, they decided it was worth the $2.50-a-day charge to leave the car where it was and avoid publicity.[5]

The following day, Clara Barker was "quite upset that the car had not been removed from the parking lot" and called Sylvia Campos to help her find the car. Campos had sold Martinez sixty rolls of film before the second break-in and subsequently told the FBI she had known Martinez since childhood in Cuba and "[had] been his girlfriend for the past ten years." She knew he was "an intelligence agent" but claimed no knowledge of his activities or a diary. Clara Barker picked her up and they drove to the airport parking lot but couldn't find the car. As they were leaving, Campos finally spotted it, "parked next to the office at the parking lot . . . some equipment had been placed in front of the car to prevent it being removed from the area." She told the FBI she wasn't aware of "any compromising material, any weapons or any contraband in [the] car."[6]

After locating the car between the fifth and sixth levels of the parking lot, the FBI had towed it to the parking concession office at 2:10 p.m. on Wednesday afternoon, while they were applying for a search warrant. This chronology suggests Barker and Campos spotted the car later that afternoon. When the FBI finally searched the car that evening, "the alarm had to be deactivated by cutting the wire." The FBI report notes that the alarm "could not be reset or reactivated without the service of the alarm key," suggesting it wasn't disturbed before they accessed it. Yolanda Toscano had a duplicate ignition key but Martinez had the only copy of the alarm key and it was taken away from him when he was arrested.[7]

Sometime later, a mutual acquaintance advised Manuel Villamanan "that he let [Martinez] down" by not helping his daughter when she needed it, but when Martinez was released on bail, Villamanan apologized and Martinez "dismissed the matter very casually."[8]

The "maritime asset" who tipped off the CIA "deep cover" officer about Martinez' car appears to be Alberto Beguiristain, a salesman at Anthony Abraham Chevrolet who was also a CIA asset. Villamanan was his supervisor at the showroom and the FBI interviewed both men about the car. During his first FBI interview, Villamanan didn't disclose the call from Clara Barker but Beguiristain persuaded him to tell the truth and come clean in a second interview two days later.[9]

A series of declassified CIA memos from the week following the Watergate arrests also help illuminate Agency connections to the burglars. On Tuesday, June 20, Agency asset IUSTEER-1 met his case officer, "Peter S.

Jasutis," and reported a recent conversation with Villamanan about the "Watergate Break-In Scandal." Villamanan was "very sympathetic to Barker" and the asset felt "he hurt Villamanan's feelings" when he was "critical of the affair." He called the dealership "a 'nest' of Cuban rumors and gossip" and noted salesman Alberto Beguiristain was a CIA asset (using the code name or cryptonym AMANCHOR-1) who had once worked as a frogman with Martinez through a CIA cover company. The dealership's chief of Security, Tony Iglesias, was the military chief of the Torriente Group and another former CIA asset, Dr. Luis Conte Aguero, was also on staff.[10]

On Wednesday, David Morales, former chief of Operations in Miami, was consulted about Barker's past CIA activities and said he was sure Barker would tell the authorities "everything he knows. He tells all to everyone. Because he was such a loudmouth, Dave recommended in 1962 that he be terminated."[11]

On Thursday, Jake Esterline wrote a still-classified memo about a meeting with Beguiristain "concerning Martinez' involvement with Barker in the Watergate episode." As Esterline claimed the FBI impounded the car on Monday, the meeting presumably happened on Monday morning at the latest. Beguiristain was thus the "Miami station maritime asset" described in the recently declassified CIA document discussed in Chapter 7, who informed Jake Esterline that "he and a business friend [his supervisor, Villamanan] had been contacted frantically by [Martinez' daughter] requesting immediate assistance in getting [his] car out of the airport parking garage since it contained deeply compromising material which had to be removed before the FBI got to it." Esterline relayed the information to headquarters and "at Esterline's request, [Beguiristain] obtained a description of the automobile and its location in the garage." This CIA document also seems to be what triggered the Deputy Special Prosecutor's investigation in October 1973.[12]

Martinez' presentence report notes that Villamanan and Beguiristain "both report they owe their lives to the defendant" and after his release from prison, Martinez worked as a manager at the Chevrolet dealership. His thank-you letter to President Reagan for his pardon in 1983 was written on Anthony Abraham Chevrolet stationery.[13]

A CIA index card indicates Martinez' Agency cryptonym was AMSNAP-3; his first case officer Ramon Gonzalez used the pseudonym "Norris G. Gervenot"; his second case officer Robert Ritchie used the name "Conrad P. Lettsome"; and the Esterline/Sternfield correspondence was between "Anthony R. Ponchay" and "Joel N. Nebecker."[14]

The day after her FBI interview, Sylvia Campos called Martinez in prison about his alleged operational diary, but he denied keeping one. He said the only notebooks he had were taken from him when he was arrested or during the search of his car. Martinez later married Campos and is still living in her apartment today.[15]

In late 1973, a *New York Times* reporter (possibly Seymour Hersh) told WSPF Assistant Special Prosecutor Nick Akerman that Miguel Suarez, the attorney for Barker Associates, had a copy of the diary. Suarez' father was a former Cuban senator and CIA asset. His son Miguel had collaborated with Barker on real estate ventures through his real estate company, Ameritas, and Barker billed the Washington hotel rooms for both break-ins through Ameritas, without—Suarez claims—his permission. Akerman told me he went down to Miami with a grand jury subpoena and confronted Suarez about the diary, but he denied having it.[16]

In mid-December, the FBI strongly resisted a request from Fred Thompson to interview Special Agents Parham and Wilson (the field supervisor who supervised the investigation by the Miami office) and refused to share "the circumstances of the search warrant" for Martinez' car. FBI director Clarence Kelley wrote to CIA director William Colby to sound out the CIA's position and his agents met with John Warner and Howard Osborn to discuss the situation. The FBI finally succumbed, and Michael Madigan and Howard Liebengood met the agents a month later but still couldn't resolve the two-day delay.[17]

Liebengood died of a heart attack in 2005 but in his papers, I found one intriguing "point of interest" eliminated from the Baker report. It reads, "COS [Chief of Station] contact with Frank Farrell (McCord) re: Martinez car." "Frank Farrell" was a pseudonym used by James McCord while at the CIA. The mind boggles as to what contact Jake Esterline had with James McCord about Martinez' car after the second break-in. This information probably came from CIA documents or Esterline's executive session testimony, both of which remain classified.[18]

THE SEPTEMBER BUG

Special Agent Joseph Parsons of the FBI Laboratory was the expert witness called by Earl Silbert to explain the bugs used by the Watergate burglars to the jury during their trial in January 1973. Parsons had examined and tested the devices recovered from the DNC and Room 723 of the Howard Johnson in June 1972, and the bug recovered from Spencer Oliver's phone in September. To the surprise of his FBI colleagues, during his testimony, Parsons disclosed that he had been a close friend of James McCord since 1942, when they attended an FBI "radio operator and technical school" together in Washington. Their families became close, but Parsons had not seen McCord for about two years.[1]

On June 17, 1972, Parsons received the three black miniature radio transmitters recovered at the DNC and labelled them Q3, Q4, and Q5. They were an inch and a half long, an inch wide and half an inch high; powered by the phone line and activated when the receiver was picked up to make or answer a call. According to Parsons' tests, Q3 "transmitted the voices on the line to a radio receiver tuned to a frequency of approximately 114.7 MHz"; Q4 transmitted at 110.3 MHz; and Q5 transmitted at 110.7 MHz but one of its components was damaged. His report also noted that Q8, the microphone transmitter in the smoke detector unit, transmitted at 110.13 MHz.[2]

As previously discussed, Alfred Baldwin was monitoring calls to and from Spencer Oliver's phone at 118.9 MHz. The bug found on Oliver's phone in

September was inoperative due to a defective transistor but once replaced, trans-mitted at 120 MHz, the closest of all four devices to the frequency mentioned by Baldwin. But as the FBI pointed out, it was impossible to know "the original operating frequency" of the device before it was damaged; the frequency after repair still did not match the frequency "reportedly received"; and Baldwin may have been monitoring another device which was never recovered.[3]

On October 16, Parsons brought Spencer Oliver's phone—"which had previously been removed and examined in our laboratory"—back to the DNC to test the three devices recovered in June, the September bug and the microphone transmitter in the smoke detector unit. Communicating by walkie-talkie, SA William Johnson tested the five bugs on Oliver's phone in his office at the DNC while SA Parsons monitored their signals from rooms 419 and 723 at the Howard Johnson, using the transceiver McCord and Baldwin had used. Parsons successfully received signals from each of the transmitters but observed that, "room 723 produced a much stronger signal than 419" and the three devices recovered in June produced a stronger signal than the September bug.[4]

While the tests were being conducted in Oliver's office, Assistant US Attorney Donald Campbell—perhaps speculating on the location of the sec-ond bug—requested that additional tests be conducted from the phone in the office formerly occupied by John Stewart. Stewart had been Director of Communications at the DNC before assuming the same role at McGovern headquarters.[5]

Two days after the September bug was found, Silbert filed charges against the Watergate burglars. Count seven of the indictment refers to the burglars' possession of "a miniature radio transmitter" matching Parson's description of the three devices recovered on June 17. All three were introduced into evidence by Campbell during the trial as Exhibits 16-A, B and C respectively.[6]

During Parsons' testimony, he explained the workings of the three tele-phone bugs, the room bug in the smoke detector unit, and his test results to the jury and was later commended by Silbert for his work on the case and his skill in doing so. But the September bug—the only bug actually found inside a phone at the DNC—was never mentioned. If Silbert believed the September bug was the device missed by the FBI and used to tap Oliver's phone, why was it never entered into evidence or discussed at the trial?[7]

Parsons also noted that Exhibit 18, a small battery-powered radio receiver recovered from Martinez' gym bag on June 17, operated above the normal FM band between 108 and 135 MHz, and was capable of receiving transmissions from the bugs. After McCord finished installing the wiretaps during the first break-in, he checked they were working with this pocket receiver. It also allowed him to monitor the bugs, independently of Baldwin.[8]

On Monday, April 9, in grand jury testimony, McCord revealed he had purchased the bugs recovered at the DNC on the night of the arrests from Michael Stevens at Stevens Research Laboratories in Chicago. Prosecutor Seymour Glanzer showed McCord a device and asked if he had purchased it from Stevens. "It looks like it," said McCord. "It's about the same size. I can't positively identify it because there's no serial numbers on it, but it has a very close appearance and I would guess it was the same." "And does it resemble the one that you placed upon Spencer Oliver's phone?" "It does," said McCord.[9]

Three weeks later, during his deposition in the DNC civil case, McCord was asked "on whose telephone the inoperative bug had been placed." After objections from his attorney about disclosing secret grand jury testimony, he gave the following evasive answer:

Let me state it this way: During the trial, a device was entered into evidence which purportedly came from Spencer Oliver's phone. Recently, during the second or third day of my testimony before the grand jury, I was shown a similar device and asked if I had ever seen it before and I stated that it looked similar to the device that had been put into DNC headquarters.

This particular second device was taken apart. The one that was entered into evidence was not. My assumption was that it had been removed from the DNC headquarters because I had read in the paper that the FBI within the preceding two or three days had been checking DNC and I assume that they had found the device because I had told the grand jury a couple of days before specifically on what phone that device had been placed.[10]

In other words, McCord thought the bug he saw on April 9 was the second bug, whose location he had given the FBI three days earlier. As we know, the devices entered into evidence during the trial had not actually come from Spencer Oliver's phone. During the trial, McCord observed the device entered into evidence on the table as it was being described by Silbert and Parsons: "I didn't examine it in detail. The FBI agent testified that it had not been disassembled." "Did it look like the one that you had installed on Spencer Oliver's phone?" "It did." McCord said the two bugs he installed at the DNC "resembled each other," inside and out. As the FBI noted, the September bug was different in design and appearance to the devices recovered on June 17 and noticeably smaller—just over an inch long and three-quarters of an inch wide.[11]

The September bug was the only device "taken apart" by the FBI, so the implication of McCord's April testimony was that he had installed one of the June 17 bugs bought from Stevens in Spencer Oliver's phone; and the September bug found in Oliver's phone in the second location. These bugs bore no similarity to each other and his testimony makes absolutely no sense, but the prosecutors let it slide.

Once McCord confirmed that the bugs recovered at the DNC were purchased from Michael Stevens, FBI headquarters ordered an immediate investigation of Stevens' "dealings with McCord" through its Chicago office. Stevens had refused to speak to the Chicago office the previous October, cryptically stating, "he was under contract to produce a certain product and could give no information on it."[12]

Stevens Research Lab was a small two-man operation Stevens ran with his partner Bernard Gordon. Stevens told Gordon he had "permission from the Federal Communication Commission (FCC) to make surveillance equipment for government agencies," including the Bureau of Narcotics and Dangerous Drugs, the FBI, and the IRS. Both men had been involved in a secret CIA-related project in Arizona in 1970, but Gordon refused to discuss it with the FBI for fear "he would be killed if he talked about it." McCord had visited their shop in May 1972 and when Stevens saw McCord's picture on TV after the second break-in, he told Gordon, "That's the guy who was in here" but didn't say another word about Watergate.[13]

When the FBI came looking for Stevens on April 10, his lab was no longer in business. Unable to pay his rent, he had closed it down during the Watergate trial in January and "completely vanished." His wife told investigators he now sold carpets and was "on the road" but Stevens was located in Chicago the same day. He refused to talk until granted immunity and his wife divorced him a week later. Mrs. Stevens later told the press her husband had sold the bugs to McCord because he thought he was with the CIA.[14]

On April 12, in heavy snow, McCord guided two FBI agents to electronic equipment he'd stashed on farmland in Maryland. The following week, the agents returned in better weather to find a further five "oral intercepting devices and one telephone intercepting device" and two Uher tape recorders "hidden in heavy underbrush." McCord had hidden the equipment shortly after his release from jail in late June 1972. Six bugs he'd stashed in storm drains were never recovered.[15]

Back in Chicago, Robert Barcal told investigators that Michael Stevens had approached him in May 1972 for help assembling bugging devices which used frequencies outside the normal FM radio band. Stevens claimed he had "secret clearance" but Barcal refused to get involved until Stevens proved it was legal. A week later, Stevens showed Barcal a bug which fit inside the mouthpiece of telephone and a "room bug," and tested both successfully. Two weeks after that, he showed Barcal a letter signed by a CIA officer, which Stevens claimed "authorized him to make bugging equipment for local police agencies and the government." A month later, Stevens showed Barcal a "pocket pager" which could pick up a bug's signal. When Watergate hit and McCord's name was in the newspapers, Stevens told Barcal: "I supplied them with the equipment." When Dorothy Hunt died in a plane crash in Chicago the following December, Stevens claimed she was bringing him money owed for his bugging equipment.[16]

Stevens reacted to the FBI probe by leaking his story to Jack Anderson and the local press, blaming his financial woes on an order for "six custom-made, high frequency transmitters and receivers" made by McCord but never picked up or paid for: "Four . . . were suitable for bugging rooms, the other two for intercepting phone conversations." McCord made two trips to Chicago to buy the equipment and "identified himself with a code name used in a previous CIA operation." When Stevens delivered the bugs recovered at the DNC to McCord at Washington National airport, McCord paid him $5400 in cash, but Stevens was never paid the balance of $13,600 for the rest of the order, which included "two room bugs and one phone bug capable of feeding into the nation's highly classified satellite communications network." Stevens claimed the $10,000 Mrs. Hunt was carrying in her purse when she died was money owed to him, "plus a bonus for keeping quiet." Press reports said investigators believed Stevens' shop had been partly-financed by the Defense Intelligence Agency (DIA) but he soon disappeared from the headlines. Stevens does not seem to have been prosecuted and is not mentioned in the final WSPF report.[17]

• • •

During McCord's Senate Watergate Committee testimony in May 1973, he was asked to examine Exhibit 16-B and identified it as "a radio transmitter which is powered by . . . the telephone line itself, and . . . was connected . . . into the telephone itself for the purpose of transmitting those conversations over the phone." The implication was that this was the bug used on Oliver's phone, but it was found in the gym bag carried by Martinez at the time of the arrests. Why wasn't McCord asked to identify the bug found in Oliver's phone in September?[18]

In a 1993 deposition, prosecutor Donald Campbell, who oversaw the investigation of the bugs for the US attorney's office, still didn't know which phones had been bugged: "Well, that gets confusing. It was probably Maxie Wells' phone . . . and Spencer Oliver's extension . . . [but] there had been more than one entry into the Watergate complex and a box had been moved from one phone to another, and the bureau didn't find the bug until sometime after. Whether that was the right bug or whether others had been removed . . . that's why it's hard to tell exactly which phones."[19]

In her memoir, Jean Westwood, who took over from Larry O'Brien as DNC chair at the 1972 convention, briefly discusses the discovery of the September bug: "We never knew whether the FBI failed to search thoroughly or if that bug had been placed there later. Possibly by the Anybody *but* McGovern people, we speculated, or by the Nixon campaign." By the "Anybody *but* McGovern people," Westwood clearly meant Spencer Oliver.[20]

In summary, the only bug found on Spencer Oliver's telephone was not entered into evidence or discussed at trial. Earl Silbert knew it was inoperative when it was found, and the FBI clearly thought it had been planted after the second break-in. In his memo of September 28 to Henry Petersen, Silbert was highly critical of the FBI and suggested they had "goofed" and missed the bug during their earlier search. But he also knew he had a problem:

Obviously, we do not want to be put in a position of challenging [the] testimony of the FBI, particularly its lab, while...relying so heavily on the FBI in general, and the lab in particular, for other important aspects of our proof.[21]

It seems he chose to avoid the issue by excluding the September bug completely from the trial. The Senate Watergate Committee didn't have access to FBI reports, so they knew nothing about Silbert's dispute with the FBI and it only surfaced after the publication of *Secret Agenda* in 1984, which analysed newly-released FBI case files for the first time. When the *New York Times* asked Earl Silbert whether he had disclosed "potentially exculpatory evidence" in the FBI memoranda to the defense attorneys twelve years earlier, he declined to comment.[22]

ACKNOWLEDGMENTS

Five years ago, I interviewed Rolando Martinez in his Miami Beach home for my documentary on the JFK assassination, *Killing Oswald*. I thought he may have been involved in a double-agent operation targeting Cuban intelligence in Mexico City shortly before Kennedy's murder in 1963 but instead, he told me about a later secret double-agent mission to Cuba, for which he'd received a full presidential pardon from Ronald Reagan.[1]

I didn't fully grasp the Cuban mission at the time but after the CIA's internal draft history of Watergate was released in August 2016 and author James Rosen suggested Martinez was a "double agent" and "CIA mole" inside the plot, I researched Martinez' story and documented his Cuban mission in FBI and CIA records five years after Watergate.[2]

I had met Anna Chennault the previous summer through my work on the Bobby Kennedy assassination. A candidate for the elusive girl in the polka dot dress seen with Sirhan Sirhan on the night of the RFK shooting in June 1968 supposedly visited Chennault in New York three days before Kennedy's murder. The late, great investigative reporter Fernando Faura asked me to

---

1 My 2013 video interview with Martinez is available online: https://vimeo.com/84462659. While I once suspected Martinez used the cryptonym "Oliver E. Fortson" in both Operation TILT and an operation targeting Cuban intelligence in Mexico City in 1963, I don't believe Martinez was "Fortson."

2 James Rosen, "Watergate: CIA withheld data on double agent," *Fox News*, 30 August 2016.

accompany him to meet Chennault in her Watergate apartment to check out the girl's claims. We found no substance to the allegation but while preparing for the interview, I researched Chennault's papers and found new evidence of her role in the 1968 election that I thought would make an interesting article as the 2016 election approached.

I asked author David Talbot's advice about pitching articles on Martinez and Chennault to U.S. publishers and he told me he was consulting for Skyhorse and asked if I had enough material for a short book. After further research, I developed a proposal for *Dirty Tricks* which he recommended to publisher Tony Lyons four days before the 2016 election.

My sincere thanks to David and Tony Lyons for their vision in supporting this book and appreciating its contemporary resonance in the current heated political climate, with Republicans and Democrats still feverishly accusing each other of "dirty tricks" two years after the election. Watergate tropes like the "smoking-gun tape" and the "Saturday Night Massacre" have returned to the daily news cycle, alongside talk of possible White House indictments and presidential impeachment.

Thank you to Rolando Martinez, whose menacing 1972 mugshot belies an extremely warm, generous and good-humored man who I had the pleasure to meet twice in Miami. It was also a great pleasure to meet Anna Chennault shortly before her death, thanks to her daughter, Cynthia Chennault, who graciously arranged our visit.

Thanks also to the others I interviewed, especially Howard Hunt's son, St. John; James Everett; Spencer Oliver; Alan Galbraith; John B. Williams—the attorney who successfully defended Gordon Liddy in the Dean and Wells lawsuits—and Jim Hougan, who very generously agreed to read the manuscript and provided extremely helpful insights into all corners of the Watergate affair. While we have notable differences of opinion, his work has been an inspiration and his constructive feedback greatly appreciated. Thanks also to Dick Russell for his comments on the manuscript.

I am also very grateful to Len Colodny for making the research interviews for his excellent book *Silent Coup* available to the next generation of researchers through the Colodny Collection at Texas A&M University, as well as the extremely valuable depositions and court filings from his dogged lawsuit with John and Maureen Dean.

I am also grateful to author James Rosen, for allowing me to read selected chapters from the "Behemoth" version of his biography of John Mitchell, *The Strong Man*, and for making his invaluable research materials available through Northwestern University Archives. My thanks to Skyler Poel for researching the collection and Kevin Leonard and Brittan Nanninga for access.

I'd like to acknowledge the dedicated work of Emma Best, whose tireless campaigning prompted the CIA to make its CREST database available online during the writing of this book; and whose Watergate-related Freedom of Information requests to federal agencies continue to uncover previously classified evidence. On the day I completed this book, she shared a 900-page FOIA release on Muckrock that had me scrambling to update several references with important new information. Thanks also to Russ Baker for supporting my work on the Sirhan case at his news site WhoWhatWhy and for his own research on Watergate.

I'd like to thank the dedicated staff at the many archive collections I contacted or visited while researching this book: Ted Jackson and Scott Taylor at the Booth Family Center for Special Collections, Georgetown University Library for helping me navigate the Richard M. Helms Papers; David Hagen at the Gerlardin New Media Center, Georgetown for providing access to Helms' interviews with David Frost; and Thomas Eisinger at the Center for Legislative Archives at the National Archives for arranging access to screened Senate Watergate Committee files and executive session testimony.

Thanks also to Dr. Jerry Jones, Vicky Eastes and their former colleague Brian Robertson, who helped me navigate the Colodny Collection and

Federal Documents Research Collection at the Central Texas Historical Archive, Texas A&M University. I'm very grateful to Hannah Abigail Dysinger for her research there and to Len Colodny for his encouragement and providing digital access to his files.

I also appreciate the help of Carol Leadenham at the Hoover Institution Archives and Tenei Nakahara for researching records there; Kris Bronstad at the Howard H. Baker Center for Public Policy and Joshua Hodge for his research there; Nicole Hartmann Hadad and Chris Banks at the LBJ Library; Mary Curry at the National Security Archive; Ryan Pettigrew at the Nixon Library; Jennifer Mandel and Jennifer Newby at the Reagan Library; Laura Peimer at the Schlesinger Library; Rebecca Bramlett and Michael Rynearson at the Special Collections Research Center, George Mason University Libraries; and Jessica Hartman (Special Access Staff) and archivist Robert Reed at the National Archives, College Park, MD, for providing access to the Watergate Grand Jury exhibits, WSPF records and the recently-screened transcript of Alfred Baldwin's *Los Angeles Times* interview. My thanks also to Edward Singer for his research at College Park.

I'm very grateful to Patricia Vice-Theron for her meticulous interview transcription; Stephen Aucutt for his advice on publishing; my colleagues at Kingston School of Art for their support during this project; and my employer, Kingston University, London, for travel grants to support my research.

At Skyhorse, sincere thanks to my editor Caroline Russomanno for her judicious work on the manuscript and patience and support throughout the process. Thanks to her team for their care and attention during production and to Andrew Geller for his assistance with contracts.

Finally, my thanks to Kanako and Koto for their love and understanding while I went down another rabbit hole and it took longer than expected to dig my way out.

BIBLIOGRAPHY

In the endnotes, CIA and FBI documents, declassified by the National Archives, are listed by RIF number. Most of these are available online and searchable by RIF number within The President John F. Kennedy Assassination Records Collection at the National Archives (https://www.archives.gov /research/jfk) and within the JFK Assassination, Watergate and Intelligence Investigation Document Collections at the Mary Ferrell Foundation (www .maryferrell.org).

FBI records relating to the Watergate investigation are listed by serial number under FBI File number 139-4089 and are available through the FBI's FOIA Library, The Vault (https://vault.fbi.gov/).

Published reports and hearings of the US House of Representatives and Senate, including House Judiciary Committee and Senate Select Committee testimony on Watergate are available at the Mary Ferrell Foundation website, HathiTrust Digital Library (www.hathitrust.org) and the Internet Archive (www.archive.org). The Silbert nomination hearings are also available through the HathiTrust Digital Library.

Watergate-related FOIA releases can be found at Muckrock: www .muckrock.com.

For the Baker Report—see Appendix to Views of Senator Baker, U.S. Senate Select Committee on Presidential Campaign Activities Within the

United States. *Final Report.* U.S. Government Printing Office, June 1974, pp. 1115–65.

For the Nedzi Hearings and Report—see U.S. House of Representatives. Committee on Armed Services. Inquiry into the Alleged Involvement of the Central Intelligence Agency in the Watergate and Ellsberg Matters.

ABBREVIATIONS

AC—Anna Chennault Papers, Schlesinger Library, Radcliffe Institute, Harvard University, Cambridge, MA.

CLA—Center for Legislative Archives, National Archives, Washington, DC.

CREST—CIA Records Search Tool, CIA Electronic Reading Room. https://www.cia.gov/library/readingroom/.

FRUS—Foreign Relations of the United States, Office of the Historian, US Department of State, Washington, DC.

HHB—Howard H. Baker, Jr. Papers, University of Tennessee, Knoxville, TN.

HSL—Howard S. Liebengood Papers. Library of Congress, Washington, DC.

HSCA—U.S. House of Representatives. Select Committee on Assassinations. *Hearings.* 1976–8.

JCH—U.S. House of Representatives. Committee on the Judiciary. *Hearings,* Washington: Government Printing Office, 1974.

JRP—James S. Rosen Papers, Northwestern University Archives, Evanston, IL.

NARA—National Archives.

RCH—Robert Charles Hill Papers, Hoover Institution Archives, Stanford University, Stanford, CA.

RCR—Commission on CIA Activities Within the United States ("The Rockefeller Commission") *Report to the President.* Washington: Government Printing Office, 1975.

RMH—Richard M. Helms Papers, Booth Family Center for Special Collections, Georgetown University Library, Washington, DC.

RVA—Richard V. Allen Papers, Hoover Institution Archives, Stanford University, Stanford, CA.

SSC—U.S. Senate. Select Committee on Presidential Campaign Activities ("Senate Watergate Committee"). *Hearings.* Washington: Government Printing Office, 1974.

SSCEX—U.S. Senate. Select Committee Executive Session testimony.

WHSF—White House Special Files, Nixon Library, Yorba Linda, CA.

WSPF—Watergate Special Prosecution Force.

X—"The X envelope." Rostow to Middleton, "Literally Eyes Only," Document O, 26 June 1973, Reference File: Anna Chennault, South Vietnam and US Politics, LBJ Library, Austin, TX.

ARCHIVE COLLECTIONS
Booth Family Center for Special Collections, Georgetown University Library, Washington, DC
Richard M. Helms Papers.

Carter Library, Atlanta, GA
Memoranda [From Maxie Wells, 11/29/76–1/15/77], Office of Staff Secretary, 1976. Campaign Transition File.
President Carter daily diary, 26 January 1977.

Central Intelligence Agency, Washington, DC
CIA Records Search Tool (CREST). CIA Electronic Reading Room. https://www.cia.gov/library/readingroom/.
"Family Jewels," Osborn to Executive Secretary, CIA Management Committee, 16 May 1973. https://www.cia.gov/library/readingroom/collection/family-jewels.

"Working Draft - CIA Watergate History," released in response to FOIA request by Judicial Watch, August 2016. https://www.judicialwatch .org/document-archive/jw-v-cia-watergate-cia-report-00146/.

"An Interview with Richard Helms," by David Frost, 22–23 May 1978.

Center for Legislative Archives, National Archives, Washington, DC

U.S. Senate. Select Committee on Presidential Campaign Activities Within the United States. *Executive Session Hearing Transcripts.*

U.S. Senate. Select Committee on Presidential Campaign Activities Within the United States. *Records.*

Central Texas Historical Archives, Texas A&M University, Killeen, TX

Martinez CIA FOIA release F-2014-01152, in response to request by Professor Luke Nichter, The Federal Documents Research Collection.

Colodny Collection:

Transcripts of Len Colodny interviews for *Silent Coup.*

Dean v. St. Martin's Press (92–1807), Motion for Summary Judgement, Subject Matter Core Categories.

Dean v. St. Martin's Press *depositions:*

Robert Allen deposition, 30 July 1996.

Alfred Baldwin depositions, July 25–6, 1996.

Jeannine Bailley-Ball deposition, 29 September 1993.

William Birely, 17 July 1996.

Phillip Mackin Bailley deposition, 25 April 1996.

Mary Banks deposition, 28 September 1993.

Donald Campbell deposition, 30 September 1993.

John Dean depositions, 12–15 September and 14–17 November 1995; 22–26 January 1996.

Maureen Dean depositions, 29–30 August 1996.

Howard Hunt depositions, 16 and 19 April and 16 September 1994.

G. Gordon Liddy depositions, 4–7 July and 6 December 1996.

Howard Liebengood deposition, 6 June 1996.

Barbara Rhoden Kennedy deposition, 17 July 1996.

John Rudy depositions, 11 April, 18–19 June and 12 July 1996.

Earl Silbert depositions, 25 and 27 June 1996.

Carl Shoffler deposition, 13 March 1995.

Robert Strauss deposition, 24 June 1996.

Ida "Maxie" Wells deposition, 7 June 1996.

Federal Bureau of Investigation, Washington, DC

FBI Watergate investigation files and summary and Howard Hunt
Pardon file.

All accessible through the FBI FOIA Library, The Vault (https://vault
.fbi.gov/). I also received the investigation file for "Watergate II" re:
the September Bug via a Freedom of Information request (FBI File
number 139-HQ-4136).

Hoover Institution Archives, Stanford University, Stanford, CA

Richard V. Allen Papers.

Robert Charles Hill Papers.

Inventory of the Cuban Freedom Committee records.

**Howard H. Baker Center for Public Policy, University of Tennessee,
Knoxville, TN**

Howard H. Baker Jr. Papers.

Howard H. Baker, Jr. Oral History Project: George F. Murphy Oral
History Interview, 19 April 1995.

LBJ Library, Austin, TX

"The X envelope." Rostow to Middleton, "Literally Eyes Only," Document O, 26 June 1973, Reference File: Anna Chennault, South Vietnam and US Politics.

"Vietnam Bombing Halt—The Chennault Affair," Huston to the President, 25 February 1970.

William Bundy Oral History Interview III, 2 June 1969, by Paige E. Mulhollan.

Ray S. Cline Oral History Interview I, 21 March 1983, by Ted Gittinger.

Bryce Harlow Oral History Interview II, 6 May 1979, by Michael L. Gillette.

Lawrence F. O'Brien Oral History Interview XXXII, 11 December 1987, by Michael L. Gillette.

Library of Congress, Washington, DC

Howard S. Liebengood Papers.

National Archives, College Park, MD

RG 21, Unsealed Materials from *U.S. v. George Gordon Liddy et al.* (1827–72):

"Transcript of interview of Alfred Baldwin" by Jack Nelson and Ronald Ostrow (*Los Angeles Times*), 5 October 1972.

Transcript of In Camera Proceedings, 17 January 1973.

Presentence reports and Bureau of Prisons evaluations on Barker, Sturgis, Martinez and Gonzalez.

RG 460, Records of the Watergate Special Prosecution Force:

Plumbers Task Force Investigation.

Transcripts of *US v. Ehrlichman, Liddy, Barker and Martinez*, 1974.

Witness File – Oliver, Spencer, US Attorney Files, Box 7.

The President John F. Kennedy Assassination Records Collection, www.archives.gov/research/jfk.

Nixon Library, Yorba Linda, CA

White House Special Files.

Richard Nixon Oral History Project:

Joseph A. Califano recorded interview by Timothy Naftali, 3 April 2007.

John Dean, recorded interview by Timothy Naftali, 30 July 2007.

Daniel Ellsberg recorded interview by Timothy Naftali, 20 May 2008.

Tom Charles Huston recorded interview by Timothy Naftali, 27 June 2008.

Egil "Bud" Krogh recorded interview by Timothy Naftali, 5 September 2007.

Eugenio Rolando Martinez recorded interview by Timothy Naftali, 25 March 2008.

Angelo Lano recorded interview by Timothy Naftali, 28 May 2009.

William Safire recorded interview by Timothy Naftali, 27 March 2008.

James Schlesinger recorded interview by Timothy Naftali, 10 December 2007.

Earl Silbert recorded interview by Timothy Naftali, 17 September 2008.

Northwestern University Archives, Evanston, IL.

James S. Rosen Papers.

Schlesinger Library, Radcliffe Institute, Harvard University, Cambridge, MA.

Anna Chennault Papers.

Senate House Library Archives, University of London

Lapping Watergate Collection.

Special Collections Research Center, George Mason University, Fairfax, VA

Arden B. Schell Watergate Collection.

OTHER DOCUMENTS

Catalog of Copyright Entries, Third Series, Vol. 19, Part 1, Number 2. July–December 1965.

CIA FOIA release F-2016-02491, in response to request by Emma Best regarding Morton Barrows "Tony" Jackson, Muckrock website.

Dean, John. Letter to Adam Parfrey (Phil Stanford's publisher), 13 August 2013. Feral House website.

Interview with Richard Allen, by Stephen F. Knott, Ronald Reagan Oral History Project, Miller Center of Public Affairs, 28 May 2002.

Interview with Ambassador Richard T. McCormack, The Association for Diplomatic Studies and Training Foreign Affairs Oral History Project, 2 January 2002.

Interview with Severin Beliveau by Mike Hastings, 5 September 2008, George J. Mitchell Oral History Project, Bowdoin College Digital Commons.

Motz, Frederic J., *Wells v. Liddy*, 1 F. Supp. 2d 532, United States District Court, D. Maryland, 13 April 1998

Motz, Frederic J., *Wells v Liddy*, 135 F. Supp. 2d 668, United States District Court, D. Maryland, 19 March 2001

Nixon, Richard. "Statements About the Watergate Investigations," 22 May 1973. Online by Gerhard Peters and John T. Woolley, *The American Presidency Project.*

Office of the Pardon Attorney, Executive Grant of Clemency—Eugenio Rolando Martinez, 11 May 1983.

Williams, John B., Reply to John Dean on behalf of Feral House and Stanford, 3 September 2013. Feral House website.

Williams, Judge, *Wells v. Liddy*, United States Court of Appeals for the Fourth Circuit, 28 July 1999

Wilkins, Williams, and Michael, Wells v Liddy, United States Court of Appeals for the Fourth Circuit, 1 March 2002.

NEWSPAPERS, WEBSITES, AND JOURNALS

AARC Library

Baltimore Sun

Boston Globe

Camden Courier-Post

CBS News

Chicago Daily News

Chicago Tribune

City Paper

Consortium News

Counterpunch

CQ Almanac

Diario de Cuba

El Nuevo Herald

Famous Trials

Fox News

Harper's

Judicial Watch

KBIR

Latin American Studies

LIFE

Los Angeles Times

Mary Ferrell Foundation

Muckrock

Miami Herald

Miami News

National Security Archive

NBC News

New York Post

New York Times

Rolling Stone

Sarasota Herald Tribune

The American Presidency Project

The Black Vault

The Education Forum

The Independent

The National Security Archive

The New Republic

The Richard Nixon Foundation

The Sunday Times

The Washingtonian

USA Today

Vanity Fair

Washington Decoded

Washington Post

Washington Star-News

BOOKS AND ARTICLES

Agee, Phillip. *Inside the Company: CIA Diary*. London: Penguin Books, 1975.

Albarelli Jr., H. P. *A Secret Order*. Walterville, OR: Trine Day, 2012.

Anderson, Jack. *Peace, War and Politics*. New York: Forge, 1999.

Baker, Russ. *Family of Secrets*. New York: Bloomsbury Press, 2008.

Bernstein, Carl, and Bob Woodward. *All the President's Men*. London: Pocket Books, 2006.

Braden, Thomas. "Can He Blame It on CIA?" *Syndicated column*, 11 December 1973.

Branch, Taylor, and George Crile. "The Kennedy Vendetta." *Harper's*, August 1975.

Buchanan, Patrick J. *Nixon's White House Wars*. New York: Crown Forum, 2017.

Bundy, William P. *A Tangled Web: The Making of Foreign Policy in the Nixon Presidency*. London: I.B. Tauris, 1998.

Califano, Joseph A. *Inside: A Public and Private Life*. New York: Public Affairs, 2004.

Chennault, Anna. *The Education of Anna*. New York: Times Books, 1980.

Colodny, Len, and Robert Gettlin. *Silent Coup: The Removal of a President*. New York: St. Martin's Press, 1991.

Commission on CIA Activities Within the United States ("The Rockefeller Commission") *Report to the President*. Washington: Government Printing Office, 1975.

Copeland, Miles. "The Unmentionable Uses of a CIA." *National Review*, 14 September 1973.

Corn, David. *Blond Ghost: Ted Shackley and the CIA's Crusades*. New York: Simon and Schuster, 1994.

Dean, John. *Blind Ambition*. New York: Simon and Schuster, 1976.

—. *The Nixon Defense*. New York: Penguin, 2014.

—. *Conservatives Without Conscience*. New York: Viking, 2006.

Dean, Maureen. *Mo: A Woman's View of Watergate*. New York: Bantam Books, 1976.

DeLoach, Cartha D. "Deke." *Hoover's FBI*. Washington, DC: Regnery Publishing, 1995.

Diem, Bui, and David Chanoff. *In the Jaws of History*. Boston: Houghton Mifflin, 1987.

Ellsberg, Daniel. *Secrets: A Memoir of Vietnam and the Pentagon Papers*. New York: Viking, 2002.

Emery, Fred. *Watergate: The Corruption and Fall of Richard Nixon*. London: Jonathan Cape, 1994.

Everett, James. *The Making and Breaking of an American Spy*. Durham, CT: Strategic Book Group, 2011.

Forslund, Catherine. *Anna Chennault: Informal Diplomacy and Asian Relations*. Wilmington, DE: Scholarly Resources, 2002.

—. *Woman of Two Worlds: Anna Chennault and Informal Diplomacy in US-Asian Relations, 1950–1990*. PhD thesis, Washington University, 1997.

Gray, Ashton. *Watergate: The Hoax*. Chalet Books, 2016.

Gray, L. Patrick III. *In Nixon's Web*. New York: Times Books, 2008.

Haldeman, Harry R., and Joseph DiMona. *The Ends of Power*. New York: Dell, 1978.

Haldeman, Harry R. *The Haldeman Diaries: Inside the Nixon White House*. New York: Putnam, 1994.

Helms, Richard. *A Look Over My Shoulder*. New York: Random House, 2003.

Hougan, Jim. *Secret Agenda: Watergate, Deep Throat, and the CIA*. New York: Random House, 1984.

—. "Hougan, Liddy, The Post and Watergate." jimhougan.com. 22 June 2011.

Hughes, Ken. *Chasing Shadows: The Nixon Tapes, the Chennault Affair, and the Origins of Watergate*. Charlottesville, VA: University of Virginia Press, 2014.

Hung, Nguyen Tien, and Jerrold L. Schechter, *The Palace File*, New York: Perennial Library, 1989.

Hunt, E. Howard, and Greg Aunapu. *American Spy: My Secret History in the CIA, Watergate and Beyond*. Hoboken, NJ: John Wiley & Sons, 2007.

Hunt, Howard. *Give Us This Day*. New Rochelle, NY: Arlington House, 1973.

—. *Undercover: Memoirs of an American Secret Agent*. London: W.H. Allen, 1975.

Hunt, St. John. *Bond of Secrecy*. Walterville, OR: Trine Day, 2012.

—. *Dorothy*. Walterville, OH: Trine Day, 2015.

Kutler, Stanley. *Abuse of Power*. New York: Touchstone, 1998.

Levenda, Peter. *Sinister Forces—A Warm Gun: A Grimoire of American Political Witchcraft. The Nine. Book One*. Walterville, OR: Trine Day, 2006.

Liddy, G. Gordon. *Will: The Autobiography of G. Gordon Liddy*. New York: St. Martin's Paperbacks, 1998.

—. *When I Was a Kid, This Was a Free Country*. Washington, DC: Regnery, 2003.

Locker, Ray. *Nixon's Gamble: How a President's Own Secret Government Destroyed His Administration*. Guilford, CT: Lyons Press, 2015.

Lukas, J. Anthony. *Nightmare: The Underside of the Nixon Years*. Athens, OH: Ohio University Press, 1999.

McCord, James W. *A Piece of Tape: The Watergate Story – Fact and Fiction*. Rockville, MD: Washington Media Services, 1974.

Magruder, Jeb Stuart. *An American Life: One Man's Road to Watergate*. New York: Atheneum, 1974.

Martinez, Eugenio, and Bernard Barker. "Mission Impossible: the Watergate bunglers," *Harper's*, October 1974.

Merrill, William H. *Watergate Prosecutor*. East Lansing, MI: Michigan State University Press, 2008.

Morgan, Charles Jr. *One Man, One Voice,* New York: Holt, Rinehart and Winston, 1979.

Newman, John. *Oswald and the CIA*, New York: Skyhorse Publishing, 2008.

Nguyen Phu Duc. *The Viet Nam Peace Negotiations: Saigon's Side of the Story*. Christiansburg, VA: Dalley Book Service, 2005.

Nixon, Richard. *RN: The Memoirs of Richard Nixon*. New York: Simon and Schuster, 2013.

Oglesby, Carl. *The Yankee and Cowboy War: Conspiracies from Dallas to Watergate*. New York: Berkley Medallion, 1977.

Powers, Thomas. *The Man Who Kept the Secrets: Richard Helms and the CIA*. New York: Alfred A. Knopf, 1979.

Ray, Andy. *Hired Gun: A Political Odyssey*. Lanham, MD: University Press of America, 2008.

Rodota, Joseph. *The Watergate: Inside America's Most Infamous Address*. New York: William Morrow, 2018.

Rosen, James. *The Strong Man: John Mitchell and the Secrets of Watergate*. New York: Doubleday, 2008.

Safire, William. *Before the Fall: An Insider's View of the Pre-Watergate House*. New York: Belmont Tower Books, 1975.

St. George, Andrew. "The Cold War Comes Home." *Harper's*, November 1973.

Smith, W. Thomas. *Encyclopaedia of the Central Intelligence Agency*. New York: Facts on File, 2003.

Stanford, Phil. *White House Call Girl*. Port Townsend, WA: Feral House, 2013.

Summers, Anthony, and Robbyn Swan. *The Arrogance of Power*. London: Victor Gollancz, 2000.

Szulc, Tad. "CIA and the Plumbers." *The New Republic*, 29 December 1973.

—. *Compulsive Spy*. New York: The Viking Press, 1974.

Thompson, Fred D. *At That Point in Time: The Inside Story of the Senate Watergate Committee*. New York: Quadrangle, 1975.

Tripodi, Tom. *Crusade: Undercover Against the Mafia and KGB*. Dulles, VA: Brassey's, 1993.

United States of America v. George Gordon Liddy, et al. (Criminal Case No. 1827–72, US District Court for the District of Columbia), Transcripts of Proceedings. 10 January to 22 March 1973. ProQuest History Vault: American Politics and Society from JFK to Watergate, 1960–1975.

United States of America v. John Ehrlichman, et al. (Criminal Case No. 74–116, US District Court for the District of Columbia), Transcripts of Proceedings. 14 March to 12 July 1974.

U.S. Department of Justice. Watergate Special Prosecution Force. Report. Washington: Government Printing Office, 1975. ProQuest History Vault: American Politics and Society from JFK to Watergate, 1960–1975.

United States of America v. John Mitchell, et al. (Criminal Case No. 74–110, US District Court for the District of Columbia), Transcripts of Proceedings. 14 October 1974 to 1 January 1975. ProQuest History

Vault: American Politics and Society from JFK to Watergate, 1960–1975.

U.S. Department of Justice. Watergate Special Prosecution Force. *Report.* Washington: Government Printing Office, 1975.

U.S. Department of State. Foreign Relations of the United States, 1964–1968, Volume VII, Vietnam, September 1968–January 1969, ed. Kent Sieg. Washington: Government Printing Office, 2003.

U.S. Department of State. Foreign Relations of the United States, 1969–1976, Volume XXI, Chile, 1969–1973, eds. James McElveen and James Siekmeier. Washington: Government Printing Office, 2014.

U.S. Department of State. Foreign Relations of the United States, 1969–1976, Volume XXXVIII, Part 2, Organization and Management of Foreign Policy; Public Diplomacy, 1973–1976, eds. M. Todd Bennett and Alexander R. Wieland. Washington: Government Printing Office, 2014.

U.S. House of Representatives. Committee on Armed Services. Inquiry into the Alleged Involvement of the Central Intelligence Agency in the Watergate and Ellsberg Matters *Hearings before the Special Subcommittee on Intelligence.* ("The Nedzi Hearings"). Washington: Government Printing Office, 1975.

U.S. House of Representatives. Committee on Armed Services. Inquiry into the Alleged Involvement of the Central Intelligence Agency in the Watergate and Ellsberg Matters. *Report of the Special Subcommittee on Intelligence.* ("The Nedzi Report"). Washington: Government Printing Office, October 23, 1973.

U.S. House of Representatives. Committee on the Judiciary. *Hearings.* Washington: Government Printing Office, 1974.

U.S. House of Representatives. Select Committee on Assassinations. *Hearings.* 1976–8.

U.S. Senate. Committee on Armed Services. *Hearings on the Nomination of William E. Colby to be Director of Central Intelligence.* July 2, 20 and 25, 1973.

U.S. Senate. Committee on Foreign Relations. *Hearings on the Nomination of Richard Helms to be Ambassador to Iran and CIA International and Domestic Activities.* February 5 and 7 and May 21, 1973.

U.S. Senate. Committee on Foreign Relations. *Hearing on CIA Foreign and Domestic Activities.* January 22, 1975.

U.S. Senate. Committee on the Judiciary. *Hearings on the Nomination of Earl J. Silbert to be United States Attorney,* April 23, 1974–May 20, 1975.

U.S. Senate. Select Committee on Presidential Campaign Activities Within the United States ("Senate Watergate Committee"). *Hearings.* Washington: Government Printing Office, 1974.

U.S. Senate. Select Committee on Presidential Campaign Activities Within the United States. *Final Report.* Washington: Government Printing Office, June 1974.

U.S. Senate. Select Committee to Study Governmental Operations with respect to Intelligence Activities ("The Church Committee"). *Hearings.* 1975–6.

U.S. Senate. Select Committee to Study Governmental Operations with respect to Intelligence Activities. *Final Report.* Washington: Government Printing Office, 1976.

Waldron, Lamar. *Watergate: The Hidden History: Nixon, The Mafia, and The CIA.* Berkeley, CA: Counterpoint, 2013.

Watergate Special Prosecution Force. *Report.* US Government Printing Office, 1975.

Wells, Tom. *Wild Man: The Life and Times of Daniel Ellsberg.* New York: Palgrave Macmillan, 2009.

Weberman, A. J. and Michael Canfield. *Coup D'État in America.* 2010 (Digital Edition).

White, Theodore. *The Making of the President 1968.* New York: Atheneum, 1969.

Wilford, Hugh. *The Mighty Wurlitzer: How the CIA Played America*. Cambridge, MA: Harvard University Press, 2009.

AUTHOR INTERVIEWS

Nick Akerman, 22 August 2018.

Robert Barcal, 20 August 2018.

Anna Chennault, 22 May 2016.

Joseph Califano, 24 August 2018.

James Everett, 6 October 2017.

Jim Hougan, 21 December 2017.

St. John Hunt, 19 April 2017.

Alan Galbraith, 11 August 2018.

Rolando Martinez, August 2013, 18 April 2017, 20 July 2018.

Robert Mirto, 24 August 2018.

Spencer Oliver, 20 July 2018.

John B. Williams, 21 February 2018.

SELECTED VIDEO

In the Eye of the Storm, American International Television, 1997.

Frost–Nixon interviews, Paradine Productions, 1977.

Frost–Helms interviews, Paradine Productions, 1978.

Paperback Vigilante. Peter Davis and Steffan Lam. Villon Films, 1974.

Richard Helms "State of the Agency" Address to CIA Staff, 30 June 1972, NARA.

Senate Watergate Committee Hearings. American Archive of Public Broadcasting. 1973. http://americanarchive.org/exhibits/watergate/the
-watergate-coverage.

The Key to Watergate. Barbara Newman for A&E "Investigative Reports," 1992.

Watergate, Brian Lapping Associates for BBC and Discovery Productions, 1994.

SELECTED AUDIO

Nixon White House Tapes and Watergate Trial Conversations. Nixon
    Library.
Presidential Recordings Digital Edition. http://prde.upress.virginia.edu/.

ENDNOTES

CAST OF CHARACTERS

1. Jail terms are sourced in Fred Emery, *Watergate: The Corruption and Fall of Richard Nixon*, (Jonathan Cape, 1994), xv–xviii.

INTRODUCTION

1. "Vietnam War U.S. Military Fatal Casualty Statistics," National Archives, https://www.archives.gov/research/military/vietnam-war/casualty-statistics.
2. Phil McCombs, "Tongsun Park's Club," *Washington Post*, 16 October 1977.
3. John A. Farrell, "Nixon's Vietnam Treachery," *New York Times*, 31 December 2016; The Richard Nixon Foundation, "Misunderstanding a Monkey Wrench," 2 June 2017. https://www.nixonfoundation.org/2017/06/misunderstanding -a-monkey-wrench/; Luke Nichter, "A Vietnam Myth That Refuses to Die," *Wall Street Journal*, 19 April 2018.
4. "Information Provided the Federal Bureau of Investigation Regarding the Watergate Incident," Walters to Acting Director, FBI, 6 July 1972, 102-10256-10273.
5. Baker report, 1118–9; Richard Nixon, "Statements About the Watergate Investigations," 22 May 1973, *The American Presidency Project*, http://www .presidency.ucsb.edu/ws/?pid=3855.
6. Baker report, 1115–7.
7. Baker report, 1119.

8. "Working Draft - CIA Watergate History," Judicial Watch, 1, http://www
.judicialwatch.org/press-room/press-releases/judicial-watch-uncovers-cia
-inspector-generals-watergate-history-report/.

9. James Rosen, "Watergate: CIA withheld data on double agent," 30 August
2016, *Fox News*; Ray Locker, "CIA director misled FBI about how agency
spied on Pentagon Papers leaker," *USA Today*, 31 August 2016; Glenn
Garvin, "Miami's Watergate mystery man at heart of newly revealed CIA
report," *Miami Herald*, 30 August 2016.

10. U.S. Senate. Committee on the Judiciary, *Hearings on the Nomination of
Earl J. Silbert to be United States Attorney*, 23 April 1974, 65.

CHAPTER 1

1. "Notification of NSC Officials of Intelligence on Missile Bases in Cuba,"
Cline Memorandum for the Record (MFR), 27 October 1962, CREST; Godfrey Hodgson, "Obituary: Ray Cline," *The Independent*, 19 March 1996.

2. Ray S. Cline Oral History Interview I, 21 March 1983, by Ted Gittinger, LBJ
Library, Austin, TX, 35–6; Ken Hughes, *Chasing Shadows: The Nixon Tapes,
the Chennault Affair, and the Origins of Watergate* (Charlottesville, VA:
University of Virginia Press, 2014), 7.

3. Tim Weiner, "Ray S. Cline, Chief C.I.A. Analyst, Is Dead at 77," *New York
Times*, 16 March 1996.

4. Chennault calendar entry, 16 March 1968, Anna Chennault Papers
(AC), Schlesinger Library, Radcliffe Institute, Harvard University,
Cambridge, MA.

5. Theodore White, *The Making of the President 1968* (New York: Atheneum,
1969), 444.

6. Anna Chennault, *The Education of Anna* (New York: Times Books, 1980), 163.

7. Ibid., 164.

8. Ibid., 166; Catherine Forslund, *Anna Chennault: Informal Diplomacy and
Asian Relations* (Wilmington, DE: Scholarly Resources, 2002), 43–4.

9. Chennault, *The Education of Anna*, 167.

10. Chennault letters to Mr. and Mrs. Melvin Gelman and Colonel William Allen, 20 March 1967, AC.

11. Chennault, *The Education of Anna,* 170. She received the cable while on a lecture tour of Asia.

12. Ibid., 171, 184–5.

13. Robert Hill memo, 19 December 1967, Robert Charles Hill Papers (RCH), Hoover Institution Archives, Stanford University, Stanford, CA.

14. Chennault calendar entries for February 16, 1968, AC. There are two calendar entries—one simply reads "10:00 A.M. Vietnam Ambassador"; Joseph Rodota, *The Watergate: Inside America's Most Infamous Address* (New York: William Morrow, 2018), 2–3.

15. Chennault calendar entry, 14 January 1968, AC.

16. John M. Crewdson, "C.I.A. Investigated Personal Life of a Top Nixon Adviser During 1968 G.O.P. Presidential Campaign," *New York Times,* 1 April 1975; Biographical Note in "Register of the Richard V. Allen Papers" (RVA), Hoover Institution Archives, Stanford, CA. Allen did not respond to my request for an interview.

17. Crewdson, "C.I.A. Investigated Personal Life of a Top Nixon Adviser . . ."

18. Calendar entries, 19–20 February 1968, AC.

19. Prescott letter to Chennault, 9 February 1968, AC; Chennault letter to Madame Chiang Kai-shek, AC; Chennault, *The Education of Anna,* 187.

20. Chennault calendar entries, 15, 20–22 March 1968, AC.

21. Chennault letter to Nixon, 25 March 1968, RCH and RVA. She also sent a copy to Hill and former Assistant Secretary of Defense Perkins McGuire with a note: "Please be sure he has a chance to read it."

22. Chenault letters to Nixon, 4 and 12 April 1968, RCH.

23. Crewdson, "C.I.A. Investigated Personal Life of a Top Nixon Adviser . . ."

24. Chennault calendar entries, 8, 18, 22 April 1968, AC.

25. Chennault letter to Thieu, 7 May 1968, AC.

26. Thomas Powers, *The Man Who Kept the Secrets: Richard Helms and the CIA* (New York: Alfred A. Knopf, 1979), 198.

27. Bui Diem and David Chanoff, *In the Jaws of History* (Boston: Houghton Mifflin, 1987), 236.

28. Allen letter to Barry Goldwater, 26 August 1968, RVA.

29. Chennault letter to Nixon, 28 June 1968, RVA.

30. Ibid.; "Massive Staff Runs Nixon–Agnew Presidential Campaign," *CQ Almanac*, 1968.

31. Crewdson, "C.I.A. Investigated Personal Life of a Top Nixon Adviser . . ."

32. Ibid.

33. Olsen/Roethe Files attached to Knoche to Belin, 22 January 1975, 104-10419-10038, 7; "Safe Drawer 2283—Drawer 4," 104-10422-10061.

34. William Safire, *Before the Fall: An Insider's View of the Pre-Watergate White House* (New York: Belmont Tower Books, 1975), 89; Interview with Richard Allen, Ronald Reagan Oral History Project, Miller Center of Public Affairs, 28 May 2002, 11.

35. Chennault letter to Nixon, 28 June 1968, RVA.

36. DC [Nixon] to Haldeman, "Re: Senator Mundt," 2 July 1968, White House Special Files, Box 35, Folder 8, Nixon Library, 41.

37. Safire, *Before the Fall*, 89.

38. Ibid.; Hughes, *Chasing Shadows*, 8–9. Hughes writes that one of Nixon's speechwriters (William Safire) kept the memo "without realizing how important it was" and "thought the meeting hadn't taken place." But the note and letters from Chennault to Nixon published in Safire's book can be found in Richard Allen's Papers today, suggesting Allen shared them with Safire for his book.

39. July 12 was a Friday, but Chennault says they met on a Monday in her book.

40. Chennault, *The Education of Anna*, 174–5.

41. Ibid., 175–6.

42. Ibid., 176. This is generally corroborated in Diem and Chanoff, *In the Jaws of History*, 237.

43. Diem and Chanoff, *In the Jaws of History*, 237. The summit was held on July 18.

44. William P. Bundy, *A Tangled Web: The Making of Foreign Policy in the Nixon Presidency* (London: I.B. Tauris, 1998), 37.

45. Chennault, *The Education of Anna*, 173–4.

46. Anthony Summers and Robbyn Swan, *The Arrogance of Power* (London: Victor Gollancz, 2000), 299.

47. Janet Chusmir, "There Will Always Be Problems," *Miami Herald*, 6 August 1968, AC.

48. "A Woman's View – Watching the GOP convention from the Grand Stand," undated, 13 August 1968, AC.

49. Chennault letters to Herbert Kalmbach, 22 August 1968 and 4 October 1968, AC; Stans letter to Chennault, 14 August 1968, AC.

50. Chennault to Nixon, 19 August 1968, RVA.

51. Chennault to Allen, 3 September 1968, RVA. The copies of the letters Chennault sent to Nixon can be found in Allen's papers and were cited in Safire's earlier book. Chennault's papers include the letter of August 19, 1968 but not the earlier correspondence with Nixon.

52. "Recent Promising Developments in Vietnam," McCormack to Allen, 13 September 1968, RVA; "Vietnam Status: Inquiries in Washington," McCormack to Allen, 8 September 1968, White House Special Files, Box 32, Folder 25, Nixon Library, 9–12; Ambassador Richard T. McCormack Oral History Interview, by Charles Stuart Kennedy, The Association for Diplomatic Studies and Training Foreign Affairs Oral History Project, 2 January 2002, 25.

53. Ibid.; Chennault to Nixon, 15 October 1968, RVA; "Key Issues Committee," White House Special Files, Box 6, Folder 10, Nixon Library, 45–6; Chennault, *The Education of Anna,* 174; Stans to Chennault, 30 September 1968, AC; Notes of "Meeting with Maury Stans," 1 October 1968, AC; Draft Chennault letter to Republican National Finance Committee, 2 October 1968, AC; Chennault to Mrs. Eisenhower, 4 October 1968, AC.

54. Chennault, *The Education of Anna,* 188; Chennault to Nixon, 15 October 1968, RVA. Only Powers references this document in Allen's papers, further suggesting Allen was his source.

55. Bundy, *A Tangled Web*, 550, fn82.

56. William Bundy Oral History Interview III, 2 June 1969, by Paige E. Mulhollan, LBJ Library, Tape 5, 4–5. Kieu is also mentioned in Nguyen Phu Duc, *The Viet Nam Peace Negotiations: Saigon's Side of the Story* (Christiansburg, VA: Dalley Book Service, 2005), 195.

57. Bryce Harlow Oral History Interview II, 6 May 1979, by Michael L. Gillette, LBJ Library, 58–63.

58. Harlow to Nixon, 22 October 1968, cited in in Richard Nixon, *RN: The Memoirs of Richard Nixon* (New York: Simon and Schuster, 2013), 326; and The Richard Nixon Foundation, "Setting the Record Straight," 5 September 2017. https://www.nixonfoundation.org/2017/09/setting-the-record-straight-vietnam/.

59. Farrell, "Nixon's Vietnam Treachery"; "HRH Handwritten Notes," White House Special Files, Box 33, Folder 8, Nixon Library, 7; Hughes, *Chasing Shadows*, 29.

60. The Richard Nixon Foundation, "Misunderstanding a Monkey Wrench," 2 June 2017.

61. "HRH Handwritten Notes," White House Special Files, Box 33, Folder 8, 8, 10.

62. Powers, *The Man Who Kept the Secrets*, 198.

63. "The X envelope." Rostow to Middleton, "Literally Eyes Only," Document O, 26 June 1973, Reference File: Anna Chennault, South Vietnam and US Politics, LBJ Library, Austin, TX.

64. Rostow to Middleton, 26 May 1973, X, Document O.

65. Powers, *The Man Who Kept the Secrets*, 198.

66. Diem and Chanoff, *In the Jaws of History*, 244.

67. Bundy, *A Tangled Web*, 42, 550, 88fn; X, Document 105.

68. Ibid.

69. X, Documents 44a, 45, 45a.

70. Hughes, *Chasing Shadows*, 35–7; X, Document O.

71. Information Memorandum from the President's Special Assistant (Rostow) to President Johnson," 29 October 1968, *Foreign Relations of the United States*

(FRUS), 1964–1968, Volume VII, Vietnam, September 1968–January 1969 (US Government Printing Office, 2003), Document 145.

72. Cartha D. DeLoach, *Hoover's FBI* (Washington, DC: Regnery Publishing, 1995), 397.

73. Ibid., 398; Hughes, *Chasing Shadows*, 186fn8.

74. Powers, *The Man Who Kept the Secrets*, 198–9.

75. "The Bombing Halt and U.S. Politics," 29 October 1968, *FRUS*, 1964–1968, VII, Document 148fn5.

76. X, Documents 35a, 36, 37, 38b.

77. X, Documents 38a, 38b; Chennault calendar entry, 30 October 1968, AC.

78. "Lyndon Johnson and Richard Russell on 30 October 1968," Conversation WH6810-10-13612-13613, *Presidential Recordings Digital Edition*, http://prde .upress.virginia.edu/conversations/4006111; Hughes, *Chasing Shadows*, 5–10.

79. X, Documents 34, 34a.

80. "HRH Handwritten Notes," 1968, White House Special Files, Box 33, Folder 8, Nixon Library.

81. "Transcript of Telephone Conversation Among President Johnson, Vice President Humphrey, Richard Nixon, and George Wallace," 31 October 1968, *FRUS*, 1964–1968, VII, Document 166.

82. Ibid., 189.

83. Ibid., 190–1.

84. "Thieu Says Saigon Cannot Join Paris Talks under Present Plan," *New York Times*, 2 November 1968.

CHAPTER 2

1. X, Document 30. Curiously, the FBI does not provide a time for the Chennault call to Bui Diem—as they did with the previous call three days earlier—but we can infer it was before she left the house at 1:45 p.m.

2. Ibid.

3. Chennault calendar entry, 2 November 1968, AC.

4. "Editorial Note," *FRUS*, 1964–1968, VII, Document 181.

5. Ibid.

6. Ibid.

7. "HRH Handwritten Notes," 1968, White House Special Files, Box 33, Folder 5, Nixon Library.

8. Harlow Oral History Interview II, 6 May 1979, 56–7.

9. Handwritten notes, 2 November 1968, RVA.

10. Catherine Forslund, *Woman of Two Worlds: Anna Chennault and Informal Diplomacy in US-Asian Relations, 1950–1990* (PhD thesis, Washington University, 1997), 227fn, citing telephone interview with Chennault, 13 April 1997; Forslund, *Anna Chennault: Informal Diplomacy and Asian Relations*, 70–1.

11. Memorandum from Valerie Bloom (office of Richard Allen) to John Mitchell (per Phil Shaffner), 28 September 1968, RVA; Nixon–Agnew Campaign Committee Staff List, RVA.

12. "The Woman Who Scared Nixon," *The Sunday Times*, 2 March 1969 (X, 60).

13. Forslund, *Woman of Two Worlds*, 227fn.

14. Forslund, *Anna Chennault: Informal Diplomacy and Asian Relations*, 70–1; "the new material" possible Rostow memo, released 1995.

15. Forslund, *Woman of Two Worlds*, 236.

16. White House memo from Jim Jones, 3 November 1968, X, Document 93.

17. "Editorial Note," *FRUS*, 1964–1968, VII, Document 186.

18. "Telephone Conversation Between President Johnson and Richard Nixon," 3 November 1968, *FRUS*, 1964–1968, VII, Document 187.

19. "Notes of Meeting," 4 November 1968, *FRUS*, 1964–1968, VII, Document 191.

20. X, Documents 86a, 89, 90, 91, 91a, 91b; Hughes, *Chasing Shadows*, 52–55.

21. Ibid.

22. X, Document 91a.

23. X, Documents 27, 28, 29.

24. "Telephone Conversation Among President Johnson, Secretary of Defense Clifford, Secretary of State Rusk, and the President's Special Assistant (Rostow)," 4 November 1968, *FRUS,* 1964–1968, VII, Document 192.

25. "Telegram from the President's Special Assistant (Rostow) to President Johnson in Texas," 4 November 1968, *FRUS,* 1964–1968, VII, Document 194.

26. Ibid.

27. *FRUS,* 1964–1968, VII, Document 192; Hughes, *Chasing Shadows,* 54–5.

28. Ibid.

29. *FRUS,* 1964–1968, VII, Document 194.

30. X, Document 46.

31. "Notes of Meeting," 5 November 1968, *FRUS,* 1964–68, VII, Document 195.

32. Chennault, *The Education of Anna,* 191.

33. White, *The Making of the President 1968,* 445.

34. Ibid., 445–7.

35. Telegram from the Central Intelligence Agency to the Stations in Saigon and [place not declassified]," 6 November 1968, *FRUS,* 1964–68, VII, Document 201.

36. Handwritten notes, 6 November 1968, RCH.

37. X, Document 23.

38. X, Documents 21a, 22.

39. Ibid.; X, Documents 81, 82, 83.

40. X, Document 21.

41. X, Document 86a.

42. Ibid.

43. Chennault, *The Education of Anna,* 194.

44. Ibid., 194–7.

45. X, Documents 81, 82, 83.

46. "Telephone Conversation Between President Johnson and President-elect Nixon," 8 November 1968, *FRUS,* 1964–1968, VII, Document 207.

47. Hughes, *Chasing Shadows*, 60–1; Johnson-Rusk conversation, 8:13 a.m., November 9.

48. "Telegram from the Director of the Federal Bureau of Investigation (Hoover) to the Executive Secretary of the National Security Council (Smith)," 10 November 1968, *FRUS*, 1964–68, VII, Document 209.

49. "Telegram from the Department of State to the Embassy in Vietnam," 10 November 1968, *FRUS*, 1964–1968, VII, Document 210.

50. Huston memo, 6; "Lyndon Johnson and Cartha 'Deke' DeLoach on 12 November 1968," Conversation WH6811-04-13730, *Presidential Recordings Digital Edition*, http://prde.upress.virginia.edu/conversations /4006139.

51. "Lyndon Johnson and Cartha 'Deke' DeLoach on 13 November 1968," Conversation WH6811-04-13733, *Presidential Recordings Digital Edition*, http:// prde.upress.virginia.edu/conversations/4006140.

52. Ibid., 52.

53. "Lyndon Johnson and Cartha 'Deke' DeLoach on 13 November 1968."

54. Ibid.

55. Ibid.

56. Tom Charles Huston recorded interview by Timothy Naftali, 27 June 2008, Richard Nixon Oral History Project, Nixon Library, 7.

57. "Vietnam Bombing Halt—The Chennault Affair," Huston to the President, 25 February 1970, LBJ Library, 7–9.

58. Ibid., 12.

59. "HRH Handwritten Notes," 1968, White House Special Files, Box 33, Folder 8, Nixon Library.

60. "Vietnam Bombing Halt—The Chennault Affair," 8.

61. DeLoach, *Hoover's FBI*, 406.

62. X, Document 71a.

63. Georgie Anne Geyer, "Saigon boast: 'We helped elect Nixon,'" *Chicago Daily News*, 15 November 1968 (X, Document 75).

64. X, Documents 16, 17, 17a, 17b, 18, 19.

65. X, Document 52.

66. X, Document 75.

67. X, Document 14a.

68. X, Document 13, 13a.

69. X, Document 12a.

70. Tom Ottenad, "Was Saigon's peace talk delay due to Republican promises?" *Boston Globe*, 6 January 1969 (X, Document 11).

71. "Memo from Rose Mary Woods to Peter Flanigan RE: Senator Everett Dirksen recommending Anna Chennault for the post of Assistant Secretary of State for Public Information," 6 January 1969, White House Special Files, Box 6, Folder 5, Nixon Library.

72. "Messrs. George Williams and Charles Whitehouse," Allen to Hill, 6 January 1969, RVA.

73. James Rosen, *The Strong Man: John Mitchell and the Secrets of Watergate* (New York: Doubleday, 2008), 59–60, citing Haldeman's notes, 25 February 1969; The *Globe* later dropped the story.

74. Ibid., 197–8.

75. Bundy Oral History Interview III, 2 June 1969, Tape 5, 4–5.

76. "Mrs. Chennault Denies Seeing Peace Talk Delay" NYT, 23 July 1969 (X, 62); "Humphrey Agrees with 'Sabotage' Charge" *The Austin American*, 11 July 1969 (X, 63).

77. Judith Viorst, "The Three Faces of Anna Chennault," *The Washingtonian*, September 1969 (X, Document 53).

78. Ibid.

79. Harlow to Haldeman, 27 August 1969, White House Special Files (December 2, 2008 Materials Release), Nixon Library.

80. "From Peter M. Flanigan to Rose Woods RE: Anna Chenault (sic)," 2 October 1969, Contested Materials Collection, Box 55, Folder 17, Nixon Library.

81. Rosen, *The Strong Man,* 59, citing a memorandum from Flanigan to Mitchell, 2 October 1969.

82. Hughes, *Chasing Shadows*, 70–1, citing Harry R. Haldeman and Joseph DiMona, *The Ends of Power* (New York: Dell, 1978), 287.

83. "Origin and Disposition of the Huston Plan," 18 February 1975, CREST; Hughes, *Chasing Shadows*, 71–4.

84. Rosen, *The Strong Man*, 60, citing Haldeman's notes, 12 April 1971 (high-level) and 18 May 1971 (finesse); "Telecon with Harlow/Sec Kissinger at 2.00 p.m.," 19 October 1973, Department of State Virtual Reading Room, https://foia.state.gov; "Memorandum of Conversation," 12 April 1971, *FRUS*, 1969–1976, Volume XVII, China, 1969–1972, Document 113fn9.

85. "Richard Nixon, John D. Ehrlichman, H. R. 'Bob' Haldeman, Henry A. Kissinger, and Ronald L. Ziegler on 17 June 1971," Conversation 525-001 (*PRDE* Excerpt A), *Presidential Recordings Digital Edition* http://prde.upress.virginia.edu/conversations/4006738; Hughes, *Chasing Shadows*, 1–2.

86. Ibid., 121.

87. Ibid., 1–3.

88. John Ehrlichman affidavit, 30 April 1974, House Judiciary Committee (HJC) Statement of Information, Book 4, 60.

89. Safire, *Before the Fall*, 89; Bundy, *A Tangled Web*, 549, 72fn.

90. Safire, *Before the Fall*, 90.

91. Ibid.

92. William Safire recorded interview by Timothy Naftali, 27 March 2008, Richard Nixon Oral History Project, Nixon Library, 6.

93. Allen Oral History Interview, 28 May 2002, 11.

94. Rosen, *The Strong Man*, 61. Rosen thanks Allen in the acknowledgments. The emails were received in January 2003.

95. Ibid.

96. Hughes, *Chasing Shadows*, 168.

97. Summers, *The Arrogance of Power*, 306.

98. Huston Oral History Interview, 30 April 2008, Nixon Library, 12.

99. "The Transformation of Anna Chenault," *Washington Post*, 15 February 1981.

100. Author interview with Anna Chennault, 22 May 2016.

101. The Richard Nixon Foundation, "*The Vietnam War* – Errors and Omissions," 25 September 2017. https://www.nixonfoundation.org/2017/09/the-vietnam -war-errors-and-omissions/.

102. John Dean, "Nixon Was Evil: Getting the Historical Evidence Right," 6 January 2017. https://verdict.justia.com/2017/01/06/nixon-evil-getting -historical-evidence-right.

103. X, Document 39.

104. Ibid., 3–5; Joseph Rodota, *The Watergate*, 3–5.

CHAPTER 3

1. Transcript of a recording between Nixon and Haldeman, 1:04–1:13 p.m., 23 June 1972, Nixon Library.

2. "CIA Op Files on E. Howard Hunt," 104-10194-10023.

3. Ibid.; E. Howard Hunt, *Undercover: Memoirs of an American Secret Agent* (London: W.H. Allen, 1975), 5, 53, 141; Hunt Pardon Petition and Investigation file, FBI Vault, https://vault.fbi.gov, 90.

4. Harriman letter to Hunt, 13 January 1949, "CIA Op Files on E. Howard Hunt," 33, 68.

5. Hunt Pardon file, 94.

6. MFR, Hunt to Garland, 22 December 1949, 104-10120-10115; Hunt, *Undercover*, 66.

7. Hunt Pardon file, 56, 58; Hunt, *Undercover*, 69, 77.

8. Ibid.; Hunt, *Undercover*, 87–90; E. Howard Hunt and Greg Aunapu, *American Spy: My Secret History in the CIA, Watergate and Beyond* (Hoboken, NJ: John Wiley & Sons, 2007), 63–65.

9. "Security Clearance of Novel – Howard Hunt," 1 December 1950, 104-10120-10107; "Clearance of Publications," 23 October 1952," 104-10120-10096; "Clearance for Publication," undated, 104-10120-10103.

10. "Clearance of Manuscript Entitled 'Darkness on the Land,'" Edwards to Chief, WHD and Director of Security, 9 April 1953, 104-10120-10092;

"Publication Clearance – Hunt, Everette Howard, Jr., 1 April 1953, 104-10120-10094.

11. Ibid.; "Bernard F. Chumley (Pseudo–OPC)," 19 September 1950, 104-10119-10341; "Manuscript: Give Us This Day," 6 February 1970, 104-10119-10185; "Everette Howard Hunt, Jr.," Evans MFR, 30 August 1971, 104-10119-10317; "Clearance for Publication," 15 September 1952, 104-10120-10101; "Clearance, Publication – Hunt, Howard," 21 January 1954, 104-10120-10089; "Clearance of Manuscript Entitled 'Darkness on the Land,'" Edwards to Chief, WHD and Director of Security, 1 May 1953, 104-10120-10070; Hunt, *Undercover*, 96; "Review of Office of Security Files on E. Howard Hunt," 13 March 1978, 180-10143-10076.

12. Hunt HSCA testimony, 3 November 1978, Part 2, 13; Hunt, *Undercover*, 96–9.

13. "Hunt Travel Order," 8 April 1954, 104-10120-10063; "Overseas Processing Sheet for Hunt, Everette Howard, Jr.," 21 May 1954, 104-10120-10066; "Everette Howard Hunt, Jr.," 104-10019-10317; Hunt, *Undercover*, 100–101; Hunt, *Undercover*, 100–101.

14. "Everette Howard Hunt, Jr.," 104-10019-10317; Hunt Pardon file, 96; "Give Us This Day," 104-10019-10185; Hunt HSCA testimony, Part 2, 13.

15. "Material from Rockefeller Commission re: E. Howard Hunt," 6 March 1975, 157-10011-10090.

16. Ibid.

17. Hunt HSCA testimony, Part 2, 24–5; "Material from Rockefeller Commission re: E. Howard Hunt," 157-10011-10090.

18. Hunt Church Committee testimony, 10 January 1976, 79–80; "Material from Rockefeller Commission re: E. Howard Hunt," 157-10011-10090.

19. Hunt Church Committee testimony, 10 January 1976, 80–1.

20. Ibid., 79–81; Hunt HSCA testimony, Part 2, 5, 16–17, 31–38.

21. Ibid., 65; Hunt HSCA testimony, Part 2, 13, 31, 38; "Everett Howard Hunt, Jr.," 19 June 1972, 104-10103-10057.

22. Hunt Church Committee testimony, 1–10–76, 65–6.

23. Ibid., 67-68b.

24. "Material from Rockefeller Commission re: E. Howard Hunt," 6 March 1975, 157-10011-10090.

25. Hunt, *Undercover*, 130, 133–4.

26. "E. Howard Hunt," Breckenridge MFR, 20 December 1973, 104-10103-10374. The memo references Stanley Woodward, another diplomat, in error. Robert Woodward was Ambassador to Uruguay from April 1958 to March 1961; and Ambassador to Spain from May 1962 to February 1965.

27. "Cause of Illness – E. Howard Hunt," 6 January 1965, 104-10194-10024, 31.

28. "The David St. John Novels," Howe to Kuhn, 6 February 1974, 104-10103-10049; "Mr. Howard Hunt," Karamessines MFR, 1 June 1967, 104-10194-10023, 205; "Everett Howard Hunt, Jr.," 104-10103-10057.

29. "E. Howard Hunt," 104-10103-10374; Hunt, *Undercover*, 34–5; "Folder on Hunt, Everette Howard Jr.," 104-10173-10130.

30. Helms letter to Hunt, 13 August 1965, Richard M. Helms Papers (RMH), Booth Family Center for Special Collections, Georgetown University Library, Washington, DC.

31. "The David St. John Novels," 104-10103-10049; Hunt HSCA testimony, Part 2, 31–38; Hunt Church Committee testimony, 10 January 1976, 64.

32. "The David St. John Novels," 104-10103-10049; Catalog of Copyright Entries, Third Series, Vol. 19, Part 1, Number 2, July–December 1965.

33. Ibid.; Hunt, *Undercover*, 134.

34. "Watergate – Frank A. O'Malley," Evans and Howe MFR, 21 February 1974, 104-10103-10042, 6; Jim Hougan, *Secret Agenda: Watergate, Deep Throat, and the CIA* (New York: Random House, 1984), 6.

35. Hunt HSCA testimony, Part 2, 31–38. He issued a similar denial to the Church Committee.

36. Hunt and Aunapu, *American Spy*, 157–8.

37. Hunt, *Undercover*, 139–40.

38. "The David St. John Novels," 104-10103-10049; Hunt letter to Helms, 16 December 1968, RMH; Helms letter to Hunt, 27 January 1969, RMH.

39. Valenti letter to Helms, 16 March 1966, RMH.

40. Valenti letter to Helms, 19 October 1968, RMH.

41. "The David St. John Novels," 104-10103-10049.

42. "General Paul F. Gaynor's Recollections," Sayle to Kuhn, 1 February 1974, Alan J. Weberman and Michael Canfield, *Coup d'État in America*, Nodule 20, http://the-puzzle-palace.com/files/nodule20.htm.

43. Ibid.; Hougan, *Secret Agenda*, 227n; "Folder on Hunt, Everette Howard Jr.," 104-10173-10130.

44. "CIA Op Files on E. Howard Hunt," 104-10194-10023.

45. "E. Howard Hunt, Jr. (Manuscript – "Give Us This Day"), Chief, LEOB/SRS to Gaynor, 104-10120-10021; "Manuscript – Give Us This Day," Chief, LEOB/SRS to Gaynor, 5 February 1970, 104-10120-10024; "Comments on Manuscript Give Us This Day: CIA and the Bay of Pigs Invasion by Edward J. Hamilton," Pforzheimer to Osborn, 104-10119-10182; "Hunt Cover History," 14 January 1970, 104-10119-10168; "Everette Howard Hunt, Jr.," 104-10119-10317.

46. Ibid.

47. "Manuscript – Give Us This Day," 104-10120-10024; "Manuscript: Give Us This Day," 104-10119-10185.

48. "Everette Howard Hunt, Jr.," 104-10119-10317.

49. Ibid.; "Gaynor MFR," 25 February 1970, 104-10119-10180.

50. "Gaynor MFR," 104-10119-10180; "Buckley," Hunt to Karamessines, 2 March 1970, 104-10119-10179.

51. "Comments on Manuscript Give Us This Day: CIA and the Bay of Pigs Invasion by Edward J. Hamilton," 104-10119-10182.

52. Ibid.

53. Howard Hunt, *Give Us This Day* (New Rochelle, NY: Arlington House, 1973), 15–6.

54. "Request for Personnel Action," 21 April 1970, 104-10119-10177; Hunt Pardon file, 96; Family Jewels, 170.

55. "Retirement Interview with E. Howard Hunt," 24 April 1970, 104-10119-10163; Hunt, *Undercover,* 139–40.

56. Helms letter to Hunt, 20 April 1970, 104-10120-10017.

57. "General Paul F. Gaynor's Recollections."

58. "Howard Hunt Interview of February 4, 1974," Liebengood and Madigan to Thompson, 12 February 1974, Box 38, Folder 6, Howard S. Liebengood Papers (HSL), Library of Congress, Washington, DC.

59. Hunt Pardon file, 90, 157; Mullen FBI interview, 28 July 1971, 124-10211-10235; "Entry into Democratic National Headquarters," 23 June 1972, 104-10256-10268.

60. "Watergate – Frank A. O'Malley," 104-10103-10042; Inventory of the Cuban Freedom Committee records, Hoover Institution Archives, Stanford, CA.

61. Ibid.

62. Bennett testimony, Nedzi hearings, 1076.

63. Ibid., 1074; Baker report, 1121; Hunt Pardon file, 90; HJC Testimony of Witnesses, Book 3, 62–3; Hunt, *Undercover*, 142.

64. "Request for Utilization of Hunt in a Project," 27 October 1970, 104-10119-10320; "Official Routing Slip," 28 October 1970, 104-10119-10321; "E. Howard Hunt – Utilization by Central Cover Staff," 104-10119-10322; "Request for CSA concerning E. Howard Hunt," Gahagen to Mahoney, 3 June 1970, 104-10119-10323.

65. "E. Howard Hunt – Utilization by Central Cover Staff," Burke to Karamessines, 14 October 1970, 104-10119-10322.

66. Ibid.; "Everette Howard Hunt, Jr.," 104-10103-10057.

67. Hunt, *Undercover*, 141–2; Hunt testimony. Nedzi hearings, 477–8.

68. Anthony J. Lukas, *Nightmare: The Underside of the Nixon Years.* (Athens, OH: Ohio University Press, 1999), 39; "With Sincere Regards, Howard Hughes," *LIFE*, 22 January 1971, 24–28; Baker staff chronology, 6 January 1974, HSL, Box 38, Folder 2.

69. Bennett testimony, Nedzi hearings, 1077–8, 1113.

70. Ibid., 1110.

71. Fred D. Thompson, *At That Point in Time: The Inside Story of the Senate Watergate Committee* (New York: Quadrangle, 1975), 184–5.

72. "Digest of Lyle Miller Secret CIA Documents," Liebengood and Madigan to Thompson, 3 February 1974, HSL, Box 38, Folder 6, 4–5. The Baker report lists the subject of the report as "association of Robert R. Mullen and Company with the Hughes Tool Company" (1122).

73. Ibid.; "Digest of Lyle Miller Secret CIA Documents," 4–5.

74. Baker report, 1122.

75. Family Jewels, 170, 432.

76. "Administrative Files on E. Howard Hunt's Post-Employment Relationship," 1993.07.23.14:37:32:250620, 27–37, 112.

CHAPTER 4

1. Lukas, *Nightmare,* 421; SSC Final Report, 119–20; Hunt, *Undercover,* 156; G. Gordon Liddy, *Will: The Autobiography of G. Gordon Liddy* (New York: St. Martin's Paperbacks, 1998), 199–200.

2. Tom Wells, *Wild Man: The Life and Times of Daniel Ellsberg.* (New York: Palgrave Macmillan, 2001), 6–7.

3. "Richard Nixon Discusses the Pentagon Papers Case: Recorded Conversations with Aides," Nixon telephone conversations with Mitchell, 29 June 1971, http://www.famous-trials.com/ellsberg/269-record.

4. Ibid.; Nixon telephone conversation with Mitchell and Kissinger, 30 June 1971.

5. Hunt, *Undercover,* 138, 141.

6. "Conversation with Howard Hunt, July 1, 1971," Exhibit 148, SSC Book 9, 3877-80; Hunt, *Undercover,* 145–8.

7. Ibid.; Bennett testimony, Nedzi hearings, 1090; "Lukoskie MFR," 10 July 1972, printed in Hougan, *Secret Agenda,* 329–331; Hunt Pardon File, 160.

8. Nedzi report, 5; CIA Watergate History, 23; Family Jewels, 286, 351; "Telephone Call to General Cushman from John Ehrlichman," 7 July 1971, HJC Statement of Information, Book 2, 467. An unredacted copy in the Arden B. Schell Watergate Collection (George Mason University, Fairfax, VA) notes that Cushman called Osborn after Ehrlichman's call. The notes were made by Cushman's secretary, Barbara Pindar.

9. "General Cushman's Call Re Howard Hunt," Osborn to Inspector General, 5 February 1974, HJC Statement of Information, Book 7, Part 2, 1040; "Everette Howard Hunt, Jr., Evans MFR, 30 August 1971, 104-10119-10317; Lukas, *Nightmare,* 91, cited in Hougan, *Secret Agenda,* 10.

10. "Colson Appointment Book," Liebengood and Madigan to Thompson, 13 February 1974. HSL, Box 38, Folder 6; Hougan, *Secret Agenda,* 56; "General Cushman's Call Re Howard Hunt"; Howard Osborn affidavit, 23 May 1973, Family Jewels, 405–9 and Nedzi hearings, 182–5; SSC report, 121. This may explain the "telephone slip asking Hunt to return a call to Mr. Osborn of the C.I.A" noted in Haldeman, *The Ends of Power,* 143 and cited in Hougan, *Secret Agenda,* 8n.

11. Administrative Files on E. Howard Hunt's Post-Employment Relationship, 28–9; Family Jewels, 420.

12. Hunt, *Undercover,* 157; Liddy, *Will,* 204.

13. Hunt HSCA testimony, Part 1, 40.

14. Ibid., 24–5.

15. Ibid., 25–7; "Cushman/Hunt Meeting," 22 July 1971, Nedzi hearings, 1125–1131; Nedzi report, 5.

16. CIA Watergate History, 28–30. Krueger briefed TSD officer Stephen Greenwood on the "Bigot case" the same day (Greenwood notes on Hunt support, CIA FOIA release F-2016-02491 regarding Morton Barrows "Tony" Jackson, Muckrock, 856).

17. Ibid., 30–31; Schlesinger statement, Nedzi report, 2; "Summary of Contacts by Mr. Stephen Carter Greenwood with Mr. E Howard Hunt," HJC Testimony of Witnesses, Book 3, 53–4; Hunt, *Undercover,* 15960.

18. Nedzi report, 6; Hunt testimony, Nedzi hearings, 483–5, 489–93, 562; Colson testimony, Nedzi hearings, 588; Bennett testimony, Nedzi hearings, 1103; Hunt, *Undercover,* 159–60; SSC Final Report, 119.

19. "Neutralization of Ellsberg," Hunt to Colson, Exhibit 150, SSC Book 9, 3886.

20. CIA Watergate History, 47–8.

21. CIA Watergate History, 48–9.

22. "Digest of Secret CIA Materials," Madigan to Baker and Thompson, 8 December 1973, HSL, Box 38, Folder 1; Osborn affidavit.

23. Helms testimony, Nedzi hearings, 88; CIA Watergate History, 50.

24. Tietjen affidavit, 9 May 1973, Nedzi hearings, 32–3; Osborn affidavit.

25. Malloy affidavit, 9 May 1973, Nedzi hearings, 33–5; "Materials Relating to the Preparation of the Psychological Assessment of Daniel Ellsberg," 104-10104-10145; CIA Watergate History, 51. An unredacted version of the Malloy affidavit can be found in SSC Book 25, 12421.

26. SSC Final Report, 121.

27. Fielding affidavit, 29 April 1973, HJC Statement of Information, Book 7, Part 2, 9748.

28. Tietjen affidavit; "Meeting with Mr. David Young"; CIA Watergate History, 52–3.

29. Osborn affidavit; "Leak Data Assessment," Young to [CIA], 11 August 1971, CREST.

30. Tietjen affidavit; "Meeting with Mr. David Young"; CIA Watergate History, 52–3.

31. "Meeting with Mr. David Young."

32. Wells, *Wild Man*, 12–13.

33. "Pentagon Papers Project – Status Report as of August 11, 1971," Krogh and Young to Ehrlichman, 11 August 1971, SSC Book 6, 2644-5.

34. Ibid.

35. Malloy affidavit; "Meeting with Mr. David Young"; "Meeting with DD/S and D/MS Regarding Daniel Ellsberg," Malloy MFR, 20 August 1971, 104-10104-10145; CIA Watergate History, 53–4; Osborn affidavit.

36. Malloy affidavit.

37. CIA Watergate History, 56–7.

38. Malloy and Tietjen affidavits; The CIA Watergate History (p.52) suggests the OMS received these from Young via the Office of Security between 5–9 August.

39. Coffey is identified in the coversheet to "Robert A. Maheu and Associates," 20 January 1971, 104-10122-10301, in various documents in the CIA's

CREST database and in his obituary: "John W. Coffey, 91; CIA Communications Expert," *Washington Post,* 7 August 2008. According to "secret CIA documents" shown to Baker's staff in December 1973, Dr. Charles Bohrer and Dr. Jerrold Post also worked on the project ("Digest of Secret CIA Materials," 2–3).

40. Wells, *Wild Man,* 6–7.

41. Malloy affidavit; CIA Watergate History, 57–9.

42. CIA Watergate History, 60–1.

43. "Digest of Secret CIA Materials," referencing Coffey affidavit, 24 May 1973; Osborn affidavit; CIA Watergate History, 61–2. The CIA Watergate History dates the Coffey–Osborn conversation to mid-October.

44. Hougan, *Secret Agenda,* 48–9; Wells, *Wild Man,* 247–8.

45. CIA Watergate History, 24; Wells, *Wild Man,* 2.

46. CIA Watergate History, 32–3; "Official Routing Slip," SSC Book 8, 3380-2.

47. Helms testimony, SSC Book 8, 3233-4.

48. CIA Watergate History, 33–7.

49. "Summary of Mr. Cleo Gephart's Contacts with Mr. E. Howard Hunt," JCH Testimony of Witnesses, Book 3, 49–50; "Technical assistance," MFR, 104-10104-10144.

50. CIA Watergate History, 33–7.

51. John Warner letter to Merrill, 1163; CIA Watergate Report, 37; "TSD Support of Hunt and CIA Psychiatric Profile on Ellsberg," Madigan to Thompson and Liebengood, 12 March 1974, HSL, Box 38, Folder 10; Hunt testimony, Nedzi hearings, 492. Greenwood's affidavit states Liddy asked for the camera and was trained in its use ("Summary of Contacts by Mr. Stephen Carter Greenwood with Mr. E Howard Hunt").

52. Helms testimony, SSC Book 8, 3233-4.

53. Hunt, *Undercover,* 164–5; Wells, *Wild Man,* 2.

54. Ibid.; Hunt testimony, 28 June 1974, *US v. Ehrlichman, Liddy, Barker and Martinez,* 807, National Archives (NARA), College Park, MD.

55. CIA Watergate History, 38; "Summary of Mr. Karl Wagner's Knowledge of CIA Assistance to Mr. E. Howard Hunt."

56. "TSD Request for Guidance on Extent of Assistance to Mr. Howard Hunt," 26 August 1971, SSC Book 8, 3393.

57. CIA Watergate report, 38; "Summary of Mr. Karl Wagner's Knowledge of CIA Assistance to Mr. E. Howard Hunt." When Greenwood discussed the case with Krueger that day, "Dick said these men are not operating under our supervision and Headquarters doesn't know what they are up to. Dick wanted to see the pictures before I delivered them to Edward that afternoon." (Greenwood notes on Hunt support, CIA FOIA release F-2016-02491, 855).

58. "Materials relating to the provisioning of Howard Hunt and Gordon Liddy," 9 September 1971, 1993.07.23.14:05:32:090620.

59. Hunt, *Undercover*, 165–6; Liddy, *Will*, 225–7.

60. "Hunt/Liddy Special Project #1," Ehrlichman to Colson, 27 August 1971, SSC Book 6, 2650-1; Wells, *Wild Man*, 14.

61. Wells, *Wild Man*, 15.

62. Warner letter to Merrill, 5 September 1973, HJC Statement of Information, Book 7, Part 2, 1162-4; Hunt testimony, Nedzi report, 504; According to Schlesinger, the Tessina camera "was returned on August 27 as unsuitable" (see also CIA Watergate History, 39).

63. Warner letter to Merrill, 5 September 1973; "Helms Re-Interview Preparation—TSD Support of Hunt," HSL, Box 38, Folder 9.

64. Ibid.; Figure 3: SSC Book 9, 3871.

65. "TSD Photographs," Exhibit 146, SSC Book 9, 3861-2.

66. Baker report, 1139; "TSD Support of Hunt and CIA Psychiatric Profile on Ellsberg."

67. CIA Watergate History, 31; "TSD Photographs." Xerox copies of the photos are printed in SSC Book 9, 3863-71. I obtained new scans for Figures 3 and 4 from Special Access Staff at the National Archives.

68. "General Cushman interview of March 7, 1974," Madigan to Thompson and Liebengood, HSL, Box 38, Folder 8, 8; "TSD Support of Hunt and CIA

Psychiatric Profile on Ellsberg"; Baker report, 1139–40; Warner letter to Merrill, 5 September 1973; RCR, 181.

69. Ibid.

70. CIA Watergate History, 41; "Summary of Mr. Karl Wagner's Knowledge of CIA Assistance to Mr. E. Howard Hunt," 21 December 1972, HJC Testimony of Witnesses, Book 3, 51.

71. CIA Watergate History, 40; Memorandum for General Cushman, 27 August 1971, Book 8, 3392.

72. Ibid.

73. CIA Watergate History, 41; "Summary of Mr. Karl Wagner's Knowledge of CIA Assistance to Mr. E. Howard Hunt."

74. "Contact with Mr. E. Howard Hunt," 10 January 1973, SSC Book 8, 3391; Schlesinger statement, Nedzi report, 3.

75. CIA Watergate History, 45.

76. William Merrill, *Watergate Prosecutor* (East Lansing, MI: Michigan State University Press, 2008), 20–1; Hunt, *Undercover*, 167.

77. Ibid.

78. "Additional Request from Mr. Howard Hunt for Agency Support," 30 August 1971, SSC Book 8, 3378-9.

79. Ibid., 3377; CIA Watergate History, 41–2.

80. CIA Watergate History, 45.

81. Wells, *Wild Man*, 15; Hunt, *Undercover*, 167; Barker says Hunt visited him in Miami two weeks before the operation (Barker testimony, SSC Book 1, 375).

82. Barker testimony, SSC Book 1, 375–6; Thomas Smith, *Encyclopedia of the Central Intelligence Agency* (New York: Facts on File, 2003), 104.

83. Hunt testimony, HJC Statement of Information, Book 7, Part 2, 1106-7, cited in Wells, *Wild Man*, 2.

84. CIA Watergate History, 43; Schlesinger statement, Nedzi report, 3.

85. Wells, *Wild Man*, 2.

86. Baker report, 1163.

87. Baker report, 1142–3.

88. Baker report, 1139–40.

89. Krogh testimony, HJC Statement of Information, Book 7, Part 3, 1257-8; Wells, *Wild Man*, 14–16.

CHAPTER 5

1. Eugenio Rolando Martinez recorded interview by Timothy Naftali, 25 March 2008, Richard Nixon Oral History Project, Nixon Library; "Investigation re Eugenio Rolando Martinez," FBI 139-4089-1205. Martinez uses "Rolando" rather than the longer form, "Eugenio Rolando," so that is the version of his name used in the text.

2. Ibid.; "Presentence reports and Bureau of Prisons evaluations on Barker, Sturgis, Martinez and Gonzalez," Unsealed Materials from *US v. Liddy*, NARA, 48, 52, 89; Martinez SSCEX testimony, 11 May 1973, 269–70, Box C74, SSC Files, Center for Legislative Archives (CLA), National Archives, Washington, DC.

3. Taylor Branch and George Crile, "The Kennedy Vendetta," *Harper's*, August 1975, 61.

4. "Summaries of Four Cubans involved in Watergate," C/WH/COG to Boylan, 22 August 1973, 1993.07.20.19:43:36:500400.

5. "Presentence reports and evaluations," 47, 91.

6. Branch and Crile, "The Kennedy Vendetta," 61.

7. Eugenio Martinez, "Mission Impossible: the Watergate bunglers," *Harper's*, October 1974.

8. Branch and Crile, "The Kennedy Vendetta," 56–7.

9. Don Bohning, "CIA figure for Bay of Pigs invasion dies," *Miami Herald*, 18 October 1999; Martinez CIA FOIA release F-2014-01152, 153, The Federal Documents Research Collection, Central Texas Historical Archive, Killeen, TX.

10. Ibid.

11. Weberman interview with Esterline, August 1993, *Coup d'État in America*, Nodule 20, http://the-puzzle palace.com/files/nodule20.htm.

12. Rockefeller Commission report (RCR), 187–8; "Presentence reports and evaluations."

13. Ibid.; Martinez, "Mission Impossible."

14. Ibid.; "Watergate Incident," Osborn to Coffey and Colby, 28 June 1972, 104-10256-10265; "Thomas James Gregory," 2; CIA memo, 22 August 1973.

15. "Potential CIA involvement."

16. Gonzalez is often spelled Gonzales in CIA documents.

17. "Presentence reports and evaluations," 47, 91, 104; "Status Report as of 19 April 1974," 1993.07.13.13:01:42:250410.

18. Martinez, "Mission Impossible"; Doug Valentine, Creating a Crime: How the CIA Commandeered the DEA," *Counterpunch,* 11 September 2015; Tom Tripodi, *Crusade: Undercover Against the Mafia and KGB* (Dulles, VA: Brassey's, 1993), 148.

19. Hunt, *Undercover,* 144–5.

20. Barker testimony, SSC Book 1, 365, 370-1, 378; "Presentence reports and evaluations," 14–16.

21. Martinez SSC testimony, 11 May 1973, 281; Martinez, "Mission Impossible."

22. Martinez, "Mission Impossible"; Doug Valentine, Creating a Crime: How the CIA Commandeered the DEA," Counterpunch, 11 September 2015; Tom Tripodi, Crusade: Undercover Against the Mafia and KGB (Dulles, VA: Brassey's, 1993), 148.

23. Don Bohning, "The Watergate-Five Mystery Thriller Spins Web of Intrigue About Miami," *Miami Herald,* 25 June 1972; Martinez, "Mission Impossible"; Martinez SSCEX testimony, 10 December 1973, 44–5, Box C74, SSC Files, CLA.

24. "Presentence reports and evaluations," 12–13, 50–51; Martinez SSC testimony, 11 May 1973, 278; Martinez SSC testimony, 10 December 1973, 60.

25. "CIA and the Plumbers," Tad Szulc, *The New Republic,* 29 December 1973, 19–21; Martinez SSC testimony, 10 December 1973, 134.

26. Martinez SSC testimony, 11 May 1973, 286, 296; Martinez SSC testimony, 10 December 1973, 160, 162.

27. Barker testimony, SSC Book 1, 365; Martinez SSC testimony, 10 December 1973, 177.

28. Martinez SSC testimony, 10 December 1973, 18–9, 22. Martinez gave the Polaroid photos to Hunt.

29. Hunt testimony, Nedzi hearings, 505, 541.

30. Martinez, "Mission Impossible."

31. Ibid.

32. Martinez SSC testimony, 11 May 1973, 286, 296.

33. Wells, *Wild Man*, 29–30; Hunt, *Undercover*, 167–76.

34. Fielding affidavit, 29 April 1973, HJC Statement of Information, Book 7, Part 2, 974-8; Wells, *Wild Man*, 26.

35. "Presentence reports and evaluations," 47, 91, 104; Martinez, "Mission Impossible."

36. RCR, 188; Wells, *Wild Man*, 24; Theo Wilson, "Files Rifled as Subject Sat in Jail," *The Philadelphia Inquirer*, 7 May 1973.

37. Martinez SSC testimony, 10 December 1973, 20–21, 35–36; "Miscellaneous Testimony before the Los Angeles Grand Jury," Liebengood and Madigan to Thompson, 18 January 1974, HSL, Box 38, Folder 4, 5.

38. De Diego testimony, HJC Statement of Information, Book 7, Part 3, 1286-1291; "Ellsberg Burglary Described," Miami Herald, 11 May 1973; De Diego SSCEX testimony, 18 June 1973, 22; Fielding affidavit, 29 April 1973, HJC Statement of Information, Book 7, Part 2, 974-8.

39. Daniel Ellsberg recorded interview by Timothy J. Naftali, 20 May 2008, Richard Nixon Oral History Project, Nixon Library, 38.

40. "Digest of Lyle Miller Secret CIA Documents."

41. RCR, 189; Martinez affidavit, quoted in Szulc, "CIA and the Plumbers," 21.

42. "Digest of Lyle Miller Secret CIA Documents."

43. RCR, 194.

44. Hunt, SSC Book 9, 3676; Nedzi hearings, 609–10, 644–5; Esterline affidavit, 19 November 1973, Fielding Break-In, Box 8, "Litigation Correspondence – CIA," RG 460, Records of the Watergate Special Prosecution Force (WSPF), NARA.

45. Wells, *Wild Man*, 30–1; Hunt testimony, SSC Book 9, 3676; Hunt claims he showed Polaroid photographs of "the violated cabinets" to Krogh and Young in Room 16.

46. Nixon–Ehrlichman recording of conversation, 8 September 1971.

47. Notes on "Hunt Informal Interview," HSL, Box 38, Folder 9; Baker report, 1139–40. Before Gottlieb's meeting with Karamessines, Stephen Greenwood briefed him "on complete Bigot [Hunt] case, gave him Xerox of second man's Alias docs [Liddy] and Xerox of film prints which were developed in TSD on 27 August" (Greenwood's notes on Hunt support, CIA FOIA release F-2016-02491, 856).

48. CIA Watergate History, 71–2; "Digest of Lyle Miller Secret CIA Documents," 2; Hougan, *Secret Agenda*, 54-5; Osborn affidavit.

49. CIA Watergate History, 61-2; Malloy and Tietjen affidavits.

50. Ibid., 62–3.

51. Malloy and Tietjen affidavits; Tietjen to Coffey, 8 November 1971, HJC Statement of Information, Book 7, Part 3, 1410-11; Coffey to Helms, 9 November 1971, Ibid., 1408-9.

52. Helms testimony, Nedzi hearings, 87; Coffey to Helms, 9 November 1971.

53. Tietjen Affidavit, 9 May 1973.

54. Malloy testimony, Nedzi hearings, 36; "Points of Interest re: Cord Meyer, Jr.," Liebengood and Madigan to Thompson, 23 February 1974, HSL, Box 38, Folder 7.

55. CIA Watergate History, 47.

56. Ibid., 69.

57. RCR, 194; Martinez, "MIssion Impossible"; RCR, 194; "Digest of Lyle Miller Secret CIA Documents"; Esterline affidavit, 19 November 1973. Esterline's affidavit states Hunt's name came up in a second meeting with Martinez on 17 March, but this conflicts with Liebengood and Madigan's later analysis of CIA documents and the reference in the Rockefeller Commission Report.

58. "Miscellaneous Points of Interest Eliminated from Final Draft of CIA Summaries," Liebengood to File, 22 March 1974, HSL, Box 38, Folder 10;

"Anti-Castro Activities," 13 September 1972, 124-10281-10068; "Ejercito de Liberacion Cubano," 19 May 1972, 124-10222-10316.

59. Esterline affidavit, 19 November 1973.

60. Weberman interview with Esterline, 1993.

61. Esterline affidavit, 19 November 1973; "Status Report as of 19 April 1974 on Material Reviewed in Relation to the Watergate Break-in; Daniel Ellsberg; and Hank Greenspun," Hopkins MFR, 18 April 1974; RCR, 194–5; "Points of Interest re: Cord Meyer, Jr."; Esterline affidavit, 19 November 1972.

62. RCR, 195.

63. "Status Report as of 19 April 1974 . . ."; "Points of Interest re: Cord Meyer, Jr."; RCR, 195.

64. Weberman interview with Esterline, 1993.

65. "Points of Interest re: Cord Meyer, Jr."

66. "Digest of Lyle Miller Secret CIA Documents"; RCR, 195.

67. Martinez, "Mission Impossible"; "Digest of Lyle Miller Secret CIA Documents," 2.

68. "Baker staff chronology."

69. Martinez Oral History Interview, 25 March 2008; Author interview with St. John Hunt, 19 April 2017; Martinez SSC testimony, 10 December 1973, 10–11, 99.

70. "HSCA Request Dated 22 Mar–10 Aug 78," 1993.08.10.17:55:39:000028, 21; "Digest of Secret CIA Materials," 9; Hunt SSCEX testimony, 18 December 1972, cited in "BM—DNC," 17.

CHAPTER 6

1. "Recommendation for Honor or Merit Award for James W. McCord, Jr.," 23 July 1970, 104-10123-10391; "James Walter McCord, Jr.," Osborn to Inspector General, 22 January 1965, 104-10123-10419 ; Lukas, *Nightmare*, 171.

2. Ibid.; "Reported Involvement of James McCord in Cuban Operations While an Agency Employee," Breckenridge to Colby, 28 June 1974, 1993.07.15.20:17:15:590380; Kammer MFR, 1 February 1961,

104-10128-10300; "Court Foster Wood," 7 October 1961, 104-10114-10162; John Newman, *Oswald and the CIA*, (New York: Skyhorse Publishing, 2008), 240-1; Gaynor testimony, Nedzi hearings, 169.

3. "Recommendation for Honor or Merit Award for James W. McCord, Jr.,"; "Summary of Agency Employment of James W. McCord, Jr.," undated, 104-10123-10382; "James Walter McCord, Jr."; "Senate Select Committee on Intelligence Operations, Request," Kane to Inspector General, 22 May 1975, 104-10123-10364; "Honor Recommendation for James W. McCord, Jr.," 4 August 1966, 104-10123-10407.

4. Ibid.

5. "Proprietaries," 1976, 157-10014-10144, 90-4.

6. Operation MERRIMACK PLAN (Remainder of FY—1968)," "Projects CHAOS/MERRIMAC/RESISTANCE," The Black Vault, 400-2; Church Committee, 682; RCR, 152–5.

7. Family Jewels, 29–30. The redacted name of the proprietary seems too short for Anderson Security Associates but, apart from the date, the description matches Osborn's testimony about them precisely.

8. "Summary of an interview with Howard Osborn," Robert Olsen to File, Commission on CIA Activities Within the United States, 13 February 1975.

9. "Entry into Democratic National Headquarters," undated, 104-10256-10268; Weberman and Canfield, *Coup d'État in America*, Nodule X31, www.archive .org; 104-10111-10157; H. P. Albarelli, Jr., *A Secret Order* (Trine Day, 2012), Chapter 3 footnotes.

10. "Project Resistance," Memo for Chief, Security Research Staff, 8 December 1967 and "Operation RESISTANCE," Deputy Director of Security (IOS) to Director of Security, "Projects CHAOS/MERRIMAC/RESISTANCE," The Black Vault, 229-230, 265-6; Church Committee Report, 681; RCR, 152-5; "Questionable Activities," Warner MFR, 8 January 1975, 104-10107-10031.

11. "Summary of an interview with Howard Osborn"; RCR, 155; "Questionable Activities"; "Operation RESISTANCE," 2 May 1968. "CI/CE" means Counterintelligence/Counterespionage.

12. "Watergate—Frank A. O'Malley," Evans and Howe MFR, 21 February 1974, 104-10103-10042.

13. Jack Anderson, "St. Clair Partner Was CIA Front Man," *Washington Post*, 22 July 1974.

14. Ibid.; Hugh Wilford, *The Mighty Wurlitzer: How the CIA Played America* (Cambridge, MA: Harvard University Press, 2009), 180.

15. "McCord, James W., Jr., OP," 104-10224-10006, 3–4, 9, 17, 20, 22.

16. "Family Jewels," Osborn to Colby, 16 May 1973, CREST, 2–3, 576–581, 646–59; "The CIA's Family Jewels," 21 June 2007, The National Security Archive, https://nsarchive2.gwu.edu.

17. "Loan of CIA Employees to Other Government Agencies for Activities Within the United States," 14 January 1972, CREST.

18. Ibid.

19. "Entry into Democratic National Headquarters," 104-10256-10268; HJC Testimony of Witnesses, Book 3, 44; Gaynor testimony, Nedzi hearings, 171–2; "Bernard L. Barker et al," SA Leman Stafford, Jr. to SAC, Miami, 19 June 1972, 139-4089-22; "Report on Plots to Assassinate Fidel Castro," Harman MFR, 23 May 1967, 104-10213-10101.

20. Lukas, *Nightmare*, 171.

21. "Entry into Democratic National Headquarters."

22. Heath FBI interview, 5 July 1972; Ruiz FBI interview, 29 June 1972, 139-4089-642.

23. "Watergate Incident," 104-10256-10265; "Entry into Democratic National Headquarters," 104-10256-10268.

24. Ibid.; "Information Provided the Federal Bureau of Investigation Regarding the Watergate Incident," Walters to Gray, 6 July 1972, 104-10256-10273; "Watergate Incident," 13 July 1972, 104-10256-10269; FBI Teletype, Baltimore to Acting Director, 26 June 1972, 139-4089-206. In late June 1972, his landlady said he had been rooming with her for six months. This contradicts the later date of 21 April 1972 given in one CIA summary.

25. Sedam FBI interviews, 23 and 27 June 1972, 139-166-131, 139-166-335.

26. James W. McCord, *A Piece of Tape: The Watergate Story – Fact and Fiction* (Rockville, MD: Washington Media Services, 1974), 12.

27. SSC Final Report, 17-8.

28. "Witness Summary—James W. McCord, Jr.," 1; McCord, *A Piece of Tape*, 11–13.

29. McCord, *A Piece of Tape*, 15; Lukas, *Nightmare*, 171.

30. Notes on "Linda Jones interview," HSL, Box 38, Folder 6; Baker report, 1121; "Watergate—Frank A. O'Malley," 104-10103-10042; "Robert A. Maheu: OS/SAG Files Provided to the HSCA," 1993.07.21.08:41:43:590620; Family Jewels, 107; CIA Watergate History, 75; FBI report on Jack Bouman, 124-10289-10440, 44.

31. Liddy, *Will*, 267, 271–6: Hougan, *Secret Agenda*, 55.

32. Lukas, *Nightmare*, 171–3; SSC Final Report, 21.

33. Lukas, *Nightmare*, 173–4 ; Dean testimony, SSC Book 3, 929-30; Magruder testimony, SSC Book 2, 789-90. The dates of Liddy's meetings with Mitchell, Magruder and Dean were January 27 and February 4. While Dean and Magruder agree these were the targets discussed, Mitchell denied it and Liddy insisted DNC headquarters was not mentioned in any of the three proposals he prepared for Mitchell (Rosen, *The Strong Man*, 280; "Behemoth Manuscript—DNC," 7, 65, Box 80, Folder 1, JRP).

34. "Thomas James Gregory," Moore to Lenzner, 30 October 1973, HSL, Box 38, Folder 3; SSC Final Report, 196.

35. SSC Final Report, 24–5; Magruder testimony, SSC Book 2, 795; "Witness Summary—James W. McCord, Jr.," 2. Mitchell later denied approving the plan. On March 8, at Liddy's request, Hunt set up a meeting with Colson, and Liddy complained they couldn't get Mitchell to approve the Gemstone plan. Colson picked up the phone to Magruder and told him "to get off the stick and get the budget approved for Mr. Liddy's plans" (Hunt testimony, SSC Book 9, 3684). To his dying day, Mitchell denied approving the plan at the meeting with Magruder and Fred LaRue in Key Biscayne on March 30 (Rosen, *The Strong Man*, 269–75).

36. SSC Final Report, 27, 197; "Thomas James Gregory."

37. Hougan, *Secret Agenda*, 111-5, 172-4; Len Colodny and Robert Gettlin, *Silent Coup: The Removal of a President* (New York: St. Martin's Press, 1991), 126–30, 143–6; Ray Locker, *Nixon's Gamble: How a President's Own Secret Government Destroyed His Administration* (Guilford, CT: Lyons Press, 2015), 172; Jim Hougan, "Hougan, Liddy, the Post and Watergate," 22 June 2011, jimhougan.com; Maureen Dean, *Mo: A Woman's View of* Watergate (New York: Bantam Books, 1976), 33–42.

38. Phil Stanford, *White House Call Girl* (Port Townsend, WA: Feral House, 2013), 81–3; Hougan, *Secret Agenda*, 118.

39. Thompson, *At That Point in Time*, 211; Hougan, *Secret Agenda*, 82, 137n, 116–8, 121; Russell FBI interview, 29 June 1972, 139-166-443.

40. Hougan, *Secret Agenda*, 112–7, 172–4; Colodny and Gettlin, *Silent Coup*, 126–30, 143–6; Locker, *Nixon's Gamble*, 172; Stanford, *White House Call Girl*, 74.

41. Author interview with Spencer Oliver, 20 July 2018.

42. "A Conversation with Secretary General Spencer Oliver," 7 October 2015, William and Mary, https://events.wm.edu/event/view/wm/61224; Oliver interview with author. Ida Wells was Oliver's first secretary at the DNC. He already had a secretary at the ACYPL, which was given office space in the Atlantic Council of the United States.

43. Ibid.; Colodny and Gettlin, *Silent Coup*, 132; Hougan, *Secret Agenda*, 116–7; Stanford, *White House Call Girl*, 85; Wells deposition in *Dean v. St. Martin's Press*, 7 June 1996, Colodny Collection; Oliver interview with author.

44. Hougan, *Secret Agenda*, 111–2; Locker, *Nixon's Gamble*, 171; Hougan, "Hougan, Liddy, the Post and Watergate."

45. "Witness Summary—James W. McCord, Jr.," Box C75, CLA, 3; McCord, *A Piece of Tape*, 17-9; Lukas, *Nightmare*, 190-1; Transcript of interview with Alfred Baldwin" by Jack Nelson and Ronald Ostrow (*Los Angeles Times*), 3 October 1972, RG 21, Unsealed Materials from *US v. Liddy*, Box 1, Folder 13, NARA; McCord deposition, *DNC v. McCord*, 30 April 1974, 41-4, 101, JRP; Liddy, *Will*, 302-3. In his book, Hunt dates the "clay impression" to May 24 (Hunt, *Undercover*, 222).

46. Rotonda, *The Watergate*, 2–4, 116, 123; *LIFE magazine*, 8 August 1969, 40–47.

47. "Alfred C. Baldwin, III," Freedman to Rotunda, 9 December 1973, Box B418, SSC Files, CLA; FBI Watergate summary, 74; Forsberg FBI interview, 6 July 1972, 139-166-745.

48. "Investigation into The Assault on Anti-War Demonstrators on the Capitol Steps on May 3, 1972," Akerman to Files, 5 June 1975.

49. McCord, *A Piece of Tape*, 16.

50. "Presentence reports and evaluations," 76; "Investigation into The Assault on Anti-War Demonstrators on the Capitol Steps on May 3, 1972," 1.

51. "Investigation into The Assault on Anti-War Demonstrators on the Capitol Steps on May 3, 1972," 6.

52. Ibid., 11–12.

53. "Presentence reports and evaluations," 51; Martinez SSC testimony, 11 May 1973, 290–1.

54. "Investigation into The Assault on Anti-War Demonstrators on the Capitol Steps on May 3, 1972," 5; "Presentence reports and evaluations," 76.

55. Daniel Ellsberg affidavit, HSCA Exhibit MLK F 430, AARC Library, 21–22; Daniel Arkin, "Daniel Ellsberg: Nixon White House Wanted to 'Shut Me Up' With Assault," *NBC News*, 19 June 2017; Daniel Ellsberg, *Secrets: A Memoir of Vietnam and the Pentagon Papers* (New York: Viking, 2003), 451–2.

56. "Presentence reports and evaluations," 13, 51, 76.

57. SSC Final report, 27, 197; "Witness Summary—James W. McCord, Jr.," 3; Hunt, *Undercover*, 210; "Presentence reports and evaluations" 63–4; Gregory interview, 5238; McCord, *A Piece of Tape,* 22.

58. Martinez, "Mission Impossible"; Lukas, *Nightmare*, 196-7; SSC Final Report, 28, 37, 514; Baker chronology; Robert Ritchie affidavit, 19 November 1973, Fielding Break-In, Box 8, "Litigation Correspondence – CIA," WSPF Records, NARA.

59. "Howard Hunt," Colson MFR, 20 June 1972, Nedzi hearings, 613–4; "Interview with Bill Bittman," Colson MFR, 5 January 1973, Nedzi hearings, 639–40; Colson testimony, Nedzi hearings, 648-9.

60. St. John Hunt, *Bond of Secrecy* (Walterville, OR: Trine Day, 2012), xiii-xiv.

61. "Administrative Files on E. Howard Hunt's Post-Employment Relationship," 113.

62. Ibid., 45, 48; Family Jewels, 170, 432.

63. Ibid., 113.

64. "Movie or TV Series on CIA Based on Books by Mr. David St. John," Isenstead to Deputy Inspector General, 104-10119-10305.

65. "Demonstrations and Violence," Box C75, SSC Files, CLA; "Alfred C. Baldwin, III"; *US v. Liddy*, Grand Jury indictment, 15 September 1972, HJC Statement of Information, Book 2, 90.

66. McCord, *A Piece of Tape*, 19–20.

67. Baldwin testimony, SSC Book 1, 412.

68. SSC Final report, 27, 197; "Witness Summary—James W. McCord, Jr.," 3; Hunt, *Undercover*, 210; "Presentence reports and evaluations," 63–4; "Thomas James Gregory"; McCord, *A Piece of Tape*, 22.

69. SSC Final Report, 129.

70. "Editorial Note," *FRUS*, 1969–1976, Volume XXI, Chile, 1969–1973, Document 300; "Chile Embassy Burglarized," *Washington Post*, 17 May 1972; Family Jewels, 384.

71. Memorandum from Levinson to Church, February 28, 1973, Digital National Security Archives, cited in FRUS, 1969–1976, Volume XXI, Chile, 1969–1973, Document 300; 104-10256-10273; 104-10256-10269; 104-10256-10265; "Entry into Democratic National Headquarters," 104-10256-10268; FBI Watergate Files 2, 250.

72. Martinez, "Mission Impossible"; Lukas, *Nightmare*, 196–7; SSC Final Report, 28; McCord testimony, SSC Book 1, 211.

73. "Alfred C. Baldwin, III"; Martinez, "Mission Impossible."

74. "McGovern National Headquarters," Box C76, SSC Files, CLA.

75. Ibid.

76. Martinez, "Mission Impossible."

77. Ibid.; McCord, *A Piece of Tape*, 24.

78. Ibid.

79. Ibid.; "Witness Summary—James W. McCord, Jr.," 3 Hunt, *Undercover*, 227.

80. SSC Final Report, 28-9; McCord, SSC Book 1, 157; McCord, *A Piece of Tape*, 25. Early press accounts suggested the O'Brien tap was installed on the phone of O'Brien's secretary Fay Abel, who sat outside his office, but I found no evidence to support this ("Break-In," *New York Times*, 22 July 1973).

81. Ibid.

82. Colodny and Gettlin, *Silent Coup*, 137–8; Barrett interview, *The Key to Watergate* (1992), cited in "BM—DNC," 58fn137. In a 1994 interview, Baldwin states: "From the conversations I had with Jim, I was led to believe that the second unit had been placed in the extreme left-hand room in the front of the [DNC]. This was a room occupied by the Deputy Chairman and not the Chairman." McCord had a basic floor plan but didn't seem to know where O'Brien's office was until after Baldwin's tour of the DNC on June 12 (Transcript of Baldwin interview for *Watergate* TV series, 49, 55, Lapping Watergate Collection, Senate House Library Archives, University of London). In his second meeting with Hunt, McCord claimed Hunt sketched a plan of the break-in on a yellow legal pad that was later found in his safe. During the first entry, McCord found O'Brien's office locked and decided to "put a device on the telephone call directory that sat on his secretary's desk . . . and pick up his line off of that . . . My task on the second mission was to actually get into Larry O'Brien's office this time. To put a device on his phone. To take a look at the call directory and see if I could figure out why that one wasn't working." (Transcript of McCord interview for *Watergate* TV series, Roll 319, 20; Roll 320, 1, 11, 14). These accounts are interesting but don't reflect either man's sharper recall and testimony in the immediate aftermath of Watergate.

83. Lawrence F. O'Brien Oral History Interview XXXII, 11 December 1987, by Michael L. Gillette, LBJ Library, 8.

84. Notes on "Linda Jones interview"; Baker report, 1123; Oliver interview with author.

85. Hunt, *Undercover*, 142; Oliver interview with author.

86. "A Conversation with Spencer Oliver," William and Mary, https://events.wm
.edu/event/view/wm/61224; "Exchanges," ACYPL, https://www.acypl.org
/calendars/exchanges/; Hunt SSCEX testimony, 10 September 1973, 14-17;
"Behemoth Manuscript—DNC," 30fn67. In 1977, CIA's Office of Legislative
Counsel assured a Congressional committee member that "CIA was not
involved in the group" ("Journal Office of Legislative Counsel," 21 April
1977, CREST).

87. Oliver interview with author.

88. McCord, *A Piece of Tape*, 26; "Witness Summary—James W. McCord, Jr.,"
3–4; SSC Final Report, 27–8.

89. Martinez, "Mission Impossible."

90. Thomas McGillicuddy FBI interview, 28 June 1972.

91. McCord interview with Fred Thompson, 9 May 1973 and "Witness
Summary—James W. McCord, Jr.," Box C75, SSC Files, CLA.

92. *US v. Liddy*, Grand Jury indictment. Figure 5: Exhibit 6, *US v. Liddy et al.*,
C.R. 1827-72, RG 21, NARA, College Park, MD. Ida Wells confirmed the
phone had three lines in her trial testimony (Wells testimony in *US v. Liddy*,
26 January 1973, 1880).

93. Hougan, *Secret Agenda*, 162–3; Liddy, *Will*, 322. McCord subsequently
bought the jack adaptors to make taping possible but didn't think it was
necessary (McCord deposition in *DNC v. McCord*, 1 May 1973, 160, 246).

94. SSC Final Report, 29.

95. Liddy, *Will*, 322-3; Transcript of Baldwin *Los Angeles Times* interview, 3
October 1972, 48, 104.

96. Ibid.; Baldwin deposition, July 25–6, 1996; Transcript of Baldwin interview
for *Watergate* TV series, 47; Earl Silbert recorded interview by Timothy Naftali, 17 September 2008, Richard Nixon Oral History Project, Nixon Library.

97. Transcript of In Camera Proceedings, 17 January 1973, Unsealed Materials
from *U.S. v. Liddy*, Box 1, Folder 8, 31, NARA; Baldwin FBI interview,
10 July 1972, 139-4089-745; 18 U.S. Code § 2515; *United States v. United*

States District Court (1972), No. 70-153. John P. MacKenzie, "Court Curbs U.S. Wiretaps," *Washington Post*, 20 June 1972. Sanford J. Ungar, "Ellsberg Wiretap Inquiry is Set." *Washington Post*, 21 June 1972. A week later, the Supreme Court "upheld the right of grand jury witnesses to refuse to answer questions which are based on illegal government wiretapping and bugging" (John P. MacKenzie, "Military Snooping Wins Test," *Washington Post*, 27 June 1972).

98. Lukas, *Nightmare*, 201; Hougan, "Hougan, Liddy, the Post and Watergate"; Hougan, *Secret Agenda*, 174-5.

99. Colodny and Gettlin, *Silent Coup*, 138-9; Lukas, *Nightmare*, 201; Hougan, *Secret Agenda*, 174.

100. Transcript of Baldwin *Los Angeles Times* interview, 3 October 1972; Baldwin testimony, SSC Book 1, 400-1, 410; McCord, SSC Book 1, 157, 232-3; Memorandum for File, 18 April 1973, Box C75, SSC Files, CLA.

101. "Watergate–Frank A. O'Malley," 104-10103-10042; "Entry into Democratic National Headquarters," 23 June 1972, 104-10256-10268; FBI Teletype, Alexandria to Acting Director, 25 July 1972, 139-4089-794.

102. Hougan, *Secret Agenda*, 185.

103. Thompson, *At That Point in Time*, 211; Hougan, *Secret Agenda*, 82, 137n; Russell FBI interview, 29 June 1972, 139-166-443; "Jack Anderson, McCord MFR, undated, CLA, Box C130; McCord notes, Nedzi hearings, 840–2.

104. Magruder testimony, SSC Book 2, 796-7; Lukas, *Nightmare*, 202. Magruder, *An American Life*, 210. According to Liddy, he met Mitchell and Magruder on June 15, left two sealed envelopes of intercept logs on Mitchell's desk and told him, "The problem we have will be corrected this weekend, sir." Liddy claims Mitchell didn't look at them (Liddy, *Will*, 328-9). Mitchell denied receiving or discussing the logs and called Magruder's account "a palpable, damnable lie" ("BM—DNC," 39fn91, 41-42).

105. SSC Final Report, 29–30.

106. "Mr. Martinez," Osborn to Parham, 20 June 1972, printed in SSC Book 9, 3426-7; Baker staff chronology.

107. McCord testimony, SSC Book 1, 200; "Security of the Doral Beach Hotel, Miami Beach, Florida, for Convention Purposes," McCord to Odle, 14 June 1972, Box C130, SSC files, CLA.

108. Family Jewels, 141.

109. SSC Final Report, 166.

110. Hunt testimony, SSC Book 9, 3688, 3786; McCord testimony, SSC Book 1, 185.

111. Hunt testimony, Nedzi hearings, 520; Hougan, *Secret Agenda*, 156.

112. Hunt testimony, SSC Book 9, 3796; Lukas, *Nightmare*, 201; 124-10289-10440: Fred Emery, *Watergate* (Simon and Schuster, 1995), 128. The National Archives cannot locate any of these photographs today.

113. Hougan, *Secret Agenda*, 157; "James McCord, Jr. and others, Burglary of Democratic Party National Headquarters, June 17, 1972, Interception of Communications," Bates to Bolz, 22 June 1972, printed in Nedzi hearings, 216-7; FBI Teletype, Miami to Washington, 22 June 1972, 139-4089-18.

114. Martinez, "Mission Impossible"; Gene Miller, "Miamian: I Developed Demo Break-in Film," *Miami Herald*, 1 September 1972).

115. "Eugenio Martinez," MFR, 22 August 1973, 1993.07.20.19:43:36:500400; Baker staff chronology; *US v. Liddy*, Grand Jury indictment.

116. Ibid.; Colodny and Gettlin, *Silent Coup*, 143–6; Locker, *Nixon's Gamble*, 172; Hougan, *Secret Agenda*, 121, 172–4. Dean denies copying the address book. His diary lists Trent as his second last call of the day (Stanford, *White House Call Girl*, 118).

117. SSC Final Report, 30–1.

118. Ibid., 32; McCord testimony, SSC Book 1, 157.

119. Hougan, "Hougan, Liddy, The Post and Watergate"; Liddy, *Will*, 325–6; Hunt, *Undercover*, 232–3.

120. This account is based on the following Baldwin testimony or interviews within a year of the Watergate arrests: Baldwin FBI interview, 10 June 1972, 139-4089-745; "Interview with 'Al'" (Baldwin interview with Alan Galbraith), 28 August 1972, JRP Box 33–1; "Interview with Baldwin in New

Haven . . .", 11 October 1972, JRP Box 33–1; Transcript of Baldwin *Los Angeles Times* interview, 3 October 1972; Baldwin testimony, *US v. Liddy*, 19 and 22 January 1973; Baldwin testimony, SSC Book 1, 401–2. See also "Alfred C. Baldwin, III"; Lukas, *Nightmare*, 202–3; Thompson, *At That Point in Time*, 210–11; Transcript of Baldwin interview for Watergate TV series, 52.

121. Wells deposition, 7 June 1996, 35–41, 238–41.

122. Ibid., 148–9.

123. Baldwin deposition in *Dean v. Liddy*, 26 July 1996, 306–7.

124. Liddy, *Will*, 325–6; Hunt, *Undercover*, 232–3.

125. "Witness Summary—James W. McCord, Jr.," 3–4.

126. Bennett testimony, Nedzi hearings, 1087–90, 1108–9.

127. Colodny and Gettlin, *Silent Coup*, 149–154; Hougan, *Secret Agenda*, 173; Stanford, *White House Call Girl*, 115–7, 121–3, 171fn81.

CHAPTER 7

1. "Presentence reports and evaluations," 47, 90; Jack Anderson, "Forgotten in Watergate: Four Cubans," *Washington Post*, 13 August 1973; Martinez SSC testimony, 11 May 1973, 301; Martinez interview, *Watergate* TV series.

2. McCord testimony, SSC Book 1, 203–5; Edwin Diamond, "November Song," *New York*, 6 November 1972, 8.

3. Anderson interview, 1994, 7–9; Jack Anderson, *Peace, War and Politics* (New York: Forge, 1999), 245–7; "Counter-Espionage Agent for the Republicans," Nedzi hearings, 838.

4. "The Mysterious A. J. Woolston-Smith Is the Low-Profile New York Private Eye Who Predicted the Watergate Break-in," *Washington Post*, 17 February 1980; Jim Matheny, "Watergate scandal began in Knoxville man's DC office," *KBIR*, 16 June 2017; "Advance Knowledge/Double Agent Investigation Draft Report," HSL, Box 35, Folder 8.

5. Hougan, *Secret Agenda*, 79, 82; Thompson, *At That Point in Time*, 211, 221–2.

6. "Entry into Democratic National Headquarters," 104-10256-10268.

7. Ibid.; "Volume 1: Support Documents for the Helms Hearing at HSCA," OLC to Darby, HSCA, 9 August 1978, 104-10406-10112, 27.

8. In a 1990 interview, Martinez implies he took a later flight from Miami and caught up with the other burglars (Martinez interview with Colodny and Becker, 1 May 1990, Colodny Collection, 4).

9. Martinez, "Mission Impossible"; Nedzi report, 12; Lukas, *Nightmare*, 204; McCord, *A Piece of Tape*, 28–9.

10. Martinez, "Mission Impossible"; Lukas, *Nightmare*, 204.

11. "Watergate Incident," 104-10256-10265; FBI Watergate summary, 17. Anderson had also met Hunt in Mexico ten years earlier, when Hunt visited the family home (Anderson FBI interview, 30 June 1972, 139-4089-2090; Lano report, 5 July 1972, 139-4089-811).

12. Hougan, *Secret Agenda*, 185–6, citing FBI interview with Gleason, 1 July 1972, 139-4089-449; WFO [FBI Washington Field Office] to Acting Director, 5 July 1972, 139-4089-432.

13. Lukas, *Nightmare*, 204; Hougan, *Secret Agenda*, 187–9. McCord thought Hunt did the first taping but Barker says it was Sturgis.

14. Ibid., 205; SSC Final Report, 1–2.

15. "Witness Summary—James W. McCord, Jr."; Baldwin testimony, SSC Book 1, 402.

16. Martinez, "Mission Impossible."

17. SSC Final Report, 1–2; Leeper testimony, SSC Book 1, 96.

18. Shoffler testimony, SSC Book 1, 118.

19. Martinez testimony, 11 May 1973, 293–4; McCord, *A Piece of Tape*, 30–1.

20. Colodny and Gettlin, *Silent Coup*, 157; Baldwin testimony, SSC Book 1, 404.

21. Ibid.; Leeper, Barrett and Shoffler testimony, SSC Book 1, 104, 112, 120. Figure 6: *US v. Liddy*, RG21, NARA, Exhibit 5.

22. Ibid.

23. Baldwin testimony, SSC Book 1, 404; Lukas, *Nightmare*, 208.

24. Leeper, Barrett and Shoffler testimony, SSC Book 1, 104, 115, 120; Baldwin testimony, Ibid., 412.

25. Colodny and Gettlin, *Silent Coup*, 157–9; FBI Marie Cunningham interview, 27 June 1972, 139-166-359. Shoffler later claimed he found a camera clamp set up on Maxie Wells' desk on June 17 but according the police evidence inventory, all photographic equipment, including both cameras, was in Martinez' bag at the time of the arrests and no photos were taken that night (Barrett testimony, *US v. Liddy*, 16 January 1973, 679; Shoffler depositions, *Dean v. Liddy*, 13 March 1995, 32–3 and 15 March 1995, 434–6). A recent photo of Exhibit 14-D, the key taped to the notebook, can be found in the photo section. Wells' calendar entry for June 17 reads: "DNC robbed. Watched TV. Jay Hodge called re key—NY" (Wells calendar, Box 47-2, JRP; "BM—DNC," 60, JRP).

26. SSC Final Report, 1–2, 31; "Alfred C. Baldwin, III"; Thompson, *At That Point in Time*, 210; Baldwin testimony, SSC Book 1, 405–6.

27. SSC Final Report, 31.

28. McCord, *A Piece of Tape*, 33–4; SSC Final Report, 1206; McCord testimony, SSC Book 1, 128–9.

29. Lukas, *Nightmare*, 204. McCord thought Hunt did the previous taping but Barker says it was Sturgis; Martinez, "Mission Impossible."

30. "Witness Summary—James W. McCord, Jr."; FBI Watergate summary, 70–1; Lukas, *Nightmare*, 212–3. ; "Burglary at Democratic National Headquarters," 139-4089-2285, 2; Bolz to Bates, 8 September 1972, 139-4089-1125; McCord deposition, *DNC v. McCord*, 30 April 1973, 173.

31. "SA Lano to SAC, WFO," 5 July 1972, 139-4089, Volume 12; Handwritten FBI notes on the Watergate arrests, 17 June 1972, 139-4089, Volume 16; Shoffler and Greigg trial testimony in *US v. Liddy*, 16 and 24 January 1973; Shoffler deposition in *Dean v. St. Martin's Press*, 13 March 1995, 34; FBI Teletype to Acting Director, 15 August 1972. 139-4089-904. I examined the notebook and other exhibits in *US v. Liddy* during a visit to the National Archives, College Park, MD, in May 2018.

32. McCord, *A Piece of Tape*, 32; Lukas, *Nightmare*, 212–3.

33. Hougan, *Secret Agenda*, 183–7, 192, 207–8; Russell FBI interview, 5 July 1972, 139-166-806. On June 16, Russell dined alone in the restaurant "for sentimental reasons." It was where he first met Ruth Thorne, allegedly a prostitute at the Columbia Plaza, who had helped him battle alcoholism as he tried to help her out of prostitution (Russell FBI interview, 5 July 1972, 139-166-806; Birely deposition in *Dean v. St. Martin's Press*, 17 July 1996, 14–15). For a detailed account of McCord's unexplained delays and absences on the night of the break-in, and possible liaison with Russell, see Hougan, *Secret Agenda*, 181–201.

34. Martinez SSC testimony, 11 May 1973, 273–4; Hunt, *Undercover*, 2246–50; "Presentence reports and evaluations," 77–8. Baldwin claims he heard Hunt call a lawyer from the motel room.

35. McCord, *A Piece of Tape*, 32; Baldwin testimony, SSC Book 1, 409.

36. "Presentence reports and evaluations," 77–8.

37. Lukas, *Nightmare*, 215–6; Liddy, *Will*, 343–7; Magruder testimony, SSC Book 2, 798.

38. Martinez testimony, 11 May 1973, 295; "SA Lano to SAC, WFO," 5 July 1972; Lukas, *Nightmare*, 212–3; "Eugenio Martinez Telephone Directory," HJC Statement of Information, Book 2, 493; Barker address book, *US v. Liddy*, RG21, NARA.

39. "Presentence reports and evaluations," 92–3.

40. Hougan, *Secret Agenda*, 82.

41. Bittenbender FBI interview, 18 July 1972, 10, 98–100; Hougan, *Secret Agenda*, 218–9.

42. Gleason FBI interview, 3 July 1972.

43. Baker report, 1157.

44. Ibid.; SSC Final Report, 31; HJC, Book 2, 93; "SA Lano to SAC, WFO," 5 July 1972; Colodny and Gettlin, *Silent Coup*, 159.

45. CIA Watergate History, 76.

46. "Interview of FBI Agents Parham and Wilson," Madigan and Liebengood to Thompson, 11 January 1974, HSL, Box 38, Folder 2; CIA FOIA release F-2016-02491, 13.

47. Richard Helms, *A Look Over My Shoulder* (New York: Random House, 2003), 3–4.

48. Ibid., 4–5.

49. "Tape Labeled "McCord Incident, 18-19 June 1972," 1 March 1974, CIA FOIA release F-2016-02491."

50. "Helms Re-Interview Preparation—Notification," undated, HSL, Box 38, Folder 9; "Minutes of DD/S staff meeting," 20 June 1972, CREST; Baker report, 1148; FBI Teletype, Miami to Acting Director, 17 June 1972, 139-4089-2.

51. FBI Teletype, Washington Field to Acting Director, 17 June 1972, 139-4089-9.

52. FBI Teletype, Alexandria to Acting Director, 17 June 1972, 139-4089-10.

53. "Minutes of DD/S staff meeting," 20 June 1972, CREST; Baker report, 1148.

54. Baker report, 1154; "Tape Labeled 'McCord Incident,' 18-19 June 1972"; Thompson, *At That Point in Time*, 159. The five-inch reel of tape was located in the Office of Security on March 1, 1974.

55. FBI Watergate summary, 17; Gleason and Houston FBI interviews, 3 and 5 July 1972, 139-4089-449.

56. Hougan, *Secret Agenda*, 236–9. Hougan calls Rikan "Tess"; "Advance Knowledge/Double Agent Investigation Draft Report," HSL, Box 35, Folder 8; "Summary of Stewart Executive Session, 10/4/73," Liebengood to Thompson, 24 October 1973; "William C. Birely," Schultz to File, 28 August 1973, HSL, Box 35, Folder 6.

57. Walter Pincus, "A Watergate Mystery: Was There a Second 'Deep Throat?'" *Washington Post*, 28 June 1992.

58. FBI Watergate summary, 77.

59. Bob Woodward, "O'Brien Sues GOP Campaign," *Washington Post*, 21 June 1972; Pincus, "A Watergate Mystery . . ."; Oliver interview with author.

60. Lukas, *Nightmare*, 222–3, 226; John Dean, *Blind Ambition* (New York: Simon and Schuster, 1976), 96–100; John Dean, *The Nixon Defense* (New York: Penguin, 2014), 9; Liddy, *Will*, 353.

61. Shoffler deposition, 13 March 1995, 32–4, 36–7, 515–6, 606; Wells deposition in *Dean v. St. Martin's Press*, 7 June 1996, 97-8. Oliver also told me there was nothing of importance in the drawer (Oliver interview with author).

62. Martinez SSCEX testimony, 10 December 1973, 94-7; Untitled and undated document, 157-10011-10084.

63. Ibid.; Baker report, 1149.

64. Family Jewels, 296, 353.

65. Helms, *A Look Over My Shoulder*, 5–6, 425.

66. Hougan, *Secret Agenda*, 220–1.

67. "Possible Taped Conversations at CIA," Madigan and Liebengood to Baker, 14 February 1974, HSL, Box 38, Folder 7, 3; Hougan, *Secret Agenda*, 110, 220–1.

68. "Digest of Secret CIA Materials," 8; "Interview of Agents Parham and Wilson," Madigan and Liebengood to Thompson, 11 January 1974, HSL, Box 38, Folder 2, 2–3.

69. "Interview with Karl Wagner," Madigan and Liebengood to Thompson, 5 March 1974, HSL, Box 38, Folder 7; "Digest of Secret CIA Materials," 4.

70. "Dear Friend" letter, 'Security File on Frank Sturgis, 1993.08.05.14:42:12:750028. A reference to the letter in the Baker report identifies its author as Shackley (Baker report, 1148).

71. Bennett testimony, Nedzi hearings, 1091.

72. Ibid., 1091–2.

73. "James A. Everett," Breckenridge MFR, 104-10059-10231.

74. Ibid.

75. Carl Bernstein and Bob Woodward, *All the President's Men* (London: Pocket Books, 2006), 11–12; Colodny and Gettlin, *Silent Coup*, 285.

76. Bernstein and Woodward, *All the President's Men*, 12.

77. Ibid., 14.

78. Ibid.

79. Bennett testimony, Nedzi hearings, 1092-3; "Presentence reports and evaluations," 77–8.

80. Jeb Magruder, *An American Life: One Man's Road to Watergate* (New York: Atheneum, 1974), 268. Magruder was alarmed when he found a transcript of a call between CRP's Harry Flemming and Spencer Oliver in the Liddy material. "My God! Flemming's a double agent!" he thought, but the call related to the American Council of Young Political Leaders. Flemming and Oliver were president and vice president respectively (Ibid., 248).

81. Family Jewels, 296, 353; Helms testimony, Senate Hearings on Nomination of Richard Helms to be Ambassador to Iran, 21 May 1973, 25.

82. "Minutes of DD/S staff meeting," 20 June 1972, CREST.

83. Helms testimony before the Senate Committee on Foreign Relations, 20 May 1972, cited in Helms nomination hearing to be Ambassador to Iran, 95.

84. "Entry into Democratic National Headquarters," 23 June 1972, 104-10256-10268; "Watergate Incident – Status Report," Osborn to Deputy Director for Support (Coffey), 26 June 1972, 1993.07.21.17:44:12:280440; "Watergate Incident," 104-10256-10265; "Watergate Incident Report," 13 July 1972, 104-10256-10269.

85. Bennett testimony, Nedzi hearings, 1093–5, 1109.

86. Baker report, 1148–9; "Digest of Lyle Miller Secret CIA Documents"; "Status Report as of 19 April 1974"; Weberman interview with Esterline.

87. Jean Martinez FBI interview, 22 June 1972, 139-4089-1205.

88. Walters to Gray, 6 July 1972; Osborn memos to Parham, 20 June 1972, JCH Testimony of Witnesses, Book 3, 14–5, 19–20.

89. Carl Rowan, "CIA's Involvement Appalling," *Washington Star-News*, 11 May 1973, published in Helms nomination hearings, 21 May 1973, 59–60.

90. Lukas, *Nightmare*, 226–7; Dean testimony, SSC Book 3, 937–8. The .25 caliber Colt automatic pistol found in Hunt's safe belonged to his wife Dorothy. The safe also contained photographs of an Argentinian she had met in Tokyo and a Uruguayan she had met in Montevideo and letters she had exchanged with them. In the late fifties and early sixties, Hunt was having extramarital affairs, so she "sought solace" through affairs of her own. When Hunt found out in the early sixties, she gave the photos and letters to him to destroy and

"was shocked to find [them] in the hands of the FBI" (Emma Best, "FBI file reveals some of the secrets of Howard Hunt's White House safe," Muckrock, 17 July 2018).

91. Martinez FBI interview, 21 June 1972; CIA memo, 22 August 1973, HSCA SC, Box 49; "Journal – Office of Legislative Counsel," 26 December 1973," CREST; "Conversation with George Murphy, Joint Committee on Atomic Energy Staff, re Watergate," 18 December 1973.

92. "Interview of FBI Agents Parham and Wilson," Madigan and Liebengood, 11 January 1974, HSL, Folder 38, Box 2; Undated note on "Martinez Diary," HSL, Box 38, Folder 6; Miami to Acting Director, 139-4089-13.

93. Hougan, *Secret Agenda*, 226–7; FBI report, 26 June 1972, 139-4089-1205; SAC Miami to Director, 6 September 1978, 139-4089-3090. The calendar notebook was sent to Washington in December 1972 but the second notebook and other materials from Martinez' car were not sent to Washington until September 1973 (SAC Miami to Director, 19 September 1973, 139-4089-2610).

94. Untitled report on Martinez, 157-10011-10084; Baker report, 1149.

95. "Potential CIA involvement"; "Martinez Diary," Liebengood to Thompson, 16 November 1973, HSL, Box 37, Folder 28.

96. Nedzi report, 15, 19; Walters MFR, 28 June 1972, Nedzi hearings, 108; Transcript of Nixon-Haldeman conversation, 23 June 1972, 2:20 to 2:45 p.m., Nixon Library.

97. SSC Final Report, 514.

98. Nedzi report, 15, 19; Walters MFR, 28 June 1972, Nedzi hearings, 108; Transcript of Nixon-Haldeman conversation, 23 June 1972, 2:20 to 2:45 p.m.

99. Gray testimony, SSC Book 9, 3451; Helms testimony, SSC Book 8, 3237-8.

100. Nedzi report, 15. On Thursday, Howard Osborn asked Leo Dunn to contact the FBI "to get a reading on their investigation of the 'McCord Incident.'" Word came down from Patrick Gray "that the FBI was not to disseminate any information about the case in oral or written form" (CIA FOIA release F-2016-02491, 15).

101. Ibid., 16-17; Helms testimony, Helms nomination hearing to be Ambassador to Iran, 21 May 1973, 94.

102. Ibid., 16-19; General Walters MFR, 28 June 1972, Nedzi hearings, 109.

103. "Supplemental Witness Summary – Alfred Baldwin," 1.

104. Ibid., 2.

105. Hougan, *Secret Agenda*, 227-8; Evans testimony, Nedzi hearings, 974; Howe testimony, Nedzi hearings, 988.

106. "Watergate Incident," Osborn to Colby, 22 February 1974, Nedzi hearings, 945-7; Evans testimony, Nedzi hearings, 972–3.

107. Helms, *A Look Over My Shoulder*, 12.

108. Ibid.; Nedzi report, 18–19; Nedzi hearings, 109.

109. Pincus, "A Watergate Mystery . . ."

110. Nedzi report, 18–19; Nedzi hearings, 108; Bates to Felt, 28 June 1972, 139-4089-2283; 38-11; "Instructions Obtained from Teletypes, Airtels and Memoranda," 139-4089-2364, referencing Ibid.; Wong FBI interview, 27 June 1972; Hougan, *Secret Agenda*, 58.

111. "Watergate Affair," Helms to Walters, 28 June 1972, HJC Statement of Information, Book 2, 472; Notes on "28 June 1972 Memo and explanation," HSL, Box 38, Folder 9.

112. Ibid.; Nedzi report, 19–20; L. Patrick Gray III, In Nixon's Web (New York: Times Books, 2008), 77-8; Felt to Bates, 28 June 1972; Gray testimony, 6 August 1973, SSC Book 9, 3519-20.

113. "CIA director misled FBI about how agency spied on Pentagon Papers leaker," *USA Today*, 31 August 2016. Helms, Wagner and Osborn discussed the FBI request before Helms intervened with Gray to stop the Wagner interview (CIA FOIA release F-2016-02491, 17). They clearly understood what was at stake. In early July, after finding Cleo Gephart's alias and number in Hunt's address book, Arnold Parham contacted the CIA to request an interview. Wagner discussed the request with Colby and General Walters, and Parham was told "senior officials from the Agency were attempting to contact Mr. Gray" (Ibid., 18).

114. "Status Report as of 19 April 1974 on Material Reviewed in Relation to the Watergate Break-In; Daniel Ellsberg' and Hank Greenspun."

115. SSC Final Report, 36–7.

116. Ibid.; Dean, *Blind Ambition*, 122–3; Angelo Lano recorded interview by Timothy Naftali, 28 May 2009, Richard Nixon Oral History Project, Nixon Library. On June 27, while handing over selected Hunt materials to the FBI, Dean told SA George Saunders he didn't want FBI agents "making any inquiries or investigations" in the White House or Executive Office Building "without his knowledge or permission" (Dean FBI interview, 27 June 1972, included in Lano report, 5 July 1972, 43, 139-4089-811).

117. Dean, *Blind Ambition*, 127; Colodny and Gettlin, *Silent Coup*, 153.

118. "Director's State of the Agency Address," 30 June 1972, CREST. A film copy of this is available in the CIA Motion Picture collection at NARA.

119. Martinez SSC testimony, 11 May 1973, 273–4; Hunt, *Undercover*, 2246–50

120. "Presentence reports and evaluations," 51.

121. Nedzi report, 20–21; "Response of L. Patrick Gray, III, to Memoranda of Lt. General Vernon A. Walters," Nedzi hearings, 283.

122. Bennett testimony, Nedzi hearings, 1109.

123. "Meeting with Robert Foster Bennett and his Comments Concerning E. Howard Hunt, Douglas Caddy and the "Watergate Five" Incident," Martin Lukoskie MFR, 10 July 1972, Nedzi hearings, 1071–3 and Hougan, *Secret Agenda*, 329–331.

124. Ibid.; Bennett testimony, Nedzi hearings, 1078–9, 1082; Baker report, 1071–2; "James A. Everett," 104-10059-10231.

125. Peter Levenda, *Sinister Forces—A Warm Gun: A Grimoire of American Political Witchcraft. The Nine. Book One* (Walterville, OR: Trine Day, 2006); "James A. Everett," 104-10059-10231; Hougan, *Secret Agenda*, 277–8.

126. Liebengood memo of telephone conversation with Agee, 6 February 1975, HSL, Box 35, Folder 19.

127. David Corn, *Blond Ghost: Ted Shackley and the CIA's Crusades* (New York: Simon and Schuster, 1994), 229–240. Shackley succeeded Bill Broe

as Chief, WH Division on 3 April 1972 (CIA FOIA release F-2016-02491, 848).

128. Lukas, *Nightmare*, 38; Phillip Agee, *Inside the Company: CIA Diary* (London: Penguin Books, 1975), 462–3, 535; "James A. Everett," 104-10059-10231; "Summary of Funds Combined Budget," 1 January 1969, CREST, 60; "Digest of Lyle Miller Secret Documents," 5. James Everett refers to the "fake acronym" LPWORLD in his self-published memoir, *The Making and Breaking of An American Spy* (Durham, CT: Strategic Book Group, 2011), 110.

129. Baker report, 1124.

130. "Working Notes, R. E. Bennett Executive Session 2/1/74," Thompson and Madigan to Liebengood, 3 February 1974, HSL, Box 38, Folder 6, 5. There is no evidence for this and Oliver denies it.

131. Schlesinger statement and testimony, Nedzi hearings, 3, 57; Hunt testimony, Nedzi hearings, 492.

132. Schlesinger testimony, Nedzi hearings, 57, cited in Hougan, *Secret Agenda*, 52; CIA Watergate History, 72–3.

133. Ibid.; "Summary of Mr. John F. Caswell's Contacts with Mr. E. Howard Hunt," HJC Testimony of Witnesses, Book 3, 52; "Digest of Secret CIA Materials," 2–3; Schlesinger statement, Nedzi hearings, 4.

134. Ibid.; "Possible Additional Agency Support Furnished Howard Hunt," 9 June 1973 and "Addendum to Chronologies on 'Watergate,'" Broe to Colby, 4 June 1973, 104-10059-10212.

135. Ibid.

136. CIA Watergate History, 124.

137. Helms to Sparkman, 25 January 1975, printed in Senate Committee on Foreign Relations Hearing on CIA Foreign and Domestic Activities, 22 January 1975, 38.

CHAPTER 8

1. "Connecticut Trip," Freedman to Hamilton, 23 January 1974 and "Supplemental Witness Summary – Alfred Baldwin," Al Baldwin, Box B418, CLA;

"Potential CIA involvement," 23 January 1974, HSL, Box 37, Folder 16, 4; Baldwin testimony, SSC Book 1, 389–90; Author interview with Robert Mirto, 24 August 2018; Nedzi report, 15; Mardian testimony, *US v. Mitchell*, 16 December 1974, 10804-10806, 10920. O'Brien also told Mardian about the diary in Martinez' car concerning "activities carried out by him in connection with this group . . . over the past year . . . indicating CIA operations that would be very embarrassing to the CIA."

2. FBI Watergate summary, 30, 79-80; Baldwin FBI interview, 5 July 1972, 139-4089-448; "Supplemental Witness Summary – Alfred Baldwin."

3. Baldwin FBI interview, 5 July 1972, 139-4089-448.

4. Baldwin FBI interview, 10 July 1972, 139-4089-745; "Interview with 'Al'," 28 August 1972, JRP Box 33-1, 10-12; "Interview with Baldwin in New Haven . . .", 11 October 1972, JRP Box 33-1, 2-3; Transcript of Baldwin *Los Angeles Times* interview, 3 October 1972, 43-48; Baldwin testimony, *US v. Liddy*, 19 January 1973, 1044-6; Hougan, *Secret Agenda*, 154-5; FBI Teletype to Acting Director, 23 October 1972, 139-4089-1422; John LaVallee FBI interview, 24 October 1972, 139-4089-1677.

5. "Supplemental Witness Summary – Alfred Baldwin"; "Diary of Earl J. Silbert," 1973-4, p. 01002553, NARA, cited in "BM—DNC," 25fn55.

6. "Violence," McCord MFR, Box C75, CLA; McCord notes, Nedzi hearings, 709, 828.

7. Alch testimony, Nedzi hearings, 714.

8. McCord note to Helms and letter to Alch, SSC Book 9, 3841-2. Carl Oglesby, *The Yankee and Cowboy War: Conspiracies from Dallas to Watergate* (New York: Berkley Medallion, 1977), 298. McCord's source for this information was Mrs. Hunt, who was later his conduit for money from CRP to cover legal fees. She told McCord that Hunt had "exploded" when he heard CRP had told Paul O'Brien it was a CIA operation. A few days later, she told him "CRP lawyers are now reporting that the administration was going to allege at trial that Liddy had stolen $16,000 and had bribed Hunt and McCord to perform the operation." McCord told her he would not "sit still

for either false story" ("Calls to Local Embassies," McCord MFR filed with McCord's SSCEX testimony, Lapping Watergate Collection).

9. Osborn affidavit.

10. CIA Watergate History, 126.

11. "Potential CIA involvement," 4; "Digest of Lyle Miller Secret Documents," 4; The notes mistakenly refer to O'Brien's "senior partner, Vern Hanson," Arthur's brother; Pete Kinsey's notes of a meeting with Colson on January 13, 1975.

12. "Central Cover Staff [redacted] Mr. Hanson Retained to Defend E. Howard Hunt," Chief, Central Cover Staff to Director of Central Intelligence, 1993.07.23.14:37:32:250620, 43. Hanson was also a Major General in the United States Marine Corps Reserve; J.Y. Smith, "Lawyer William O. Bittman Dies," *Washington Post*, 3 March 2001.

13. McCord letter to Alch, 23 August 1972, Nedzi hearings, 835–6.

14. Ibid.; "Exhibit C," McCord to Alch, Nedzi hearings, 716; "What is Needed," McCord note to Gaynor, 29 December 1972, Book 9, 3836.

15. "The Lee J. Pennington Matter," Evans to Inspector General, 25 February 1974, HSL, Box 38, Folder 8 and Nedzi hearings, 978–80.

16. Notes on "Pennington Matter," HSL, Box 38, Folder 8; "Office of Security Organizational Chart," HSL, Box 38, Folder 8.

17. Pennington testimony, Nedzi hearings, 1023–4.

18. Gaynor testimony, Nedzi hearings, 1037.

19. "Watergate Incident," Osborn to Colby, 22 February 1974, Nedzi hearings, 945–7; "The Lee J. Pennington Matter."

20. "Watergate Incident," Nedzi hearings, 945–7; Cecil Pennington FBI interview, 5 September 1972, FBI 139-182-112.

21. "Interview with 'Al'," Galbraith memo, 28 August 1972, Box 33-1, JRP; "Connecticut Trip," 23 January 1974; Hougan, *Secret Agenda*, 241; Joseph A. Califano, *Inside: A Public and Private Life* (New York: Public Affairs, 2004), 271–3; Pincus, "A Watergate Mystery . . ."; Author interview with Alan Galbraith, 11 August 2018 and subsequent email correspondence. Galbraith told Pincus the meeting was on August 5 but after I sent him his original memo, he agreed it

was on August 26. Two other DNC attorneys had a further meeting with Baldwin on 3 October, in response to the discovery of the September bug ("Interview with Baldwin in New Haven . . . ," 3 October 1972, Box 33–1, JRP).

22. Ibid.

23. O'Brien, Interview XXXII, 18.

24. Ibid.; "Connecticut Trip"; Cassidento obituary, *New York Times*, 12 June 1974.

25. Max Holland, "Richard Nixon's Own Deep Throat," *Washington Decoded*, 3 November 2009; "Bugging 'Participant' Gives Details," *Washington Post*, 11 September 1972; Hougan, *Secret Agenda*, 241–3.

26. Thompson, *At That Point in Time*, 208; "Alfred C. Baldwin, III," 3.

27. "Watergate Defense Seeks to Query Democrat Chiefs," *Camden Courier-Post*, 6 September 1972; Thomas Foley, "Bugging of McGovern Offices Failed," *Los Angeles Times*, 8 September 1972; Mitchell deposition in *O'Brien v. McCord*, 5 September 1972, cited in Rosen, *The Strong Man*, 287.

28. Oliver deposition in *O'Brien v. McCord*, Civil Action 1233-72, 8 September 1972, 94-5, 151, James Rosen Papers (JRP), Northwestern University Archives, Evanston, IL; Wells testimony in *US v. Liddy*, 26 January 1973; Wells letter, referenced in Motz (2002); Oliver interview with author. Characteristic of Rothblatt's bumbling performance, he had Sanford's name but genuinely didn't know who he was. "Forgive my ignorance," he said. "Your ignorance is unforgivable," said DNC attorney Harold Ungar.

29. Hougan, *Secret Agenda*, 244–6; "Watergate Lawsuit Trial Drops Names"; Richard Walter Blackman FBI interview, 21 September 1972 and Haldane FBI interviews, 13 and 15 September 1972, WSPF Records, NARA. Haldane told the FBI a different story. After returning from the lobby, Blackman showed her a metal "transmitter" (two and a half inches wide), which he had replaced with a new one.

30. Silbert nomination hearings, 30 April 1974, 198–9.

31. Oliver FBI interview, 15 September 1972; Wells FBI interview, 15 September 1972; Haldane FBI interviews, 15 and 18 September 1972; Richard Walter Blackman FBI interview, 21 September 1972; Lawrence J. Capone FBI

interviews, 13 and 15 September 1972; John H. Williams FBI interviews, 13 and 15 September 1972; Roger Fewell FBI interviews, 13 and 20 September 1972; Earl Connor FBI interviews, 13 and 18 September 1972; FBI report on examination of Oliver's phone, 14 September 1972. These reports can be found in Witness File – Oliver, Spencer, US Attorney Files, Box 7, WSPF Records, NARA. The defective transistor is mentioned in Bureau airtel to WFO, 26 September 1972, 139-4136-18.

32. Ibid.; FBI Teletype, WFO to Acting Director, 4 October 1972, 139-4136-68; Bates to Felt, 15 September 1972, 139-4136-61; FBI Teletype, WFO to Chicago, 18 September 1972, 139-4136-2; Hougan, *Secret Agenda*, 244–6; Galbraith interview with author; Wells deposition in *Dean v. St. Martin's Press*, 7 June 1996, 161–2.

33. Hougan, *Secret Agenda*, 254–6; Wolff FBI interview, 18 September 1972, Witness File – Oliver, Spencer, U.S. Attorney Files, Box 7, WSPF Records, NARA; "Wayne Barber, William Pierce—Nicholas Beltrante," Schultz to Thompson, 19 October 1973, HSL, Box 35, Folder 7.

34. Lukas, *Nightmare*, 245–6; *US v. Liddy*, Grand Jury indictment.

35. Conversation between The President, Haldeman and Dean, 15 September 1972 (5:27–6:17 pm), Exhibit 4, *US v. Mitchell*, Nixon Library and HJC Statement of Information, Book 2, 594.

36. Ibid.; In a memo to Haldeman on September 12 titled "Counter Actions (Watergate)," Dean noted the depositions "are wide ranging and will cover everything from Larry O'Brien's sources of income . . . to certain sexual activities of employees of the DNC. They should cause considerable problems for those being deposed" (Silbert nomination hearings, 20 April 1975, 270); Lawrence Meyer, "Trial of Watergate Suit Before Nov. 7 Held 'Impossible," *Washington Post*, 22 September 1972. On September 12, Richey had already put all depositions and discovery on hold, pending a ruling on a motion to dismiss (Galbraith interview with author).

37. FBI Watergate summary, 34–7, 70–1; SA Dennis W. Fiene to SAC, WFO, 19 June 1972, FBI 139-4089-2001; Bradley to Conrad, 2 October 1972, FBI

139-4089-1455; FBI investigative summary and WFO to Acting Director, 22 June 1972, 139-4089, Volume 16; Bradley to Conrad, 12 April 1973, 139-4089-2001; Summary of Stan Greigg DNC Deposition," Liebengood to Thompson, 25 October 1973, HSL, Box 36, Folder 19. The secretarial cubicle where the burglars were caught seems to have belonged to Bush or Greigg's secretary, Marie Cunningham.

38. Ibid.; Stevens to Bradley, 14 September 1972, 139-4089-1115; Bates to Felt, 14 September 1972, 139-4089-970; "Society of Former Special Agents of the FBI" (Paducah, KY: Turner Publishing, 1998), 232; "Democratic 'Bug' Set After June 17," *New York Times*, 22 September 1972.

39. *New York Post*, 26 September 1972, cited in Silbert nomination hearings, 23 April 1974, 36–7.

40. "Electronic Device Removed from Spencer Oliver's telephone on September 13, 1972," Silbert to Petersen, 28 September 1972, 139-4089-1454. Silbert was perhaps justifiably upset because the FBI report he was given on the discovery of the bug on Oliver's phone contained no statements by FBI personnel detailing the "nature of their sweep of the [DNC] in late June or July as a basis for establishing that the device had to be installed after the sweep." In response, the FBI claimed it had "never received the results of the lab search in writing" but Wilbur Stevens sent a memo to Bradley the day after the Oliver bug was found (FBI reply to Silbert comments, "L. Patrick Gray's Notes," 139-4089-2757X, Item 189).

41. Ibid.; Bradley to Conrad, 2 October 1972, FBI 139-4089-1455; Kunkel to Felt, 21 September 1972, 139-4136-17; FBI memoranda relating to the transmitter tests and Silbert's memo above: 139-4089-1449 to 139-4089-1453.

42. Galbraith interview with author.

43. Ibid.; FBI Watergate summary, 34-7, 70-1; SA Fiene to SAC, WFO, 19 June 1972, 139-4089-2001; FBI memo, 24 June 1972; FBI summary of investigation, 22 June 1972 and WFO to Director, 22 June 1972, 139-4089-2757; Silbert nomination hearings, 30 April 1974, 198–9; Robert Parry, "Robert Strauss's Watergate Secret," *Consortium News*, 20 March 2014.

44. Hougan, *Secret Agenda*, 95, 183–5, 254–6.

45. "Exhibit C," McCord to Alch, Nedzi hearings, 716; "What is Needed," McCord note to Gaynor, 29 December 1972, Book 9, 3836; Hunt, *Undercover*, 274; Alch testimony, Nedzi hearings, 775–6.

46. Alch testimony, Nedzi hearings, 714–5, 775–6.

47. "Meeting with Charles Colson on January 13, 1975," Pete Kinsey MFR, HSL, Box 36, Folder 5, 8.

48. Lukas, *Nightmare*, 245; Colodny and Gettlin, *Silent Coup*, 229–231; "Hougan, Liddy, The Post and Watergate."

49. Silbert nomination hearings, 23 April 1974, 66.

50. Ibid., 129–130.

51. Ibid., 130–1.

52. Ibid., 65.

53. Hunt, *Undercover*, 277, 283–4; Dean, *Conservatives Without Conscience* (New York: Viking, 2006), xiv.

54. "Review and Statement of Problem," 14 November 1972, attached to FBI serial 139-4089-2934; Lukas, *Nightmare*, 256-9; SSC Final Report, 55-6; "Conversation with Howard Hunt," 14 November 1972, SSC Book 9, 3888; Helms, *A Look Over My Shoulder*, 11, 13. The date of this meeting seems to be 20 November 1972, a couple of weeks after the election.

55. "Watergate Case," Warner MFR, 27 November 1972, Colby nomination hearings, 164–6; "Meeting at the White House on December 15, 1972, re: Watergate Case," Colby MFR, Colby nomination hearings, 163–4.

56. Ibid.; RCR, 201.

57. Ibid.

58. Notes on "Pennington Matter"; Thompson, *At That Point in Time*, 163; Baker staff chronology, 6 January 1974, HSL, Box 38, Folder 2; "Necessary CIA Interviews and Documents," Liebengood and Madigan to Thompson, 8 January 1974, HSL, Box 38, Folder 2. Figure 7: HSL, Box 38, Folder 8.

59. Paul Gaynor affidavit, Nedzi hearings, 201–2; Evans and Colby testimony, Nedzi hearings, 981–2.

60. Evans and Colby testimony, Nedzi hearings, 981–2.

61. Hougan, *Secret Agenda*, 303; SSC Book 9, 3839; Hunt, *Undercover*, 269–81; Dean, *Blind Ambition*, 124, 168; Notes on "Dorothy Hunt," HSL, Box 38, Folder 6. Dorothy Hunt's memos of monies received to her husband's attorney, dated 19 September and 2 October 1972, are attached to FBI serial 139-4089-2934. Rivers was the maiden name of Caulfield's wife (Caulfield résumé, Nixon Library).

62. "Meeting at the White House on December 15, 1972, re: Watergate Case"

63. "Watergate Incident," Warner to Petersen, 21 December 1973, HJC Testimony of Witnesses, Book 3, 48; Colby nomination hearings, 167.

64. "Discussions with Staff Members of the Senate Judiciary Committee," 26 June 1975, CREST; Ehrlichman Log, December 15, 1972, HJC Statement of Information, Book 2, 652; RCR, 201; "Digest of Secret CIA Materials," 4, 7.

65. Dean, *Blind Ambition*, 169–71.

66. Charles Morgan, *One Man, One Voice* (New York: Holt, Rinehart and Winston, 1979), 211–2; Silbert nomination hearings, 20 May 1975, 39fn93.

67. Morgan, *One Man, One Voice*, 213–5; Silbert nomination hearings, 23 April 1974, 50.

68. Alch testimony, Nedzi hearings, 714–5.

69. Ibid.

70. Hougan, *Secret Agenda*, 303; "McCord letter to Gaynor," 29 December 1972, SSC Book 9, 3839.

71. Gaynor testimony, Nedzi hearings, 169. He returned in September 1959.

72. The first letter was sent to Gaynor's son.

73. Gaynor testimony, Nedzi hearings, 170.

74. "McCord letter to Gaynor," 29 December 1972, SSC Book 9, 3839; Hougan, *Secret Agenda*, 303.

75. SSC report, 64.

76. Gaynor testimony, Nedzi hearings, 171–2; Gaynor affidavit.

77. "McCord letter to Gaynor," 29 December 1972, SSC Book 9, 3838.

78. Ibid., 3837.

79. Ibid., 3836.

80. Gaynor testimony, Nedzi hearings, 173–4.

81. SSC Final Report, 66–7; Dean testimony, SSC Book 3, 973–4.

82. McCord letter to Gaynor, 3 January 1972, SSC Book 9, 3835.

83. Gaynor testimony, Nedzi hearings, 176–7.

84. Silbert nomination hearings, 23 April 1974, 131-2.

85. Ibid., 130–1.

86. Silbert nomination hearings, 19 June, 1974, 392 and 24 June 1974, 446–8.

87. Silbert nomination hearings, 24 June 1974, 504–12; Anthony Ripley, "Petersen Says Prosecutors Failed to Check 'Plumbers' Evidence," *New York Times*, 27 June 1974; Stephen Green, "Watergate Prosecutors Admit Error," *Washington Post*, 27 June 1974. Silbert never admitted his mistake.

88. Tunney memo, 18 June 1975, Silbert nomination hearings, 20 May 1975, 85–6.

89. Petersen testimony and Goldin receipt, HJC Testimony of Witnesses, Book 3, 71–3; McCord, *A Piece of Tape*, 147, 315–6.

90. Dean testimony, SSC Book 3, 978-9, 1087; Ehrlichman testimony, SSC Book 6, 2553.

91. "Notes," McCord to Gaynor, 5 January 1973, SSC Book 9, Exhibit 138, 3834.

92. Gaynor testimony, Nedzi hearings, 170, 201.

93. Ibid., 171, 181–2.

94. Osborn testimony, Nedzi hearings, 959.

95. CIA Watergate History, 126–7.

96. Gaynor testimony, Nedzi hearings, 179–80.

97. Ibid., 178

98. Ibid., 171–2.

99. McCord, *A Piece of Tape*, 152-8; SSC Final Report, 63–6.

100. SSC Final Report, 1217.

101. "Digest of Secret CIA Materials," 8–9.

102. Seymour Hersh, "4 Watergate Defendants Reported Still Being Paid," *New York Times*, 14 January 1973; Helms, *A Look Over My Shoulder*, 23–4, 27–33.

103. Martinez testimony, 11 May 1973, 275–6, 280.

104. Martin Schram, "Watergate Case Called Broad Plot," *Washington Post*, 7 January 1973, printed in Helms nomination hearing to be Ambassador to Iran, 60–1.

105. "Digest of Secret CIA Materials," 9.

106. Rockefeller Commission Deposition of Frank Sturgis, 4 April 1975, 29, 34; "Alleged Burglary . . . ," SAC New York to FBI Director, 17 August 1973, 124-10292-10149.

107. "Alleged Burglary . . ."

108. Ibid.; Rockefeller Commission Deposition of Frank Sturgis, 4 April 1975, 29, 34; Shackley memo to Deputy Director for Operations, 8 March 1973, CREST; "ITT Denies Connection with Watergate Figure," *Washington Post*, 9 March 1973.

109. Dean, *Blind Ambition*, 182; SSC Final Report, 36.

110. Transcript of Baldwin *Los Angeles Times* interview, 41–2.

111. Ibid., 73–4, 89-90.

112. Morgan, *One Man, One Voice*, 225–30; Silbert nomination hearings, 20 May 1975, 88–9; *US v. Liddy*, Transcript of In Camera Proceedings, 17 January 1972, NARA, 1010–12. Morgan incorrectly states it was January 16 in his book.

113. RCR, 203-4; Baker report, 1131–2.

114. "Helms Re-Interview Preparation - Martinez Relationship," undated, HSL, Box 38, Folder 9.

115. SSC Book 8, 3247-8; Cary cable to Helms, 16 November 1973, "HSCA Request Dated 22 Mar–10 Aug 78," 25.

116. Dean, *The Nixon Defense*, 673fn11; Kleindienst to Petersen, 15 April 1973, SSC Book 9, 3860; Hunt to Gray, 17 February 1973, 139-4089-1924.

117. McCord letter to Sirica, 19 March 1973, HJC Statement of Information, Book 4, Part 1, 221–225.

118. McCord testimony, SSC Book 1, 193–8; SSC Final Report, 1203.

119. Ibid., 129–130.

120. Gebhardt to Felt, 6 April 1973, 139-4089-1975; Bradley to Conrad, 9 April 1973, 139-4089-1988; FBI Teletype, 6 April 1973, 139-4089-1976; John Everett FBI interview, 11 April 1973, 139-4089-2393; Lano report, 5 June 1973, 139-4089-2393, D-F; McCord deposition in *DNC v. McCord*, 30 April 1973, 145-6, 173; "Digest of Susan David Cantril Interview," Madigan to Thompson, 9 November 1973, HSL, Box 35, Folder 7; FBI Watergate summary, 34-7. On the night of the arrests, LeBow's home number was the first one police found on June 17 so they notified her of the break-in and she called Stan Greigg.

121. McCord deposition in *DNC v. McCord*, 30 April 1973, 141-7.

122. McCord testimony, SSC Book 1, 156-7; McCord, *A Piece of Tape*, 25. McCord told the prosecutors he put the second bug in a "call directory" and "gave them an exact description of where within the call directory it was located, and they sent a man out, and picked it up, and brought it back. So presumably, it was still transmitting . . . during that period" (Transcript of McCord interview for *Watergate* TV series, Roll 320, 17).

123. SSC Book 9, 3630; Lukas, *Nightmare*, 329. Earlier in his testimony, Petersen claimed, "we didn't relate those [photographs] to the Ellsberg case, I think, until the time of Mr. Krogh's affidavit [dated 4 May 1973] in connection with the Ellsberg matter." (SSC Book 9, 3623). This seems unlikely.

124. Gray, *In Nixon's Web*, 237–42.

125. HJC Statement of Information, Book 7, Part 1, 123, 130; Petersen testimony, HJC Testimony of Witnesses, Book 3, 119.

126. Richard Nixon, "Statements About the Watergate Investigations," 22 May 1973.

127. Gray, *In Nixon's Web*, 242-3.

128. Ehrlichman testimony, SSC Book 6, 2552; HJC Statement of Information Book 7, Part 1, 123, 130.

129. Gray, *In Nixon's Web*, 244–5; Fielding affidavit.

130. Lukas, *Nightmare*, 335–6; Richard Nixon: "Address to the Nation About the Watergate Investigations," April 30, 1973. *The American Presidency Project*. http://www.presidency.ucsb.edu/ws/?pid=3824.

131. Thompson, *At That Point in Time*, 145.

132. Byrne Statement and Order of Dismissal, *US v. Russo*, 11 May 1973, HJC Statement of Information, Book 7, Part 4, 2076–83.

133. Stanley Kutler, *Abuse of Power* (New York: Touchstone, 1998), 473.

134. Rowan, "CIA's Involvement Appalling," *Washington Star-News*, 11 May 1973.

135. SSC Final Report, 122–3; Ehrlichman testimony, 24 July 1973, SSC Book 6, 2542, 2594; Lukas, *Nightmare*, 101.

CHAPTER 9

1. Mary DePue death notice, *Washington Post*, 23 September 2011; "Possible Additional Agency Support Furnished Howard Hunt," Breckenridge MFR, 9 June 1973, 104-10059-10212.

2. Hougan, *Secret Agenda*, 328fn.

3. "CIA Employee Statement," Ratliff MFR, 17 January 1974, HJC Statement of Information, Book 2, 298–9 and Hougan, *Secret Agenda*, 328–9. While the previously published Ratliff statement is redacted, I located an unredacted copy in the Arden B. Schell Watergate Collection, Box 2, Folder 25, George Mason University, Fairfax, VA.

4. Family Jewels, 424.

5. "CIA Employee Statement."

6. Ibid.; "Official Routing Slip", Chamberlain to Colby, 17 January 1974 and partial list of "CIA Materials Furnished to the Special Counsel, [HJC]," Arden B. Schell Watergate Schell Collection, Box 2, Folder 25. Chamberlain was Inspector General from 1973 until his retirement in 1976 ("Ex-CIA Inspector General Donald Chamberlain Dies," 6 April 1991.) In March 1974, the CIA's Office of

Legislative Counsel was still worried about Ratliff's admission that he had destroyed the receipts for the envelopes used "to pass materials on Ellsberg" from Hunt through the Agency NSC liaison to Dr. Tietjen: "The above admission, as well as others present in [related] memos, could be big problems if the wrong people got hold of them" ("Unresolved Watergate Items," OLC to Lyle Miller, 25 March 1974, CIA FOIA release F-2016-02491, 34).

7. CIA Watergate History, 153. Richards died in December 1974.

8. "Colson Hits CIA on Date," *Washington Star-News*, 22 January 1975.

9. Hougan, *Secret Agenda*, 50–2.

10. Both are titled "Addendum to Conversation, Wednesday, October 27, 1971" and were filed in JFK Box 37, Folder 10 at the National Archives and declassified in 1995.

11. Ibid.

12. Hunt, *Undercover*, 161.

13. Hunt HSCA testimony, Part 1, 30.

14. "Memorandum from Director of Central Intelligence Schlesinger to All Central Intelligence Agency Employees," 9 May 1973, *FRUS*, 1969-76, Volume XXXVIII, Part 2, Document 6; John Crewdson, "C.I.A. and Congress Investigate Ellsberg Burglary Authorization," *New York Times*, 8 May 1973.

15. Nedzi report, 4; Family Jewels, 420–422a.

16. "Memorandum from Director of Central Intelligence Schlesinger to All Central Intelligence Agency Employees"; Family Jewels, 418–9, 430–1.

17. Thompson, *At That Point in Time*, 157.

18. Helms testimony, Helms nomination hearing to be Ambassador to Iran, 21 May 1973, 57–66.

19. Petersen testimony and Goldin receipt, HJC Testimony of Witnesses, Book 3, 71–3.

20. CIA Watergate History, 125, 129; "Memorandum from the Executive Secretary of the Central Intelligence Agency Management Committee (Colby) to All Central Intelligence Agency Employees," 23 May 1973, *FRUS*, 1969–76, Volume XXXVIII, Part 2, Document 7fn1.

21. "Memorandum from the Executive Secretary of the Central Intelligence Agency Management Committee (Colby) to All Central Intelligence Agency Employees"; Family Jewels, 411–3.

22. Family Jewels, 401.

23. Osborn affidavit; Family Jewels, 411–2; Family Jewels, 399–400.

24. Family Jewels, 392.

25. CIA Watergate History, 127–8.

26. Conversation between Nixon and Buzhardt, 16 May 1973, White House Tapes (920–9), Nixon Library, cited in *FRUS*, 1969–1976, Volume XXI, Chile, 1969–1973, Document 300.

27. "Chilean Embassy Burglary," 21 June 1973, Box 5, 6, RG 460, Plumbers Task Force, Investigations of Alleged Illegal Activities, NARA, cited in *FRUS*, 1969–1976, Volume XXI, Chile, 1969-1973, Document 300.

28. WSPF Report, 66.

29. Author interview with Eugenio Rolando Martinez, 18 April 2017.

30. "Zero aka Cero," 15 May 1974, http://www.latinamericanstudies.org /belligerence/Cero-FBI.pdf; "Defector believes Cuban agents killed exile leader," *Miami Herald,* 31 May 1988, http://www.latinamericanstudies.org /belligerence/torriente.htm. See also the excellent article by Dick Russell, "Little Havana's Reign of Terror," News Times, 29 October 1976.

31. Watergate Special Prosecution Force Final Report, U.S. Government Printing Office, 1975, 4–5, 8; Charles Morgan, Jr. "Report to the Special Prosecutor on Certain Aspects of the Watergate Affair," 18 June 1973, printed in Silbert nomination hearings, 23 April 1974, 5.

32. WSPF Final Report, 6; Lukas, *Nightmare*, 341–2; "The Watergate Coverage," American Archive of Public Broadcasting. http://americanarchive.org/exhibits /watergate/the-watergate-coverage.

33. SSC Final Report, 1080–1.

34. "Presentence reports and evaluations," 48.

35. Hunt testimony, Nedzi hearings, 540–3; Silbert nomination hearings, 23 April 1974, 129–30.

36. Merrill, *Watergate Prosecutor*, 23.

37. Helms testimony, 2 August 1973, SSC Book 8, 3234, 3277; "Helms' Prior Testimony," HSL, Box 38, Folder 10.

38. Ibid.

39. Helms testimony, 2 August 1973, SSC Book 8, 3265-6.

40. "Highlights of Ambassador Helms interview, August 1, 1973," Liebengood to Thompson, 17 January 1974; Notes on "Helms Public Testimony – August 2," Liebengood to Thompson, HSL, Box 38, Folder 9.

41. Helms testimony, SSC Book 8, 3260.

42. Cushman testimony, 2 August 1973, SSC Book 8, 3294, 3308; "General Cushman interview of March 7, 1974," Madigan to Thompson and Liebengood, 6 March 1974, HSL, Box 38, Folder 8.

43. SSC Book 9, 3441-7; "The Lee R. Pennington Matter," Evans to Inspector General, CIA, Nedzi report, 978.

44. Miles Copeland, "The Unmentionable Uses of a CIA," *National Review*, 14 September 1973.

45. Hunt testimony, SSC Book 9, 3739, 3751, 3757; *Silent Coup*, 140–1; *Dean v. St. Martin's Press*, Motion for Summary Judgement, Subject Matter Core Category 11, 1996, 12–14. A year later, in *US. v. Mitchell*, Hunt admitted the notebooks did not contain "the full operational story of Watergate" or "Liddy's principals by name" - see later in the chapter.

46. SSC Final Report, 1080–1.

47. Nedzi report, 23 October 1973, 4–5, 10-11, 22.

48. Dean, *Blind Ambition*, 182.

49. Andrew St. George, "The Cold War Comes Home," *Harper's*, November 1973.

50. Maury affidavit, 20 November 1972.

51. Colby to Senator Fulbright, 16 November 1973, "HSCA Request Dated 22 Mar–10 Aug 78," 8–10; Maury, Esterline and Ritchie affidavits and Gonzalez cable, 19–20 November 1973, Fielding Break-In, Box 8, "Litigation Correspondence – CIA," WSPF Records, NARA.

52. Cary cable to Helms, 16 November 1973, and Miller MFR on St. George testimony, "HSCA Request Dated 22 Mar – 10 Aug 78."

53. Baker report, 1119.

54. Baker report, 1120.

55. "Potential CIA Involvement," 23 January 1974, HSL, Box 37, Folder 16.

56. "Martinez Diary," Liebengood to Thompson, 16 November 1973, HSL, Box 37, Folder 28.

57. Reinaldo Pico SSC testimony, 20 November 1973, CLA, 38–44.

58. "Clarification of 'The Yeoman Story,'" Helms cable to CIA headquarters, 4 December 1973; Rosen, *The Strong Man*, 283-4; "Conference with Senator Baker," Liebengood to File, 7 December 1973, HSL, Box 38, Folder 1; "Martinez Diary," Liebengood and Madigan to Thompson, 7 December 1973, HSL Box 37, Folder 28; George F. Murphy Oral History Interview, 19 April 1995, Howard H. Baker, Jr. Oral History Project, University of Tennessee, Knoxville, TN; "Special Report Interagency Committee on Intelligence (Ad Hoc)," Houston to Chief, Counterintelligence Operations, DDO, 11 July 1973, CREST. The Page-a-Day calendar notebook was unsealed by the National Archives in 2013 and can be found in Unsealed Materials from *U.S. v. Liddy*, Box 3, Item 35, NARA: www.archives.gov/research/investigations/watergate/us-v-liddy.html.

59. Martinez SSC testimony, 10 December 1973, 78.

60. Ibid., 79, 84.

61. Ibid., 80–1.

62. Ibid., 81–2.

63. Ibid., 83.

64. Ibid., 86–8.

65. Hougan, *Secret Agenda*, 333-4; Thompson, *At That Point in Time*, 148, 169, 177–8; Thomas Braden, "Can He Blame It on CIA?", reproduced in "HSCA Request Dated 22 Mar–10 Aug 78," 33–6.

66. Braden, "Can He Blame It on CIA?"

67. Ibid.

68. "The Lee R. Pennington, Jr. Matter," Nedzi hearings, 978.

69. Ibid., 979.

70. Ibid.

71. Ibid.

72. Ibid.; Weberman and Canfield, *Coup d'État in America*, Nodule 20.

73. "Office of Legislative Counsel Annual Report FY 1974," CREST; Colby to Baker, 28 June 1974, Baker report, 1158; Thompson, 157–8, *At That Point in Time*, 167.

74. 25–6, 41–2; 104-10096-10131; Hougan, *Secret Agenda*, 220–1; "Requests of CIA," Thompson to Baker, 20 February 1974, HSL, Box 38, Folder 7.

75. Ibid., 2.

76. Ibid., 3. The Agency later told Thompson that Ritchie "took over Martinez on 14 April 1972 at a meeting at the Tien Kiu restaurant" in Miami (CIA FOIA release F-2016-02491, 849). Strangely, Ritchie did not include this meeting in his November 1973 affidavit.

77. Molly O'Neill, "Where Adventure Shapes the Menu," *New York Times*, 1 April 1992.

78. Ibid.; Thompson, *At That Point in Time*, 160–1.

79. Ibid.

80. "Watergate Incident," Osborn to Colby, 22 February 1974, Nedzi hearings, 946; "The Lee R. Pennington Jr. Matter," Ibid., 978–81.

81. Ibid., 945–7. Pennington "refused to cooperate in the termination." One CIA document describes him as "a right-wing political activist." The FBI was informed of his CIA relationship in 1966 "for operational reasons" but Pennington did not reveal his CIA links when questioned by the FBI about Watergate ("Unresolved Watergate Items," OLC to Miller, 25 March 1974, CIA FOIA release F-2016-02491, Muckrock, 36).

82. Ibid.

83. Thompson, *At That Point in Time,* 161.

84. "The Lee R. Pennington Jr. Matter," Nedzi hearings, 978–81.

85. Pennington testimony, Nedzi hearings, 1023–9.

86. Thompson, *At That Point in Time*, 169-71; Baker report, 1156.

87. Ibid., 163; Baker report, 1129–30.

88. "Points of Interest re: Cord Meyer, Jr."

89. Ibid.

90. "Interview with Karl Wagner – Summarized Highlights," Madigan and Liebengood to Thompson, 5 March 1974, HSL, Box 38, Folder 7; "Digest of
Secret CIA Materials," 3.

91. Thompson, *At That Point in Time*, 172–4.

92. Ibid.

93. Baker report, 1154; "Baker Report: A Sequel," Box 8, Folder 26, 1–3, Howard
H. Baker, Jr. Papers (HHB), University of Tennessee, Knoxville, TN;
Thompson, *At That Point in Time*, 180.

94. "Administrative Files on E. Howard Hunt's Post-Employment Relationship,"
12, 14, 18.

95. "Memo for The Record with Several Letters Attached, Re James McCord
Manuscript", Warner MFR, 24 April 1974, CIA, 1993.

96. McCord, *A Piece of Tape*, x.

97. "Office of Legislative Counsel Annual Report FY 1974," CREST; Colby to
Baker, 28 June 1974, Baker report, 1158.

98. Baker report, 1161–5; Thompson, *At That Point in Time*, 181–2.

99. Ibid., 1139–40, 1163.

100. Ibid.

101. Ibid., 1142–3, 1163.

102. Ibid., 1144; "Baker Report: A Sequel," HHB, Box 8, Folder 26, 1–3.

103. Ibid., 1150–7.

104. "Office of Legislative Counsel Annual Report FY 1974," CREST.

105. Administrative Files on E. Howard Hunt's Post-Employment Relationship,
52, 58–64.

106. Ibid., 55, 61, 102; Hunt, *Undercover*, 87.

107. Ibid., 103–4.

108. Ibid., 105; "Re: Autobiography of Mr. E. Howard Hunt, Jr.," Snyder to Morrison, 1 October 1974, 104-10119-10312; Hunt testimony in *US v. Mitchell*, 29 October 1974, 4372-7 and 22 November 1974, 7613-21; The false quote was printed on page 277 of the US edition of *Undercover*. Hunt said he only had one Hermès notebook—a desk diary and address book from a French department store. His safe had also contained a pop-up address book.

109. "Memorandum from the Executive Secretary of the Central Intelligence Agency Management Committee (Colby) to All Central Intelligence Agency Employees," *FRUS*, 1969–1976, volume XXXVIII, Part 2, 1973–1976, Document 7fn5; Seymour Hersh, "Huge C.I.A. Operation Reported in U.S. against Antiwar Forces, Other Dissidents in Nixon Years," *New York Times*, 22 December 1974.

110. "Editorial Note," *FRUS*, Ibid., Document 17; "Letter from Director of Central Intelligence Colby to President Ford," 24 December 1974, Ibid., Document 19.

111. "Memorandum of Conversation," 3 January 1975, Ibid., Document 21.

112. RCR, ix–x.

113. "Memorandum of Conversation," 4 January 1975, Ibid., Document 24.

114. "Note from the Secretary of State's Executive Assistant (Eagleburger) to Secretary of State Kissinger," 7 January 1975, Ibid., Document 25.

115. Helms testimony, 22 January 1975.

116. Helms, *A Look Over My Shoulder*, 414–5, 445.

117. "Final report of the Select Committee to Study Governmental Operations with Respect to Intelligence Activities," Book 1, 26 April 1976, 2–4.

118. RCR, 188.

119. RCR, 189.

120. RCR, 190.

121. RCR, 195.

122. RCR, 199–203.

123. RCR, 205–7.

124. "About the Committee," U.S. Senate Select Committee on Intelligence, https://www.intelligence.senate.gov/about.

125. "Baker Report: A Sequel," HHB. Baker filed his new report with the permanent oversight committee, appending new evidence he had compiled which remains classified.

126. Ibid.

127. Author interview with Jim Hougan, 21 December 2017.

128. "Meeting with the Special Prosecutor with regard to the McCord Letters," 8 June 1976, CREST.

129. "Letter from James McCord with Affidavit Attached," 1993.07.20.16:40:35:900590, 5; "McCord, James Walter, Jr.," Solie MFR, CIA, 104-10123-10362.

130. "Letter from James McCord with Affidavit Attached," 6.

131. Hunt HSCA testimony, Part 2, 9, 42–3. Hunt also stated he did not visit Mexico in 1963, where he was accused of meeting Lee Harvey Oswald.

CHAPTER 10

1. Martinez, "Mission Impossible."

2. Valentine, "Creating a Crime: How the CIA Commandeered the DEA"; "Anti-Fidel Castro Activities," FBI report by SA Robert James Dwyer, 124-10306-10071.

3. "Aldo Vera Serafin," SAC San Juan to Director, FBI, 9 July 1975, 124-10279-10050.

4. "Internal Security – Cuba," Priority cable from CIA to FBI, 24 May 1977, 104-10422-10258.

5. Alfonso Chardy, "Former CIA agent talks about the trip to Cuba of 'Musculito', Cuban condemned by Watergate," El Nuevo Herald, 1 November 2016.

6. "Internal Security – Cuba," Priority cable from CIA to FBI, 27 May 1977, 104-10422-10256.

7. Camilo Loret de Mola, "El último de los Plomeros" ("The Last of the Plumbers"), Diario de Cuba, 27 April 2015.

8. Alejandro Armengol, "Tema del traidor y del héroe en Miami" ("Traitor and Hero Theme in Miami"), 18 October 2016, www.cubaencuentro.com; Chardy, "Former CIA Agent talks . . ."; Martinez recorded interview, 25 March 2008, Nixon Library.

9. FBI "Spot Report," 2 June 1977, 104-10422-10251.

10. "Internal Security – Cuba," FBI Director Kelley to Director of Central Intelligence, 104-10428-10209.

11. "Aldereguia claims FBI framed him to get to WFC president," *Miami News*, 27 March 1978. http://www.latinamericanstudies.org/espionage/aldereguia-samuel.htm

12. "Aldereguia once worked with FBI," *Miami News*, 27 March 1978.

13. "Cuban Secret Police Letter to Spy in Miami Is Found," *Miami Herald*, 15 March 1978. http://www.latinamericanstudies.org/espionage/aldereguia.htm

14. "Aldereguia claims FBI framed him to get to WFC president."

15. "Cuban Secret Police Letter to Spy in Miami Is Found."

16. "Aldereguia claims FBI framed him to get to WFC president."

17. "International Fraud Hinted in Passport Affair," *Sarasota Herald Tribune*, 8 March 1978.

18. "Cuban Secret Police Letter to Spy in Miami Is Found."

19. "Aldereguia claims FBI framed him to get to WFC president."

20. "Aldereguia once worked with FBI."

21. Ibid.

22. Ibid.

23. Interview with Antonio Veciana for the documentary *638 Ways to Kill Castro* (2006), shared with me by producer Peter Moore; "Exile was carrying Cuban documents, police say," *Miami Herald*, 2 February 1984; "Veterinarian Suspected as Front Man Loses His License," *Miami Herald*, 7 October 1989.

24. "El último de los Plomeros."

25. "Watergate Thief Denies Portrayal in Fuentes' Book," *Miami Herald*, 20 November 1999.

26. Ibid.

27. "Traitor and Hero Theme in Miami."

28. "Watergate Thief Denies Portrayal in Fuentes' Book."

29. Ibid.

30. "Activist Denies He Collaborated with Castro," *El Nuevo Herald*, 20 November 1999.

31. Ibid.; Gibbons' "expertise was dealing with complex foreign counter-intelligence cases," according his 2014 obituary ("Francis E. Gibbons," www.coxgiffordseawinds.com).

32. "Traitor and Hero Theme in Miami"; "El último de los Plomeros."

33. Chardy, "Former CIA agent talks . . ."

34. "Executive Grant of Clemency," 11 May 1983, Office of the Pardon Attorney; "Pardon of Watergate Burglar Eugenio Rolando Martinez," Holland Memo for Central Files, 25 May 1983, Reagan Library; David Hoffman, "Reagan Grants Martinez Pardon for Watergate," *Washington Post*, 14 May 1983.

CHAPTER 11

1. Frederic J. Motz, *Wells v. Liddy*, 1 F. Supp. 2d 532, United States District Court, D. Maryland, 13 April 1998.

2. Ibid.

3. Manuel Rogia-Francia, "Watergate Lawsuit Trial Drops Names," *Washington Post*, 18 January 2001; Dean letter to Phil Stanford's publisher Adam Parfrey, 13 August 2013, www.feralhouse.com. The inclusion of Mitchell's former personal assistant Kristen Forsberg led him to conclude Bailley's story was a "scam" ("Behemoth Manuscript—DNC," 65fn153, JRP). All five women have denied the allegations.

4. Wilkins, Williams, and Michael, *Wells v. Liddy*, United States Court of Appeals for the Fourth Circuit, 1 March 2002; James Rosen, "Under Watergate," *City Paper*, 25 May 2001; Colodny and Gettlin, *Silent Coup*, 136.

5. Martinez interview with Colodny and Becker, 1 May 1990, 7–10, 13, 17, 28–9; Colodny and Gettlin, *Silent Coup*, 130–1, 145, 157. My summary is

based on my interpretation of the unedited interview with Martinez rather than the conclusions drawn in *Silent Coup*.

6. Hunt interview with Colodny, 16 January 1991, 27, 30, 55–6.

7. Ibid., 6, 23–4.

8. Hunt letter to Colodny, 19 January 1991, quoted in Hunt deposition in *Dean v. St. Martin's Press*, 16 September 1994, 76–9; Hunt depositions in *Dean v. St. Martin's Press*, 16 April 1995, 80 and 19 April 1995, 673.

9. *Dean v. St. Martin's Press*, Motion for Summary Judgement, Subject Matter Core Category 6, 11.

10. Ibid.; Ibid., Subject Matter Core Category 5, 28, 32–3. Wells and Maureen Dean depositions in *Dean v. St. Martin's Press*.

11. Motz (1998).

12. Judge Williams, *Wells v. Liddy*, United States Court of Appeals for the Fourth Circuit, 28 July 1999; Wilkins, Williams, and Michael (2002).

13. Hougan, "Hougan, Liddy, The Post and Watergate."

14. Ibid.; Dean letter to Parfrey, 13 August 2013; "Watergate Lawsuit Trial Drops Names"; "Under Watergate."

15. Jeannine Bailley Ball deposition in *Dean v. St. Martin's Press*, 29 September 1993.

16. Hougan, *Secret Agenda*, 118–9.

17. Rudy deposition in *Dean v. St. Martin's Press*, 18 June 1996, 151–3; Rudy deposition, 19 June 1996, 319–20; *Dean v. St. Martin's Press*, Motion for Summary Judgement, Subject Matter Core Category 5, 25.

18. Rudy depositions, 11 April 1996, 62–3 and 12 July 1996, 450–2; Colodny and Gettlin, *Silent Coup*, 132–3.

19. Hougan, *Secret Agenda*, 114.

20. Motz (2001); Rudy depositions in *Dean v. St. Martin's Press*, 11 April 1996, 223–5; 19 June 1996, 210–11, 318–22; and 12 July 1996, 508; Rudy declaration, 24 June 1997, JRP, Box 68–3.

21. Rudy deposition, 19 June 1996, 203, 216.

22. Ibid., 246–50.

23. Motz (1998).

24. *Dean v. St. Martin's Press*, Motion for Summary Judgement, Subject Matter Core Category 5, 10–14; Higby interview with Len Colodny, cited in "BM—DNC," 48; Maureen Dean, *Mo*, 30–1; Maureen Dean deposition in *Dean v. St. Martin's Press*.

25. Ibid., 14–23; Stanford, *White House Call Girl*, 28.

26. Banks deposition in *Dean v. St. Martin's Press*, 28 September 1993, 11, 23; Summers, *The Arrogance of Power*, 422; Stanford, *White House Call Girl*, 18, 61, 70, 93, 94, 177; Nixon's Gamble, 171.

27. Summers, *The Arrogance of Power*, 419–20.

28. Hougan email to author, 3 July 2018.

29. Baldwin deposition in *Dean v. St. Martin's Press*, July 25–6, 1996; A year later, Baldwin testified it would be very easy to read one of the logs and take it out of context—"eight out of ten people [reading a transcript] would have said, 'that's a call girl ring. This is a prostitution ring'" (Baldwin deposition in *Wells v. Liddy*, 28 July 1997, 156-7). This quote has since been taken out of context to support the call-girl theory.

30. Shoffler deposition, 15 March 1995, 278, 325–6, 329, 460; Hougan email to author, 27 June 2018.

31. Dean, *Conservatives Without Conscience*, xv, xvi.

32. "L.A. Woman Sues Liddy for Comments About Watergate," *Washington Post*, 9 April 1997; Motz (2002). Liddy is exaggerating here. Baldwin brought a camera back from Connecticut on June 12 and took some pictures of people have lunch on the sixth-floor terrace but his camera wouldn't focus correctly and he threw them away (Baldwin deposition, 25 July 1996, 209).

33. *Dean v. St. Martin's Press*, Motion for Summary Judgement, Subject Matter Core Category 5, 30–1 Wells deposition in *Dean v. St. Martin's Press*, 7 June 1996, 42-46, 50, 252-263; Interview with Severin Beliveau by Mike Hastings, 5 September 2008, George J. Mitchell Oral History Project, Bowdoin College Digital Commons.

34. Wells' letter to Joann Roberts is cited in Motz (2001) and copies can be found in box 47-5, JRP.

35. Summers, *The Arrogance of Power*, 417-8; Andy Ray, *Hired Gun: A Political Odyssey* (Lanham, MD: University Press of America, 2008), 33-5. It's not clear how Ray discovered this reference. Wells depicted herself as a demure church organist from Mississippi but her calendar included a visit to a strip club with DNC colleagues at the Miami convention, watching a pornographic film (possibly *Deep Throat*, which was released June 12) and attending a "wine and pot party" (Wells' calendar entries, cited in "BM—DNC," 31-2; Wells 1972 calendar, JRP, Box 47-2).

36. Motz (1998); "Under Watergate."

37. Williams (1999), cited in Hougan, "Hougan, Liddy, The Post and Watergate."

38. Manuel Rogia-Francia, "Watergate Has Liddy In Court Once Again," *Washington Post,* 17 Jan 2001; "Watergate Lawsuit Trial Drops Names."

39. Motz (1998); "G. Gordon Liddy Gives First Testimony on Watergate Break-In," *New York Times*, 30 January 2001.

40. "Watergate Lawsuit Trial Drops Names"; Frederic J. Motz, *Wells v. Liddy*, 135 F. Supp. 2d 668, United States District Court, D. Maryland, 19 March 2001; Wells testimony in *Wells v. Liddy*, 17 January 2001, 122-3, referenced in "BM—DNC," 62-4.

41. "Liddy Case Dismissed," *CBS News*, 29 January 2001; "Liddy Hangs Tough on Watergate Theory," *CBS News*, 2 February 2001.

42. Motz (2001).

43. Shoffler deposition, 13 March 1995, 36–7, referenced in Motz (2001).

44. Ibid.

45. Wilkins, Williams, and Michael (2002).

46. Liddy, *Will*, 214-220; Darragh Johnson, "Second Trial Opens in Watergate Case," *Washington Post*, 25 June 2002; Gail Gibson, "Judge says Liddy theory is strong but 'debatable'," *Baltimore Sun*, 3 July 2002; Shoffler interview, *The Key to Watergate* (1992).

47. Locker, *Nixon's Gamble*, 171; Stanford, *White House Call Girl*, 85; Dean letter to Parfrey, 13 August 2013; Maureen Dean, *Mo*, 46; Dean White House telephone log, 8 June 1972, Colodny Collection; Stanford to Colodny, 18 October 2012, Colodny Collection.

48. Stanford, *White House Call Girl*, 92, 94.

49. Hougan, "Hougan, Liddy, The Post and Watergate."

50. Ibid.

51. Transcript of Martinez interview with Becker and Colodny, 1 May 1990, Colodny Collection, 7–9. Hougan received a copy of the June 27 FBI memo matching the key to Maxie Wells desk through a FOIA request.

52. Baldwin deposition, 26 June 1996, 306; Transcript of Baldwin *Los Angeles Times* interview, 3 October 1972, 112; Shoffler deposition, 13 March 1995, 34.

53. Liebengood deposition in *Dean v. St. Martin's Press*, 6 June 1996 37, 44; Howard Liebengood interview, *The Key to Watergate* (1992).

54. "A Conversation with Secretary General Spencer Oliver"; "Digest of Lyle Miller Secret Documents," 4; "About CSCE—Frequently Asked Questions," CSCE, https://www.csce.gov/about-csce/our-structure/frequently-asked -questions; Robert Allen deposition in *Dean v. St. Martin's Press*, 30 July 1996, 47; FBI Teletype to Acting Director, 5 October 1972, 139-4136-74; Oliver deposition in *R. Spencer Oliver v. Village Voice* (Civil Action 74—4105), 1977, 39-41, 50, Box 43-5, JRP. The offending article by Ron Rosenbaum, "What Were They Hoping to Hear on Larry O'Brien's Phone?" was based on Senate Watergate Committee investigator Scott Armstrong's debriefing of Hunt. I have found no evidence to substantiate the allegations.

55. Buchanan/Khachigian to Mitchell and Haldeman, 12 April 1972, SSC Book 10, 4233; Buchanan to Mitchell and Haldeman, 27 April 1972, Ibid., 4235.

56. Robert Parry, "Robert Strauss's Watergate Secret," *Consortium News*, 20 March 2014; Eileen Shanahan, "Connally to Work to Re-Elect Nixon," *New York Times*, 15 July 1972. Severin Beliveau joined Oliver's civil suit and

believes the "Republican U.S. attorney under Nixon was investigating and he wanted to disclose the contents of our telephone conversations . . . ostensibly to embarrass us." He thinks DNC chair Robert Strauss wanted them to drop the suit "because he and Nixon were very good friends. Why do you think he was ultimately appointed ambassador to Russia?" (Interview with Severin Beliveau by Mike Hastings, 5 September 2008).

57. Colson to Dean, 16 June 1972, SSC Book 10, 4247.

58. Summers, *The Arrogance of Power*, 417, 528–9fn11. The Greenville reference is redacted in Baldwin's FBI interview but discussed in Donald Campbell's deposition in *Dean v Liddy*, 30 September 1993, 44 and Wells' deposition in *Wells v. Liddy*, 19 September 1997, 171-3; Oliver email to author, 4 September 2018.

59. Barbara Rhoden Kennedy deposition in *Dean v. St. Martin's Press*, 17 July 1996.

60. Robert Strauss deposition in *Dean v. St. Martin's Press*, 24 June 1996.

61. Rosen testimony in *Wells v. Liddy*, cited in Hougan, "Hougan, Liddy, The Post and Watergate."

62. Oliver interview with author. McCord joined Morgan's unsuccessful motion to Judge Sirica to set aside his conviction due to perjured testimony (Morgan, *One Man, One Voice*, 252–4).

63. Ibid.; Oliver email to author, 8 September 2018.

64. Patrick J. Buchanan, *Nixon's White House Wars* (New York: Crown Forum, 2017), 271-272; Theodore Shabad, "Young Americans End Soviet Visit," *New York Times*, 14 November 1971; Oliver interview with author. After the break-in, some at the DNC suspected Oliver was leaking information to Buchanan.

65. Hougan, "Hougan, Liddy, The Post and Watergate"; Baldwin deposition in *Dean v. Liddy*, 26 July 1996, 306–7.

66. Wells deposition, 7 June 1996, 13-4; Memoranda [From Maxie Wells, 11/29/76-1/15/77], Office of Staff Secretary, 1976 Campaign Transition File, Carter Library; President Carter daily diary, 26 January 1977, Carter Library.

67. Phillip Mackin Bailley Twitter account, 15 October 2013; Phillip Mackin Bailley Esq. LinkedIn profile, https://www.linkedin.com/in/phillip-mackin-bailley-esq-9ba42664/; "YDA officers of the past 50 years," *Young Democrats of America*, www.yda.org/past-officers. Oliver calls Bailley "a complete nut job": "Someone told me that he was a member of the Young Democratic Club in Prince George's County in Maryland where I was also a member, along with Steny Hoyer and Pete O'Malley, who were my campaign managers when I ran for National President of the Young Democrats, neither of whom remember ever meeting him" (Oliver email to author, 8 September 2018).

68. Baldwin interview with James Rosen, 19 August 1995, 15-6, JRP, Box 32-7; Baldwin interview with Rosen, 9 September 1995, 22-25, 51, JRP, Box 32-7.

69. Nodule X31; Hougan, *Secret Agenda*, 306, 310-11, 326; Birely deposition, 17 July 1996, 21-22; Love FBI interview, 3 July 1972, 139-166-787.

70. Hougan, *Secret Agenda*, 305.

71. Ibid., 306, 310–11; Love FBI interview, 3 July 1972.

72. Hougan email to author, 3 July 2018 Hougan, *Secret Agenda*, 254–5.

73. Hougan, *Secret Agenda*, 308.

74. Ibid., 309.

75. Ibid.

76. Jim Hougan, "Carl Shoffler, Robert Merritt and the Scandal That Dare Not Speak Its Name," 22 July 2011, jimhougan.com.

77. Malloy affidavit, Nedzi hearings, 33-4; Hunt testimony, Nedzi hearings, 506. The name of the supervisor is redacted.

78. Hougan, *Secret Agenda*, 302; Hougan comment on Jim Hougan, "Throat: Mark Felt, Robert Bennett and the Post's Cointelpro Problem," 25 March 2018, jimhougan.com; Hougan comment on "Hougan, Liddy, the Post and Watergate," 11 January 2015, jimhougan.com.

79. Lano Oral History Interview, 28 May 2009.

80. Erik Hedegaard, "The Last Confessions of E. Howard Hunt," *Rolling Stone*, 5 April 2007; "Confession of Howard Hunt," www.maryferrell.org; author interview with Robert Mirto, 24 August 2018; Baldwin interview with

Rosen, 19 August 1995, 10, 15-6, 26-7; Baldwin interview with Rosen, 9 September 1995, 91; "BM—DNC," 65, JRP. McCord's niece confirmed the details of his death to me. Baldwin's scenario suggests a possible connection to the Moorer-Radford affair, covered by Ray Locker in *Nixon's Gamble*. The Dallas reference is odd because in March 1973, McCord hired Bernard 'Bud' Fensterwald to be his attorney. In 1969, Fensterwald had founded the Committee to Investigate Assassinations and employed Lou Russell as an investigator. Russell persuaded him to represent McCord and put up $40,000 of McCord's bail (Hougan, *Secret Agenda*, 116, 118, 303-4). I have found nothing to substantiate Cuban exile leader Harry Ruiz-Williams' claims that he met Desmond FitzGerald with Hunt and McCord on the morning of the Kennedy assassination about "another murderous scheme" to kill Castro "promoted by Robert Kennedy" (Anthony Summers and Robbyn Swan, "The Ghosts of November," *Vanity Fair*, November 2001).

81. Author interview with Eugenio Rolando Martinez, 20 July 2018; "Weddings; Ofelia Trevino, Ramon Gonzalez," *New York Times*, 2 July 1995.

APPENDIX 1

1. FBI memo, 5 November 1973, 139-4089-2646.
2. SAC Miami to Director, 22 December 1972, 139-4089-1766; Felt to SAC Miami, 26 December 1972, 139-4089-1719.
3. Ibid.; SAC Miami to Director, 19 September 1973, 139-4089-2610; Transcript of Proceedings, 15 January 1973, *US v. Liddy*, 449–450.
4. FBI Teletype, Miami to Director, 18 October 1973, 139-4089-2631.
5. Villamanan FBI interview, 16 October 1973, 139-4089-2644; Toscano FBI interview, 17 and 19 October 1973, Ibid.
6. Sylvia Campos FBI interview, 19 October 1973, 139-4089-2632.
7. Ibid.; FBI report by SA Stiles and Knight, 23 June 1972.
8. Villamanan FBI interview, 18 October 1973, 139-4089-2646.
9. Villamanan FBI interviews, 16 and 18 October 1973; Beguiristain FBI interviews, 17 and 18 October 1973, 139-4089-2646.

10. 104-10166-10016; "IUSTEER-1 – Anthony Abraham Chevrolet, Miami," 30 June 1972, 104-10221-10021.

11. "Conversation 21 June with Dave Morales re AMCLATTER-1, Hopkins MFR, 104-10164-10186. Barker was eventually terminated in 1966.

12. "Status Report as of 19 April 1974 . . ."; Untitled and undated document, 157-10011-10084.

13. Martinez Presentence report, 91; Ashley Halsey, "The Watergate Cubans – burglars with a cause," *Philadelphia Enquirer*, 9 August 1984.

14. Index card dated 7 June 1973, found in "Card Lists re Frank Sturgis, E. Howard Hunt, et al.," 104-10096-10131 ; "Inventory of Rockefeller Commission Files," 178-10004-10420, 108; "Handwritten Bernard Barker chronology," 104-10164-10015.

15. FBI Teletype, Miami to Director, 24 October 1973, 139-4089-2633; Sylvia Campos FBI interview, 24 October 1973.

16. Author interview with Nick Akerman, 20 August 2018; "Watergate Incident Report," 13 July 1972, 104-10256-10269; Suarez trial testimony, US v Liddy, 26 January 1973.

17. Kelley to Colby, 2 January 1974, 139-4089-2677; "Select Committee Request to Interview Special Agents of the FBI," Legal Counsel to Director, 17 December 1973, 139-4089-2671; "Request to Interview Special Agents Arnold L. Parham and Robert L. Wilson," Legal Counsel to Director, 12 December 1973, 139-4089-2672; "Select Committee Request to Interview Special Agents of the FBI," Long to Gebhardt, 20 December 1973, Ibid.

18. "Miscellaneous Points of Interest Eliminated from Final Draft of CIA Summaries," Liebengood to File, Box 38, Folder 10, HSL.

APPENDIX 2

1. Parsons trial testimony in US v Liddy, 24 January 1973. Parsons had not seen McCord for two years prior to the trial.

2. Ibid.; FBI Laboratory report, 26 June 1972

3. Bradley to Conrad, 2 October 1972, FBI 139-4089-1455

4. Ibid.

5. Bradley to Conrad, 17 October 1972, 139-4089-1450 (21, 44). The current occupant was Mrs. Harriet Cipriani. The tests were observed by Oliver and Galbraith. According to the FBI, "Galbraith observed the tests very closely and took detailed notes including description of devices tested, test equipment used [and] instrument settings."

6. *US v. Liddy*, Grand Jury indictment, 15 September 1972, HJC Statement of Information, Book 2, 90.

7. "Summary of Watergate Trial Testimony – January 24, 1973," 139-4089-2144; Silbert and Titus to Gray, 1 February 1973, 139-4089-1915; 27, 15–17; "Watergate in Court"

8. Parsons trial testimony, 24 January 1973, 1582–3; FBI Laboratory report, 26 June 1972; McCord testimony, 147, 153.

9. Jack Anderson, "Watergate Team Hit Democrats Twice," *Washington Post*, 16 April 1973.

10. McCord deposition in *DNC v. McCord*, 30 April 1973, 77–9.

11. Ibid.; Transcript of CBS News report, 14 September 1972, Box 43–5, JRP, 87; McCord, *A Piece of Tape*, 25. McCord told the prosecutors he put the second bug in a "call directory" and "gave them an exact description of where within the call directory it was located, and they sent a man out, and picked it up, and brought it back. So presumably, it was still transmitting . . . during that period" (Transcript of McCord interview for *Watergate* TV series, Roll 320, 17).

12. FBI report on Stevens, 7 May 1973, 139-4089-2374; FBI investigative notes, 9 and 11 April 1973, 139-4089-1985, 1986.

13. Bernard Gordon FBI interview, 17 May 1973; Chicago to WFO, 15 June 1973, 139-4089-2398.

14. Adrian Stevens FBI interview, 10 April 1973; Michael Marcus Stevens FBI interview, 10 April 1973; "Bug bill unpaid, paper is told," *The Morning News*, 3 May 1974; Ronald Koziol, "President's group owes bug bill here," *Chicago Tribune*, 16 May 1973.

15. Teletype to Acting Director, 12 and 16 April 1973, 139-4089-1994 and -2004; FBI reports, 13 and 25 April 1973, 139-4089-2393.

16. Barcal FBI interview, 21 May 1973.

17. Jack Anderson, "Watergate Follies Would Make Splendid Comic Opera," *Argus-Leader*, 30 April 1973; "Dealer Ties CIA to Watergate, Paper Says," *The Indianapolis Star*, 18 May 1973; Howard S. Marks, "McCord Sought Secret Sky Spy Bug Devices," *The Indianapolis Star*, 5 June 1973.

18. McCord testimony, 22 May 1973, SSC Book 1, 235.

19. Donald Campbell deposition, 30 September 1993.

20. Jean Westwood, *Madame Chair* (Logan, UT, Utah State University Press), 157.

21. "Electronic Device Removed from Spencer Oliver's telephone on September 13, 1972," Silbert to Petersen, 28 September 1972, 139-4089-1454.

22. Phillip Taubman, "'72 Data Show F.B.I. Questioned If Burglars Bugged the Watergate," *New York Times*, 6 November 1984.

INDEX